D1075398

Twentieth-Century Japan: The Emergence of a World Power

Irwin Scheiner, Editor

The City as Subject

*Seki Hajime and the
Reinvention of Modern Osaka*

JEFFREY E. HANES

University of California Press

BERKELEY   LOS ANGELES   LONDON

University of California Press
Berkeley and Los Angeles, California

University of California Press, Ltd.
London, England

Library of Congress Cataloging-in-Publication Data

Hanes, Jeffrey E.
  The city as subject : Seki Hajime and the reinvention of modern
Osaka / Jeffrey E. Hanes.
      p.   cm.—(Twentieth-century Japan)
  Includes bibliographical references and index.
  ISBN 0-520-22849-9 (alk. paper)
  1. Seki, Hajime, 1873–1935. 2. Economists—Japan—Biography.
3. Mayors—Japan—Biography. 4. Osaka (Japan)—Economic
conditions. 5. Japan—Economic conditions—1918–1945. I. Seki,
Hajime, 1873–1935. II. Title. III. Series.
HB126.J4 S374 2002
307.1'26'092—dc21   2001027321
[B]

Manufactured in the United States of America
11 10 09 08 07 06 05 04 03 02
10 9 8 7 6 5 4 3 2 1

The paper used in this publication meets the minimum requirements of
ANSI/NISO Z39.48–1992 (R 1997) (Permanence of Paper). ∞

To Miyamoto-sensei

Contents

Illustrations

Acknowledgments

This book has taken me years to complete. Along the way, I have benefited from the advice of many friends and colleagues as well as the assistance of numerous universities, libraries, archives, and research groups. I owe special thanks to my teachers for their encouragement, support, and keen criticism. Professors Irwin Scheiner and Thomas C. Smith generously shared their knowledge and wisdom with me when I was a graduate student, and they have since kept on my case to see the dissertation become a book. Professor Miyamoto Ken'ichi has offered unwavering support for this project since I arrived on his doorstep in Osaka. Having made him work so hard and wait so long for this book, it seems only fitting that I should dedicate it to him.

Along the way, a whole host of friends and colleagues have offered me advice and encouragement. They include Gary Allinson, Marston Anderson, Taylor Atkins, Sarah Baldwin, Laura Fair, Josh Fogel, Charlie Fox, Tak Fujitani, Bryna Goodman, Jim Grossman, Carol and Eldon Hanes, Tom Havens, Laura Hein, Ellen Herman, Hirano Takayuki, Hotta Akio, Ishida Yorifusa, Kamo Toshio, Karen Kelsky, David Luebke, Glenn May, Karl Mendel, Miko-Burauni and Orenji, Miyamoto Eiko, Miyano Yūichi, Masao Miyoshi, Jim Mohr, Risa Palm, Dan Pope, Jennifer Rondeau, Blair Ruble, Barbara Sato, Andre Sorenson, George Sheridan, Shibamura Atsuki, Henry Smith, Teddy and Masuyo Saleh, Larry Tritle, David Tucker, Ron Toby, Kathy Uno, Andy Verner, Louise Wade, Paul Waley, Brett Walker, Alan Wolfe, and two anonymous readers for the University of California Press. All these individuals and more gave me reason to believe that I had something important to say and also gave me the sort of criticism that made me want to say it right. Finally, I have benefited from the invaluable help and support of several editors at the University of California Press, including Sheila Levine, Laura Harger, and Julie Brand. My copyeditor, Pamela Fischer, is a whiz.

I could not have completed this book without the generous financial assistance of the Fulbright-Hays Program and the Social Science Research Council. In addition, the University of Illinois and the University of Oregon gave me valuable time off to work on the manuscript. The following institutions and associations helped me in various different ways to accomplish the research and writing: the East Asiatic Library at the University of California (Berkeley), the Osaka City University Library, the Osaka City History Archive, the Osaka City Library, the Tokyo Institute for Municipal Research, the University of Illinois Library, the University of Oregon Library and the statewide ORBIS system, the Seki Hajime Research Association, the Social History Group at the University of Illinois, and the Miyamoto Zemi at Osaka City University.

Finally, I want to offer my heartfelt gratitude to family and friends for their faith and forbearance. My parents' unqualified love and support have helped keep me afloat. Three sets of friends—Ann Billingsley and Jim Grossman, Charlie Fox and Sawako Murotani, and Ron Toby and Yuko Toby—have been surrogate families, offering me shelter from the storm whenever I needed it. Last but in no way least, Sarah Baldwin provided just the right measure of tough love and tough criticism to see me safely and happily to the Promised Land of Done. Thank you, one and all.

Introduction

*Seki Hajime and Social Progressivism
in Prewar Japan*

On Nakanoshima, at the center of the city of Osaka, stands the weather-worn statue of Mayor Seki Hajime (1873–1935). Nestled in the trees across from Osaka's Central Town Hall, a stone's throw from the City Hall, Seki gazes benevolently over the city he served from 1914 to 1935. Suitably modern and dignified in crisply creased trousers, starched collar, cravat, vest, and morning coat, he truly looks the part of the cosmopolitan "scholar-mayor" *(gakusha shichō)* who each morning reputedly ate an international breakfast of miso soup and toast in his book-lined study. Seki's fame was such that the city he served mourned his death with great pomp and circumstance. Hundreds of local and national luminaries attended the funeral, which began with a grand processional from the family home in Uehonmachi and wound south to Tennōji Park, and thousands more of the city's residents followed the proceedings live over JOBK radio.[1]

Attached to the grimy stone pedestal on which Seki's figure stands is a commemorative plaque that forgettably proclaims him a paragon of civic virtue and a master of municipal management. This unremarkable monument to the remarkable interwar mayor who vowed to transform the Capital of Smoke (Kemuri no Miyako) into the Livable City (Sumigoko-chiyoki Toshi) is sadly appropriate, for while Seki achieved many things in interwar Osaka, livability was not one of them. His visionary plan to reinvent the city, which pivoted on the creation of working-class "garden suburbs" *(den'en kōgai)*, itself went up in smoke—done in by the actions of greedy landed capitalists in the hinterlands of Osaka and the inaction of shortsighted, office-bound bureaucrats in Tokyo. Soon after they went up, Seki's model public-housing tracts were enveloped by urban sprawl.

Seki did not sit idly by as the combined forces of capitalism and statism quashed his plan. He fought mightily for metropolitan autonomy *(daitoshi jichi)* in hope of freeing the municipal government to extend urban planning to Osaka's still-undeveloped hinterlands and in this way to prevent urban sprawl rather than merely treating its symptoms. In Seki's mind, this was more than a battle over conflicting economic priorities and political jurisdictions; it was a battle over urban identity. His main adversaries, local landowners and state bureaucrats, treated the city as an economic object. By contrast, Seki treated it as a social subject. The defining characteristic of his perspective on the city was insistent social-ism. To him, the city was a dynamic social organism whose development and well-being were predicated on the welfare of the classes, families, and other groups who inhabited it.

Seki came by his social-ism honestly. He was a man of his times in the most fundamental sense: a man of what I call the "younger generation" of Meiji Japan, whose own journey to adulthood traced a course parallel to his nation's quest for progress. Following the Sino-Japanese War (1894–1895), at precisely the moment when Japan shifted the locus of national concern from state building to economic development, Seki found himself in business school at the Tokyo Commercial College. Since, like many of his cohort, he was eager to help Japan become powerful and prosperous, he elected to focus on the new social science of building national wealth: political economics.

Yet Seki was not one to accede easily to the prevailing orthodoxy. Although he did not question the priority that Japan's national leadership had placed on increasing industrial production *(shokusan kōgyō)*, he definitely had opinions of his own about how best to achieve it. When the headmaster of the Tokyo Commercial College narrowly interpreted the government's new slogan as a call for technical training—and unilaterally altered the curriculum to answer it—the nineteen-year-old Seki and other students rose up in righteous rebellion. Identified by the headmaster as a ringleader of this student protest, Seki was unceremoniously dismissed from school. Before long, men in high places intervened to reinstate him, going on to sack the headmaster himself. Seki was a *wunderkind,* it seems, whose intellectual talent was sufficiently valued to merit indulgence of his moral fervor.

Following a brief stint in government, Seki returned to the Tokyo Commercial College as a professor of economics. He was soon recognized in academic and government circles as a rising star—one of several young scholars on the cutting edge of political economics. Like all his peers, Seki looked to the West for economic models of progress and alighted initially on the state-centered national economics of Friedrich List. List's perspective on modernization, which issued from his firsthand appreciation of the political and economic challenges faced by the emerging German nation-state, resonated powerfully with the national imperatives that faced Japan in the Meiji Era. Although Seki was taken in by List's alluring identification of the nation as the central figure of modernity, he was left unconvinced by List's characterization of the nation as a power- and wealth-hungry entity.

Seki found what he was looking for in the people-centered political economics of Wilhelm Roscher. Doyen of the revisionist German historical school of political economy, Roscher had helped to humanize List's national economics. His redefinition of national economics as activities designed primarily to achieve "resource maximization" rather than power and wealth at last provided Seki with a compelling alternative to the state-centered developmental model sanctioned by the Meiji leadership. Identifying the nation as a social collectivity and declaring the state its hand-maiden, Seki recast the Japanese national economy as a "people's national economy" *(kokumin keizai)*. This critical shift in emphasis from the state to the people changed Seki's world-view. Thereafter, he opened himself up to a social perspective on economic affairs that was rapidly gaining currency worldwide: progressivism.

Had Seki remained ensconced in his position at the Tokyo Commercial College, he might well have continued to plug away at political economics. But his destiny lay elsewhere. Awarded a prestigious traveling research fellowship in economics by the Ministry of Education, Seki soon found himself in Europe. Initially posted to Belgium, where he conducted transport surveys and thus came to appreciate the importance of railway systems to the exchange economies *(Verkehrswirtschaft)* at the heart of capitalism, Seki later received permission to study in Germany. There, he had the opportunity to work with the guiding lights of the Verein für Sozialpolitik ([German] Association for Social Policy), Gustav Schmoller and Adolf Wagner. Sometimes referred to as the "younger historical school," these intellectual descendants of Roscher so powerfully extended the reach of their mentor's people-centered political economics that they unwittingly opened up a new field of study: social economics.

Seki's exposure to social economics in the lectures of Schmoller and Wagner changed his life. When he delved into the progressivism at the core of the Verein's critique of capitalist society, he also found himself reaching out effortlessly to a wider, transnational fellowship of like-minded reformers. As Daniel T. Rodgers has demonstrated in his path-breaking book *Atlantic Crossings,* a whole host of Americans and Europeans were making the same intellectual pilgrimage as Seki to the fount of social-economic thought in Germany. These reform-minded social-ists were drawn together—at a time when nationalist convictions and aspirations ran deep on both continents—by their common observation that the forces of industrial capitalism spanned oceans.

As Rodgers explains the emerging fellowship between North American and European social progressives, initially, at least, it was the product of circumstance:

> Two phenomena of the late nineteenth century made the North Atlantic progressive connection possible. The first was the rapidly convergent economic development of the key nations of the North Atlantic basin. Across the older, intricately varied political and cultural checkerwork of Europe and North America began to appear, in thicker and thicker concentrations, economic institutions instantly recognizable from one end of the North Atlantic region to the other. Nothing was more important for sustained trade in social policies than this dramatic expansion of the social landscapes of industrial capitalism. In a world of nation-states, economic forces were particularly aggressive trespassers and powerful centralizers of experience.[2]

Mesmerized by the common "new landscapes of fact" that they beheld—and gripped by the "intertwined landscapes of mind" that defined their common response to this sight—these "cosmopolitan progressives" of *fin-de-siècle* Europe and North America soon forged "transnational social-political networks." Eager to rein in the awesome power of industrial capitalism by placing economic wealth at the service of social peace and prosperity, this unlikely and ungainly fellowship of social reformers suddenly found themselves celebrating their relatedness.[3]

Given the looming presence of nationalism as a divisive political and cultural force at the time, it is more than a bit surprising that such a fellowship even existed. But, as Rodgers points out, "enough of the real and imagined distance between the nation-states shrank in this era to make a trade in social policy possible." In explaining how budding North American social progressives in particular found themselves almost effortlessly engaged in this new transatlantic traffic in ideas and idealism, Rodgers reminds us that the United States was an "outpost nation" that began as an "imperial project" and that continued to see the Atlantic "less as a barrier than as a connective lifeline—a seaway for the movement of people, goods, ideas, and aspirations."[4]

While Japanese progressives had no such geographical or historical advantage—and remained distant from the eyes and the minds of most

Americans and Europeans at the turn of the century—they nonetheless forged a transpacific progressive connection whose intellectual trajectory (if not also its ethos) paralleled that of the transatlantic fellowship described by Rodgers.[5] A handful of North American and European figures such as John Dewey and Charles Beard clearly appreciated this fact and apparently accepted invitations to visit Japan so that they might decide for themselves just how deeply the common currents ran.[6] After six months of work in Tokyo on municipal affairs, Beard, for his part, was forced to admit that "the difficulties of Tokyo do not lie in any lack of knowledge about local needs or about modern methods of meeting those needs." In Tokyo, as in many big cities in Europe and North America, bureaucratism and the lack of "public spirit" were the undoing of progressivism.[7]

Although reformers such as Beard carried the message back to Europe and North America that progressivism was alive and well in Japan, Japan was not brought into the loop. Japanese progressives were never able to generate a transoceanic exchange of the sort that flourished across the North Atlantic. And, arguably, they failed to do so for a reason that Rodgers has unwittingly elicited: Japan simply did not fit the Euro-American mold that rendered transatlantic interchange possible:

> For social policies to be borrowable across political boundaries, there must be not only a foundation of common economic and social experience but also a recognition of underlying kinship. The polities in question must be seen to face similar needs and problems, to move within shared historic frames, and to strive toward a commonly imagined future. Relatedness is the core assumption. Where there is only comparison or culturally-imagined difference there can be envy or pride in abundance, but there can be no sustained trade in social policy.[8]

The key to understanding Japan's enthusiasm for social progressivism lies, paradoxically, with its "recognition of underlying kinship" with Europe and North America. But it must be clear to readers by now that this recognition was unilateral. Despite the perceived gulf between Japan and the West—a condition variously described at the time as geographical, historical, linguistic, cultural, ethnic, or racial (or some combination of these) by Europeans, Americans, and a growing number of Japanese— Japanese progressives such as Seki Hajime staunchly maintained that the similarities outweighed the differences. Like their North American and European progressive counterparts, they stressed the transnational, universalist character of economic forces such as industrial capitalism. However, if the Japanese version of transnational progressivism was admittedly unidirectional, it was not built on mimicry or on envy or pride. As I hope to demonstrate in this biography of Seki Hajime, Japanese progressives could be just as searching in their prescriptions for social reform as their North American and European cousins.

It is hard to imagine what Seki must have been thinking and feeling as economic development took off in the early 1900s and he began to recognize a family resemblance between European and Japanese industrial capitalism—one that he had seen with his own eyes during his three-year sojourn in Europe. However bracing it must have been to see and believe that there was indeed a transnational kinship of modern nations, it must have been frightening as well to concede that the modern economic forces that had forged this kinship were purveyors of both good and evil. Sufficiently powerful to generate untold wealth, they were also capable of undermining the very foundation of the societies they touched in the process. That late-modernizing nations such as Germany and Japan had thus far proven themselves incapable of administering an effective prophylactic to the class conflicts produced by industrialization—seemingly the same conflicts that continued to afflict early modernizers—took Seki up short.

No sooner did Seki confront this grim reality in the early 1900s than he made the leap from political economics to social economics. Picking up Marx for the first time—and engaging Marx's incisive interpretation of the evils of capitalism—Seki was forced to concede that classes were no less central figures of modernity than were nations. When he finally took a fresh look at the people's national economy *(kokumin keizai)*, he made a shocking discovery: antagonistic classes within his organismic nation had spawned a social problem *(shakai mondai)* of looming proportions. Like his progressive cousins in the West, Seki found himself militating for what Rodgers aptly terms the "de-commodification" of labor.[9]

Rather than simply preaching reform from his lectern at the Tokyo Commercial College, Seki swung into action at this critical juncture. Transforming himself from a scholarly social economist into an impassioned labor reformer, he fought tirelessly not merely for a factory law *(kōjō hō)* but for worker protection *(rōdōsha hogo)*. While he remained firmly committed to the goal of national economic development, he proposed to sustain that development by promoting socioeconomic justice and thus restoring social peace. In effect, Seki identified worker protection as the legal linchpin of a moral economy for the industrial age.

When Seki embraced the mission of worker protection, his progressivist eyes naturally followed workers from the factories in which they labored to the homes in which they lived. There he found living conditions no less appalling in their way than the working conditions he had already helped expose. Noting that Japan's industrial working class was overwhelmingly concentrated in cities but that the Meiji leadership continued to objectify these cities as urban markets *(toshi)*, Seki pointedly subjectified them as urban communities *(tokai)*. He then went on to radically recast urban reform *(toshi kairyō)* as a social imperative rather than an economic opportunity.

No sooner did Seki set the scholarly groundwork for his transformation from labor reformer to urban reformer than he was afforded the extraordinary opportunity to begin practicing what he preached. Named deputy mayor of the industrial metropolis of Osaka in 1914, Seki threw himself into the pursuit of urban social reform *(toshi shakai kairyō)*. By the time he was appointed mayor in 1923, he had made residential reform the pillar of his urban social reformism and the creation of working-class garden suburbs its central objective. This brings us full circle—back to my initial observation about Seki's urban progressivism: it was a visionary ideology, yes, but one that fell victim in the end to the very forces it had endeavored to contain, capitalism and statism.

In the coming pages, I tell the story of this ardent reformer and his remarkable progressivism. But before beginning, I propose to bring the reader's attention to a story line embedded in my narrative that arguably lends coherence to the story as a whole. As I see it, Seki spent a lifetime concerned with the idea and the experience of family. In chapter 1, where I attempt to bring Seki's youth to life through a thick description of studio portraits, family is key. Many of the images I read are family portraits, and they arguably reveal two important things: first, the Seki family, like most other families of the day, was tacitly implicated in the essentializing national/ethnic logic of the family-state *(kazoku kokka)*;[10] second, Seki Hajime's palpable ambivalence toward family portraiture as a young man—an unfortunate by-product of his sadly abnormal family circumstances—masked his fierce loyalty to family and, by extension, to family solidarity as a national ideal.

As a fledgling political economist in the orthodox Listian national economic tradition endorsed by the Meiji state, this free-thinking young man reinvented the family-state as a family-nation and promptly identified it as the foundation of the people's national economy *(kokumin keizai)*. When he left for Europe in 1898, Seki remained utterly convinced that the Japanese people's national economy was no less intrinsically unitary than the family-nation that generated its activities. But no sooner did Seki encounter the social economics of Schmoller and Wagner than his political economics was shaken free from its Listian underpinnings. On his return to Japan in 1901, as I argue in chapter 2, Seki continued to place his faith in creative entrepreneurs to keep the family-nation intact and solvent. As evidence of labor abuses mounted in the early 1900s, however, he was compelled at last to accede to a disturbing point confidently asserted and reasserted by his German mentors: that class conflict between industrialists and workers was an unavoidable consequence of capitalist development.

Chapter 3 witnesses Seki's struggle to find a way of rescuing the family-nation from its contentious fate at the hands of industrial capitalism. Revisiting his tumultuous interchange with the quixotic Japanese Marxist Kawakami Hajime—and reexamining his critical engagement with Marx's own writings—I rehearse Seki's rebirth as a progressive social economist who held that the state might conciliate in the disputes between Japan's rival classes and impel them to acknowledge their common interests as constituents of the nation/subject. Chapter 4 explores the labor reformism elicited by this rebirth, plumbing the depths of Seki's nascent progressivism. It suggests that his call for worker protection issued from the pragmatic recognition of increasing class abrasion within the Japanese family-nation—tensions that he tellingly likened to the conflicts that often divided different national peoples (kokumin)—and it shows that he expected the state to rise above the fray and restore family-nation unity.

After delineating the critical changes in Seki's understanding of the Japanese family writ large, I devote chapter 5 to a historical contextualization of his growing concern with the Japanese family writ small. This chapter recounts Seki's awakening to a brutal fact of modern urban industrial life: working-class families were no less in need of protection at home than their breadwinners were in need of protection at work. Tracing the logic of Seki's changing priorities as a municipal policymaker, from a broad-gauged commitment to urban social reform to a focused agenda of residential reform (jūtaku kairyō), chapter 6 goes on to remind us that, for Seki, family remained the fundamental social building block of modern civilization.

If only Seki's story ended here, with the triumph of his visionary progressivist agenda to create working-class garden suburbs on the outskirts of the industrial metropolis and thus to defuse class conflict, achieve social peace, and assure continued prosperity. But, as the residential segregation of these working-class garden suburbs suggests, classism lurked between the lines of Seki's pioneering plan. Although working-class families were to be placed in comfortable neighborhoods of owner-occupied row houses, their isolation from both new middle-class suburbs and old downtown neighborhoods suggests the degree to which Seki had begun to see the social subjects of his reformist zeal as social objects of his professional expertise. Sadly, under the triple threat of landed capitalism, state bureaucratism, and municipal insolvency, Seki's social reformism slowly began to devolve into technocratic authoritarianism; happily, he did not live to see the day that his progressivism crossed over the line into behaviorism.[11]

1 A Portrait of the Economist as a Young Man

The studio portrait opposite (figure 1), which somberly memorializes an unspecified family anniversary, was never intended for public display. It was placed in the Seki family album more than a century ago and, by all accounts, remained there until 1982, when Seki Jun'ichi released his grandfather's papers to the newly formed Seki Hajime Research Association (Seki Hajime Kenkyūkai). Together with a diary, letters, manuscripts, notebooks, photographs, and other miscellany, the portrait found its way into the Osaka City History Archive (Ōsaka-shi Shi Hensanjo) two years later. Not until 1989 did it complete its passage from the private to the public realm. As reproduced in Shibamura Atsuki's biography of Seki Hajime, it offers us a window on the subject's youth. Except for an innocuous caption that identifies the subjects and dates the studio session, however, the portrait goes unremarked in the text. What passes for context is a bare-bones biographical narrative that raises many more questions than it answers.[1] Thus radically decontextualized—extracted from its private context, deprived of its nostalgic associations, and objectified by the biographer—this family portrait has been cast into a kind of historical purgatory, along with other photographs from the Seki family album.

In this chapter, I rescue a number of portraits from this same fate by inserting them into narrated time. Although Shibamura Atsuki and one earlier biographer, Kawabata Naomasa, gestured toward such a representational strategy in their books on Seki, neither took the critical semiotic turn that I propose here.[2] Like most biographers with access to modern family albums, they elected to decorate their books with photographic portraits, to caption these perfunctorily, then to frame the images with their biographical narratives. Rather than engaging the portraits on their own terms, no less integrating them into the biographical narrative, these

Figure 1.   Seki Yoshi and her three sons (1896). *Right to left:* Hajime, Giichi, and Yoshinori. Courtesy of the Seki family and the Osaka City History Archive.

writers compelled their readers to connect text and context. What they left to the reader's imagination in their biographies I intend to explore in mine.

THE STUDIO PORTRAIT AS A BIOGRAPHICAL TEXT

My decision to integrate photographs from the family album into this book on Seki Hajime issued from the most conventional biographical motive—the desire to show readers what my subject looked like—but it has been fueled by the growing conviction that such personal portraits can and should be much more than window dressing. After all, as Pierre Bourdieu has poignantly observed, family albums are "the essence of social memory":

> The images of the past arranged in chronological order, the logical
> order of social memory, evoke and communicate the memory of events
> which deserve to be preserved because the group sees a factor of
> unification in the monuments of its past unity or—which amounts to
> the same thing—because it draws confirmation of its present unity
> from its past: this is why there is nothing more decent, reassuring and
> edifying than a family album.[3]

Because most biographers are not members of the families whose portraits they reproduce—and yet can legitimately lay claim to a privileged perspective of the family history—they hold great promise as recorders of memory. With this role in mind, I have trained my biographical lens on the Seki family album and selected several portraits for reproduction and interpretation here.

When the pictures in a family album are posed photographic portraits, as they are in this case, the biographical plot thickens. As Susan Sontag points out in her epoch-making book *On Photography*, photographs capture reality in a way that other pictures cannot—by preserving a visual "trace" of the past:

> [A] photograph is not only an image (as a painting is an image), an
> interpretation of the real; it is also a trace, something stenciled off the
> real, like a footprint or a death mask. While a painting, even one
> that meets photographic standards of resemblance, is never more than
> the stating of an interpretation, a photograph is never less than the
> registering of an emanation (light waves reflected by objects)—a
> material vestige of its subject in a way that no painting can be.[4]

Precisely because they preserve a "material vestige" of their subjects, photographic portraits are of extraordinary value to the biographer. Yet although they preserve vivid traces of lives and times past, they are anything but transparent reflections of reality. John Berger reminds us that "unlike memory, photographs do not in themselves preserve meaning. They offer appearances—with all the credibility and gravity we normally lend to appearances—prised away from their meaning."[5] Accordingly, the biographer who endeavors to weave family portraits into a biographical narrative, as I do here, faces the daunting task of reintegrating appearance and meaning—of placing displaced photographic traces of the subject into narrated time.

While we cannot hope to re-create the private context in which Seki family portraits were appreciated, or to restore the private meanings they evoked, we can re-place them in social and historical time. The key is to listen to Mnemosyne. As Berger poses the challenge, "If we want to put a photograph back into the context of experience, social experience, social memory, we have to respect the laws of memory. We have to situate the printed photograph so that it acquires something of the surprising conclusiveness of that which *was* and *is*."[6] By folding family portraits into this chapter—namely, by reproducing select images, siting them strategically, reading their visual signs, drawing them into the biographical narrative, and thus (re)infusing them with historical meaning—I hope to recover and reassemble some of the scattered pieces of Seki Hajime's young life.

While photographs arm the biographer with a powerful source of insight and information, they are not easy to employ (no less deploy) in a biographical narrative. The biographer who hopes to use them meaningfully must first learn to "read" the visual vocabularies they employ. As Yamaori Tetsuo reminds us in his fascinating study *The Face(s) of Japanese*, reading portraits is not simply about "*looking at* the 'face(s)' presented by Japanese; it is about *deciphering* their cultural context."[7] In this case, the photographic record enables us to follow the course of Seki Hajime's journey from boyhood to adulthood. It preserves traces of his youth that, when interwoven with written sources, permit us to put flesh on the bones of our biographical narrative. Placed one after the other, in chronological order, Hajime's portraits serve as signposts of a sort. Not only do they record the biological transformation of the boy into the man, but they trace the course of his youthful socialization.

Read metonymically by their visual signs, these portraits tell a story of personal and professional successes: of the son of an ex-samurai who graduated from the elite Tokyo Commercial College; of a promising teacher who, after completing his apprenticeship in Kobe and Niigata, was invited back to teach at his alma mater; of a talented young scholar who won a prestigious government fellowship to study in Europe; and, finally, of a successful academic professional who married, had children, and assumed the family headship. Read empathetically, with the privileged eye of the biographer, these portraits give up even more. They reveal a young boy who was nurtured by a loving father; an adolescent who learned the value of discipline and perseverance from his mother; a teenager who was abruptly thrust into manhood; a gifted student who later distinguished himself as a respected teacher; a serious scholar whose experience abroad wrought a transformative influence on his work; a mature young adult who learned to make his own way in the world; a proud son, brother, husband, and father who epitomized the modern family values promoted in Meiji Japan; and a passionate citizen with a profound personal and professional commitment to his nation's future. Thus, at one and the same time, these portraits help explain where a young man found his place in society and how he forged his identity as an individual.

How we read such photographic images depends, in the first instance, on what sort of images they are. The extant images of Seki Hajime as a young man are similar in one important respect: they are all studio portraits. What makes this especially intriguing from the biographer's perspective is that Meiji studio portraiture, like its British Victorian progenitor, was a highly conventionalized craft. Initially, Japanese studio photographers largely imitated Western portraiture, replicating Victorian visual conventions in the interest of creating a generically modern social image for their native subjects. Later, they assimilated these conventions into a higher, and more specifically Japanese, purpose: the promotion of a new national imaginary under the public rubric of the family-state *(kazoku kokka)*. Because such portraits (including those of Seki Hajime) were typically taken on certain special occasions—at New Year's, on graduation day, for leave-takings, during family and school excursions—studio photographers were able to fine-tune their craft and to refine their visual aesthetic.

At the beginning of the Meiji Era, the Japanese studio photographer endeavored to depict his subjects in an idealized state of modern normalcy: he produced portraits that made his subjects appear modern, thus easing them into modern life.[8] The studio photographer accomplished this delicate task for Japanese families by placing them in contrived Western domestic settings—where they would look at home with modernity, so to speak. The Meiji portrait studio, in this sense, was a liminal space in which people gained what Julia Hirsch terms "temporary immunity from reality."[9] Here, the photographer and his subjects collaborated to manufacture idealized images of social reality. The family albums in which these portraits were thereafter preserved—albums that, according to John Dower, "became an almost obsessive part of popular culture"—were liminal worlds of another sort. In early Meiji, when "traditional family relationships were being eroded by urbanization and modernization,"[10] family albums provided people with a new way to preserve memories and to confabulate family narratives for themselves and for posterity.

Needless to say, considerable artifice was involved in the production of such images of the family. Early Meiji studio photographers assembled an impressive array of state-of-the-art cameras, lights, backdrops, props, and darkroom equipment—most of it imported. Not only did they emulate the professional technique of Western studio photographers, but they culti-vated a visual aesthetic that virtually replicated Western conventions of family portraiture. These early photographers did not emulate the visual aesthetic of traditional woodblock printing or of ink painting. Indeed, as Dower observes incredulously, they "appear to have been uninfluenced by these traditional ways of seeing."[11] It is important to recall, however, that their failure to invoke traditional ways of seeing was consistent with their disinterest in what we might call "traditional ways of being." While Jap-anese masters of the photograph *(shashinshi)* were busy testing the limits of photography as an art form[12]—and their Western counterparts were busy manufacturing exoticized images of traditional life[13]—studio por-traitists were hard at work developing a repertoire of photographic tech-niques and visual conventions capable of capturing the ethos of Japan's emergent modern society.

Commissioned mainly to produce images that assimilated the family into modernity, early Meiji studio photographers did so in the spirit of *bunmei-kaika* (civilization and enlightenment). They modeled their family portraits after Western ones, thereby reaffirming the popular belief that modernization was synonymous with Westernization. Many of their ear-liest portraits reproduced Western ways of seeing and being down to the smallest detail. Often featuring aristocratic elites in European drag, posed before lavish Occidental backdrops, these photographs poignantly docu-mented the facile modus operandi of *bunmei-kaika* believers. Their sub-jects, who look like nothing so much as poseurs,[14] tragicomically witness the hypnotic power that the Occidental imaginary wielded over early Meiji Japanese.

The aura that surrounded the camera itself accounts, at least in part, for such facile photography. As one of the "seven standard paraphernalia of civilization and enlightenment" *(bunmei kaika no nanatsu dōgu)*, cameras, together with newspapers, the postal system, gaslights, steam engines, ex-hibitions, and dirigible balloons,[15] were accorded virtually magical trans-formative powers. Although photography was demystified by the 1890s—demoted from modern magic to technical wizardry—people continued to value its transformative capabilities. Eager to assimilate gracefully into modern life, yet trapped in a real world where grace was a social affectation monopolized by the hereditary aristocracy, mid-Meiji families found solace in the fact that studio photographers could simulate the ideal world they envisioned. In modern Japan, as in the modern West, studio photographers were consummate makeover artists. Their ability to simulate a strategic social transformation, and to preserve a photographic trace of it for posterity, made them indispensable to modern families who felt besieged by change. As Dower puts it, they "offered comforting scrapbook evidence that everyone had a place and everything was proceeding well—and in the same gesture . . . offered seductive models of harmony to emulate."[16]

Meiji studio portraits fall into two broad aesthetic categories: those with and those without scenic backdrops. While both styles of portraiture left revealing visual traces of their subjects, they revealed different elements of the subjects' identities. Hirsch's observations about these same two styles of portraiture in the West are equally relevant to Japan:

> The plain background . . . frees the person in the picture from the grip
> of any spatial allusions at all—he seems to be both everywhere and
> nowhere—and allows the photographer and the viewer to look at faces
> and bodies unencumbered by allusions to place, to time, to work,
> and to possessions. The family photograph taken without such clues
> focuses far more on personalities and relationships than on activity
> and experience. The photographer who takes his subject in a scenic
> background—painted or biographical—acts as a producer putting
> together a stage design; the photographer taking his subject in front of
> a plain background becomes a psychologist, perhaps even a philosopher,
> concerned with ultimate human values.[17]

As we shall see, Seki Hajime was subject to the photographic imaginations of "producers" and "psychologists" alike during his youth. But while we can easily establish which of these photographic imaginations was at play in a given portrait simply by glancing at the backdrop, we cannot so easily determine what exactly was being imagined. Which is another way of saying that Meiji studio photographers, once mimetic in their practice, quickly learned to play producer and psychologist in a specifically Japanese context. They were initially enabled to do so by their growing familiarity with photographic technology, and their resolve was fueled by the huge consumer market created by the revolutionary technology of dry-plate processing.

Unlike the self-consciously artistic masters of the photograph of early Meiji, who pioneered the Western-born craft of photography in Japan, mid-Meiji studio photographers were pragmatic merchants of the photograph. Capitalizing on the efficient, new dry-plate technique to reduce unit costs, they made studio portraiture affordable to the general populace. So successfully did studio photographers court consumers, in fact, that the public came to call the photographers themselves *shashinya*, or photographic studios.[18]

By the turn of the century, studio portraiture had become so popular and affordable that enterprising entrepreneurs opened spacious new studios. One well-documented example of such a business is the Tomishige Photographic Studio (Tomishige Shashinjo) in Kumamoto. This expansive complex of production and processing facilities featured a capacious second-story studio with floor-to-ceiling windows on one side and high transoms on the other.[19] Such photographic studios were worlds unto themselves in more ways than one. Like their counterparts in the West, as described by Suren Lalvani, they contained reception rooms (full of "iconic representations"), studios ("where the subjects were transformed into images"), and laboratories ("the concealed factory space of production").[20] Here, under one roof, Meiji merchants of the photograph promoted, produced, and processed their images.

In Japan, as in the West, photographers made the studio itself into what Lalvani calls "a fabricated space, a theatrical space outfitted with props designed to promote the public self of portraiture." The studio was thus a liminal space "for constructing metonymic signs that evoke[d] the necessary impressions and experiences."[21] What makes such studios interesting for our purposes is that studio photographers in Japan constructed their metonymic signs from the same material cultural repertoire drawn on by studio photographers in the West. Not only did they strive to simulate the Victorian parlors that their Western counterparts did, but they used identical backdrops and props. The Tomishige Photographic Studio, for example, employed a sizeable collection of "Western" background cloths, Gobelin chairs, armchairs, benches, wooden tables, ornamental columns, statuettes, blacked-out mirrors, and other props. Using these to set distinctly Victorian-looking scenes, its photographers then posed their subjects with the help of marking rods and metal headrests; took portraits with J. H. Dallmeyer (London), C. A. Steinheil (Prussia), or Wollensak Verito (United States) lenses and Thornton-Pickard (London) shutters; and processed the prints on Ilford (United Kingdom) dry plates.[22]

Although mid-Meiji studio photographers re-created Victorian parlors in their studios, then posed and shot their subjects with Victorian photographic equipment, they did not re-create the Victorian ethos in their photographs. In other words, while they adopted Western studio conventions, they adapted these conventions to a distinctly Japanese purpose. Even as Western studio photographers were bourgeoisifying the Victorian parlor,[23] their Japanese counterparts were nationalizing it.

In the West, parlors had become the consummate bourgeois status symbol by the 1880s, and Victorian families accordingly expected photographers to simulate them in their studios. As Hirsch describes the effect, "In photographic studios, standing in front of elaborate furnishings, [people] shed their histories, and assumed a homogenized air of propriety."[24] But for many status-seeking Americans, it seems such simulations were not sufficient, for, rather than going to portrait studios, they invited studio portraitists into their homes. Whether taken in a studio or in a home, however, the artistic, soft-focus, "cabinet-card" photographs that soon dominated family portraiture in the West eloquently witnessed the Victorian proclivity for bourgeois social display.[25]

In Japan, by contrast, the virtual Victorian parlors in which Meiji studio photographers posed their subjects were liminal spaces in the extreme. They did not simulate actual parlors, which were rare in Japan, nor did they embody an image of "home" that Meiji families either recognized or desired. Indeed, most families neither had nor had use for such parlors, not to mention the cabinets and mantel pieces on which their Western cousins displayed family portraits. While Victorian parlors in and of themselves were culturally irrelevant to late Meiji Japanese, the virtual parlors in which they posed for family portraits could hardly have been made more culturally meaningful: They embodied a modern Japanese model of domesticity.

In these virtual Victorian parlors, late Meiji studio photographers produced uniform, hard-focus portraits that were intended to show families not as they were seen or even as they wished to be seen but as they should be. Their adaptation of Victorian bourgeois imagery to Japanese social idealism was the by-product of a public agenda to modernize and stabilize the Japanese family system.

This public agenda, which pivoted on the invented tradition of the family-state, was introduced in the Imperial Rescript on Education of 1890 and codified in the new "family administration policy." Under the influence of family-state ideology, as Wilbur Fridell has pointed out, "Japanese leaders and ideologues referred to the nation more and more as an 'extended family,' not by way of analogy, but as a historical fact. The nation was not *like* a family, it *was* a family."[26] Inoue Tetsujirō, the most prominent spokesman for the family-state ideology, was soon speaking grandiloquently of Japan as "one nation, one family."[27] And by the 1890s, as T. Fujitani has compelling argued, the Meiji leaders were eager to move from rhetoric to reality:

> [S]ince . . . the nation was coming to be represented in the dominant discourse of the time as a family writ large, as a "nation-state family" *(kazoku kokka)*, in which the imperial household and the people

were mystically bound together as a family and where "the righteousness *(gi)* between the ruler and his subjects and the intimacy between father and child are absolutely the same," it was imperative that the family itself be a properly ordered model for the nation. In other words, for the metonymic relationship between the family and the nation to work as an effective mechanism of control, it was necessary that the part, the family, be understood as the stable and properly hierarchized whole, the nation.[28]

In an effort to promote this new perspective of "national community," the Meiji leaders mediated a visual transformation of the monarchy, producing and disseminating prints and photographs that represented the emperor and empress as role models of the modern family-state.[29] By 1910, ethics textbooks were replete with lessons and admonitions that linked family values to emperor worship, such as the following passage on loyalty and filial piety: "Our country is based on the family system. The whole country is one great family, and the Imperial House is the Head Family *(sōka)*. It is with the feeling of filial love and respect for parents that we Japanese people express our reverence toward the Throne of unbroken imperial line."[30]

The Meiji leaders brought their message to the people through a variety of means, but most effectively in illustrated elementary school ethics primers. Here, they enshrined family-state values with captioned depictions of the proper parent-child relationship *(oyako)*, parental benevolence *(on)*, well-adjusted siblings *(nakayoki kyōdai)*, and family enjoyment *(katei no tanoshimi)*.[31] As propagated in the schools and elsewhere, family-state ideology presented the family *(katei)* as the essence of the household *(ie)* and reflexively identified the family with home *(hōmu)*.[32]

By the early 1900s, such ideas had taken root in the popular imagination. As Muta Kazue points out, "The 'home' became the symbol of an affective union of family members and at the same time was considered to be the foundation for the development of the Japanese nation state."[33] So widely was this notion diffused that one popular magazine felt compelled to remark on it in 1906: "The home, the home *(katei katei)*, everywhere in the country people are paying attention to it now. Whether one talks of state or society, the foundation is the home, where all social reform must originate."[34]

It is hardly surprising that studio photographers jumped on the family-state bandwagon. As family portraitists in the main, it was their job to translate the popular enthusiasm for modern family values into appropriate photographic images. While their early Meiji predecessors had gestured suggestively at ideals such as social harmony, late Meiji studio photographers produced portraits that objectified the family values enshrined by the Meiji state by suffusing their portraits with symbolic power. Not only did they carefully choreograph the compositions, posing their subjects in such a way as to project the image of an ideal family, but they manufactured sets designed to project a generic image of familial modernity. By domesticating Western cultural iconography—that is, by severing signifier from signified—late Meiji studio photographers managed to transform the drawing room from a Victorian symbol of bourgeois social status into a Japanese emblem of modern familism.

The family portraits produced by studio photographers were all the more meaningful because the families themselves were anthropomorphic icons of nation-statehood. While nations in the West were typically symbolized by abstractly heroic figures, such as Britannia for Britain and Marianne for France, Japan accorded living, breathing families this distinction. When photographers posed late Meiji families for studio portraits, they took pains to cast them in precisely this light—as the bedrock of modern Japan.

For modern, urban, nuclear families, whose social status remained painfully ambiguous, such symbolic association with the nation-state was arguably significant in the extreme.[35] The Seki family is a prime example. In 1896, when they crossed the threshold of an unnamed Tokyo portrait studio to pose for the portrait with which we opened this chapter, they crossed over into a liminal space in which they hoped to reinvent themselves for the camera. With the help of the studio photographer, whose expertise as a cultural producer enabled him to finesse that objective, the Sekis were portrayed as both dutifully filial and comfortingly familistic.

A cursory glance at this portrait might suggest that the Sekis were able to effortlessly project this image. But a closer look belies that impression, and a privileged one demolishes it. What the casual observer recognizes as uneasiness in facial expressions and postures, the biographer can explain; what such an observer recognizes as material and social signs of the times, the historian can interpret; and what such an observer notices about the artifice of the studio photographer, the careful researcher can explicate. The key is to weave these biographical, historical, and analytical elements together into a "thick description" of the studio portrait that breathes life into its subjects and its subject matter.

To look at this studio portrait out of its private context is to gaze on a dignified Meiji family of some social standing. All four members of the family are formally attired in the fashion of former samurai, presumably in the tradition of their forebears. The matriarch wears this distinction with notable grace. In her dark-hued kimono—with a white underkimono pulled up high and tight about her neck and split-toed socks called *tabi* covering her ankles—Yoshi is the picture of propriety. But this portrait holds surprises. The figure seated next to Yoshi is not her husband, as we might expect and the photographer might have preferred; rather, it is her eldest son, Hajime, the subject of this biography. In this portrait, Hajime literally wears honor and tradition on his sleeve: The formal *haori* (or half-coat) over his kimono, tied by a silk ceremonial braid, bears the Seki family crest. Finally, standing at their mother's side, as befits their status as younger sons, are Hajime's brothers, Giichi and Yoshinori.

On closer inspection, this traditionally clad family betrays a curiously modern aspect as well. Not only is Hajime holding a modish bowler hat in his hands, tipped toward the camera for effect, he is seated alongside his mother in one of two matching fringed chairs with upholstered seats and finely turned legs. These props, we soon recognize, are a central element of the contrived Western domestic space in which the studio photographer suspended his subjects. Carefully positioned on a patterned surface intended to simulate a parquet floor, before a painted backdrop rendered in perspective, the figures cast receding shadows under lights that enhance the illusion of depth. Flanked by plush satin curtains and an elaborately carved armoire, the subjects have been made to appear as if they had gathered in a Western drawing room.

In this liminal space, enveloped by icons of modern domesticity appropriated from Western bourgeois society, we might reasonably expect the Seki family to exude the "homogenized air of propriety" that the photographer worked so cleverly to achieve. But they do not. Their forced expressions and awkward postures betray the limitations of studio portraiture. Photographers were restricted to one or two takes—a restriction that severely limited their ability to produce powerful illusions—and they were compelled to take subjects as they were. No matter how adept they were at molding their subjects, studio photographers could hardly hope to change them. In this respect especially, as we shall illustrate, the Sekis set their photographer an almost insurmountable challenge.

Any success the Sekis' photographer had in projecting the illusion of familial normalcy is attributable almost entirely to his technical and artistic expertise. He carefully positioned his subjects on a set whose striking Occidentalism sufficiently generalized a Western setting to make it appear generically modern. Which is to say, he compellingly domesticated Western domesticity, naturalizing it to modern Japan. The photographer then posed the family in such a way as to accentuate the effect: Pressing its members in on one another, in uncomfortably intimate proximity, he clearly coaxed the figures into assuming appropriately "modern" seated and standing postures.

Notwithstanding this masterfully contrived illusion, one would be hard-pressed to describe the final product as a flattering family portrait. Paradoxically, the scrupulous composition of the portrait betrays the false illusion of comfortable domesticity manufactured by the photographer. Precisely because the figures have been drawn into an unnaturally tight semicircle in order to suggest family intimacy, their discomfort and disorientation is obvious.[36] Clearly asked to keep their eyes on the birdie, Yoshi and her younger sons fixed their eyes on a point to the right of the camera—she intensely, they blankly. But not Hajime: He can be seen sternly staring the camera down.

So, how do we explain the awkwardness of this portrait? It arguably derives, in large part, from the artifice of the studio photographer. When he objectified Seki Hajime and his family, subjecting them to the homogenizing gaze of the family-state, he unwittingly confronted them with their inability to meet its familistic ideal. He did so by seating Hajime in the position of family head. By sharpening this symbolic presence, the photographer likely hoped to blur a real-life absence whose commemoration had brought the family to his studio in the first place. He would have known immediately from the Sekis' dark-hued formal attire—identifiable by its somber colors as the semimourning clothes typically worn to memorial services for the deceased—that these were mourners. In all likelihood, the Sekis themselves envisioned the portrait session as an opportunity both to honor the spirit of the departed and to witness their own ability to move on with dignity. They seemingly did not anticipate just how awkward it would be to suspend disbelief. As the conventions of family portraiture reminded them, they were far removed from the familistic ideal promoted by the Meiji nation-state. They could not conceal the fact that they were not a "norm-al" family at all, despite the effort of the studio photographer to reinvent them. They carried the discomfiting evidence of this on their backs and in their faces, and the studio photographer unwittingly accentuated it.

The Sekis' awkwardness can be traced to a fateful turn of events six years earlier that had shattered their lives: the premature death of Seki Chikanori, husband and father. Compelled to confront the impact of that painful event on their lives, the Sekis witnessed it in their expressions and in their postures. The disarmingly fresh-faced Hajime, an unmarried twenty-three-year-old high school headmaster at the time of this portrait, stands in uncomfortably and incongruously for the father he has lost; his sorrowfully stern-faced mother—compelled in widowhood to find employment and to adopt out her infant daughter, Shige, in order to keep the family together—wears a look of weariness on her face and the weight of personal loss on her sleeve; Hajime's abashedly blank-faced brothers share the vacant expression of adolescent boys deprived of a paternal role model. Albeit at the Sekis' expense, this studio portrait reminds us that Meiji familism was an invented tradition that conspicuously elided social reality.[37]

While it does not give up its secrets easily, this portrait ultimately speaks volumes about Seki Hajime's youth. By similarly deconstructing other such portraits in the coming pages, I hope to work a biographical metamorphosis. Specifically, I propose to read the bare-bones written record of Hajime's youth into several other photographs gleaned from the Seki family album. If I am thus able to breathe some life back into the two-dimensional figure who haunts the narratives of Seki Hajime's earlier biographers—to restore his integrity as a historical subject—then perhaps I can also write him into modern Japanese history as the seminal figure that I believe him to be.

THE MAKING OF AN ECONOMIST

The earliest extant image of Seki Hajime dates to 1876. Then age three, he sat for a commemorative photograph (figure 2) alongside his kimono-clad father. The tiny Hajime, easily identifiable by his protuberant ears, is seated *seiza* (formally upright) on a nondescript chair in his ceremonial best. Judging from the scowl on his face, he was not a willing subject. His father, by contrast, looks the part of the proud patriarch. Leaning into his son slightly, with one arm steadying the boy from behind, he has assumed an almost protective position. This gentle gesture of paternal affection, combined with the quiet intelligence that animates his expression, speaks eloquently for the man and his humanity. These qualities resonate resoundingly because this particular studio portrait, taken before a nearly blank backdrop, placed the photographer in the role of psychologist. By all appearances it is a production-line portrait—probably commemorating a visit to the local shrine—but its spare (though not completely bare) backdrop heightens our awareness, as it must have the photographer's, of the subjects' expressions.

While this photograph reveals precious little about Hajime except that

Figure 2.   Seki Chikanori with Hajime (1876). Courtesy of the Seki family and the Osaka City History Archive.

he was the treasured first son of a former samurai, it is a revealing study in the character of his father. Born Nemoto Saburōbei in the post town of Yokkaichi along the Tōkaidō Highway, he was adopted at age five into the family of Seki Kangorō, a low-ranking Tokugawa retainer from Shimōsa, and renamed Seki Chikanori. This adoptive son was educated as a youngster in literature and mathematics by a Hosokura clan tutor, then went on to study accounting and English at the renowned Numazu Military Academy and at the Finance Ministry's Currency Institute. Early in the Meiji Era, Chikanori settled on a career in teaching. He opened a private academy in the port town of Nishi Izu and moved his young wife, Yoshi, there from the castle/post town of Numazu. On September 26, 1873, Yoshi gave birth to their first child, Hajime, in Hōgenji Temple at nearby Nichinahama.

Our portrait of father and son, taken three years later, suggests that Chikanori understood the importance of nurturing his young son—a sentiment likely reinforced by memories of his own uprooted childhood. We might compellingly associate the self-evident paternalism expressed in this photograph with the momentous decision that Chikanori soon made to relocate his family from the backwoods of Izu to the metropole of Tokyo. According to local lore in Nishi Izu, he uprooted his family for one reason alone: to make certain that his young son received a top-flight education.[38]

With the help of his father-in-law, who had relocated his own household to the lively Shitamchi (downtown) district of Asakusa, Chikanori settled his family into metropolitan life in the upscale Yamanote (hillside) district of Yotsuya in 1877. Here, amid the families of other ex-samurai, who had gravitated in some numbers to Yamanote,[39] he doubtless hoped to provide his son with social advantages. Over the next dozen years, the family flourished. Yoshi gave birth to two more sons and a daughter, and Chikanori established himself as a respected educator, first at the Tokyo Girls' Normal School and later at the Second Prefectural Middle School in nearby Ibaraki Prefecture. In keeping with his legendary pledge to secure Hajime the best education possible, Chikanori placed him in the preparatory program of the prestigious Tokyo Commercial College (Tokyo Shōgyō Gakkō) at Hitotsubashi. In 1890, the father's dreams for his son were realized: Hajime gained admission to the school's regular degree program.

That same year, however, the family's fortunes took a tragic turn: Chikanori was struck down suddenly by a fatal illness. While this dutiful husband and father left a legacy of loyalty to family and respect for education, he also left behind a wife and four children. As the portrait with which we opened this chapter suggests, the family struggled in the coming years to survive his loss intact. Its success, as I soon argue, resulted from the extraordinary fortitude exhibited by Yoshi. Forced to give up her infant daughter for adoption, she managed nonetheless to land a teaching job and to raise three sons as a single working mother.

Barely seventeen when his father died, Hajime might easily have lost his way. But he was apparently unslowed by the personal tragedy that had befallen him and his family. He studied hard enough and well enough to be named class salutatorian upon his graduation from the Tokyo Commercial College in 1893. His graduation portrait (figure 3) reveals a baby-faced young man of twenty with the close-cropped hair then typical of male students. Clad in one of the ubiquitous, German-inspired school uniforms that held the day, Hajime would look entirely unremarkable were it not for his intense expression. Indeed, although the unflattering camera angle infelicitously magnified one of his conspicuous ears, the earnestness written on his face easily eclipses the ungainly impression made by his features.

While the expression is vintage Hajime—one he reproduced time and again for later portraits—we have the studio photographer to thank for capturing it with such dramatic results here. The photographer achieved this effect by means of a time-tested technique commonly associated with political portraits: the three-quarter profile. As described by Sontag, this technique produces "a gaze that soars rather than confronts, suggesting instead of the relation to the viewer, to the present, the more ennobling abstract relation to the future."[40] Especially significant, Hajime's photographer chose not to follow the more common Western convention for graduation photos—the frontal shot, which "signifies solemnity, frankness, the disclosure of the subject's essence."[41] This was no ordinary college graduate, but one of Japan's best and brightest. Already a bureaucratic appointee to the Ministry of Finance at the time of this portrait, Seki Hajime, by all accounts, was a public man on the rise.

In this revealing psychological portrait, Hajime's eyes convey the same quiet intelligence of his father. Yet his lips convey something more—an emotional intensity that we cannot read in Chikanori's face nor trace to what we know of his life history. This intensity reminds us of the obvious: that Hajime was his mother's, as well as his father's, son. Caught here at an impressionable age—at the crossroads between adolescence and adulthood—Hajime's emotions are written on his face. The look he wears in this graduation portrait displays the same intensity that his mother would exhibit in the family portrait of 1896. Not only had Hajime's character been formed by the time he graduated from college, but it arguably combined personal qualities traceable to both his parents.

Figure 3. Graduation day (1893). Courtesy of the Seki family and the Osaka City History Archive.

From 1890 on, Hajime lived up to the academic legacy left by his father but lived after the ethical example of his mother. If he inherited his talent for economics from Chikanori, he surely realized that talent because he possessed the personal and professional tenacity of Yoshi. His mother's life, which was quite literally transformed in the wake of Chikanori's death, provided Hajime with a character-building example of true grit. This now-single mother of four, who succeeded suddenly to the dual responsibility of breadwinning and child rearing in 1890, was forced to give up her baby daughter for adoption. In the coming years, Yoshi raised her three sons on her own, apparently with the help of a live-in maid.[42]

In order to make ends meet, Yoshi accepted a teaching position at an unidentified girls' occupational school in Tokyo. If this school was at all like those examined by Kawashima Yasuyoshi—the most famous of which, ironically, was located near the Tokyo Commercial College campus at Hitotsubashi—Yoshi was already practicing what she would preach to her students: the central purpose of such schools was to teach young girls from the lower classes how to fend for themselves (jikatsu).[43] In both her personal and her professional life, as this sketch suggests, Yoshi was anything but the "good wife, wise mother" (ryōsai kenbo) prescribed by Meiji family-state ideology.[44] Rather than presenting her boys with a properly subservient model of womanhood, Yoshi showed them the value of tenacious independence and perseverance, not to mention fierce family loyalty. These same personal qualities stare out at us from Hajime's graduation portrait, testifying powerfully to the influence of the mother on the son.

Aside from offering clues to his personal character, Hajime's graduation portrait holds hints about his professional trajectory. The intelligent-looking young man in the photograph wears the Western uniform of a student schooled in the knowledge and the manners of the modern world. Yet while this knowledge brought him recognition at graduation, the manners nearly cost him his career. In the rarefied world of Meiji colleges, where the nation's educated elite were groomed for prominent positions in government and business,[45] Hajime was a square intellectual peg who refused to conform to the round academic hole of practical education.

The college that Hajime attended would soon become one of the most elite institutions in the land. The brainchild of Mori Arinori (1847–1889), father of the Meiji educational system, the Tokyo Commercial College was Japan's first business school. Its establishment at Hitotsubashi in 1875 was due to Mori's conviction, formed during his posting to Washington as Japanese ambassador in the early 1870s, that business education and nationhood went hand in hand.[46] Fukuzawa Yukichi (1835–1901), brought on board as a trustee, waxed eloquent about the school's lofty mission: "In fighting one another by means of the sword one cannot go to the battlefield without learning the art of fencing beforehand. Likewise, in the age of battles by means of business, one cannot confront foreigners without learning the art of business."[47] Appropriately, given the importance accorded business education, the central government's Ministry of Agriculture and Commerce assumed administrative control of the Tokyo Commercial College in 1884. Subsequently certified by the Ministry of Education as one of five public commercial schools in the nation, it had a curriculum patterned after Europe's finest such school, the Belgian Institut Supérieur de Commerce d'Anvers.[48]

In 1890, the year Seki Hajime enrolled in its regular program, the Tokyo Commercial College was granted the elevated status of a higher school (or what I am calling a college). From the outset, it established itself as an elite institution, if also a slightly controversial one. From 1889, its students competed each year in a boat race with highly vaunted Ichikō, the top-ranking higher school in the nation. According to Donald Roden, Ichikō students saw the race as a yearly reenactment of the Punic Wars: the "manly virtues" of Rome were represented by Ichikō, the "Carthaginian lust for business and material extravagance" by the Tokyo Commercial College.[49] In fact, the Ichikō students were not far off the mark in characterizing the educational ethos of their rival institution. "According to the revised regulations issued in 1886," write Sugiyama and Nishizawa, "the new Tokyo Commercial School was to be the 'place where the future administrators and managers of commercial affairs, or the future directors and teachers in the commercial schools were to be trained.'"[50] Under the controversial leadership of Yano Jirō, who began in the late 1880s to steer the curriculum away from its Belgian-inspired emphasis on research and toward the U.S. model of practical commercial education, the Tokyo Commercial College was rapidly devolving into the crassest sort of business school.

Yano's educational "reforms" aroused heated debate at the school, splitting the student body into two distinct factions: the research-minded "reformist clique" *(kaikaku-ha)* and the bookkeeping-oriented "apron clique" *(maedare-ha).*[51] Not only was Hajime one of the seven student activists who formed the reformist group, but he was reputedly the one who penned its manifesto. Railing against the "spiritless, passionless gentleman merchants of the world of commerce in Japan" and their woeful ignorance of the wider world, he urged his fellow students to make the student community a "home of righteousness" where all lived by the watchwords of "social improvement" and "progress."[52] Specifically, Hajime and his fellow reformers "were eager to pursue the new and advanced arts of commerce and foreign languages, in order to confront and compete with the foreign merchants" who held sway over Japan's foreign trade.[53]

In 1892, when Headmaster Yano announced his intention to phase out academic research in favor of practical training for government clerkships, the reformist clique put their convictions on the line: they demanded the headmaster's resignation. Yano, whose autocratic tendencies were so pronounced that his successor once wondered aloud whether it might have been more correct to speak of "Yano's Commercial College" than of "the Commercial College's Yano,"[54] was so incensed at the hubris of his adolescent detractors that he expelled fifty-five of them in 1893.

Conspicuously missing from the list of student protesters unceremoniously dismissed by Yano was Seki Hajime.[55] How and why he eluded the dire fate of his classmates remains something of a mystery. One apocryphal story has it that the administration took pity on Hajime as a misguided idealist who had inadvertently jeopardized the fragile future of his fatherless family. While there is little reason to believe this tall tale of benevolent officials seized by compassion for a hapless, teenage household head, there is every reason to believe a slightly different variant of it: that beleaguered school officials, eager to make the best of a bad situation, were persuaded by certain influential national figures to cut a promising student considerable slack.

Reliable rumor has it that no less a national figure than Shibusawa Eiichi, the patron saint of Japanese business, interceded on Hajime's behalf. Shibusawa, it is said, acted on the advice of acquaintances only slightly less powerful than himself who had identified Hajime as a rising star. One of these individuals was almost certainly Soeda Juichi. This reform-minded economist from the Ministry of Finance, who later penned the foreword to Hajime's first economic treatise, had already recruited him for government service. Working behind the scenes to reinstate Hajime, these same national figures apparently forced Yano to tender his resignation as headmaster later in 1893. Not only did this move pave the way for a thorough institutional housecleaning at the Tokyo Commercial College, but it opened the door for Hajime's eleventh-hour reprieve. Cast briefly into academic limbo, Hajime was ultimately permitted to take a special senior examination. In July 1893, he was graduated along with thirty-six of his classmates in a ceremony conducted at Tokyo Imperial University.

At about this time, Hajime posed for two different portraits that tell us much about the man he would soon become. In the first (figure 4), a family portrait taken with his brothers, Hajime has adopted the style and the posture of the family head. He sits stiffly erect in his kimono and haori, one hand tucked manfully into his sleeve, with the bearing of a man twice his age. This is the portrait of a young man who has acknowledged his responsibility to honor the family name and to maintain the family line.

In the second portrait, taken with a classmate, Hajime has adopted a very different persona. Figure 5 is a study in contrasts that accentuates

Figure 4.   Seki Hajime and his brothers (1893). Courtesy of the Seki family and the Osaka City History Archive.

Figure 5.   Seki Hajime (standing) with a Tokyo Commercial College classmate (ca. 1893). Courtesy of the Seki family and the Osaka City History Archive.

the differences in public style adopted by Meiji elites from various walks of life. Hajime's seated classmate, whose apron identifies him as a traditional scion of commerce, has adopted a hybrid style of dress common for the day: a kimono topped with a straw boater. By contrast, Hajime, every bit the modern man of his times, has affected a casual Western appearance. Similarly sporting a straw boater, he has otherwise outfitted himself as a modern gentleman in dress shirt, vest, waistcoat, pleated trousers, and leather boots. His erect figure, accentuated by the bamboo cane at his side, looms imposingly over that of his classmate in what might almost be interpreted as a metonymic representation of the ascendancy of the "modern" professional over his "traditional" predecessor. Secure with his past and hopeful at last for his future, Hajime cut a figure of self-confidence that mirrored the growing confidence of his maturing nation.

Hajime had every reason to feel self-confident in 1893. With degree in hand, he had accepted a post in the Banking Section of the Ministry of Finance. Yet his career as a government bureaucrat was destined to be short-lived. Apparently uninspired by his bureaucratic duties, he leapt at the opportunity to join the Kobe Commercial College faculty less than a year after joining the government, choosing the life of the scholar over that of the bureaucrat. Only much later, when he was offered the opportunity to combine these two worlds in the service of his nation, as a deputy mayor of the city of Osaka, did Hajime return to public life.

Surrounded by his Kobe Commercial College students in 1894 for the obligatory commemorative photograph of a school excursion to Kyoto (figure 6), Hajime looks like nothing so much as an English country squire. The tailored suit, calf-high riding boots, bowler hat, and walking-stick umbrella distinguish him from his uniformed students and also distinguish him as a modern man of mid-Meiji. Within two years, this bright, ambitious young economist had risen to the next rung of the academic ladder: he was named headmaster of the Niigata Commercial College in 1896.

About this time Hajime returned to Tokyo for the memorial service that occasioned the family portrait of 1896 with which we opened this chapter. To look at this photograph in sequence now, along the trajectory we have traced for Hajime from boyhood to manhood, is to be reminded, among other things, that the more things change, the more things remain the same. If the clothes can truly be said to make the man, then Hajime expressed his identity clearly: he was every bit the modern man of his times, sporting modish Western fashions in public but adopting Japanese dress in private.

No less intriguing than the distinct personae that Hajime adopted in

Figure 6.   Seki Hajime with his students on a school trip (1894). Courtesy of the Seki family and the Osaka City History Archive.

public and private, as evidenced by his seeming sartorial schizophrenia, is the emotional consistency that he displayed in all his youthful portraits. Aside from his baby picture, taken in 1876, Hajime exudes the intensity and intelligence that defined his character from adolescence into adulthood. These portraits eloquently depict a young man certain of his modern identity. Unlike the young men who reached adulthood at the beginning of the Meiji Era, whom Kenneth Pyle has dubbed the "new generation,"[56] Hajime never struggled with his cultural identity. He was typical, in this sense, of what I will call the "younger generation"—young men who, literally and figuratively, grew up with modern Japan. Unlike the new generation, whose profound sense of cultural discontinuity both heightened their awareness of tradition and caused them to stigmatize it,[57] the younger generation was unfazed equally by aesthetic eclecticism, cultural fluidity, and ideological syncretism. They were children of the new age; and the modern world, with its accent on change, was the only world they knew.

As we pore over portraits taken of Hajime in his youth—of this young man who was arguably typical of the younger generation—we can see the self-confidence in his eyes. Only later, in portraits of Hajime as an adult, do we also begin to sense the impatience that it bred. Much like mid-Meiji Japan itself, Hajime knew he was going places and couldn't wait to get there. Less than a year after he accepted the headmaster's position in Niigata, he was offered a lectureship in commercial science at his alma mater. Of this move from Niigata to Tokyo, like his earlier one from Kobe to Niigata, he says only that it was made "for my own [selfish] reasons" *(jiko no tsugō)*.[58] We can reasonably surmise from Hajime's stunning rise within the academic profession, however, that political patronage also came into the picture—or, to put it more bluntly, that he was quietly placed on the fast track to professional success.

But what distinguished Hajime from other promising young academics? In a nutshell, it was his genius for political economics. By the time Hajime was taken back into the academic fold at his alma mater, Yano Jirō had been replaced by a headmaster who shared Hajime's belief that research lay at the core of a modern business school's mission. Koyama Kenzō, formerly a functionary in the Ministry of Education, had long been an outspoken advocate of industrial studies. His appointment as headmaster of the Tokyo Commercial College marked the beginning of a new era in Japanese business education. Declaring it his principal intention to implement a curriculum consistent with Japan's renewed mission of "increasing production and promoting [new] industry" *(shokusan kōgyō)*, Koyama made the study of political economy and law the fulcrum of his educational program. Perhaps largely because the school's new academic agenda resonated loudly with Japan's renewed sense of national purpose following the Sino-Japanese War, the school experienced soaring popularity among students. As Earl Kinmonth notes, business schools had generally become more selective in admissions, but none became more so than the Tokyo Commercial College: With nearly five applicants for each available seat by 1904, it was more highly selective even than Ichikō, whose graduates were destined for admission to Tokyo Imperial University.[59]

Aside from excellent students, Koyama attracted first-rate scholars and teachers to the new and improved Tokyo Commercial College. He attracted them from higher schools, universities, government ministries, and the business community,[60] and Hajime was one of his prize recruits. Already a seasoned academic at age twenty-three, Hajime made an immediate impact. In the process, it seems, he also won Koyama's undying respect: twenty years later, when the mayor of Osaka endeavored to lure Hajime from academia to city government, it was Koyama, by then a powerful Osaka banker, who acted as official intermediary.

Before Hajime made his much-celebrated leap from the ivory tower into the real world, however, he made his mark as what has come to be termed a "scholar of practical learning" (*jitsugakusha*). Such men, who made it their business to promote a kind of applied social science, tended to be unrelenting empiricists. Brought back to his alma mater as a lecturer in economics, Hajime published his first treatise in the field of commercial science. His book, released in 1898, was entitled *Shōgyō keizai taii* (An outline of commercial economics).[61] It came complete with a rousing recommendation from Soeda Juichi, the reform-minded official who had earlier recruited him into the Ministry of Finance. In his foreword, which challenged the Japanese "to regenerate national feelings that ha[d] been infused with political theorizing and to face Japan's destiny as the greatest commercial-industrial nation in the East," Soeda hailed *An Outline of Commercial Economics* as a bible for future commercial policymakers.[62]

This was heady praise for the first book of a twenty-five-year-old political economist—praise whose substance and merit I address and assess in the following chapter. Of greater interest to us now, however, as we continue to trace Hajime's youth, is what this early critical acclaim won him: an all-expenses-paid, three-year study tour to the birthplace of modern economics. Awarded a Ministry of Education research fellowship to study commercial education and transport economics in Europe, Hajime left for Belgium in August 1898. He joined five other young Tokyo Commercial College economists in Europe: Fukuda Tokuzō, Sano Zensaku, Tsumura Hidematsu, Takimoto Hideo, and Ishikawa Bungo. Although the diary kept by Hajime during his three-year sojourn on the Continent rarely invites us into his intellectual life, it does afford us a tantalizing glimpse of the setting in which he matured from a journeyman scholar into an accomplished political economist.

In 1899, Hajime tells us, he began his European studies at the Belgian "railroad school," where he conducted research into transport policy and interviewed state railway officials.[63] This was a defining experience in the young scholar's life. Already well-versed in commercial economics—and particularly fascinated by the infrastructures used to enhance commercial exchange—he had been afforded the opportunity to study one of Europe's foremost railway networks. Unlike the railway systems of neighboring countries, which were designed with domestic commerce and national defense in mind, the Belgian railway system was explicitly conceived to promote inter-European communications and commerce.[64] This model network of modern transportation was a central element of the nineteenth-century Belgian project of nation-state building. And as I suggest in the next chapter, this fact had a profound impact on Hajime's emerging identity as a political economist.

During his stay in Belgium, Hajime went on to study commercial science at Anvers.[65] But he longed to make his way to Germany. An ardent admirer of the economic reformers who had formed the so-called German historical school of political economy (hereafter, the German historical school), he petitioned the Japanese Ministry of Education for permission to study at their feet in the University of Berlin. Hajime's request was granted, and if his *"Anmelds Buch"* (class record) is to be believed, his wish was also fulfilled. In October 1900, he was enrolled in classes with two of Germany's most prominent political economists, Adolf Wagner and Gustav Schmoller, and with one its most renowned sociologists, Georg Simmel.[66]

At this time, Wagner and Schmoller especially wielded immense scholarly influence. Along with Lujo Brentano, they were the most famous of the internationally renowned *Kathedersozialisten* (academic socialists), who, as Volker Berghahn has aptly expressed their purpose, "were looking for a third way between Marxism and classical economic liberalism."[67] Not only many aspiring Japanese scholars but legions of Americans parked on the doorstep of these reform-minded scholars.[68] This global migration of foreign students to lecture halls at the University of Berlin was triggered by the fresh perspective that Wagner and Schmoller brought to the study of economics. These now-forgotten political economists—Wagner "a theorist full of ethical furor," Schmoller "a man of history and piecemeal reform"[69]—were then high-profile leaders of a gathering revolt against laissez-faire ideology. By the turn of the century, they and their fellow revisionists from the German historical school had attracted a loyal and influential cohort of young American devotees of what Daniel Rodgers aptly terms "the remoralization of economic life."[70] If smaller in number, an equally stalwart cohort of young Japanese economists were infected with the same enthusiasm. Leading the way, as I argue in the following two chapters, was Seki Hajime.

Swept up in this bracing ideological revolt, whose relevance to the modernization of Japan seemed self-evident, Hajime took every opportunity to further his education and to put his newly acquired knowledge and newfound convictions to the test. Aside from attending lectures, doing language study, reading, and gathering data, he managed to complete a detailed study of European commercial education for the Tokyo Commercial College; to represent his school at the International Congress of Commercial Schools in Paris, where he presented a paper in French; and to coauthor the so-called Berlin Declaration, which demanded the establishment of commercial universities in Japan. Given his obvious engagement and industriousness, it is little wonder that Hajime, alone among his peers, managed to stretch the meager government stipend to the end of each month.[71]

For all the attention that Hajime lavished on his studies, however, he was by no means oblivious to the brave new world surrounding him. Among other things, he made his way to Paris for the grand Exposition Universelle of 1900. As described by a French writer at the time, the Exposition created "a new and ephemeral city hidden in the centre of the other, a whole quarter of Paris in fancy dress, a ball, where the buildings were the masqueraders. To our childish eyes it was a marvel, a coloured picture book, a cave filled by strangers with treasure."[72] This great exposition was conducted on such an immense scale that another Japanese visitor, the novelist Natsume Sōseki, observed that even two weeks would not be enough time to drink in its wonders.[73]

The Paris Exposition was many things, but, as Rodgers has poignantly argued, it was first and foremost a celebration of the triumph of industrial capitalism.[74] Modern nation-states especially were eager to display their technological accomplishments, and several ended up in a vicious competition for space that reproduced national rivalries. Perhaps the biggest loser in this political sweepstakes was Japan. "A distant power with little impact on the administrators or deputies in Paris," explains Richard Mandell, "Japan had her request for more space repeatedly turned down and her allocation diminished."[75] When the Japanese exhibitors arrived, as they themselves tell the story, "the insufficiency of the space became still more shocking."[76] Not surprisingly, Hajime the political economist was struck by the "small scale of the Japanese goods" on display. Equally important, however, he was shocked by the fact that these goods, which included boilers, armor plating, and guns,[77] paled in comparison with the "manufactured goods of Western peoples."[78] It is not difficult to imagine Hajime carrying his impressions of the Exposition back to Japan and integrating them into his prescription for national economic change.

On a second excursion to Paris, just three weeks after his first, Hajime marveled again at Western technology—this time recording his impressions of the Métro, the Parisian underground. He enviously looked over this spanking-new example of twentieth-century technology with the discerning eyes of a modern transport expert and proceeded to produce a detailed description of its equipment. Whether Hajime was able to visit the equally, but differently, path-breaking social-economy pavilion at the

Exposition remains unclear. But, given the shift in perspective from political to social economics that would soon reorient his work, it is tantalizing to imagine him soaking in the exhibits.

As Rodgers has eloquently encapsulated the social-economy pavilion, it was where "the fair's managers gave vent to the anxieties that, beneath the surface, bourgeois confidence, permeated the world of iron."[79] Organized by the Musée Social, a Paris emporium of information on the social economy, the pavilion housed a bewildering array of national exhibits that addressed the unanswered *question sociale* that had cast a troubling shadow over the triumph of industrial capitalism: How were different nations addressing the social problems that attended industrial-capitalist development? The French economist Charles Gide, whose work on social economy Hajime would later praise, contrasted social economy to political economy in his revealing summary of the exhibits. As Rodgers has paraphrased his remarks, "Political economy was the science of the augmentation of wealth. . . . The field of social economy, by contrast, embraced every effort—within the constraints of political economy itself—to temper, socialize, and mutualize the pains of the capitalist transformation. It was the science of 'practical realities and possible amelioration,' the science of 'social peace.' "[80] Whether or not Hajime visited the social-economy pavilion at the Exposition or read Gide's summary of it, he clearly had begun to subject his political economics to critical scrutiny and to plant the seed of social revisionism.

While Seki likely left Paris full of hope for his own nation on its journey toward industrial progress, he surely left Berlin with a touch of anxiety on the same account. Not only had he studied with Schmoller and Wagner, two of the founding fathers of the social-reformist Verein für Sozialpolitik ([German] Association for Social Policy), but he had likely been subjected by Wagner to some scathing criticism of Berlin itself. One historian has noted that Wagner, a resident of this rapidly growing industrial city since 1870, had found himself morally repulsed by its capitalist excesses and had gone on a public crusade to expurgate them.[81]

Although Hajime did not say much about the city that Wagner loved to hate, it is worth providing a capsule portrait of the Berlin that he experienced. Then the third largest metropolis in Europe, Berlin was not merely the recently unified Germany's political capital but also its financial and commercial center.[82] In many ways, Berlin in 1900 embodied the modern city. As Peter Fritzsche has observed, "What was true for the industrial city in general was epitomized by Berlin."[83] However consumed by his studies, Hajime could hardly have been oblivious to the fact of Berlin's "ceaseless mutability."[84] Indeed, it is entirely likely that at least two of his professors addressed the subject directly in their lectures: Wagner with contempt for real estate speculators, whose rapaciousness had convinced him that "everything turns on a reform of the idea of property,"[85] and Simmel, who had long since evinced a palpable ambivalence toward modern city life.[86] While Hajime did not share Simmel's fear of escalating urban alienation, he did share Wagner's contempt for real estate speculators. Later, as I illustrate, he went head to head with Osaka's landed capitalists on exactly the same account.

Although Berlin was his home base by 1900, Hajime apparently did a good deal of traveling throughout Germany. Aside from hitting tourist hot spots such as the childhood home of Johann Goethe in Frankfurt, he also made his way along less-traveled roads. One of the places he visited had already become a minor mecca for European and American social reformers: the model worker community that had been erected by Krupp near its manufacturing center in Essen.[87] We don't know what Hajime thought of this facility at the time he visited it, but we do know that he later proposed the corporate establishment of similar communities in Japan.

All these connections suggest that the hardened young political economist who made his way to Europe in 1898 was irrevocably softened by his experience abroad—made aware that nation building was not only about building wealth but about using it to achieve social progress. Buffeted about by new ideas and new experiences, Hajime soon found himself challenged to transform them into an ideology. Almost literally on the eve of his departure from Europe, Hajime was reunited in Brussels with his Tokyo Commercial College colleague Fukuda Tokuzō. Paradoxically, this encounter with a fellow Japanese economist was the intellectual climax of his three years in Europe. In an unusually introspective diary entry, Hajime recounts the debate into which he was lured by this fellow professor who would later become one of Japan's most renowned economic thinkers—a debate over the very nature of progress. Figure 7, a photograph taken during their reunion in Brussels, captures the combination of cultural cosmopolitanism and intellectual intensity that animated the relationship between Hajime and Tokuzō.

Here we see two of Japan's international elite: young economists sent off to the putative fount of modern civilization to drink up the knowledge needed to guide Japan toward a glorious future in the twentieth century. They wear this lofty purpose in their bearing and in their expressions, and they wear it in distinctive ways that accord with what we know of their respective qualities of mind: Tokuzō, the loquacious intellectual, staring

Figure 7.   Seki Hajime (seated) and Fukuda Tokuzō in Brussels (1900). Courtesy of the Seki family and the Osaka City History Archive.

off wistfully into space, a cigarette dangling from his slender fingers; Hajime, the no-nonsense political economist, sitting powerfully erect with his jaw set. Full of ideas and seemingly full of themselves as well, these driven young men had begun an animated intellectual dialogue that would continue for the next thirty years.

Not only did Hajime and Tokuzō meet regularly in Brussels to outline their respective positions on the subject of national progress, they also exchanged letters clarifying the points they had made. Tokuzō outlined what he took to be universal laws of historical development, while Hajime argued passionately for the notion of "historical relativity" (what he termed *relativität*), in keeping with the orthodoxy of the German historical school. In the end, as Shibamura Atsuki has compellingly argued, these two young scholars set out the methodological perspectives that would later define them as mature economists: Hajime embracing historical empiricism, Tokuzō promoting logical positivism.[88] Equally important, however, these idealistic young men evinced a common commitment to capitalist reform for Japan that bred mutual respect and enduring friendship. Following their return to Japan in 1901, the two collaborated on a monograph that carried their theoretical debate into a practical discussion of foreign trade, taught political economy together for several years at the Tokyo Commercial College, remained regular drinking companions, and continued to debate economic theory until Tokuzō's death in 1930.

In 1901, Hajime and his Tokyo Commercial College colleagues began their long journey back to Japan. They embarked from Southampton by steamship in early September and reached New York in ten days. In his travel diary, Hajime recalled the sights: Wall Street, Broadway, the Brooklyn Bridge, Riverside Park, Grant's Tomb, and, finally, Columbia University. Characteristically, he managed to arrange academic audiences at Columbia: one with the political scientist John W. Burgess, the other with the economist Edwin R. A. Seligman. Both were members of the cosmopolitan fellowship of progressives, which included Japanese scholars, such as Hajime, who had made their way to the lecture halls of reform-minded German scholars since the latter part of the nineteenth century.[89] Burgess was a one-time student of Wilhelm Roscher, founder of the German historical school and a man whose work Hajime both revered and emulated as a young economist;[90] Seligman was a German-trained national economist and cofounder of the American Economic Association, the U.S. version of the social-reformist Verein für Sozialpolitik ([German] Association for Social Policy), founded by Hajime's own German mentors, Schmoller and Wagner.[91]

On October 4, after touring New York and making contact with fellow progressives at Columbia, Hajime and his Japanese colleagues began their cross-country journey by railroad. They traveled from New York to Buffalo with a stopover at Niagara Falls, then on to Chicago, where Hajime caught a glimpse of that city's celebrated elevated railway. Finally, after sweeping across the northern plains to the Pacific, they boarded a ship from Seattle bound for Yokohama.

Of all the sights he saw in the United States, the cities of New York and Chicago seem to have made the deepest impression on Hajime: New York as a universal figure of modernity, Chicago as its specifically American incarnation. Utterly astounded by the technologies he encountered in New York—as he put it, "the newest machines, on the cutting edge of civilization"[92]—Hajime represented the city as a living monument to modern industrial civilization.[93] Among other wonders, he confessed to utter amazement at the combination of speed and danger that attended New York's rapid-transit system.[94] Aside from trains that reached "the highest speed yet attained on first-class railways,"[95] as one New York transit planner boasted at the time, Seki encountered a metropolis awash in electric light, with telephones, elevators, and other technological marvels around every corner.[96]

Finally, Hajime found himself astonished by the stark contrasts that defined urban society. In New York, "twenty- and thirty-story skyscrapers built with the latest technology sit beside crumbling three- and four-story tenements," he lamented. "Here, in the world's wealthiest city, one also finds the world's worst tenements."[97] In this impression, likely left by a tour that took him past both Fifth Avenue chateaux and Lower East Side tenements, Hajime echoed what Theodore Dreiser and other social critics had poignantly observed about New York: that the city displayed a "sharp, and at the same time immense, contrast between the dull and the shrewd, the strong and the weak, the rich and the poor, the wise and the ignorant."[98] Wondering aloud whether the coexistence of great wealth and dire poverty was "a natural product of life in the new world,"[99] Hajime had clearly initiated the interrogation of modern urban life that would ultimately become the focus not only of his scholarship but of his own life.

In this social commentary on New York, as in his subsequent critique of life in Chicago, Hajime forecast his growing concern with the social economy of modern cities. If New York reminded him of European cities, despite the "new world" edge to its society, Chicago struck him as uniquely and troublingly American. "The conditions of [Chicago's] rapid advancement are astonishing," wrote Hajime after his brief stopover in October

1901. "In a word, what one sees is an assemblage of colonists, without order—each individual walking about with only his or her own concerns in mind."[100] Whether Hajime witnessed this rootlessness or whether he imagined it through Professor's Simmel's somewhat cynical social lens is impossible to determine. But here, too, Hajime's views echoed those of other contemporary critics. As quoted by William Cronon in his sweeping history of Chicago and the Great West, the novelist Henry Blake Fuller depicted the city as one in which "nobody really knows who he is, or who his people are, or where he is from. . . . [It is] a town full to overflowing with single young men . . . from everywhere."[101]

Ultimately, it seems, Hajime apprehended both New York and Chicago as abstract figures of modernity. In the contrast between these two metropolises of the new world, which were not defined by history to the extent that European and Japanese cities were, he discovered ample food for thought concerning the nature of modern urban life.

With New York and Chicago still fresh in his mind, Hajime boarded a ship for home in the fall of 1901. On November 3, after three years abroad, he finally stepped back onto Japanese soil.[102] The sparsity and reticence of Hajime's diary entries belie the ample benefit he derived from his time abroad. He had the opportunity to see the wider world he had read and dreamt about as a student; to learn foreign languages and to experience foreign cultures; and to study at the feet of some of the greatest scholars in the Western world. Equally important, however, he had the opportunity to witness modern civilization(s) at work. Coming home to Japan with "civilized" ideas in his head and tangible impressions of "civilization" on his mind, Hajime also arrived with the resolve to bring his ideas and experience to bear on the Japanese enterprise of national progress.

Unlike Fukuda Tokuzō, who seemingly left Europe as a true believer in the metanarrative of progress, Seki Hajime left with a kaleidoscopic range of impressions that affirmed the diversity of the modern experience. With his own eyes, he had seen what recent history had wrought: a richness of modern possibilities that belied the enduring myth of unilinear progress. If this insight gave him pause, as it did when he encountered the disconcerting, historyless human "assemblage" of Chicago, it also gave him hope, for it witnessed the possibility that Japan might yet manufacture its own distinct and distinctly powerful version of modernity.

Like the young, idealistic European and American social progressives described by Rodgers, Hajime longed at once to bring his nation up to modern speed and to do so with appropriate style. Speaking as a leader of what we might call the Pacific progressive connection, he echoed the sentiments attributed by Rodgers to its Atlantic branch: "Others might talk of distinctive national geniuses and incomparable political destinies, but it was the mark of those who shaped the Atlantic progressive connection to see the world as a long line of runners pumping down a track of progress, some in advance, others straggling in the rear."[103] It was also the nature of both transatlantic and transpacific social progressives, we should add, to see themselves as national competitors in this global footrace.

As conveyed by the commemorative photograph, figure 8, for which Hajime posed with his Japanese friends in Berlin, the man who left Europe in 1901 was different from the one who had arrived there three years earlier. The youthful visage of Hajime's graduation portrait is gone, replaced by a heavier face with just the hint of a moustache. Gone, too, is the closely cropped hairstyle that Hajime kept even as a young teacher. Now cut close around the ears, his hair is meticulously greased and combed in the European fashion of the day. He looks every bit the part of the modern professional in his dark suit, silk tie, and starched collar. Peering through slightly weary eyes beyond the camera to the right, Hajime's is the most intense of the four faces in the photograph. His is also the most erect figure. Serious and self-confident, as always, he now projects both conviction and determination. Unlike his colleagues, who clearly followed the photographer's invitation to mug for the camera, Hajime remained either unable or unwilling to do so. We see him not as the photographer wished him to look, nor even as he might have wished himself to be seen, but as he was. And, in three-quarter profile against the blank backdrop of a Berlin portrait studio, Hajime looks every bit the powerful intellectual and passionate ideologue he would soon show himself to have become.

Seki hit the ground running on his return to Japan in 1901. Not only did he resume his regular teaching duties at the Tokyo Commercial College in Hitotsubashi, but he immediately formed a research group with Fukuda Tokuzō and Sano Zensaku—appropriately named the Berlin Association. The group's intellectual agenda was much the same as that of the political economists with whom its founders had studied in Germany, and its work was so high-powered that the three earned themselves a catchy sobriquet: the Hitotsubashi Triumvirate.[104] Seki himself, who was praised by students for his "decisive personality and powerful intellect," soon became the driving force behind the College's newly formed Research Section.[105]

In 1902, at age twenty-nine, Seki finally settled down: he was married to Ōtsuka Gen, the daughter of a prominent ex-samurai from nearby Narita-chō in Chiba Prefecture. After honeymooning at Nikkō and Matsushima, Seki and his wife started a family and adopted a domestic routine

Figure 8. Commemorative photograph of Monbusho Fellows in Berlin (1900). *Left to right:* Tsumura Hidematsu, Seki Hajime, Fukuda Tokuzō, and Takimoto Hideo. Courtesy of the Seki family and the Osaka City History Archive.

that soon moved to the rhythm of seven children. In the studio portrait, figure 9, taken to commemorate the induction of his brother Giichi into the imperial army in 1904, Seki towers over the rest of his family. What is more, his once-timid brothers have assumed a comparable air of dignity. As if to smother the timid impression they left in the portrait of 1896, the Seki men have assumed a virtually iconic modern aspect: Hajime, the young patriarch, flying the traditional family colors; his brother, the officer, seated at attention in his stately waistcoat, gloves in hand; and their bespectacled young sibling, sharp in his brass-buttoned school uniform. Here, too, is their perseverant mother—holding up her infant granddaughter for all to see and looking all the grander for the submissive pos-

Figure 9.   Seki Hajime and family (1904). Courtesy of the Seki family and the Osaka City History Archive.

ture and meek expression that her daughter-in-law has assumed—staring smugly at the camera. What this portrait says is "We've arrived," and it is said with conviction.

If this sentiment issued from the family's personal and professional successes, and most especially from those of Seki Hajime, it also resonated loudly with the nation's advancement. Six years earlier, in the preface to his first book, Seki observed sardonically that Japan's efforts "to achieve national power and authority" had come under "increasing scrutiny from the world powers."[106] In the years immediately following, which carried many Japanese (including Seki) into the Western world, the Japanese subjected the world powers themselves to scrutiny. Rather than wilting under the Western gaze in submissive acceptance of Japan's inadequacy, however, they came to recognize Western scrutiny for what it was: a signal that their nation, thanks to its rapid advancement, had appeared on the political radar of the world powers as a national power in the making.

If we are correct in our reading of mid-Meiji family portraits as symbolic representations of the family-state ideology of the Japanese nation-state, then the Seki studio portrait of 1904 conveyed much more than resilience: it witnessed the family's identification with national progress itself. Much as Japan had triumphed over adversity, successfully redoubling the national commitment to modernization after its humiliating diplomatic defeat at the hands of the Western powers following the Sino-Japanese War in 1895, the Seki family had triumphed over daunting trials and tribulations. About to send his brother into battle against Russia, one of the powers that had humbled his nation a decade before, Seki betrayed not the slightest doubt about the outcome.

The confident figure of authority that Seki assumed for the family portrait, not to mention the dashing figure of cosmopolitanism that he cut in public as a rower, hiker, and tennis player, mirrored the modern figure of Japan's national destiny that he was then confidently projecting. As an educator, he took up this cause as a tutelary challenge and brought it home to his colleagues and students. This young turk, who had been militating for change since he was a student, soon made his mark nationally as an educational reformer. In 1908, following the introduction of a long-awaited resolution in the Diet to award business schools university accreditation, Seki spearheaded the campaign at the Tokyo Commercial College. Passionately debating the purpose of business education with Fukuda Tokuzō and Sano Zensaku— Fukuda an advocate of survey research, Sano a supporter of technical training—he eloquently took up the cause of a balanced curriculum that combined the benefits of the two approaches.[107]

In the years immediately following the Russo-Japanese War (1904–1905), Seki began to extend his scholarly reach and to expand his professional scope. Bringing his knowledge and experience to bear on the diverse range of developmental challenges that faced modern nation-states, he read and researched widely in German, English, and French. Together with Fukuda Tokuzō, in 1906 he founded the *Kokumin keizai zasshi* (Journal of the people's national economics), which soon published the work of intellectual luminaries such as Kuwata Kumazō, Kawakami Hajime, and Minobe Tatsukichi. About this time as well, Seki was watching his star rise within the influential Nihon Shakai Seisaku Gakkai (Japan Association for Social Policy), where he had established himself as an authoritative voice for the younger generation of Japanese political economists.[108] Even during the after hours, it seems, Seki ran with a high-powered intellectual crowd: his regular drinking companions were the constitutional theorist Minobe Tatsukichi and the theoretical economist Fukuda Tokuzō.[109]

Arguably, Seki was propelled from the relative obscurity of his business school professorship into public life by the range and the relevance of his practical studies *(jitsugaku)* of the Japanese political economy. In the next chapter, I scrutinize those studies, which confronted the critical economic challenges that faced Japan in late Meiji. It will be important not merely to explore the provenance of Seki's political economics, distinguishing his perspective on the national economy from that of the aging Meiji leadership, but also to establish the whys and wherefores of his ultimate transformation from a political economist into a social economist.

But first things first. Although Seki would later find himself engaged in battles with the Meiji leadership over social economics, he was initially challenged simply to set them thinking creatively and systematically about the economy more generally. From early Meiji, this leadership had subscribed to an arrestingly archaic definition of the economy *(keizai)*, derived from the neo-Confucian term *keikoku saimin* (as translated by Tessa Morris-Suzuki, "administering the nation and relieving the suffering of the people"). Presenting themselves as "virtuous rulers" of the Meiji state, who had been enjoined by their emperor to hold "together the social fabric of the nation,"[110] Japan's leaders took it on themselves not merely to guard the popular interest but also to determine it. The national economy, as they understood it, was the state economy *(kokka keizai)* writ small.

Working from a radically different definition of the economy—simply put, the multitude of exchanges through which human beings fulfill their wants and needs—late Meiji political economists such as Seki inverted the early Meiji model of economic policymaking. While they similarly regarded the nation as the most important locus of economic action, they identified it primarily with the people rather than the state. In his reconceptualization of the national economy as a people's national economy *(kokumin keizai)*, Seki located the source of public authority with the people *(kokumin)* rather than with the emperor, portraying the nation as society writ large. The state, in his heterodox model, was thus transformed from the institutional extension of imperial power into the subject(ive) *(shutai)* embodiment of popular authority.[111] Unlike the Meiji leadership, which clung to the belief that only the state could ascertain the best interest of the people, Seki argued that the interests of the people should determine those of the state. "The central obligation of the state," he argued bluntly, "is to ascertain [and act on] the interest of the Japanese people as a body."[112]

Seki derived his definitions of the nation and the state from those generated by the German historical school. As a long-time admirer of List and Roscher, as well as a recent student of Schmoller and Wagner, Seki was steeped in German political economics and had become a confirmed believer in the people-centered *Nationalökonomie* that was central to their ideology. His convictions concerning national economic policymaking initially recapitulated those of Roscher and Bruno Hildebrand, the doyens of the German historical school. Echoing their views in 1903, he pronounced his firm commitment to proactive national economic policymaking: "Economic phenomena are not subject solely to natural laws of development, nor can the natural, historical course of a national economy's development be altered in any significant way by [individual] human action. If we are to achieve cultural progress [*bunka shinpo*], then we must strive to achieve full development of the national economy by means of [state] policies based on proper principle [*shinri*]."[113] Not only did Seki virtually reproduce Roscher's model of the "rational" state as the institutional facilitator of modern national progress, he evinced a similar faith in the "*ur*-rationality" of the *Volk* to set the course of such progress. His appeal to "proper principle" as the basis of "cultural progress" was redolent with *kokumin-teki* (ethnic nationalist) associations that echoed Roscher's *Volk*-ish sentiments.

Only rarely, however, did Seki venture further into discussion of the genesis of nations and nationalisms. His relative silence on the subject betrays his ambivalence toward the presumptions of ethnic nationalism (*minzokushugi*) used by so many during his lifetime to bolster their claims of uniqueness for the Japanese nation-state or to justify their arguments for colonial assimilationism.[114] While Seki followed the logic of the German historical school in arguing that nations were the historical product of ethnic coalescences that had formed over centuries, he also acknowledged the causal importance of transnational historical forces such as social progress. In the end, Seki's emergent transnational identity as a social progressive—which was arguably based in equal parts on the conceptual influence of the German historical school and on his own global experience—impelled him to view ethnicity as but one of a cluster of factors that explained national identity.

Despite the powerful influence that the German historical school exerted over his views on the national political economy, Seki was no mere cipher. Not only did he adopt and adapt German ideas to the Japanese context, as I illustrate in chapter 2, but he did so in a way that brought them into harmony with progressive Japanese thinking at the time. A good example is his characterization of the relationship between nation and state, which echoed the ideas of his longtime friend Minobe Tatsukichi. Much as Minobe identified corporate social life (*kyōdō seikatsu*) as the precursor to state development,[115] Seki identified corporate self-interest *(dantaiteki shirishin)* and collective responsibility *(kyōdō sekinin)* as social preconditions to nation-state formation. Identifying the state as facilitator of the collective interest of the nation—that is, of the corporate self-interest of the Japanese people—he echoed Minobe in the view that officials and politicians were properly conceived as humble servants of the people, not as autocratic agents of the emperor.[116] In short, Seki enthusiastically endorsed the principles of social democracy enunciated by late Meiji political progressives.

In the studio portraits that grace this chapter, Seki Hajime witnesses his personal identification with this public ideal of the nation. The Japanese nation, which was portrayed by the state as an extended family, came to life in his scholarship as a collective social subject. As Seki plotted the development of the people's national economy, therefore, he was careful to identify the groups who composed it and to define their respective roles. No less than the members of a real family, each member of this figurative family had his or her proper place. The merchant, the industrialist, the worker, the banker, the bureaucrat, the farmer, the city dweller—all these and more played a role in meeting the needs of the national collectivity.

Still, time and again, Seki came back to the family as the most basic unit of society. "The foundation of social organization is the family system," he would later write.[117] If Seki also came to affirm the importance of classes to Japan's modern social structure—and to openly acknowledge the appearance of classes as a transnational historical development—his concept of nation continued to rest on family *(katei)*. Paradoxically, given his un-normal personal background, Seki subscribed wholeheartedly to the invented tradition of family sanctioned by the Meiji family-state. Whether he yearned for the stability of fixed role models or wished to overcome his own past, we will never know for sure. But, throughout his life, Seki preached normalcy publicly and pursued the ideal within his own family.

By all accounts, Seki was himself a model family man. Not only does the record he kept of his comings and goings reveal a nurturing father who faithfully took his children on weekend excursions and enthusiastically attended to their needs and concerns, it reveals a loving one whose pain during the tragic illness and death of a daughter was palpable.[118] Seki also tried to be an exemplary husband, it would seem. Following his wife's premature death in 1932, he penned a moving testimonial to her life as a "good wife and wise mother."[119] Based on Seki's behavior as a husband and father, one is tempted to argue that this ardent believer in the nation as a collectivity was simply practicing what he preached.

However we choose to explain the connection, Seki projected this same normative model of family into his notion of the Japanese people's national economy. In that economy, with all its diverse groups and all their divergent interests, the collective nation/subject was the glue that held society together. This was the "family" of Japan, and it was doubtless comforting to think of it as such at the turn of the century. After all, progressives like Seki lived in a brave new world in which the aggressive force of industrial capitalism leapt effortlessly across the political boundaries that divided nation-states. Although this force generated great economic wealth in the process, it also created troubling social problems that only unified nations could hope to solve—nations such as the family-nation of Japan.

2 The People's National Economy

On New Year's Day 1900, admitting to a certain dreaminess, Seki Hajime exhorted his countrymen "to make ready" for "the approaching dawn of the Pacific Age [*taiheiyō jidai*]":

> Considering the challenges we face from an economic vantage point, we should not get sidetracked by trifling issues such as how to cultivate industriousness or how to attract foreign capital. The real challenge is to cultivate the spirit of [capitalist] enterprise among the Japanese people . . . and to prepare for this great [new] age by effecting a transformation of the nation's economic structure.[1]

Thus challenging the Meiji leaders to reassess the nation's developmental priorities—and most especially, it would seem, to cut short their futile search for modern magic elixirs—Seki called for a complete overhaul of the Japanese economy. Over the following decade, in word and in deed, Seki committed himself to this grand objective. As a scholar, teacher, and government advisor, he endeavored to identify the most critical economic challenges facing Japan and to develop a far-reaching program of structural change conceived to meet them. Toward this end, Seki reconceptualized the Japanese economy as a people's national economy *(kokumin keizai)*. Urging the Meiji leadership to shift the locus of national concern from the polity to the economy, in recognition of the developmental challenges that loomed ahead, he actively promoted the model of national economic policymaking invented by his mentors, the political economists of the German historical school.

THE *TOPOS* OF EXCHANGE

The German historical model rested on a linked set of premises concerning human nature, social progress, and the nation. Identifying human beings

53

as economic animals whose primary motivation was to satisfy material needs and desires, the political economists of the German historical school maintained that history had witnessed the formation of communities collectively dedicated to this purpose. In modern times, these communities had coalesced as nations, and this development, in turn, had stimulated the formation of nation-states. As the political embodiment of these national communities, they concluded, nation-states were duty-bound to implement economic policies that addressed the needs and desires of the whole.

As this argument suggests, the German historical school of political economy was named for the insistent historicism with which its proponents scrutinized the relationship between economic, political, and social development. Through its identification of flexible economic laws that might be translated into timely national economic policies, their scholarship was a natural extension of the so-called national economics *(Nationalökonomie)* introduced by Friedrich List at the beginning of the nineteenth century. The "older historical school" rejected what Karl Knies called the "absolutism of theory" perpetrated by liberal economists and forged a new historical understanding of progress.[2] As Keith Tribe has astutely observed of the result, scholars of the German historical school strove to "redirect *Nationalökonomie* into a doctrine of the economic laws of the development of peoples" by promoting a sweeping "reform of economic understanding."[3]

With this grand purpose in mind, the political economists of the German historical school conducted extensive empirical research, working inductively to derive general economic laws from historical example and statistical evidence. According to their findings, national peoples had steadily developed a distinct "realm of economic activity" in modern times— one that helped them satisfy their collective needs and desires. They termed this realm *Verkehr* (traffic[king]). As described by Tribe, "*Verkehr* is the axiom that unites studies of telegraphs, railways, stock exchanges, banks, and trade with a conception of the marketplace as a location at which the activities of individuals transmuted into an ordered whole."[4]

As Tribe sees it, in fact, the distinguishing characteristic of the German historical school was not so much its insistent historicism as its steady focus on *Verkehr*. Pronouncing *Verkehr* pivotal to modern national economies, the political economists of the German historical school identified such economies as *Verkehrswirtschaft* (exchange economies). As Tribe notes, "The exchanges that occurred in this realm [of human needs and wants] were summarized in the all-embracing *topos* of *Verkehr*—communication, commerce, social intercourse, traffic, exchange. Economic man was here conceived as *der verkehrende Mensch*."[5]

While Seki was drawn to the inductive method as well as to the historicism of the German historical school, he was mesmerized by the "axiom of *verkehr*" that defined its political economics. Less interested himself in deriving general laws of economic development than in exploring those that other like-minded economists had already postulated, Seki conducted a wide range of practical studies *(jitsugaku)* that fit the general description of what we now call applied social science. These studies, which were conceived to address the economic challenges and to rectify the economic problems faced by Japan at the turn of the century, were part and parcel of Seki's larger practical project: to effect a thoroughgoing reform of Japan's political economy.

Seki's economic scholarship was breathtakingly broad in its scope. Between 1898 and 1913, he conducted a sweeping examination of the structure and the infrastructure of the Japanese economy, producing a searching anatomy of Japanese capitalism that peeled back its skin and probed its organs. Seki wrote a series of path-breaking monographs on Japan's *Verkehrswirtschaft* that focused successively on commercial economics, commercial economic policy, industrial policy, and industrial-worker protection. Along the way, as he produced dozens of case studies and translations of everything from foreign-trade policy to labor legislation, he also steadily shifted his gaze from the political economy to the social economy.

In much the same spirit as the German political economists he emulated, Seki kept up with the changing economic challenges that faced his nation and fashioned research agendas designed to meet them. From the beginning of his career, when he first trained the wide-angle lens of the *Verkehrswirtschaft* paradigm on Japan's developing exchange economy, Seki appears to have envisioned that economy in spatial terms. Devoting himself initially to the study of railway development, he moved straight to the core concern of emerging exchange economies: the infrastructures necessary to move people and goods.

In his fascination with railroads, Seki evinced a studied appreciation of what Henri Lefebvre has called "the production of space."[6] Railroads, as Seki saw them, were quintessentially modern, constructed spaces that promised to revolutionize the people's national economy by breaking down barriers of space and time within Japan. When he returned from Europe in 1901, Seki was so obsessed with railroads that his students at the Tokyo Commercial College nicknamed him "Railroad Seki" (Tetsudō Seki).[7]

If Seki's interest in railway development grew directly out his intellec-

tual conviction that a lively exchange economy was key to national progress, his passion for railway development issued from the belief that Japan's modern economy was in dire need of rational ordering. Seki was
turned on to the importance of this national developmental problem, as
well as to the spatial solution railways offered, by the renowned German
economist Friedrich List (1789–1846). List, in turn, came initially to the
issue as a staunch supporter of German confederation.

List argued presciently that railway networks would facilitate the "creation of interior unity" in modern economies.[8] As Tribe astutely observes
about his reasoning on the subject, "[He] perceived that the revolution in
transportation that the railway brought with it would have profound social
and economic consequences. The free movement of persons and goods
within the nation would intensify economic relationships, providing a material framework for economic progress and market development."[9] Similarly, Seki promoted railways as an essential infrastructural element of
modern national economic development in Japan.

As arteries of the modern economy, and as conduits of the political,
social, and cultural interchange essential to modern nation building, railways possessed tremendous practical and symbolic value. For his part, Seki
considered railways the lifeblood of the people's national economy. Unlike
waterways, whose development was initially promoted by the early Meiji
leaders as the infrastructural means to modernization, railways could be
laid virtually wherever their creators desired.[10] Simply put, they offered
Japan a valuable means to produce modern space.

Seki closely identified railway technology with "human economic development" and, even more specifically, with the "dramatic progress of
people's national economies."[11] Because "the railroad reorganized space,"
as Wolfgang Schivelbusch has so eloquently argued, it offered modern
nation-states a powerful means of directing national economic development.[12] Not only did the location of railway lines determine where and
how natural resources, labor, and capital were allocated, but it also fixed
the routes by which finished goods were conveyed to market. As the basic
infrastructural framework of Japan's modern exchange economy, railways
offered the nation-state a golden opportunity to set the course of its economic development.

What Tribe has observed of List and his commitment to national railway
development goes doubly for Seki: "It was not a matter simply of con-
necting one city with another, but of creating a network and so lending
structure to enlarged markets."[13] In an article on state-owned railways

(kangyō tetsudō), written in anticipation of the Railway Nationalization Law of 1906, Seki heaped Listian praise on the initiative. Japan's expanded national railway network, he predicted, would permit "the comprehensive development of commerce, industry, and agriculture and thereby promote the advancement of the people's national economy."[14]

By sanctioning the purchase of over fifteen regional railway lines—and thus facilitating critical links to the nation's existing trunk lines—the Railway Nationalization Law at last enabled Japan to lay the foundation for its powerful national railway network. "As a result of [this law]," observes Steven Ericson, "the state's share of the total length of railway line open leaped from about 30 percent in 1905 to 90 percent in 1907."[15]

It was no accident that the state pressed this initiative in the wake of the Russo-Japanese War (1904–1905). Having publicly redoubled their commitment to the national goal of *shokusan kōgyō* (fostering industry and promoting enterprise), the Meiji leaders were understandably eager to create a transportation infrastructure capable of supporting rapid national economic growth.[16] Since the beginning of the Meiji Era, they had envisioned a national railway network as the spatial frame for Japan's rapidly developing national economy.[17] Now they had it: the Railway Nationalization Law of 1906 enabled them to set the spatial parameters of national economic development.

Seki viewed this expanded national railway network as the infrastructural foundation for a structural transformation of the Japanese economy. Keen to iron out what he deemed kinks in the new law, in 1906 and 1907 he addressed one particularly troubling ambiguity. In a two-part article on light railways, Seki challenged the notion that local railways should be limited to local transport and therefore be deprived of government subsidies. He maintained that this restriction would seriously compromise the objective of "interior unity" made possible by railway networking and prevent Japan from inscribing the structure of a modern exchange economy onto the "homogenized internal space"[18] that the new national railway network promised to create. Proposing a program of public-private cooperation designed to bring local railways into the national railway network, Seki urged the state to provide strategic subsidies for light railways. Such railways, he maintained, were productive *(seisanteki)* lines of transport that carried freight and passengers alike, and as such they constituted the lifeblood of the regional social economies that fortified the people's national economy.[19] Not only did light railways fuel the growth of regional industry and thwart the decline of regional agriculture by promoting economic exchange, noted Seki, they spurred social integration by providing postal service and facilitating social and economic contact between villagers and urbanites.[20]

For all of these reasons and more, Seki urged the state to subsidize the expansion of Japan's light railway network and to treat new construction projects as public enterprises *(kō kigyō)*.[21] In 1907, the Meiji leaders adopted just such a policy, but with a predictably statist twist. After heavily subsidizing several construction projects in the Kantō area, they served notice on the railway owners that their lines might one day be nationalized.[22]

By fostering the development of a national railway network, Seki believed, Japan might one day possess a modern transport infrastructure capable of facilitating the systematic exchange essential to a modern national economy. But he recognized that this ambitious goal would not be realized until several critical problems had been resolved. With these problems in mind, he investigated as many different angles as seemed relevant to the ultimate objective. In an effort to find the proper balance of public and private railway ownership in Japan, he conducted comprehensive surveys of a number of different railway systems in Europe and North America;[23] in hope of putting the Japanese national railway network on solid financial footing, he investigated different models of railway economics;[24] and in an effort to maximize the benefit of railways to the Japanese people as a whole, he explored various methods of making passenger fares affordable.[25]

Always, it remained Seki's main concern to make railways serve the collective economic interest of the Japanese nation and its citizenry. Even when he turned to the thorny example of the South Manchurian Railway, which Japan exploited for its own benefit and decidedly not for that of the Manchurians or the Chinese, the issue of "collective economic interest" remained foremost in his mind. In Manchuria, he argued, proper railway development would ultimately redound to the benefit of China and Japan alike—with the Chinese gaining a critical vehicle of "civilization" and the Japanese a foundation for the "development of commercial power."[26]

Increasingly in the 1910s, Seki's research on railway development was focused on urban transit in direct response to the spatial model of *Verkehrswirtschaft* that List and others had introduced. Writing on the spatial significance of railways to the European nations in 1836, List had noted that "the needs of industry and communication will compel the railway systems of the larger Continental nations to assume the form of a network, concentrating on the interior principal points and radiating from the centre to the frontiers."[27] Reading List on the subject doubtless called to Seki's mind the iron-bound railway network he had studied in Belgium. His own proposal for the development of a comprehensive national railway network in Japan identified several specific "interior principal points" as critical to the nation's emerging exchange economy: the nation's largest cities.

At the annual meeting of the Japan Association for Social Policy in 1909, with his eyes trained at last on cities, Seki finally brought his views on transit into accord with his views on the people's national economy. While he had earlier portrayed railways primarily as vehicles of economic exchange, highlighting their capacity to carry freight, he was compelled in the urban context also to scrutinize their socioeconomic function as transporters of labor. By 1909, he had distinguished two essential types of urban transit: intraurban transit *(shinai kōtsū)* and interurban transit *(shinai to shigai no kōtsū)*.[28] In discussing these critical conduits of goods and people, he projected an image of cities within the people's national economy that had quietly been gathering strength in his writing—that is, cities as social subjects rather than economic objects.

As the foregoing observation illustrates, Seki would not long remain content to define cities solely as the central markets of Japan's exchange economy. By identifying them with the people who composed them— that is, by treating them as animated human communities rather than treating them as abstract economic entities—Seki began to bring his people's national economy into social perspective. Ultimately, this social perspective of the national economy came to define his political economics. As he told his colleagues in the Japan Association for Social Policy in 1909, "Advancement of the people's national economy in the present day may involve the acquisition of 'concrete things,' but the foundation is people."[29]

Seki never lost sight of this fact in his sweeping studies of Japan's exchange economy. He remained alert to the fact that the people's national economy had been forged by the people: industrialists, merchants, bankers, investors, laborers, farmers, tenants, consumers, families, and more. As he took stock of the state of Japan's economy in late Meiji, and as he conducted practical studies conceived to spark economic reform, he always returned axiomatically to this core belief. He called on the state to mediate the people's national economy by creating frameworks of economic exchange designed to meet the collective needs and desires of the people, giving the axiom of *Verkehr* a palpably social inflection.

THE POLITICAL ECONOMY

Seki Hajime was one of a handful of young economists who challenged the late Meiji state to keep the economy in human perspective—even as it was stridently promoting *shokusan kōgyō*. These young turks, who counseled the Meiji leaders to harmonize the means and ends of their economic programs, spoke rather like the social conscience of the state. Although the voices of these economic reformers initially fell on deaf official ears, by the 1910s they had started to get through to Japan's national economic policymakers. In his study of *Economic Ideology and Japanese Industrial Policy,* Bai Gao acknowledges their influence on both state and economic thought. But, like so many before him, Gao glosses the Japan Association for Social Policy so superficially as to obscure its contribution to prewar national economic policymaking.[30] This study will flesh out the historical narrative, tracing the influence of political economists such as Seki on the movers and shakers of Japan's developmental state.

Seki first took the nation's pulse in the late 1890s, as a young political economist freshly graduated from the Tokyo Commercial College. In *An Outline of Commercial Economics* (1898), his first major work, he observed at the outset that Japan's efforts "to achieve national power and authority" had come under "increasing scrutiny from the world powers."[31] This wry reference to the international attention paid to Japan in the wake of its stunning victory in the Sino-Japanese War (1894–1895) betrayed Seki's growing conviction that his nation was on the verge of becoming a major world power.

Seki was hardly alone in this conviction, of course. As Akira Iriye points out, the war filled most Japanese with pride: "By waging war, Japan would establish a beachhead in Asia and be recognized as an expanding nation, a symbol of its great-power status."[32] Yet the highly contested treaty that soon emasculated Japan's victory left a bitter aftertaste in the mouths of many. Forced by the so-called Triple Intervention of the Western powers to retrocede hard-won territorial gains in China, Japan was rudely awakened to the harsh realities of global politics. It had met the accepted Western standard of great-power status—imperialistic expansion—but still the world powers denied it membership in the Western imperialist fraternity.

The European emasculation of Japan's victory in the Sino-Japanese War, which was clearly intended to bridle Japan's dramatic development as a modern nation-state, shattered the faith of many Japanese in the putative "laws" of progress. Among the most deeply disillusioned were the Westernizing modernizers that Kenneth Pyle has termed the "new generation" of Meiji Japan—young men who self-consciously identified themselves as a "new generation of 'Meiji youth.' "[33] "As a result of the Triple Intervention," lamented one of these idealists, "I was baptized to the gospel of power."[34]

In sharp contrast to the "new generation," whose wild-eyed faith in the laws of progress seemingly set them up for a fall, what I call the "younger generation" was infinitely more realistic. As Meiji babies, they had literally grown up with their nation, and they thus gauged its progress in much more measured terms. Disappointed, not disillusioned, by the Triple Intervention, the "younger generation" took this national setback in stride, then placed it in historical perspective. Political economists like Seki Hajime identified the war as a critical turning point and, from the late 1890s, pressed for a new national agenda that would shift the locus of national concern from political prestige to economic development.

On this basic point, the Meiji leaders were in utter agreement, as evidenced by the fact that they soon made *shokusan kōgyō* the pillar of their national(ist) agenda. While this new national agenda might seem an inevitable development in historical retrospect, it is important to recall the inchoate condition of national economic ideology at the time. Economists of several different stripes, ranging from scholars to bureaucrats, emerged as self-styled reformers at this critical juncture. Schooled in exotic theories "borrowed" from Western economic discourse—theories ranging from laissez-faireism to protectionism—they spoke in an esoteric language that must have seemed incomprehensible to many at the time.

It is instructive in this connection to review the history of economics in Japan. As Tessa Morris-Suzuki has aptly observed, the modern Japanese term for economics *(keizaigaku)* was derived from the traditional term for "administering the nation and relieving the suffering of the people" *(keikoku saimin)*. The term *keikoku saimin,* which was Confucian in origin, had powerful historical associations with Tokugawa neo-Confucianism, and these associations became connotations of the modern term. Thus, notes Morris-Suzuki ironically, the term *keizai* "bore overtones far removed from twentieth-century notions of economics as the science of efficiently allocating scarce resources amongst alternative uses."[35]

From early in the Meiji Era, Japanese economists strove to extricate economics from this murky moralism and to reconstitute it as a modern science. When self-styled liberal economists such as Tsuda Mamichi, Kanda Takahira, and Taguchi Ukichi fired the first volley of translations and commentaries in the 1870s, they did so in the naive belief that they were apprising their countrymen of the universal laws governing progress.

Taguchi Ukichi best exemplifies this "scientific" approach. Unlike members of the so-called enlightenment school such as Fukuzawa Yukichi, who equated modernization with Westernization, Taguchi elevated the process of "cultural borrowing" to a higher plain. "We study physics, psychology, economics, and the other sciences, not because the West discovered them," he preached, "but because they are the universal truth."[36]

Despite the early Meiji enthusiasm for classical and neoclassical economic ideas, historical circumstance minimized their public influence. As Morris-Suzuki points out, "The economic circumstances of early Meiji Japan were, after all, very different than those of Victorian England. There was no extensive industrial capitalist class, whose members might desire to carry on their business unhindered by government interference."[37] Thus, while classical economics had powerful abstract appeal as an explanatory framework for historical progress, it had weak practical appeal as a policymaking framework for national development.

Much more influential in both the long and short terms was the antithesis of classical economics, protectionism. The adherents of this doctrine, whose faith in government to guard the national economy rivaled the faith of laissez-faireists in the marketplace to grow the universal economy, were equally doctrinaire.[38] Far more than the laissez-faireists, however, protectionists were attuned to the tenor of the times and familiar with the lay of the land. In place of the liberal economists' emphasis on high-risk investment in a freewheeling economic system—a perspective that glorified free enterprise and free trade in the belief that the global marketplace was self-adjusting—protectionists proposed low-risk investment in a tightly run economic ship of state that placed a priority on tariff protections in the interest of national economic development.

To self-described late developers such as the Japanese, protectionism held great appeal. Wakayama Norikazu, one its earliest proponents, promoted protectionism as a matter of common sense: "[I]t is clear as day that an economic policy suitable to one country is not necessarily so to another; . . . it is absurd to believe that there is a general rule which applies in any country."[39] In this belief, protectionists constantly reaffirmed Japan's identity as a late developer and harped on the state's obligation to use tariffs as a means of defending infant industries against a commercial invasion by advanced foreign competitors.

If reform-minded political economists like Seki had serious reservations about protectionism, they nonetheless shared the protectionists' ardent commitment to the nation as the central locus of modern economies. Identifying the nation as the guide and guardian of economic development,

they recast economic progress as a multifaceted historical process generated by a multitude of causal factors, including ethnicity, religion, and
culture. Unlike the elegant laissez-faire theoreticians whose theology of
progress impelled them to look for common developmental denominators
that confirmed the operation of natural law, these hard-nosed political
economists painstakingly retraced the developmental pathways that illustrated the importance of human agency to economic change.

In search of a new paradigm of national economic development, Japanese political economists located a kindred spirit in List. Noting that List's
concern with Germany's plight as a late developer paralleled their own
economic concerns, they plumbed his work for inspiration and positive
reinforcement. Godfather of the German historical school, List traced the
mistaken belief in unilinear progress directly to classical economics.[40] He
held that Adam Smith, Jean Baptiste Say, François Quesnay, and their
disciples had superimposed the laws of nature over the story of human
progress and thereby obscured the lessons of history. Morris-Suzuki has
elegantly paraphrased List's basic criticism of classical economics as follows: "Instead of basing their theories on the real world, which consisted
of separate nations at differing stages of development, they postulated a
fictitious 'cosmopolitical' world in which national boundaries were assumed away."[41]

Challenging "the key assumption of laissez-faire theory that only markets and individuals exist,"[42] List appealed to "the laws of logic and of the
nature of things":

> If we wish to remain true to the laws of logic and of the nature of
> things, we must set the economy of individuals against the economy
> of societies, and discriminate in respect to the latter between true
> political or national economy (which, emanating from the idea and
> nature of the nation, teaches how a given *nation* in the present state
> of the world and its own special national relations can maintain and
> improve its economical conditions) and cosmo-political economy,
> which originates in the assumption that all nations of the earth form
> but one society living in a perpetual state of peace.[43]

Going on to challenge the classical economists' model of historical progress, which asserted positivistically that "commercial union" had produced "political union," List argued on strictly empirical grounds that this
"confound[ed] effects with causes."[44]

When List thus reversed the terms of the classical model of economic
development, rendering "political union" as the cause of progress and
"commercial union" as its effect, he put the nation-state front and center.

In sharp contrast to laissez-faire theorists, who viewed nation-states as a drag on the innately progressive forces of free enterprise and free trade, List cast them as guardians of progress. Foremost in his mind were the "less advanced nations" of the world, for whom economic progress was a dream rather than a reality. The developmental dilemma that continued to plague such nations, argued List, gave the lie to laissez-faire theory: "[That,] . . . under the existing conditions of the world, the result of general free trade would not be a universal republic, but, on the contrary, a universal subjection of the less advanced nations to the supremacy of the predominant manufacturing, commercial, and naval powers, is a conclusion for which the reasons are very strong and, according to our views, irrefragable."[45]

To resolve the problems faced by "less advanced nations," List advocated the systematic study of *Nationalökonomie* (national economy), or national economics, whose parameters he defined in the following way: "National economy appears from this point of view to be that science which, correctly appreciating the existing interests and the individual circumstances of nations, teaches how *every separate nation* can be raised to that stage of industrial development in which union with other nations equally well developed, and consequently freedom of trade, can become possible and useful to it."[46]

List's tacit acknowledgment of the special challenges that faced late developers won the Japanese over to his prescription for progress. While Japan had certainly been alert to these challenges prior to the Sino-Japanese War, their significance was accentuated by the Triple Intervention. Still laboring under tariff restrictions enforced by the most powerful nations in the world—states that guiltlessly pressed their trading advantage as a natural right under the universal law of free trade—Japan had become increasingly incredulous of liberal economic logic and increasingly suspicious of its economically privileged proponents.

List gave the Japanese exactly the argument they needed to cast the motives of the Western powers into question. In his attack on classical economics, he argued compellingly that Adam Smith had deduced the principle of free trade from the British historical experience of economic development. That the British still knew a distinct developmental advantage in the 1890s went a long way toward explaining their continued enthusiasm for free trade, insisted List, and it did not take a genius to see that this advantage had worked to the demonstrable detriment of late-developing economies.[47]

At mid-century, German economic nationalists almost ritually invoked

List when they criticized classical economics. As Tribe wryly observes, they derided the "Smithian system" for "pretending to a generosity that it does not possess, it being rather an expression of the prevailing money economy."[48] By century's end, Japanese economic nationalists were making the same criticisms.[49]

From the late 1890s, in keeping with the spirit and the letter of List's argument for foreign-trade regulation, the Japanese leadership openly endorsed protectionism and with it List's much-vaunted principle of "infant industry protection."[50] While List's influence on late Meiji economic policymaking is legendary, it is important to recall that his ideas had been circulating freely since the Restoration. Ōkubo Toshimichi, who was introduced to List's ideas at the beginning of the Meiji Era, integrated many of them into the economic program he introduced in 1874.[51] And Inukai Tsuyoshi, a staunch supporter of trade protection, later paraphrased List so closely that his arguments virtually reproduced List's rhetoric.[52]

Ōkubo and Inukai arguably paved the way for the "List Boom" that first began to gather momentum in 1890. Spearheaded by the powerful National Economics Association (Kokka Keizai Kai), Japan's first professional economics society, the List Boom went off with a bang. In 1890, in its founding declaration, the Association enthusiastically endorsed Listian protectionism:

> Power is created by wealth. It is unheard of that power can exist where there is no wealth. The competition which is occurring at present between nation and nation is nothing but a competition of strength and of productive power. Thus the problem of independence is a problem of wealth. The problem of a country's wealth is of more importance than the system of trade. This is particularly true in the present circumstances of our country. In these circumstances the only approach which we should adopt is that of national economics, i.e. the economic philosophy that each nation must treat its own self-defence and independent development as the most important factors. It is now urgent that we should exert ourselves to investigate the ways of pursuing this economic philosophy.[53]

Because of their influence in government circles, the economists of the National Economics Association easily worked their protectionist philosophy into public policy. Japan soon began to chip away at the so-called unequal treaties—that is, at the grossly inequitable trading agreements that the Western nations had virtually dictated to Japan. If it was the government's immediate goal to establish tariff autonomy, its long-term objective was much more sweeping: to use tariffs as a means of protecting infant industries from the ravages of foreign competition and thereby to buy Japan the time necessary to gain equal footing with the Western capitalist economies.

No less convinced than the nation's leaders that Japan was fast approaching a critical developmental crossroads, Seki Hajime inaugurated his career as a political economist with the lengthy treatise *An Outline of Commercial Economics* (1898). Yet, despite the Listian tilt of this early work, it was clear that he had already begun to question some of List's most cherished principles. Increasingly skeptical of List's unqualified emphasis on power and wealth as the foundation of political economies, Seki and several other like-minded revisionists began to stray from the Listian fold. Economic historians of Japan have elided this critical development, myopically asserting that the list of theoretical influences on Meiji economics begins and ends with List.[54] The time has come to correct that impression.

Seki did not repudiate List; rather, he progressed beyond the Listian paradigm. In doing so, it is crucial to note, he followed a revisionist course blazed by the political economists of the German historical school. Although most economic historians concerned with these political economists continue to characterize their work as a sharp departure from Listian *Nationalökonomie*, Tribe has convincingly demonstrated that "in substance the work of Roscher, Knies, and Hildebrand marks a development of, rather than a departure from, the German economics of the 1820s and 1830s."[55]

These political economists were distinguished from List by their refusal to assess national economies by the crude standards of power and wealth. In place of the Listian calculus, which reflected List's hostility to classical economics, Roscher and his followers from the German historical school applied the subtler standard of "resource maximization." In contrast to List, Roscher reserved his invective for neoclassical economics. Complaining that the disciples of Adam Smith had hopelessly distorted his historical insights by rendering them as inviolable laws of economic behavior, he promoted a notion of progress that highlighted the history of modern economic development. In place of "laws," as Fritz Ringer has astutely observed, Knies proposed "analogies":

> First, he argued that in his field, the action of causes was not universal, but modified by specific cultural conditions. This accounted for the centrality of "the individual and the concrete" in history. Second, he claimed that "analogies" might be discovered where strict laws could not be found. Incomplete regularities might be detected not only

within the several subsections of a culture, but also in the steps or stages that followed one another in the historical development of nations. Thus both synchronic and diachronic analogies might do for the economic historian what laws did for the natural scientist.[56]

While Roscher concurred with neoclassical economists in the view that all men naturally seek material power, he dismissed their assertion that this impulse could be attributed to blind human instinct. Attributing the ability of humankind to achieve economic progress to creative faculties unique to the human species, Roscher held that the economy "is neither the invention of man nor the revelation of God. It is the natural product of the faculties and the propensities which make man man."[57]

Above all, Roscher stressed the human capacity to reason. Allowing that progress was subject to certain natural laws that governed the material world, he insisted that it was also subject to the human laws that governed society. While human beings responded instinctively to the demands of the material world, argued Roscher, they invoked their innate capacity to reason when negotiating the social world. Characterizing instinct as the native impulse that impelled human beings to improve their condition—that is, as the impulse that caused them to seek progress—Roscher identified reason, in turn, as the motive force through which human beings achieved progress. Thus, when he contemplated human society, he saw "rational human beings . . . capable of progress" acting in their collective interest.[58]

Given that all societies acted naturally to promote their own material well-being, according to Roscher, they were inevitably propelled along similar historical trajectories. But since each society was endowed with the capacity to reason out a developmental strategy suitable to its unique interests and circumstances, Roscher insisted that each was also capable of making its own history. While Roscher thus identified reason as the universal agent of progress in human societies, he insisted that each society reasoned differently.[59] Arguing that people who shared a common tradition tended to reason in ways that reflected their own distinct history, Roscher celebrated the propensity of national peoples to implement strategies of "resource maximization" consonant with their unique laws, languages, and customs. But he did not hold out equal hope to all. The only peoples who would succeed, declared Roscher, were those who actively employed reason to ascertain the proper means of coordinating material and cultural progress.[60]

Roscher likened progress to the process of human socialization rather than to that of biological evolution. Much as parents raised their children, he believed, nations should nurture new socioeconomic relationships consonant with their unique personalities and needs.[61] Roscher remanded this responsibility to the national collectivity, calling attention to the reciprocal relationship between cultural tradition and state authority:

> The systematization of the public economy of a people finds its clearest expression in economic laws, and in the institutions of the state. But it finds expression also, without the intervention of the state, in the laws established by use, and by the opinions of jurists or courts, in community of speech, of customs and tastes etc., things which have an important economic meaning, which depend on the common nature of the land, of race and history, and which influence the state, as much as they are influenced by it.[62]

In Roscher's view, nations were organismic entities whose capacity to achieve progress—progress witnessed fundamentally by the "systematization of the public economy"—issued from the people who constituted them and the traditions they had established. As the personification of the nation, the state bore primary responsibility for cultivating progress. Its bureaucrats and politicians—respectively, the appointive and elective servants of the people—represented the nation. To them fell the task of converting the nation's "rational spirit" into state policy.[63]

The most appropriate measure of a state's success in advancing the cause of progress, according to Roscher, was socioeconomic development. Appraising progress by a subjective standard he termed "the notion of value in use of the resources of the nation," Roscher identified specific indices of "national wealth": treatment of the lower classes; the use of social capital; the introduction of material improvements such as buildings, roads, and canals; the size of commercial payments; and the frequency of foreign loans.[64] In application, this socioeconomic standard measured the degree to which states had fulfilled their obligation to the people by facilitating economic exchange.

By 1898, when he published *An Outline of Commercial Economics*, Seki was already a devotee of Roscher. Indeed, as the national economic policymaker Soeda Juichi made clear in his forward to the book, *An Outline of Commercial Economics* was nothing less than the Japanese incarnation of Roscher's *Principles of Political Economy*. In this early work, Seki recapitulated Roscher's theoretical position and emulated his historical method. His book detailed virtually every commercial function the state might regulate, proffered numerous examples of effective commercial policymaking in the West, and measured national economic progress by a standard that vividly recalled Roscher's "notion of value in use of the resources of a nation" (in Seki's model, consumer benefit, national productive capacity, health and public-safety regulations, labor protection, and the capacity to relieve short-term economic difficulties).[65]

Seki argued that Japan faced the immediate challenge of stimulating domestic production and deflecting foreign competition, and he accordingly urged the state to create a modern *Verkehrswirtschaft* by actively overseeing currency exchange, banking, taxation, trade, and transport.[66] Yet *An Outline of Commercial Economics* was otherwise silent regarding the economic challenges that faced the nation. It went only so far as to suggest that Japan, like every other nation, should "develop an [economic] system in accordance with its national circumstances and characteristics."[67] In short, Seki's book was much longer on description than on prescription.

Thus, while *An Outline of Commercial Economics* demonstrated Seki's scholarly range and suggested his theoretical potential, it was hardly the masterwork Soeda proclaimed it to be. In the coming years, Seki would build on the theoretical foundation he set in 1898, drawing methodological and historical insights from the West and harnessing these to the Japanese experience. Promoting an unerringly historical perspective on progress— a perspective that rendered national development as a dynamic process of socioeconomic change—Seki strove to identify each new challenge as it appeared and to persuade his countrymen to meet each in its turn. Not only did he monitor the course of Japan's development, repeatedly taking the national pulse and insistently diagnosing national problems, but he also adjusted his own scholarly and professional course to meet the challenges facing his nation.

The issue that commanded Seki's attention toward the turn of the century was the very same issue that obsessed the Japanese leadership: foreign trade. Foremost in the minds of this leadership was protection of the nation from the debilitating economic influence of a long-standing import surplus that had drained Japan's currency reserves and stultified domestic industrial production. List addressed this problem in a manner that the Meiji leaders found especially appealing, and Richard Samuels has paraphrased the Listian argument as they likely understood it: "List argued, against Smith, that comparative advantage is not only bequeathed; it can be *created*. Its creation requires a nation to 'sacrifice some present advantages in order to insure itself future ones.' In the short term, protection is undoubtedly less efficient than free competition, because the protected goods are more costly. In the long term, however, the price paid to protect infant industry might well prove a good investment."[68]

If Listian protectionism had much to offer Japan, it also posed a hidden challenge. Little different than "neomercantilism," as Samuels has observed, Listian protectionism was a double-edged sword. On the one hand, it promised to protect the nation from rapacious foreign competition; on the other hand, it threatened to prevent the nation from realizing its productive potential. If David Williams is to be believed—and he seems to speak for many economic historians—the late Meiji state passed this test of leadership with flying colors. Calling attention to List's enduring intellectual influence, Williams suggests that Japan adopted and adapted his ideas with alacrity.[69] Though Williams is right to emphasize the Listian influence on Japanese economic policymaking, he vastly overstates its historical significance. I would suggest that the "reasoned clarity" Williams pointedly attributes to List, then projects into the minds of his supposed Japanese disciples, actually owes much more to the influence of Roscher and the political economists of the German historical school.

I am prompted to offer this alternate view by evidence of a moderating influence at work on state policymakers who were steeped in Listian protectionism. That moderating influence, I argue in the following discussion of late Meiji commercial policymaking, issued from the work of revisionist economists such as Seki Hajime. Putting the Japanese leadership on notice from the late 1890s that protectionism was a poor substitute for trade policy, Seki and others helped put the brakes on Japan's slide into "neomercantilism." For his part, Seki mercilessly attacked examples of protectionist foreign-trade policy, especially when they smacked of the facile Listian logic of national "power and wealth."

Seki applied Roscher's subtle calculus of national "resource maximization" to his own reasoned proposals for trade regulation, thus invoking a different sort of "reasoned clarity." He urged Japan to formulate foreign-trade policies that reflected the short-term imperative of infant-industry protection and projected the long-term goal of global competitiveness. If Christopher Howe is correct in his observation that "the Japanese were remarkably successful in achieving mutually supportive patterns of external and internal expansion,"[70] then we might reasonably surmise that the Japanese leadership acted on the advice of revisionist economists like Seki Hajime. After all, exchange was the name of the game.

BEYOND PROTECTIONISM

In 1902, soon after he returned from Europe, Seki trained his sights on the German debate over foreign-trade policy and, together with Fukuda Tokuzō, translated an influential collection of essays on the subject.[71] Written by Lujo Brentano and Adolf Wagner, two of the guiding lights of the younger generation of the German historical school, the essays were essentially position papers on German commercial policy. To their Japanese translators, however, these essays offered much more than a window on current events in Germany: They witnessed the struggle of another late-developing economy to negotiate the treacherous journey toward national progress. As Seki saw it, the challenge of the day was not merely to secure Japan against the ravages of foreign competition but also to prepare it for economic battle in the global marketplace. When he engaged the German debate over foreign trade, therefore, he was ever mindful of the lessons that Japan might learn as it confronted the looming issue of protective tariffs.

Seki's searching discussion of foreign-trade policymaking pivoted on a critique of the divergent positions of Brentano and Wagner. Taking issue with Brentano's case for free trade, which was premised on an "inflexibly laissez-faire" model, Seki laid bare its faulty logic. He noted that this unerring advocate of industrial progress had allowed his blind faith in German enterprise to drown out the voice of reason. Much as he had inflated Germany's prospects as an industrial exporter, Brentano had dismissed the foreign threat of industrial imports. Seki attributed Brentano's stunning myopia to the insidious influence of laissez-faire theory. The still-unexamined faith in free trade permeated modern economic thought—even that of the German historical school, which had ostensibly repudiated liberal economics. Seki cautioned Japanese economists against a similar inclination to render economics as a natural, rather than as a social, science.[72]

Seki urged Japan instead to heed the advice of Wagner, who called on all modern nations to promote flexible foreign-trade policies closely attuned to the dynamic socioeconomic interests of their respective citizenries. In the case of Germany, maintained Wagner, the prospect of reaping untold profits from industrial exports had blinded economists and policymakers alike to the broader national implications of a freewheeling free-trade arrangement. He cited the plight of Germany's agricultural sector as a powerful case in point. Already in decline, he observed, it was certain to be decimated without the imposition of strategic tariffs.

Wagner's argument called up a central theme of Seki's nascent commercial ideology, and he thus concluded his commentary with a formal proposal for Japan.[73] Arguing that the Meiji leadership had mistakenly cast foreign trade as a diplomatic issue, Seki urged them to reconceive it as an economic one. As he had argued before, "It is not the purpose of commercial policy to promote trade, but to coordinate it with [other, national] economic concerns."[74]

Seki's attention to the foreign-trade policymaking process was anything but academic. In urging the Japanese leadership to formulate foreign-trade policies based on domestic economic considerations rather than on international diplomatic ones, he was confronting one of the thorniest issues then facing his nation. In 1902, after all, Japan still remained subject to unequal treaties signed in 1866.[75] These treaties with the West, which had kept customs duties below 5 percent on average,[76] had placed Japan in a nerve-wracking economic dilemma. As Kent Calder has compelling argued, the continuing combination of low tariff rates and unpredictable foreign markets had compelled the government to rethink its highly vaunted *shokusan kōgyō* program. In order to increase industrial production rapidly, as the program envisioned, the Meiji leaders had elected to ply the course of what Calder terms "strategic capitalism." In the aftermath of the Sino-Japanese War, in the midst of a national identity crisis, they placed large amounts of government funds in private hands. The recipients were mainly industrial conglomerates and banking institutions, and as Calder rightly observes, they used their new-found influence to lasting effect by laying the groundwork for Japan's (in)famous "hybrid public-private system."[77]

One equally star-crossed strategy used by the government to place Japan on a more equal trade footing with the Western powers was currency reform. Finding itself flush with cash from the indemnity paid by China in the wake of the Sino-Japanese War, the government embarked on a bold program conceived to place Japan on the international gold standard. Finance Minister Matsukata Masayoshi, the initiative's main sponsor, steadfastly maintained that this project would attract needed capital imports to Japan. Even more sweepingly, as the popular view had it, the gold standard signified a higher level of civilization.[78]

Yet the anticipated boom in foreign trade never materialized. Although bullion valued at seventy-four million yen was duly shipped to and minted in Japan,[79] the nation was instead beset by a coincidental concatenation of calamitous events in 1896–1897. Owing to domestic crop failures and factory building in Japan itself, imports rather than exports increased; because of an economic recession in the United States, raw-silk exports declined; and thanks to the devaluation of China's silver-based currency vis-à-vis Japan's gold-based commodity prices, cotton-yarn exports fell off as well. The net result was a negative balance of payments that began to sap Japan's currency reserves.[80] Ostensibly in an effort to stabilize the financial situation, the government nervously began to manipulate prices on Japan's money and stock markets. But these manipulations only put Japan one step closer to disaster.

In 1898, when the textile business centered in Osaka fell on hard times, the bottom nearly fell out of the national economy. Only a belated government offer of export assistance enabled the nation to avert a more widespread financial collapse. But, by this time, the Japanese economy was living on borrowed time. In 1900, no such heroic scenario developed to save Japan from financial disaster. No sooner did the United States slide into an economic depression, further slashing Japanese silk imports, than China was torn asunder by the Boxer Rebellion and cut back on Japanese cotton-yarn imports. To make matters worse, Japan already had been compelled to borrow against its own currency reserves for military expenditures related to the unstable situation in China. The unavoidable result was the so-called Panic of 1900–1901. Once the first big bank failed, fifty smaller ones fell like dominoes. It took direct intervention by the Bank of Japan—to the tune of seven million yen in bail-out funds—to avert a complete financial collapse.[81]

Had all these calamities occurred in a political vacuum it would have been bad enough, but they happened even as the Western powers were placing Japan in a vise and steadily tightening it. Resistant still to Japan's repeated demand that the unequal treaties be revised—though they had made modest concessions toward Japanese tariff autonomy from 1899—the Western powers were instead erecting new tariff barriers of their own.[82] Given that some of these same nations were complicit in the Triple Intervention by the West following the Sino-Japanese War, the issue was nothing if not political. And because so many in Japan continued to put this political spin on the issue of foreign trade, Seki evinced concern. He was fearful, in particular, that government leaders would fashion foreign-trade policies that measured success by an international diplomatic yardstick rather than by a national economic one.

With this concern in mind, Seki sketched out the parameters of proper commercial policymaking: "Since the foundation of today's people's national economy is the political body of the 'folk,' the state [that represents them] and [that] formulates commercial policy cannot assume a neutral position toward commercial activities that reach beyond the boundaries of this political body. Conversely, the state must assume a neutral position with respect to commercial activities that take place within the body of the people's national economy."[83] Identifying "foreign-trade policy [as] the domestic economic policy of a nation as encountered from without,"[84] Seki maintained that truly modern nations formulated foreign-trade policies based on a thoroughgoing assessment of their domestic developmental priorities.[85] But, as he knew, no such reasoned assessment could take place until the irrational instincts of Japan's influential protectionist lobby were overridden.

As the self-appointed knights of protectionism, the chauvinistic economists of the National Economics Association were not the least bit shy in throwing down the gauntlet. But as Seki and others lamented, they invariably put the political horse before the economic cart. At once envious and suspicious of the Western powers, they urged state leaders not simply to nullify the unequal treaties but to impose tariffs, too, as a defensive weapon of economic war. Seki was no less suspicious of the chauvinistic instincts of late Meiji protectionists than he was of the free-trade faith of early Meiji liberal economists. Critical of liberal economists for their misguided principles, he was critical of protectionists for their misguided policies. Seki's dispute with the National Economics Association and its statist proponents in government came down to a single seminal issue: defining the national interest.

Seki rejected the model of a production-centered economy designed fundamentally to enhance national power. Instead, he proposed the establishment of a citizen-centered economy conceived to advance the collective interest of the Japanese people. Having redefined the state as the agent of the people, not the servant of the emperor, he encouraged its leaders to formulate foreign-trade policies in the collective interest of Japanese producers and consumers alike. Not only did this shift in Seki's perspective on the political economy foreshadow his growing concern with the social economy, but it hinted at a parallel development related to his political identity: increasing sympathy for social-democratic ideas.[86]

Announcing Japan's emergence into the "era of the people's national economy" (kokumin keizai jidai),[87] Seki put the nation on notice that commerce had taken on new meaning. In the preface of Shōgyō keizai seisaku (Commercial economic policy), a new monograph that reworked many of the themes in An Outline of Commercial Economics, he argued that "the time is past when national economic development could be advanced by profit-seeking merchants alone. The ebb and flow of commerce [today] is linked to . . . the national destiny."[88] This argument reinforced a historical observation Seki had made in 1902: that the demise of agricultural economies and the development of modern commercial-industrial ones signaled the supersedence of "conservative, quietistic, national" economies by "progressive, energetic, international" ones.[89]

As an emerging industrial economy on the cusp of epoch-making change, Japan, Seki had long maintained, should devote its fullest attention to the promotion of trade. Now in defense of that proposition—at what seemed a particularly critical juncture—he provided an explicitly historical justification. Seki began his historical narrative by questioning the most cherished assumption of liberal economists: that trade is a human phenomenon dictated by natural law. Dismissing as hopelessly "abstract" and "incorrect" their assertion that fishermen and hunters in "primitive tribal societies" naturally engaged in trade, he cited the research of anthropologists to the contrary. "The phenomenon of [commercial] exchange," noted Seki, "has progressed gradually by various means over long periods [of historical change]." He went on to observe that "the division of labor was a necessary precondition of [commercial] exchange" and that none existed in tribal societies, where self-sufficiency remained the rule. This, intoned Seki, was an inescapably "scientific" conclusion based on the latest "social science" *(shakai kagaku).*[90]

Among the various historical forms that this division of labor had taken, Seki cited occupational differentiation *(shokugyō no bunritsu)* as the most important: "With occupational differentiation, the phenomenon of [commercial] exchange infiltrated economic life, and in the end, in today's advanced economic societies, commerce has come to be tinged with important occupational distinctions." Noting that these distinctions were not innate to human society but were the result of human agency, Seki endeavored to illustrate the process of historical development through which they had evolved. In ancient societies, he observed, kings and chieftains had monopolized commercial exchange and thereby limited its scope. Only with the appearance of seafaring societies, which not only traded goods but also introduced "commercial spirit and commercial customs" wherever they landed, did a merchant class devoted exclusively to commerce begin developing. Such "[commercial] exchange," concluded Seki, "gradually changed into what [we] now [call] foreign trade."[91]

At the beginning of this historical process of foreign-trade development, Seki maintained that "[trade] had affected only the outward appearance [*gaimen*] of the economic life of ethnic groups. Within ethnic groups [socioeconomically speaking], production and consumption were one and the same." If self-sufficiency had remained the rule within ancient societies, domestic commerce became the rule in medieval ones. Seki traced the origins of domestic commerce to medieval Europe, in particular, where "the appearance of cities and towns gave rise to an urban-rural distinction that resulted in the separation of artisans from agriculturalists, ultimately necessitating the initiation of [commercial] exchange."[92]

In this view, Seki echoed the German historical school's emphasis on urban markets as the epicenters of exchange economies and anticipated his own lifelong fascination with cities. He attributed the steady development of domestic commerce to the growth of urban markets: "The economy of cities and towns was intimately related to the growth of markets, and [these] markets grew as a function of the direct exchange between producers and consumers." Not only did this development plant the "seed" for "domestic commerce," argued Seki, but it formed the basis for people's national economies: "Within the large economic groups that national peoples became, one [began to] see occupational differentiation as well as occupational and residential freedom. Commerce was indispensable in linking producers to consumers, and this [ultimately] triggered the growth of a [commercial] exchange economy, the birth of industrial enterprise, and the increase of capital, among other things."[93]

Before this development could reach fruition, it was necessary to reduce the powers enjoyed by city(-states) since the beginning of the medieval "era of city and town economies." These powers, which included the prerogative to restrict transport and to assess tariffs, were lost for good during the age of discovery. As new trade routes were opened and colonies were formed, national peoples became increasingly conscious of their common interest. By asserting that common interest against the established special interests of cities and guilds, argued Seki, they built a solid foundation for the new economic "body" *(dantai)* of "greater national peoples" *(ōinaru kokumin).* The end result was the demise of special city powers and the corresponding rise of nation-centered mercantilism—whereby nations ripped down internal barriers to domestic commerce and erected external ones to foreign competition in their place. In short, the establishment of maritime power by nations during the age of discovery precipitated the elimination of special city and guild powers; and the elimination of these powers, in turn, facilitated "the unification of national peoples" *(kokumin tōitsu).*[94]

Looking back over the subsequent development of mercantilist regimes in seventeenth-century Europe and assessing their historical influence on modern exchange economies, Seki concluded that they had put national peoples in a position to reap the benefits of world economic development for centuries to come: "The tremendous commercial progress of the present day is not the result of the independent power of each [different] national people, but the result of [several] national peoples grasping central authority over commerce following several thousands of years [of gradual commercial development]." Having identified mercantilism as a historical development spearheaded by seventeenth-century European states, Seki denied that it was the inevitable product of some innate "tradition" that dictated their unilinear development: "It is a mistake to conclude that commerce and the commercial system of the present day developed uniformly through the transmission of oral traditions. Especially since the formation of people's national economies, the [modern economic] system that emerged out of a [shared] tradition has been adapted to the unique spiritual and material character of each [different] national people."[95] Thus, Seki traced the development of modern economic systems to the "transmission" *(denshō)* of shared traditions by the advanced nations, and he traced the inter-national diversity of national economies to the influence of national peoples and their "unique spiritual and material character." In short, he attributed modern economic development to the operation of historical, rather than natural, law.

Seki then went on to summarize the history of commercial development: "Foreign trade sprouted in ancient times; domestic commerce grew over the past few hundred years. Together, these became the constituent parts of the people's national economy. From this point forward, [such] people's national economies will describe [the course of] commercial change and the systemic changes accompanying it."[96] Consistent with the historical logic of Roscher and the German historical school, then, Seki traced the rise of modern national economies to the commercial developments that issued from the creative enterprise of their constituent national peoples. In short, he identified the birth of modern exchange economies with national peoples rather than with national states.

Japan, of course, was subject to the same historical laws of economic development as the Western world. Yet because it was a relatively "backward nation" *(kōshinkoku)* compared to the "advanced nations" *(senshinkoku)* of Europe—and because, like all nations, its history and spirit were in certain respects unique—Seki sought not to identify developmental parallels but instead to sketch analogies.[97] He noted that Japan had conducted foreign trade in ancient times within the broader framework of a China-centered tribute system and that trade had been expanded and specialized during the Ashikaga period. Convinced that Japan had compromised its own commercial development under the legendary *sakoku* (closed-country) policy of the Tokugawa era,[98] Seki nonetheless acknowledged that the nation had made significant advances in the area of domestic commerce through "occupational specialization" *(bungyō).*[99]

The Meiji Restoration of 1868, however, had changed the name of the game. According to Seki, this pivotal event offered Japan "the authentic basis for commercial progress."[100] And as Samir Amin and others have since suggested, the fact that Japan coincidentally thwarted Western colonization as it was establishing nation-statehood helped to set it on a unique course of economic development: "From the start . . . Japan gave birth to its own autocentric capitalism. The fact that it came later, so that it was able to draw inspiration from the European development, did not do it any harm, as would have been the case had the country been colonized."[101] Indeed, seen from this perspective, Japanese developmentalism looks the more impressive, for, unlike "outpost nations" such as the United States, whose history as a European "imperial project" remained a powerful and complicating leitmotif of national comparison, Japan approached the same challenge as a tabula rasa.[102]

Seki maintained that the Meiji Restoration had placed Japan in a unique position: It might now share the common "tradition" of the advanced nations yet also craft a modern economic system all its own. In this belief, he strove to distill the historical lessons conveyed by that common "tradition" into a developmental paradigm tailored to the needs and desires of his own nation. Sketching the outline of an efficient exchange economy, Seki urged the Meiji leaders to focus initially on the critical task of commercial policymaking. Specifically, he called on them to harmonize the interests of Japanese producers and consumers through the judicious enactment of appropriate commercial regulations.

Seki readily acknowledged, however, that this would be no easy task. Among other things, it would require national economic policymakers to draw the necessary functional distinction between domestic commerce (*naikoku shōgyō*) and foreign commerce (*gaikoku shōgyō*). With respect to domestic commerce, Seki urged the state to expand consumption networks by nurturing trade and to render the interests of producers and consumers "compatible" by cultivating commercial enterprise. With respect to foreign commerce, he counseled the state to guard the interests of the national collectivity by regulating foreign competition. While Seki eschewed state control of domestic commerce, characterizing it as a needless brake on entrepreneurial freedom and consumer choice, he welcomed state intervention in foreign commerce as a necessary concession to global "power politics" (*kensei seisaku; Machtpolitik*).[103]

When he wrote *Commercial Economic Policy* in 1903, Seki bent himself to the task of articulating the proper principles of commercial policymaking for people's national economies. Pitting Friedrich List against Adam Smith, he argued that List had correctly indexed economic progress to the collective benefit of each national people, while Smith had mistakenly indexed it to the "benefits that individuals might obtain as consumers." Seki concluded that Smith had misconstrued the "national benefit" as a simple sum of the individual social parts of which the nation was made.[104] Taking the Listian view instead that the corporate self-interest is greater than the sum of the individual interests that compose it, Seki concluded that Japan's foreign-trade policies should be fashioned in accordance with the "interests of the people as a whole" *(kokumin zenpan no rigai)*, not just with those of one or another social class.[105]

Seki spoke directly to the issue of the national interest in his defense of tariffs, portraying tariffs at once as the most effective means of protecting developing economies from better-established competitors in the world market and as a necessary complement to domestic production priorities. As he saw it, proactive foreign-trade policymaking offered a multitude of benefits to nations such as Japan: "It harmonizes the benefits of producers, consumers, and workers; it prevents the spread of 'dangerous contagious diseases' that may obstruct the improvement of industrial conditions [i.e., social conflict in the workplace]; and it manages and controls commerce with foreign countries, thereby preventing important national industries from succumbing to foreign competition."[106]

While Seki continued to treat freedom of commerce as a laudable ideal, he distinguished it quite explicitly from "free trade-ism" *(jiyū bōeki shugi)*. Hence, while he promoted tariffs as an essential means of protecting infant industries, he also advocated the negotiation of multilateral trade agreements to promote international commerce. Preeminently, argued Seki, these agreements should accommodate cultural and economic differences:

> We should work out the particulars of each pivotal commercial treaty individually, considering the pros and cons of each tariff agreement or most-favored-nation clause in the context of an evaluation of cultural differences, disparities in productive capacity, and trade friction between the nations involved. These days, the countries on each continent of the world exhibit distinct cultures. Generally speaking, we need to be aware of the fact that treaties among European countries, those between European and American countries, and those between European and Asian countries will be concluded under different terms.[107]

Seki argued for this cultural relativism with explicit reference to the challenges that faced Japan at the time. If the Sino-Japanese War (1894–1895) had earlier convinced him of the need to develop commercial policies consistent with the objective of rapid industrial development, the Russo-Japanese War (1904–1905) reinforced his commitment to the active promotion of industry. Writing in 1908, he advised the state to conclude international trading agreements that promised to protect domestic industry against the threat of foreign competition:

> Even if our [elevated] position [in the world] today, following the Russo-Japanese War, cannot be compared to our [low] position before, the Western powers are paying increased attention to Japan's economic fluctuations. Given the [protectionist] trend in Western commercial policymaking, we must do something [to ensure] the protection and defense of [our own] national advantage by concluding trade agreements. There is nothing more important to our [national] economic policy [than this].[108]

Ultimately, the Meiji leadership implemented many of the basic measures that Seki and other like-minded political economists were promoting. Among other measures, as Howe points out, they introduced a "tariff policy [that] was based on the protection of industries with either strong import-substitution or export potential."[109] Only when the government began to levy supplemental tariffs designed to shield domestic industry from "unfair competition" (that is, from countervailing, retaliatory, and antidumping duties)[110] did Seki see fit to question the wisdom of its foreign-trade policies, warning Japan against protectionist overkill.

When the issue of national priorities was raised in discussions of trade regulation and international trading agreements, as it was during the annual meeting of the Association for Social Policy in 1909, Seki espoused the view that Japan should assess tariffs on processed and semiprocessed goods but not on either raw materials or foodstuffs.[111] Significantly, this recommendation was precisely the opposite of that which he had advocated for Germany in 1902. Rather than holding up Germany's foreign-trade policy as a model for all late developers, in other words, Seki based his recommendations for Japan on a close reading of its own specific developmental needs. He argued against agricultural tariffs, in this connection, on the grounds that the state had been overprotective of Japan's traditional agricultural sector.

Seki was joined in this opinion by a raucous chorus of industrialists who soon found themselves embroiled in an acrimonious dispute with rural landowners over agricultural protectionism. Depicting the advocates of agricultural tariffs as reactionary agrarianists whose anachronistic rhetoric of "economic stability" hearkened back to the "isolationist" Tokugawa

Era, Seki railed against the hopelessly archaic ideal of economic self-sufficiency that they uncritically endorsed. He drove the point home during the rancorous debate over grain tariffs that raged toward the end of the Meiji Era—tariffs that had been set in 1905 at 15 percent on rice and between 5 and 15 percent on wheat and barley.[112] Arguing that demand would continue to outstrip supply as Japan's population steadily increased, Seki criticized grain tariffs as a misguided effort to prop up Japan's traditional economy.[113]

Drawing a parallel between the government's obstinate advocacy of grain tariffs and its misguided subsidization of cottage industry, Seki insisted that reactionary policies such as these would soon condemn the nation to economic backwardness. He then wondered aloud whether the Meiji leaders would welcome the revolution in production afforded by industrialization, or whether they would blindly sacrifice progress in an effort to preserve the traditional way of life represented by farming and handicraft production. Protecting village sidelines would not merely retard the development of advanced factory systems, he maintained, but would also deprive the export industry of quality products to trade. Only by developing modern mass-production systems capable of manufacturing marketable exports in volume could Japan become competitive in the world market.

As he summarized his argument against grain tariffs and cottage-industry subsidies in 1909, Seki drew a telling comparison between Qing China and Meiji Japan. Both nations had mistakenly dragged "backward commercial values" into the modern era, he contended, but only Qing China had thus far condemned itself to economic stagnation. By refusing to succumb to the Confucian anticommercial bias that was China's undoing, argued Seki, Meiji Japan might yet overcome its past. He noted, indeed, that Japan had already begun to relinquish its archaic commercial ethic and that it remained only for the nation to implement modern systems of production and distribution.[114] With this goal in mind, Seki threw down the gauntlet. "It has come time for Japan to reach the various levels of economic development that the advanced nations of the world have already passed through . . . ," he intoned. "An industrial revolution is inevitable."[115]

Even as he was advising Japan to lay the foundation for a forward-looking people's national economy, Seki remained alert to the potential problems that threatened its growth.[116] Foremost among these difficulties was a demographic crisis that seemingly loomed on the horizon. "Japan is a small country with a rapidly increasing population," wrote Seki in 1912.

"It would be extremely risky to rely permanently on a policy of self-sufficiency [jikyū-jisoku]."[117]

Where staples such as rice were concerned, one potential solution was grain imports. And this was the solution that Seki favored, but with a critical twist. He proposed that Japan feed its growing industrial society— and thus also fuel the development of its expanding industrial economy— by transforming Korea into Japan's breadbasket. Initially at least, while Korea remained a Japanese protectorate under the provisions of the Portsmouth Treaty following the Russo-Japanese War, Seki called for the creation of a customs league *(kanzei dōmei)*. Such leagues typically accomplished the dismantling of internal barriers to domestic commerce and the erection of external barriers to foreign competition. Seki envisioned much more than an economic entente between Japan and Korea, however. As early as 1902, he had made the argument that customs leagues were the direct precursors of nation-states. He cited Germany as an example, noting that its "political unification" was enabled by the prior formation of "economic alliances" between previously autonomous regions.[118] When he proposed the creation of a Japan-Korea customs league, he was clearly projecting the future absorption of Korea into the Japanese nation-state. In short, Seki had started to redraw Japan's economic boundaries in anticipation of the seemingly certain expansion of its political boundaries.

In 1908, two years prior to Japan's formal annexation of Korea, Seki proposed an intimately symbiotic relationship between the two. Calling on Korea to "promote agriculture" and on Japan to implement "advanced systems of industrial production," he spoke of the Japanese and Korean economies together as a *"greater* people's national economy" *(dai kokumin keizai;* italics mine).[119] This strategic expansion of the "body of the people's national economy" *(kokumin keizai dantai),* according to Seki, would result in its maturation into a "international imperial economy" *(sekaiteki teikoku keizai)* capable of propelling Japan into the global economic age.[120]

To my knowledge, Seki did not explore the obvious racial and cultural implications of his position—implications that prompted others to reconceive postannexation Japan/Korea as an extended family-state—but he at least tacitly endorsed the assimilationist stance that the Meiji leadership would soon adopt. Peter Duus has summarized the assimilationist position:

> The adoption of assimilationist rhetoric allowed the Japanese to argue that Korea was not a colony at all, at least not in the sense that European overseas possessions were. In European colonies the rulers were completely alone, with no basis for commonality with the dominated peoples; hence, in the Japanese view, they tended to be

rapacious, selfish, and exploitative. But in a territory like Korea, where the people not only shared culture and history with the Japanese but were also part of one common "family," exploitation was ipso facto impossible, . . . The conclusion was obvious: Japan was helping the Koreans to improve themselves; it was not exploiting them. The relationship was not oppressive but reciprocal or complementary like the two wheels of the cart or like two brothers in a family.[121]

If Seki believed that the relationship between Japan and Korea was altogether different than the one between Britain and India, he was hardly oblivious to its imperialist cast. With this similarity in mind, perhaps, in 1910 he conducted an exploration of early-twentieth-century British imperialist ideology. He identified two different strains: political imperialism *(seijiteki teikokushugi)* and political economic imperialism *(seiji oyobi keizaiteki teikokushugi)*. The political economic form of British imperialism, which Seki went on to characterize as "constructive imperialism" *(kensetsuteki teikokushugi),* recalled Adam Smith's observation that imperialism had everything to do with political economy and that its central purpose was twofold: national defense and revenue. Echoing Smith's contention that trade within an empire is ultimately a better source of revenue than trade external to it, Seki justified imperialism as a national socioeconomic imperative.[122]

For fear that the Meiji leadership was about to squander the economic opportunity that the annexation of Korea had afforded Japan, Seki urged all those who supported the notion of a Japan-Korea customs league to read and reread *The Wealth of Nations*. Parroting Smith, he insisted that the real benefit derived from colonies was not a "monopoly over trade" but a monopoly over the "national defense and revenue."[123] In other words, the political and economic integration of Japan and Korea should not be viewed as a means of establishing global power and status but as a means of advancing national security and increasing national wealth.[124]

In 1911, Japan moved one step closer to the precious goal of economic independence: It finally achieved tariff autonomy. If this event signaled Japan's ability at last to formulate a foreign-trade policy beneficial to the people's national economy, it also raised the central question of how and at what levels tariffs should be levied against foreign competition. In 1913, after turning his scholarly attention inward to domestic industrial production for a time, Seki returned to the topic of foreign trade. He jumped back into the fray, it seems, for one overriding reason: to demonstrate to his countrymen that the nation's continuing import surplus was no cause for alarm. In an effort to calm nervous domestic producers, whose fear of

the import surplus had driven them to publicly equate buying Japanese
(naikoku shinamono) with love of country (aikokushin), Seki patiently
explained that the import surplus was actually a statistical chimera based
on a misreading of government trade figures. Once such data as currency
fluctuations and foreign-loan figures were taken into account, he maintained, the illusion of a deficit in the balance of trade would evaporate into
thin air.[125]

After spending over a decade researching, writing, and speaking about
commerce, Seki shifted intellectual gears toward the end of the Meiji Era.
He remained focused on the Japanese *Verkehrswirtschaft*—on the networks of exchange that drove the people's national economy and those
who promised to help them grow—but his focus shifted from commerce
to industry. What prompted this shift was historical circumstance: aside
from expanding its national economic boundaries to Korea and thereby
reducing the pressure to live or die by foreign trade, Japan had managed
to achieve tariff autonomy. Between them, these seminal developments
placed the Japanese people's national economy in a novel position: At last,
as Seki saw it, the people were truly free to pursue *shokusan kōgyō*.

If Japan were to successfully foster industry and promote enterprise,
the rules of economic engagement would have to be changed. Those days
were gone, maintained Seki, when the Japanese leadership could unconditionally throw its support behind Japan's most powerful industrial conglomerates and banking institutions on the pretext that their unmatched
financial and productive resources enabled them alone to compete effectively in the world market. The time had come, Seki would argue, to stunt
the growth of monopoly capitalism in Japan and to stimulate the growth
of the people's national economy.

In the coming years, guided by this conviction, Seki steadily shifted the
focus of his scholarship from commercial to industrial policy. A strident
supporter of industrial innovation, he acknowledged the seminal importance of *shokusan kōgyō*. Although he applauded the goal that this state
policy envisioned, he also questioned the means by which the state proposed to achieve it. Highly critical of the production-centered economic
ideology that guided the *shokusan kōgyō* program—and particularly alert
to the social dangers that attended its unremittingly mechanistic perspective of industrial progress—Seki turned his attention toward the people of
the people's national economy. Resisting the temptation to measure the
success of *shokusan kōgyō* in cold statistical terms as industrial output, he
embraced the challenge to put a human face on the people's national economy and thus began to redefine himself as a social economist.

PRODUCTION-SIDE ECONOMICS IN A NEW KEY

The sign on Seki Hajime's office door in the Tokyo Commercial College read "Trade Section." Given his growing concern with domestic industrial production in the wake of the Russo-Japanese War, however, it should probably have been changed to read "Industrial Section." By 1909, Seki had virtually abandoned the study of foreign trade and had embarked on a related project: a comprehensive analysis of Japanese industrial development focused on the infant industries whose protection he had advocated in his earlier work on tariff policies. Looking for the first time at the inner workings of the people's national economy and ever alert to the national agenda of *shokusan kōgyō*, Seki initiated his exploration of Japanese industry with a production-side portrait of modern enterprise that featured its central protagonists: industrial entrepreneurs.

Seki got the ball rolling with a rousing defense of the system of private enterprise. The rise of all industrial economies, he contended, could be traced to the capitalist instincts of creative entrepreneurs. Declaring them heroes of the industrial era, crediting them with the technological and organizational advances that had propelled industrial progress, Seki strove to define their proper role in a healthy industrial economy.[126] First and foremost, he recognized entrepreneurs as innovators. Cleverly contrasting their social contribution to that of capitalists, Seki maintained that "the development of society is advanced by [acts of] creation, and it is the function of the industrialist to create. The capitalist does not participate in this."[127]

Synthesizing the diverse perspectives of Roscher, Schmoller, J. A. Hobson, and Thorstein Veblen, among others, Seki went on to promote the principle of entrepreneurial independence. He did not seek merely to guard the managerial prerogatives of industrialists, however; he sought to ensure their proprietary interests as well. Sharply distinguishing industrialists *(kigyōsha)* from their sponsors *(hokkinin)*, he evinced a healthy skepticism of capitalist financial practices.[128] In this spirit, Seki called on the state to champion the cause of the owner-manager by circumscribing the influence of stockholders, bankers, and financiers over the operation of industrial enterprise.

Notwithstanding his mistrust of investors, Seki realized full well that the industrialist could not indulge his entrepreneurial talents without capital. He thus made two related proposals: first, that industrialists incorporate their businesses, and, second, that they seek out appropriate sources of venture capital.

Seki advocated incorporation as a means of freeing the industrialist from the financial constraints of Japan's traditional family economy. Under the principle of limited liability, he observed, the industrialist could build up his business without jeopardizing his personal property.[129] While incorporation promised to provide the industrialist with increased incentive to innovate, it did not necessarily secure him the financial means to do so. Seki therefore endeavored to identify sources of industrial capital in late Meiji Japan that would not compromise entrepreneurial independence. Poignantly observing that "the growth of credit institutions has acted to encourage the differentiation of capitalists from industrialists," he hastened to add that it had also "caused industrialists to lose their individualistic status and to be treated as commodities."[130] This worrisome development did not just threaten the entrepreneurial integrity of individual industrialists; it posed a perilous threat to the system of private enterprise itself. Once a business had lost the personal imprimatur of its founder, Seki cautioned, it soon lost direction as well. The challenge was to identify financial arrangements that would preserve the integrity of the individual industrial firm.

As a staunch supporter of incorporation, Seki predictably proposed that enterprising entrepreneurs offer shares of stock in their companies to well-heeled investors. Noting that this strategy had been effectively employed by Western corporations to acquire working capital, Seki was cautious nonetheless in his endorsement of it. His reservations concerning joint-stock incorporation reflected his palpable disdain for the "financiers" *(fuainanshā)* who had come to control the stock market. Although Seki acknowledged the advantages of a financial arrangement that would permit industrialists to attract investors, he was adamant in the conviction that it should not compromise the managerial autonomy of the entrepreneur.[131] Seki most feared that industrialists might succumb to financial pressure from individual and institutional investors.

In late Meiji Japan, as William Wray has observed, such fears were well founded. Japanese stockholders, who tended to regard large dividends as their due, often acted as though they were owners rather than sponsors of the enterprises in which they held a financial interest.[132] Understanding this belief at the time, Seki voiced a justifiable fear that stockholders and their agents would systematically appropriate industrial profits for their own short-term gain: "The acquisition of immense profits is demanding of attention . . . by reason of the [demonstrable] temptation to obtain [such] profits by unjust means. A variety of abuses related to joint-stock companies can be traced to the capitalization of profits."[133] Not only did

Seki fear that greedy stockholders and their agents would prevent the industrialist from reinvesting capital in his enterprise, but he feared that they would usurp his managerial authority as well.[134]

For all the contempt he generally heaped on stockholding practices, Seki reserved the lion's share of his anticapitalist invective for the "financiers."[135] He maintained that financiers were not true capitalists *(shihonka)*, but rather "procurers of capital" *(shihon no chōtatsusha)*, who typically maneuvered to become majority stockholders of the enterprises they underwrote. Left unchecked, argued Seki, these freewheeling speculators would do whatever was necessary to wrest control from corporate executives and managers.[136]

For fear that industrial operations would soon fall under the monopolistic control of financiers, Seki pressed the government to circumscribe the financial prerogatives of corporate stockholders.[137] Otherwise, he warned, "common investors" *(futsū hōshisha)* and "petty capitalists" *(koshihonka)* would become powerless and the wealthy would literally inherit the earth: "When the distribution of wealth in the nation [thus] becomes increasingly unbalanced, ... the very foundation of our [national] economic structure is endangered."[138]

In this same critical vein, Seki raised the specter of robber barons such as those who had seized economic control in the United States.[139] But he feared even more the enervation that had seized Great Britain's economy under the impact of monopoly capitalism. There, declared Seki, "financiers and the idlers who accompany them" had become so adept at manipulating the stock market that they had effectively taken command of national economic affairs.[140] Adding that this takeover had left the British people in the lurch, with virtually no influence over their own nation's economic destiny, he noted ominously that the citizenry had grown spiritually demoralized.[141] The Japanese people, warned Seki, would do well to read the writing on the wall: "It is no exaggeration to say that [our] current crisis in economic organization is traceable to the wealth amassed in the hands of financiers and the right to control over industrial production that has come with it."[142]

To whom, then, did Seki propose that Japanese industrialists turn for the capital they needed? The answer, of course, is to banks.[143] Having made this predictable pronouncement, however, Seki hastened to qualify it in recognition of the pressing problems that continued to plague the modern Japanese banking system. Observing that Japanese industrialists regularly encountered difficulty in securing loans, Seki advocated comprehensive banking reform: "If we wish to secure substantial industrial capital, we must make certain that the movement of capital is smooth. But the [smooth] flow of capital requires the regulation of a wide range of financial institutions."[144] Should Japan succeed in "smoothing out the relationship between industrialists and banks," declared Seki, "the benefit to our national economy will be immeasurable."[145]

Aside from spurring industrial development, this reform promised to get at another problem that had plagued Japanese capitalism since the beginning of the Meiji Era: the excessive concentration of banking capital in a few select financial institutions. Modern banking, as it was introduced to Japan in the 1880s and 1890s, was dominated by the Bank of Japan and two huge private institutions, the Yasuda and Mitsui banks. While the Bank of Japan acted as a financial clearing house of sorts—managing Japan's money supply, regulating fluctuations on the stock market, and supplying funds for economic development—the Yasuda and Mitsui banks served as prime lenders. According to one estimate, 50 percent of the deposits and 27 percent of the loans traceable to commercial banks in 1893 were with one or the other of these two institutions.[146] With the addition of the Dai-Ichi, Sumitomo, and Mitsubishi banks in 1910, the number of prime lenders expanded to five (the so-called Big Five), significantly broadening Japan's national banking structure.[147]

Consistent with the trend toward strategic capitalism, the government had placed its weight behind banks closely affiliated with industrial conglomerates. As well, in an effort to take up the economic slack in areas of extraordinary developmental concern to the nation as a whole, the government had itself established a number of special banks: the Yokohama Specie Bank, the Bank of Taiwan, the Hypothec Bank of Japan, the Hokkaido Colonial Bank, the Industrial Bank of Japan, and later the Bank of Chōsen (Korea). None of these special financial institutions, however, did much to alter the overall banking picture. As Calder has observed, the Japanese leadership had created a banking system that accorded private banks an "unusually prominent role . . . as financial intermediaries and industrial organizers."[148] In short, despite a diversified banking system, large private banks were exercising steadily increasing influence within the national economy.

To make matters worse, the Japanese banking system was rife with abuse. Because the biggest banks routinely denied loans to small commercial and manufacturing enterprises, smaller banks and "quasi-banks" (ginkō ruiji kaisha) had flourished locally—many of them engaging in shady business practices.[149] The smaller banks typically harbored speculators who gambled away ordinary deposits on risk-laden investments and recycled low-interest government loans through "arbitrage profiteering" *(sayatori)*; the quasi-banks resembled nothing so much as glorified moneylenders; and, as the Panic of 1900–1901 painfully illustrated, both sorts of banks were precariously leveraged.[150] Despite a state initiative to promote local bank mergers, Japan's financial landscape was also littered with so-called organ banks by the 1910s. Succinctly described by William Tsutsui as "institutions founded or managed solely to provide funds for a single client,"[151] these freewheeling operations offered their well-heeled clientele every imaginable speculative financial service. By doing so, argued Seki, they encouraged the worst sort of capitalist excess.[152]

Fearful that the financial free-for-all that defined Japanese banking in the 1910s would ultimately stifle responsible industrial investment, Seki worked up a sweeping proposal for banking reform that mitigated the problems created by a banking system that was alternately too big, too small, too private, or some combination thereof. While he readily acknowledged the central role played by the Industrial Bank of Japan in the area of industrial investment, he placed his faith in "ordinary banks" *(futsū ginkō)* to step into that role in the future. Such banks, he suggested, were exactly what the nation needed to reorder a banking system that had drifted dangerously into disarray.

Seki thus championed an innovative strategy of banking reform: "If we wish local banks to become institutional suppliers of fixed capital, we must increase banking capital, facilitate bank mergers and consolidation, and seek changes in industrial organization." Most important, however, he urged the government to "forge an intimate connection between local banks and industry" by helping to place industrial entrepreneurs with financial institutions sensitive to their immediate needs and committed to their long-term success. In thus encouraging the government to arrange a reliable and economical source of credit for industrial entrepreneurs, Seki strove, once and for all, to shift Japan's developmental focus from the cultivation of "capitalist spirit" to the creation of a "capitalist [economic] structure."[153]

If Seki thus readily acknowledged the integral role of capitalists in the provision of funds earmarked for the establishment and expansion of industrialist production, he considered credit a necessary evil of the capitalist system. Paradoxically, he proposed to restrict the prerogatives of the capitalist by securing the legal status of industrialists: "If, under the law, he [the industrialist] is [recognized as] the largest stockholder, promoter, director, consultant, supervisor, and general manager, there will be no question whatsoever about who is competent . . . to direct the establishment and operation of industrial enterprise."[154]

While Seki aimed to protect industrialists from the pressure of stockholders and from the manipulation of financiers, he was by no means oblivious to the drawbacks of a private-enterprise system dominated by freewheeling entrepreneurs. He noted that the industrialist's notion of free enterprise was informed by a belief in freedom founded on the principle of individual rights. Most industrialists, he observed, operated under the assumption that the free-enterprise system guaranteed them the right to set up businesses as they liked and to direct them without state interference.

The industrialist's rendering of economic freedom as the freedom to act in one's own interest had produced two nagging problems in industrial society. First, it had reinforced his "natural" impulse to place personal profit before the good of society; and, second, it had prompted him to treat labor as the mechanical means to realize economic success. All too often, declared Seki, "individual freedom has become the freedom to oppress workers, the freedom to make speculative investments and to reap speculative profits, and the freedom to commit fraud and to declare bankruptcy, until finally the fear takes root [among us all] that the basis of social organization [itself] may be shaken."[155] Characterizing such "freedoms" as abuses of the private-enterprise system, Seki lamented the failure of industrialists to subordinate self-interest to social responsibility. He urged them accordingly to cease rendering freedom as an inviolable principle of economic behavior and to begin treating it as a social prerogative.[156]

Although Seki thus attributed Japan's economic success in large part to the creativity of industrialists, he did not subscribe to the then-conventional wisdom that their social instincts led them naturally to address the needs of the nation. In sharp contrast to the rhetoric of industrialists, who commonly represented themselves as selfless "social capitalists" committed to the greater good of the nation, Seki drew attention to their intrinsic greed. Laying the lion's share of blame for Japan's developmental problems squarely at the feet of industrialists, he traced many of the ills of industrial society to the materialistic inclinations they had increasingly indulged under the free-enterprise system. In short, Seki derided industrialists for precisely the vice that they publicly repudiated: the implacable impulse to maximize profits for personal gain.

Challenging the view that wealth naturally yields progress, Seki declared that "the increase of 'wealth' is anything but synonymous with the furtherance of human welfare." So long as the Japanese failed to recognize this fact, he added, they would "not be able to avoid the various abuses occasioned by that system of industrial freedom which is premised on the demands of industrialists." While Seki expected industrialists themselves to address this problem by showing greater self-control, he was not so naive as to believe that they would rise to the challenge. He therefore called on the state to assume responsibility for the welfare of industrial society, and he suggested that its leaders begin by regulating the behavior of industrialists: "We cannot allow industrialists complete freedom in industrial operations. We need to set various restrictions [on them], addressing such considerations as public safety, social policy, and economic [order]."[157]

Seki advocated state regulation of industry in two specific arenas: economic policy *(keizai seisaku)* and social policy *(shakai seisaku)*. Under the aegis of economic policy, he proposed state regulations that would govern industrial organization by addressing broad structural issues related to ownership and management; under the aegis of social policy, he proposed a factory law that would govern industrial relations by emphasizing labor protection.

With respect to economic policy, Seki focused his attention on big business. He was particularly ambivalent about "big operations" that had grown larger through "specialization and synthesis" *(tokka-gōsei)*—that is, trusts and cartels—and accordingly called for their strict regulation. If such conglomerates were evidence of the evolution of Japanese industry to a level of "complex cooperation/interaction" that signaled the maturity of the people's national economy as well as its capacity to compete in the world economy, they were also monopolistic enterprises that posed a palpable threat to the domestic system of private enterprise. Ostensibly established to meet consumer demand for better products at lower prices, trusts and cartels were being employed instead to restrict industrial competition.[158] Not only did their exponents intend to corner markets, wrote Seki, but they aimed to manipulate the marketplace: "Instead of [engaging in] free, individual competition, trusts and cartels operate under [a form of] systematic, organized competition. . . . As we pass out of the era of competition between individual industrialists, we are witnessing the birth of the age of trusts and cartels."[159]

As Seki celebrated the "birth of the age of trusts and cartels" as incontrovertible evidence that Japan had developed into an "advanced nation," he also understood that this development brought with it a host of new problems. As a case in point, Seki cited the common practice of "dumping" products on the world market. By selling products abroad at significantly lower prices than at home, he observed, cartels made the Japanese consumer pay for their mistakes.[160] Only through the enactment of regulatory policies *(torishimari seisaku)* did Seki believe that the manipulative economic practices of trusts and cartels could be curtailed.[161]

Seki supplemented his demand for economic policies designed to preserve domestic economic competition and to protect the interests of domestic consumers with a demand for social policies designed to deal with the unique labor problems produced by large and complex industries. He was concerned primarily with the alienation of labor that had ensued from the growing automation and specialization of industrial production. Treated as interchangeable part of the machines they operated, not as producers in their own right, industrial wage laborers had become increasingly alienated from their work as well as from their employers.

Seki identified the alienation of industrial wage labor as the root cause of Japan's growing "industrial-laborer problem" *(kōgyō rōdōsha mondai)* and pronounced this problem modern Japan's worst nightmare. Initially triggered by the proliferation of wage laborers, the worker problem (as I will call it) was exacerbated by worsening working conditions, the deterioration of workers' daily lives, and the rise of working-class consciousness. To resolve these problems, Seki proposed the implementation of state-sponsored social policies aimed at improving the lives of the working poor.

In keeping with his growing concern with the worker problem, Seki steadily shifted the emphasis of his scholarship from industrial organization to industrial relations. Between 1909 and 1913, he produced three searching studies that help us trace the logic of his steady transformation from an advocate of industry into a labor reformer: *Shōkō seisaku kōryō* (An outline of commercial and industrial policy, 1909), *Rōdōsha hogo hō ron* (On a worker-protection law, 1910), and *Kōgyō seisaku* (Industrial policy, two volumes, 1911 and 1913). In *Shōkō seisaku kōryō*, Seki confronted the stark realities of factory production that he had glossed in his earlier work on industrial development. In *Rōdōsha hogo hō ron*, he confronted the manifold labor problems plaguing Japanese industry, seizing on industrial relations as the key to industrial reform and reconceptualizing the "labor problem" *(rōdō mondai)* as the "worker problem" *(rōdōsha mondai)*. And in *Kōgyō seisaku*, a two-volume tome compiled from his class lectures at the Tokyo Commercial College, he made the case for a comprehensive national industrial policy that promoted creative entrepreneurship on the one hand and worker protection on the other.

These pioneering studies brought Seki's people-centered economic perspective to bear on what was arguably the most urgent socioeconomic challenge facing Japan in the early 1910s: industrial labor reform. They also signaled his effort to bridge the gap between political economics and social economics. *Kōgyō seisaku*, which was devoted in equal parts to industrial organization and to industrial relations, embodied this larger purpose. By placing these concerns side by side, Seki made it crystal clear that national wealth and social prosperity went hand in hand.

CAPITALISM AND ITS DISCONTENTS

I have observed in this chapter that as the Japanese people's national economy sank roots and began to grow in the modern era, Seki's economic concerns shifted steadily from foreign-trade policy to domestic industrial policy. Much as his economic concerns shifted with the changing times so, too, did his theoretical perspective. Early on, when infant-industry protection remained one of Japan's paramount concerns, Seki leaned toward List and his economic creed of national wealth and power; later, when the industrial economy began to develop, he progressed to Roscher and his socioeconomic calculus of national resource maximization. In the process, Seki steadily humanized the Listian trope of the unitary nation/subject, in which the state loomed larger than the people, redefining the nation/subject as the national people writ large.

Once the people's national economy *(kokumin keizai)* began to mature, however, Seki was compelled to acknowledge that the modern nation/subject was not an organismic social entity but a rationalized social matrix. Within Japan's sophisticated, modern, capitalist society, with its highly specialized and concentrated industrial economy, the interests of the nation/subject's constituents were becoming increasingly distinct. As the old family economy gave way to the new industrial economy, argued Seki, new constituencies appeared. These new constituencies were "classes," and the newest among them was the industrial working class. Despite the central role that this class played in Japan's modernizing industrial economy, Seki noted dismally that it had been denied its proper place in society: "Thus, the worker problem addresses the challenge of liberating the many workers among the Japanese people. As a new class [*shin kaikyū*], the workers deserve to occupy their proper place [*chii*] within the traditional social structure of the nation."[162]

Acknowledging that this worker problem was a problem that engendered a conflict of interest between social classes *(shakai kaikyū)* within the nation, Seki was compelled to question the Listian/Roscheran trope of the unitary nation/subject that had been the mainstay of his argument for the development of a people's national economy. By the end of the Meiji Era, he was forced to admit that his people's national economy was rife with class inequities. Well aware that a similar "laborer question" *(Arbei-ter-frage)* hung heavily on the minds of his European cousins, the political economists of the German historical school, Seki was similarly impelled to acknowledge that this question was really a class question.

Seki owed his reconceptualization of the laborer question as a class question preeminently to the ideas of an economist whom he had heretofore ignored: Karl Marx. Along with many other reform-minded political economists at this critical juncture, Seki now subjected Marx's work to the closest scrutiny. Most important, Marx compelled Seki to entertain the possibility that classes, rather than nations, were the central figures of modernity. At once impressed and appalled by Marxism, Seki combed Marx's masterwork, *Das Kapital,* for theoretical and historical insight; he then put Marxist class analysis to the test in Japan.

Seki's exploration of Marx resulted in a searching commentary on Japanese capitalism that confirmed that classes mattered no less than nations in the modern industrial world. Just like the advanced industrial nations of the West, argued Seki, Japan had begun to show symptoms of an impending class conflict *(kaikyū tōsō)* between the owners of the means of industrial production and the propertyless workers who toiled in their factories. Japan's industrial revolution, which had forged an entirely new relationship between capital and labor, had also ushered in a new era: what Seki called the "age of classes" *(kaikyū jidai).*[163]

Notably, Seki did not mourn the advent of the "age of classes" in Japan but instead celebrated its arrival as evidence of social progress. Echoing Marx himself, Seki argued that industrialization had wrought critical changes in the means of industrial production that heralded the advent not merely of a new economy but of a new society as well. If industrialization had triggered technological "specialization" *(tokka)* and "synthesis" *(gō-sei),* necessitating new forms of factory organization,[164] it had also "precipitated a complete transformation of the organization of work."[165] More specifically, industrialization engendered a division of labor between the owners of the means of production and the wage laborers in their employ—between the "leaders of industry and the obedient who follow their orders," as Seki portrayed them—a division that had precipitated social "specialization" and "synthesis." In the end, concluded Seki, social "specialization" and "synthesis" in the industrial age had also produced unprecedented "social compartmentalization" *(sōsei bunshi).*[166]

Seki celebrated the process of social "specialization" through which classes had been produced as the means by which modern societies were made increasingly orderly: "The appearance of hierarchically ordered groups and classes within society is unavoidable. [Indeed,] the phenomenon of [social] specialization is the very thing that promotes social action and advancement."[167] Rather than identifying the "social compartmentalization" of industrialists and workers as a harbinger of the coming class revolution, as Marxists did, Seki identified it as proof positive of social progress. In short, he broke ranks with Marx not over the historical fact, but over the historical thrust, of class formation.

Seki took Marx to task for his bold prediction that the proletariat would one day rise in revolution and thereby trigger the creation of a classless paradise. Identifying this formulation as an example of backward-looking socialist utopianism whose objective was to revive the "communal life" *(kyōdō seikatsu)* of yore, Seki reiterated his belief that class formation signified social progress. Seki then went on to warn his readers off the reactionary romanticism intrinsic to Marx's projection of a classless paradise in the future: "Given that sophisticated cultures first appeared with the division of classes and [advanced] with their interaction, the elimination of classes [certainly] would signify cultural retrogression."[168]

Seki envisioned, in short, not a classless society, but a class-ful[l] one. Unlike Marx, who projected an impending proletarian revolution, Seki anticipated continuing social evolution. Nevertheless, he had few illusions about the obstacles that stood in Japan's path. Openly acknowledging the evils of the capitalist system, Seki urged the people of the people's national economy to generate a "new system" *(shin seido):*

> We cannot deny that historical development is basically social development. The structure of today's capitalist system, being the result of thousands of years of development, cannot be destroyed with a single blow. We must eliminate the evils of the capitalist system, step by step, through a process of organic evolution. We cannot form a new society by struggling against state power in a violent revolution. By the same token, we should not turn to state intervention . . . to destroy the foundation of the system, altering the structure of the capitalist system such that it reverts to the patriarchal social structure of the past. Instead, we must generate a new system that reflects the uninterrupted continuities of social development.[169]

In the "new [social] system" that Seki envisioned for Japan, the classes that collectively constituted the modern nation/subject would occupy subject positions of their own within the people's national economy. Seki laid the foundation for this remarkable new figure of modernity by forging common ground between List and Marx. Much as he had earlier humanized the Listian *Nationalökonomie* with the help of Roscher's socioeconomic calculus of "national resource maximization," he now endeavored to humanize the Marxist class model. How Seki accomplished this humanization—and how he came to envision industrialists and workers as the constituent subjects of a unified (though not unitary), modern nation/ subject—is the topic of the chapter that follows.

3 Class and Nation

In the waning years of Meiji, as the laborer question reared its ugly head, Seki Hajime was compelled to acknowledge that the Japanese nation/subject was not an organismic community *(Gemeinschaft)* comprised of the "folk" but a complex society *(Gesellschaft)* internally divided among classes. Questioning the universalist argument made by Listian nationalists that the nation was a unitary collectivity whose health could be measured by its wealth and power, he also questioned the universalist argument made by Meiji Marxists that the nation was a constructed community whose seeming unity actually masked irreconcilable class differences among its constituents. Rather than rejecting one or the other of these competing views of modernity, Seki searched for common ground between nationalism and Marxism.

PROLOGUE: MARX VERSUS LIST

Seki could not have known that Marx himself had earlier confronted nationalism with many of the same concerns that he later would, but Marx had done precisely that in an unpublished criticism of Friedrich List. Writing in 1845, Marx pointedly dismissed and disparaged List's contention that nations, rather than classes, were the primary subjects of modernity. Because Marx's essay brings Seki's concerns into high relief—and because Seki ultimately managed to find common ground between Marx and List— I begin this chapter with a rehearsal of the battle that Marx fought with his self-declared ideological nemesis.

Thanks to the scholarship of Ernest Gellner and Roman Szporluk, who have wondered aloud how and why Marx so vehemently rejected List's contention that nations were the central protagonists in the modern metanarrative of progress, we have a leg up on the critical conceptual dilemma with which Seki grappled as he forged his ideology of social reform: the seeming incompatibility of nationalism and Marxism. Since List was the foundational figure of Seki's people's national economics, and since Marx provided the intellectual inspiration for his conversion to social reformism, it seems entirely appropriate that we examine their differences here.

"Structural change of human society means, if it means anything, some basic alteration in the relationship of the parts or elements of which mankind is composed. The dramatis personae of history change their positions relative to each other. But who or what exactly are those dramatis personae?" asks Gellner in his provocative essay "Nationalism and Marxism." With respect to the "radical, structural change" that swept European society in the nineteenth century, Gellner contends that "there are two principal candidates for the crucial role: classes and nations."[1] Following the lead of Szporluk,[2] he pits Marx against List as spokesmen for "classes" and "nations," respectively.

Gellner and Szporluk both begin their studies by recalling the vicious criticism that Marx leveled at List in an unpublished manuscript written in 1845. That polemic, which represents List as an apologist for the German bourgeoisie in the name of the German nation, bears reproducing here in all its rhetorical excess:

> What then does the German philistine want? He wants to be a *bourgeois*, an exploiter, inside the country, but he wants also not to be exploited outside the country. He puffs himself up into being the "nation" in relation to foreign countries and says: I do not submit to the laws of competition; that is contrary to my national dignity; as the nation I am a being superior to huckstering.
>
> The nationality of the worker is neither French, nor English, nor German, it is *labour, free slavery, self-huckstering.* His government is neither French, nor English, nor German, it is *capital.* His native air is neither French, nor German, nor English, it is *factory air.* The land belonging to him is neither French, nor English, nor German, it lies a few feet *below the ground.* Within the country, money is the fatherland of the industrialist. Thus, the German philistine wants the laws of competition, of exchange value, of huckstering, to lose their power at the frontier barriers of his country! He is willing to recognise the power of bourgeois society only in so far as it is in accord with *his interests*, the interests of his class! He does not want to fall victim to a power to which he wants to *sacrifice* others, and to which he sacrifices himself inside his own country! Outside the country he wants to show himself and be treated as a different being from what he is within the country and how he himself behaves within the country!

He wants to leave the *cause* in existence and to abolish one of its *effects!* We shall prove to him that selling oneself out inside the country has as its necessary consequence selling out outside; that competition, which gives him his power inside the country, cannot prevent him from becoming powerless outside the country; that the state, which subordinates to bourgeois society inside the country, cannot protect him from the action of bourgeois society outside the country.

However much the individual bourgeois fights against the others, as a *class* the bourgeois have a common interest, and this community of interest, which is directed against the proletariat inside the country, is directed against the bourgeois of other nations outside the country. This the bourgeois calls his *nationality*.[3]

Thus identifying the nation as its bourgeoisie writ large, Marx took List to task for obfuscating what Gellner terms "the central intuition of Marxism": that "all history of all hitherto existing society is the history of class struggles."[4]

Gellner calls our attention not to the obvious philosophical gulf that separated Marx, the "international socialist," from List, the "national capitalist," but to the common ideological enemy that these strange bedfellows shared: "The point of overlap between List and the founding fathers of Marxism is their shared perception of the invalidity of the legitimating ideology of the new industrial order, i.e. of the *laissez-faire* doctrine of free trade."[5] Both recognized free trade as an impediment to, not a stimulus for, socioeconomic progress, but they cast their arguments against it in different terms. For his part, List ridiculed the liberal economic assumption that free trade would put all producers on an equal footing. Noting that England and France already had a significant productive advantage when they began promoting the cause of free trade and that they broke "the rules" whenever it was in their economic interest to do so, List urged late developers such as Germany "to protect themselves against such free or early riders." Marx, however, welcomed the conflict ignited by free trade as an inevitable consequence of capitalist development. As Gellner observes,

> [Marx was] inspired by the conviction that unequal terms were not a contingent flaw, but an inherent and necessary feature of the system: even if there were no inequality of strength at the start (though there was), the sheer natural workings of the system would eventually ensure its appearance and its aggravation. There was for him no special need to protect late developers, since their suffering would be no worse than that of the victims of early, and hence all the more painfully protracted, development of capitalism.[6]

While Gellner acknowledges that Marx had fundamental differences with List, he also wonders at the extraordinary vehemence of Marx's objections to Listian economics. What prompted this vehemence, Gellner goes on to surmise, was Marx's own suspicion that he had misjudged "the relation between nationalism and industrialization."[7]

Gellner does not go so far as to argue, as Szporluk does, that "Marx got it wrong, and List got it right";[8] instead, he plays up the hypocrisy of Marx's position on free trade. Noting that Marx paradoxically advocated free trade for Germany as a revolutionary strategy—as a means, in Marx's own words, of "break[ing] up old nationalities and carry[ing] antagonism of the proletariat and bourgeoisie to the uttermost point"[9]—Gellner goes on to remind us that Marx publicly opposed Listian protectionism on the grounds that the German bourgeoisie had no "chance of succeeding" in the effort "to develop its own 'national road to capitalism' (Szporluk's phrase)."[10]

Similarly, Harold Laski has argued that Marx's visceral ambivalence toward nationalism even found its way into the *Communist Manifesto*, which reads strangely like an " 'antinationalist manifesto' by someone who had confronted German nationalism through the works of its main spokesman—Friedrich List."[11] While Szporluk goes on to infer dramatically that Marx learned both nationalist theory and laissez-faire economics from his nemesis and that "latter-day Marxists" became "crypto-Listians" when they integrated these ideas into their Marxian ideologies, Gellner more modestly interprets Marx's palpable hostility toward Listian political economy as a kind of railing against historical reality.[12] In the end, writes Gellner, Marx dogmatically wrote himself into a theoretical corner:

> Free trade internally, protectionism outwardly he held to be a contradiction, and the idea of nationalism was simply a smokescreen intended to hide the absurdity of it all from those who propounded it.
>
> In the event, the alleged absurdity turned out to be the crucial reality of the nineteenth and twentieth centuries. It was both feasible and terrifyingly effective. Worse still: the actual role of Marxism in the form in which it actually came to be implemented in the real world, was Listian. The national road to either capitalism or socialism was not only viable, but mandatory. It was the *national* path to industrialism that was essential. Capitalism and socialism are single variants of it—though one may add that capitalism seems considerably more efficient, and commits the society undergoing it to far less false consciousness concerning its own organization, than does socialism.[13]

This discussion of Marx and List—and, more pointedly, the story it tells of the ideological rivalry between nationalism and Marxism in the twentieth century—resonates profoundly with the ideological dilemma that confronted Seki once he was compelled to acknowledge the existence of antagonistic classes within the organismic nation that had once seemed the mainstay of his people's national economy. If Marx, with his unrelenting historicism, gave Seki insight into this issue, he also gave him fits with his uncompromising materialism and universalistic theoretical pretensions. Paradoxically, as we shall see, it was by deconstructing the addled musings of a self-styled Japanese Marxist that Seki developed a critical perspective on Marxism. This view, in turn, enabled him to take the essential first step toward the domestication and the subsequent integration of Marxist insights into his analytical model of the people's national economy.

METHOD AND MADNESS IN JAPANESE MARXISM

Question: When did Seki begin to take Marxism seriously? Answer: The moment the Ministry of Agriculture and Commerce released *Shokkō jijō* (The condition of the workers) in 1903. This ground-breaking government survey of industrial labor awakened many, including Seki, to the sorry plight of the working classes in Japan. A shocking exposé of working conditions in Japanese factories, *Shokkō jijō* irrefutably illustrated that Japan was anything but immune to the labor problems that plagued other industrial nations.[14] Its extensive interviews with factory workers put such a disturbingly human face on the labor problem that government leaders who had once banished the problem from their economic field of vision suddenly found themselves haunted by the waking nightmare of impending labor unrest. No longer could these leaders argue that the labor problem was a hysterical projection of the *Arbeiter-frage* onto the Japanese industrial landscape. It had become all too real.

Japan's political leadership was not alone in awakening late to the stark realities of the labor problem. If we can reasonably extrapolate from the experience of Seki Hajime, then many former economic nationalists were compelled by the testimony recorded in *Shokkō jijō* to reinvent themselves as economic reformers. Writing later about the significance of this survey to the epoch-making debate over labor legislation that raged in the coming years, Seki likened *Shokkō jijō* to the pioneering surveys of laboring life in nineteenth-century England that had precipitated the introduction of the world's first factory laws: "We can demonstrate unequivocally that free enterprise gives rise to numerous abuses related to working conditions . . . based on the surveys of laboring life repeatedly conducted in England since the beginning of the nineteenth century, and now based as well on the surveys entitled *Shokkō jijō*, conducted by our own Ministry of Agriculture and Commerce."[15]

If *Shokkō jijō* educated Seki to the magnitude of Japan's labor problem, it did not define his reaction to it. When he recast the labor problem as the "worker problem," he did not do so solely out of compassion for the pitiful workers portrayed in *Shokkō jijō*; when he militated for a worker protection law *(rōdōsha hogo hō)* rather than for a factory law *(kōjōhō)*, he was engaged in a much further-reaching critique of industrial society than *Shokkō jijō* intended. Embedded in the unique vocabulary that Seki came to employ were critical conceptual distinctions, not merely semantic ones, concerning the challenge of industrial-labor reform. In making these distinctions as he did, Seki defined the new social logic of his economic nationalism. While he echoed the sentiments of many other late Meiji labor reformers, who similarly redefined the labor problem as a "social problem" *(shakai mondai)*, his redefinition of "the social" brought class into focus as the central issue.

While *Shokkō jijō* provided budding social reformers such as Seki with ample empirical evidence of a growing industrial-labor problem in Japan, this problem assumed even greater significance in their eyes for two related reasons: first, because it revealed a far-reaching pattern of exploitation that affected not merely individual workers here and there but the industrial working classes as a whole; second, because it mirrored the experience of other industrialized and industrializing nations. The seeming similarity between Japan's labor problems and those of the Western nations impelled Seki to conduct a wide-ranging survey of the European industrial working classes. One economist in particular helped him to place the results in comparative perspective: Marx. Repeating the praise of Schmoller, Seki declared Marx's "scientific socialism" a new and revolutionary type of economics: "[Socialist] research on class conflict and class war has helped explain the imbalance of power in political and social relationships, and it has illustrated the pitiable insecurity and poverty of workers. Having thus uncovered a new national economic phenomenon, [socialism] can be said to constitute a new type of economics."[16]

While Seki was just as impressed as Schmoller with the putatively universal implications of Marx's sweepingly comparative perspective on class conflict, as well as its attendant promise as a positivist historical paradigm, he was won over to class analysis as a heuristic method by Marx's reliance on painstaking empirical research. Seki called attention specifically to the "scientific" analysis of English industrial development on which Marx had based his masterwork, *Das Kapital:* "As Marx himself writes in the preface to his theory of capital, 'the physicist . . . observes natural processes where they occur in their most significant form.' . . . By [similarly] focusing his own research on English government reports and statistics, Marx managed to produce an indisputable account of [the condition of] industrial workers."[17]

Initially, then, Marx was recommended to Seki as a formidable economic thinker by the rigorous combination of empiricism and positivism that described his scholarship. That Seki's own political economics was characterized by a similar methodological balance helps explain why he could so deliberately integrate class analysis into his scholarship. He strove to achieve in his work the sort of methodological blend of empiricism and positivism that David Williams has aptly described as being a "compound" rather than a "mix."[18] This said, however, it was not a simple matter for Seki to mix Marxism into his national economics to produce a stable compound. Not only did the Marxist model of socioeconomic development pretend to deterministic universalism, but it did so by confounding the critical distinction between social science and natural science that Seki and the economists of the historical school so carefully guarded. Seki's criticism of Marxism, in this respect, recalled his earlier criticism of neoclassical economics: he decried their mutual predilection to deduce natural laws of socioeconomic development from the evidence of history—natural laws that, in his view, literally and figuratively defied human reason.

While Seki was contemptuous of the deterministic universalism that pervaded both Marxist and neoclassical economics, he did not extend this criticism uncritically to their foundational texts. Much as he had resurrected the historical wisdom of Adam Smith from a close reading of *The Wealth of Nations* earlier in his career, Seki now drew historical insight from Marx as he waded through *Das Kapital.* His critical reading of Marx's masterwork led him neither to swallow Marxist theory whole nor to dismiss it out of hand, but rather to domesticate it in appreciation of its demonstrable relevance to the nascent labor problems of Japanese industrial capitalism.

Whether Seki was the exception to the rule among political economists of his day remains an open question, but the story of his selective integration of Marxist class analysis into Japanese national economics certainly cuts against the historiographical grain. While it is old news that Marxism spawned a lively debate over national development among left-wing Japanese economists in the 1920s[19]—and though it has come to our attention that government bureaucrats, of all people, were well versed in Marxism in the late 1930s[20]—the influence of Marxist thought on economists in the early 1900s has yet to be adequately acknowledged.[21]

One historian who has attempted to correct the misimpression that Marxism mattered little to Meiji economists is Tessa Morris-Suzuki. In her sweeping survey of Japanese economic thought, she calls attention specifically to Fukuda Tokuzō's early engagement with Marxism. While Morris-Suzuki convincingly illustrates that scholars such as Fukuda integrated Marxism into their economics as young men, she goes on to emphasize that they soon repudiated it. Noting that Fukuda later "read and drew inspiration from a wide range of sources" that included "the newly-emerging theories of the European neo-classical school," she recounts his disenchantment with Marxism and his eventual conversion into an anti-Marxist.[22]

Not all young Meiji political economists who engaged Marxism early in their careers followed Fukuda's example, however. Among those whose ideological development traced a different trajectory was Fukuda's friend and colleague Seki Hajime. No less critical than Fukuda of Marxist historical materialism, Seki declined nonetheless to throw the baby out with the bath water. Rather than rejecting Marxism outright, contemptuous of its rigid determinism and fantastical internationalism, he painstakingly historicized Marxist class analysis and integrated it into his prescription for labor reform in Japan's late-developing capitalist society.

Seki's earliest excursion into Marxist economics led him to initiate this process of domestication. In a memorable commentary penned in 1910, he took Marx to task for his historical determinism. His argument pivoted on the observation that Marx had proven to be a poor prognosticator. Noting that recent trends in economic development were running counter to Marx's predictions, Seki provided two critical examples. First, he observed that monopoly capitalism had not taken root in the modern industrial world; rather, petty capitalists had flourished collectively under the joint-stock system. Second, he pointed out that the working classes had not descended precipitously into proletarianism; instead, industrial society had witnessed the growth of a middle class *(chūsan kaikyū)* that included factory workers on the rise.[23]

Armed with ample evidence of troublesome flaws in Marxist class analysis, many of which indicated that Marx had overestimated the generalizability of his historical paradigm, Seki endeavored to identify its limitations. What leapt out at him, as it would to Gellner and Szporluk seventy years later, was that Marx had compellingly cast classes, not nations, as the dramatic leads in the epic of modern history. That neither Marx's nor

List's historical script left room for a co-star cast Seki into a quandary. Increasingly, he was convinced that the modern nation/subject comprised class/subjects whose conflicting interests could and should be mediated by the state in the interest of peace and order—not to mention social progress.

In the end, Seki was able to conflate the competing visions of modernity proffered by Marx and List through his domestication of class analysis. He had initiated this process by working through Marx's major writings, including *Das Kapital;* he now completed it by working over the quasi-Marxian treatise *Jisei no hen* (The changing spirit of the times; hereafter, *Changing Times*), written by Kawakami Hajime.[24] Seki's critique of this quirky book sparked a lively public debate with Kawakami that impelled both author and critic to come to terms with Marxism.

Changing Times marked the beginning of Kawakami's lifelong affair with Marxism and arguably set an agenda for the European study tour that would soon change his life.[25] In *Changing Times*, Kawakami argued that social change issued fundamentally from changes in the means of production and that this connection was particularly obvious in the present day with its "culture of machines." He contended that the development of machines had wrought revolutionary social and cultural change and that those who possessed machines knew true power.

Kawakami went on to argue, quite unremarkably for the day, that "the wealth and strength of a nation correspond to [its] mechanical advancement." It was his embellishment of this argument that provoked controversy. Making materialism the pillar of his nascent Marxist creed, Kawakami traced the "changing spirit of the times" throughout history to "materialistic trends." He termed this approach the economic materialist historical perspective *(keizaiteki yuibutsu shikan)* and applied it wholesale to Japan. Following the Meiji Restoration, observed Kawakami, Japan had dispensed with its archaic "tool civilization" and replaced it with a "machine civilization." In hope of transforming the Japanese into a "new race" *(shinjinrui)*, he added, the state had forced the pace of this transition and thereby triggered the troubling social (i.e., class) differences that had come to plague the nation.[26]

Kawakami explicitly distinguished his "economic materialist historical perspective" from the base materialism of the "historical school"—by which he meant the economics of scholars such as Seki, who were profoundly influenced by the German historical school of political economy. Characterizing their work as hopelessly positivistic *(jisshōteki)* and descriptive *(kijutsuteki)*, Kawakami described his own as the epitome of idealism *(risōron)*.[27]

No sooner did Kawakami publish his essay than he found himself embroiled in a heated dispute with the "historical school" economists whose work he had so disdainfully dismissed. Taking issue with Kawakami's economic materialism, Seki Hajime bluntly accused him of nihilism *(West-nihilismus)*.[28] Although the label did not then carry the pejorative connotation it does today, it was damning nonetheless: Seki insinuated that Kawakami had denied human values their proper place in history, and, as we shall see, Kawakami heard him loud and clear.

Seki first made his case against Kawakami in a critique of *Changing Times*. His review, which appeared in 1912, was carried by *Kokumin keizai zasshi* (The people's national economics), the journal of economics that Seki had founded with Fukuda Tokuzō in 1906. Terse and to the point, Seki's review was devastatingly brief. In barely two pages of criticism, he managed not merely to raise serious questions about Kawakami's methodology but to impugn his honor. The critique began with a jibe at the author. Seki pointedly recalled Kawakami's past commitment to reactionary economic causes and most especially his strident support of "agrarianism." Is this the same man, intoned the critic, who once blithely called for grain imports and now speaks of mechanization as the "spirit of the times"?[29]

Having berated Kawakami for being ideologically inconsistent, Seki proceeded directly to the text of *Changing Times*, intent on demolishing the case made there for historical materialism. His critique was anything but even-handed: he immediately launched a frontal attack on the premises of Kawakami's argument. Seki's criticisms laid bare the basic methodological differences between economists of his own persuasion, the social reformers of the "historical school," and those of Kawakami's, the new breed of radical materialists. Seki argued that Kawakami had baselessly attributed "all the great [historical] changes in economy and thought" to technological advances. Protesting this reductionism in the strongest possible terms, he cautioned that "the [school of] thought based on historical materialism will lead [us] toward nihilism and cannot help but lead [us] ultimately to [reductive] internationalism."[30]

Seki's ruthless criticism was understandable: Kawakami had struck at the fundamental beliefs of reformers like himself. Not only had Kawakami attributed social change in the modern world exclusively to mechanization—denying, in effect, the causal importance of customs, traditions, and ideas—but he had rendered social change as a unilinear process, ignoring the historical influence of national differences. As if to demonstrate the sheer folly of historical materialism, Seki drew the reader's attention to logical inconsistencies in Kawakami's argument. He seized first on an obscure Buddhist reference buried in the text. Quoting the medieval Buddhist theologian Nichiren, Kawakami had suggested that the "laws" applicable to other nations might not always be applicable to Japan. Seki called him out on this perplexing point, wondering aloud how so radical a universalist could so readily endorse historical particularism.[31]

Yet Kawakami's perplexing argument about the relationship between technological change and social progress truly baffled Seki. He cited the following passage as evidence of a fatal contradiction in Kawakami's reasoning: "There are people who use tools the way lions and tigers use their jaws, but there are also people who, like ants, thrive on the wealth of collective activity. . . . The Japanese are akin to the latter."[32] Noting that Kawakami had contradicted himself, refuting his own argument for the parallel advance of technological and social change, Seki remarked that "the author may be leaning toward historical materialism, but cannot seem to abandon a dualistic world view *(nigenron)*."[33]

It is hard to escape the conclusion that Seki meant this criticism to be read in two ways: first, as a frontal assault on Kawakami's methodological inconsistency, and, second, as a sarcastic jibe at his fanciful comparison of the lives of human beings to those of tigers, lions, and ants. Thoroughly exasperated by Kawakami's essay, which he adjudged "one great contradiction," Seki concluded his review as sarcastically as he had begun it. "Perhaps this is one of those books that you have to read 'between the lines,' " he quipped. "If so, I'll gladly shut my mouth."[34]

Seki's critique of Kawakami precipitated a series of volatile exchanges symptomatic of the serious methodological differences that then separated historical idealists and historical materialists. The ultimate source of conflict between Seki and Kawakami was their different philosophies of history. Although each was concerned in his way with the issue of social change, they were at opposite poles in identifying its causes. Kawakami maintained that social change was essentially a function of "the [natural] law of cause and effect," Seki that it reflected the natural propensity of human beings to adapt to new circumstances as they maximized their resources. Kawakami looked outside the human world for his explanation of social change—to universal laws of material progress. Seki looked within the world for his—to the creative faculties innate to human beings. The heated debate between these true believers witnesses the passion and conviction that Japanese economists brought to the late Meiji search for a paradigm of national progress.

Predictably, Kawakami did not take kindly to Seki's terse review of

Changing Times. In his rebuttal, which appeared in the April 1912 issue of *Kokumin keizai zasshi*, Kawakami parried each of Seki's thrusts, then introduced some jabs of his own. As if to chasten Seki for the sarcasm of his parting remarks, Kawakami prefaced his rebuttal with a courteous acknowledgment of the review: "I wish to thank Doctor Seki at the outset for granting me the honor of his esteemed criticism. It is my distinct academic privilege [to reply]." Kawakami then wasted no time in identifying the motives of his distinguished detractor. Accusing Seki of "thought control," which he defined as the intent "to suppress new ideas and restrain freedom of thought," Kawakami cited the lengthy passage from Seki's review in which he had been accused of both nihilism and internationalism. "The [criticism] is so simplistic," he asserted, "that I have not yet received the benefit of enlightenment. . . . I can only guess at Seki's intent."[35]

Notwithstanding this expression of bemusement, Kawakami fully appreciated the gravity of Seki's accusations. With his ears still ringing, he raised a spirited defense of historical materialism that was intended simultaneously to establish its methodological integrity as a philosophy of history and to restore the intellectual reputation of its practitioners. In an effort to establish the philosophical credibility of historical materialism, Kawakami represented it as a visionary "ism" in the pragmatic tradition: "The historical materialist view may not be completely compatible with 'theoretical idealism,' but it does not clash with 'practical idealism.' " Adding that historical materialists were no less ethical than the next person, Kawakami adamantly defended his own moral standards: "Even those like myself who stress the materialist view of history have a sense of right and wrong."[36]

Evidently, Kawakami understood that not merely his academic reputation but his philosophy of history was on trial, for he answered each of Seki's objections to *Changing Times* with a sharp eye to the ideological controversy sparked by his newly adopted methodology. In distinguishing "theoretical idealism" from "practical idealism," for example, Kawakami strove not only to refute the charge of nihilism but to advance the cause of historical materialism as a value-laden rather than a value-free ideology of social change. He suggested along the way that "theoretical idealists" like Seki had mystified the concept of historical change. Observing that historical materialists like himself were intent on identifying "the source of social change" rather than "the source of social difference,"[37] Kawakami meant to bring "historical idealists" back down to earth. Throughout his rebuttal, Kawakami intimated that the materialist perspective would at last enable economists to advance a coherent causal interpretation of history.

Yet Seki had passionately criticized Kawakami not because he attributed social change to material causes but because he denied ideas and customs any causal importance at all. True to form, Kawakami provided his antagonist with added ammunition on this count in the closing paragraphs of his rebuttal. Challenged to defend the methodological assumptions that had led him to depict social change as a monocausal process, Kawakami laid bare the logic of his philosophical system. Rather than estranging himself from the "dualistic" world-view that Seki deemed logically inconsistent with historical materialism, Kawakami identified it as the foundation of his theory of history: "Since the 'history' of historical materialism refers to human history [*jinrui shi*], not biological history [*seibutsu shi*], even if I adhere completely to a dialectical view of biological evolution— conceived broadly as the prosperity and decline of living creatures—this does not contradict the materialist view of history, which is [exclusively] concerned with the advancement of human society."[38]

This point made, Kawakami admitted to the operation of "material laws" independent of those that ruled the plant and animal worlds. These laws applied exclusively to the evolution of human society, he maintained, and directed the development of human "productive capacity." Activated by two "dynamic forces"—technological advancement and the division of labor—these laws presupposed the natural propensity of human beings to seek material progress. Further, claimed Kawakami, these two forces were linked to each other in a causal relationship. Identifying "technological advancement" as the "root cause" of a widening "economic division of labor" in human society, he revealed the true depth of his materialist assumptions.[39]

In June 1912, Seki published his first rejoinder to Kawakami's rebuttal. In answer to Kawakami's unambiguous defense of historical materialism, Seki divulged the unacknowledged source of the author's world-view: "Professor Kawakami's materialist view of history is not materialist theory in the broad sense of the term. It is the historical materialism of Karl Marx. . . . It rejects moral-ethical value judgments, being based as it is on a monistic adherence to nihilism."[40] Quoting the "evolutionary socialist" Eduard Bernstein, Seki likened "historical materialists" to "Calvinists dedicated to atheism."[41] Seki meant to suggest that, except for their atheism, Marxists were just as narrowly fanatical about their beliefs. Not only had they seized on historical materialism with religious intensity, but they had done so in the name of a monistic ideology that denied human values historical agency. This contention was more than Seki could swallow: "In Marx's material view of history, climate and customs—even the influence of people—are not considered sources of social change. . . . Marx recognizes no national borders, nor [even] distinct peoples. He maintains that society finds its origins in the material [technological] means of production."[42]

Although Seki readily acknowledged the causal influences of technological advancement and the division of labor on the process of social change, he rejected the Marxist assertion that social change had been precipitated by material forces beyond human control. In place of this monocausal explanation of social change—and in answer to the deterministic slant that Marxism lent it—Seki proffered a multicausal historical paradigm.

Contending that historical materialists had mistakenly attributed the process of social change to irreducible "root causes" when it should properly be understood in terms of "causal relationships," he highlighted the human capacity to modulate the social effects of material advancement. Here, Seki called attention to the work of German economists, reserving his highest praise for Werner Sombart, who had demonstrated that it was the reflexive relationship between "common tendencies" *(tōitsu no keikō)* and "national particularities" *(kokuminteki tokusei)* that animated the process of historical change. Seki noted, in brief, that Sombart had affirmed the causal importance of national character to social change.[43]

Despite his outspoken criticism of Kawakami, Seki held out hope that this closet Marxist might redeem himself. If only he would acknowledge the difference between idealism and materialism by "harmonizing" his understanding of the materialist aspect of social change with an appreciation of national differences, maintained Seki, Kawakami might yet escape the trap of "internationalism." Seki sensed rightly, it would seem, that Kawakami himself had not yet resolved this ideological dilemma—that he stood precariously between an "organic" and a "material" world-view.

Kawakami wasted no time in fashioning a reply to Seki's latest challenge. Entitling his rejoinder "From the Materialist Historical Perspective to the Materialist Spiritual Perspective," he published it in two parts, in July and August 1912. The essay, which totals a full forty pages, is as frank a defense of Kawakami's peculiar brand of historical materialism as one is likely to find. In it, Kawakami spells out his methodological assumptions in excruciating detail. Unwilling to concede that idealism and materialism were mutually exclusive, Kawakami resolved to demonstrate their compatibility. Earlier, he had begun to recast himself as a "practical idealist"; now, he proposed to back up the claim.

Reiterating his earlier assertion that historical materialists were less committed to tracing the diverse origins of social differences than they were to identifying the "root cause of social change," Kawakami proceeded to extemporize on the methods and objectives of his ideology. In stark contrast to what he considered the humanistic subjectivity of economists like Seki, Kawakami proposed scientific objectivity as a methodological ideal: "The materialist view of history provides us with the means to examine social phenomena scientifically." Looking to the natural sciences for a model, Kawakami passionately outlined the responsibilities of the empiricist:

> The world of science is the world of "death," the world of "objects."
> In other words, it is the world of "inanimate objects." It is not the
> world of "life," nor is it a world of "spirit." . . . The inanimate world is
> a "cold-blooded" world, not a world of "warm feeling." As scientists,
> we must be certain not to mix lukewarm blood into this cold-blooded
> world. Though I have a "heart," I cannot allow it to influence my
> scientific persona.[44]

Turning his attention to the role of historians in particular, Kawakami characterized them as natural scientists. He cautioned historians to treat people as "heart-less objects" *(mushin no buttai)*—to treat them in the same manner as they would "metal, stone, earth, or ingots." Above all, warned Kawakami, historians should remain "cool" *(reisei)* toward their subject matter, avoiding at all costs the intrusive influence of their feelings *(kanjō)*: "[Historians must] look at things objectively, rather than subjectively, peering at them from the outside rather than the inside." Since the world of science is restricted to "space, time, objects, and power," added Kawakami, the historian who conducts himself as a scientist can do no better than to assess the influence of these causal factors on social relationships. Because scientists cannot measure differences in quality *(hinshitsu)*, but only in quantity *(bunryō)*, Kawakami warned historians that they would make a shocking discovery when they applied the scientific method to social relationships. Though people may be different, he warned, they look the same to the scientist: "[The world contains] aristocrats, beauties, zealots, patients, whites, and blacks, but in the eyes of the scientist they are all of the same type, and they are all equal."[45]

Much of what Kawakami had to say about the scientific responsibilities of the historian must have seemed old hat to his readers. Long familiar with the scientific method, most economists had already adapted its empiricism to their discipline. But few had laid bare their methodological assumptions as openly and publicly as had Kawakami. Judging from the manner in which he presented them, it would appear that Kawakami meant to convince not only his readers but himself of their indispensability to the future of social research. Indeed, it is difficult to escape the impression that Kawakami had not yet resolved the conflict between his feelings as a human being and his obligations as a social scientist.

As if to defend his own humanity against the assaults of economists like Seki, Kawakami spent the remainder of his essay sketching out the philosophical foundations of his historical materialism. Openly acknowledging an indebtedness to Marx for the first time in his exchange with Seki, he urged readers to guard the distinction between objective research and subjective interpretation. Marx's purpose was not to render amoral judgments about the character of social change, insisted Kawakami, but to enable human beings to make critical judgments objectively. In an effort to demonstrate the superiority of this approach, Kawakami probed Marx's epistemological assumptions. Like all scientists, he argued, Marx understood that in the beginning every object in the universe was in a state of inertia:

> Movement as such is not "automatic" [*jidōteki*] but "induced" [*tadōteki*]. Hence, we must look for the cause of movement outside of objects themselves. We may conclude from this that the movement of a single object can [only] be comprehended in terms of its "causal relationship" [*inga kankei*] to others. Therefore, the world of science is a world of "cause and effect" [*inga*], of "transmigration" [*rinne*], of "secondary causes" [*shukuin*], and of "fate" [*teimei*]. A certain cause will always produce a certain effect, and a certain effect always emanates from a certain cause.[46]

Kawakami identified this law of cause and effect as the objective principle, or natural law *(shizen hōsoku)*, governing the process of historical change.[47] Alert to the teleological implications of his assertion, however, he proceeded immediately to a discussion of the manner in which this law of cause and effect affected human action. Although we enter into action as conscious beings with our own "meanings, purposes, and ideals," he wrote, we nevertheless operate within limits fixed by natural laws.[48] These laws serve to "restrain," even to "obstruct," our capacity to initiate social change since they restrict the degree to which we can manipulate our material circumstances. Terming this condition of human experience "subconscious spirit" *(muishikiteki no seishin)*, Kawakami declared it the governing force of human existence: "The material world is the world of cause and effect, of restraint and obstruction."[49]

While Kawakami contended that the "laws of cause and effect" governed the human condition, he did not go so far as to argue that humankind was helpless before this material force. "The material world may be one of inevitability," he insisted, "but the world of purpose is a world of free will, a world of accommodation and of freedom from obstacles. It is a world of original creation." Kawakami maintained that human beings possessed the capacity to coordinate their actions toward a common purpose through "moral restraint," arguing implicitly that they might guide their own history within the limits set by natural (social) law.[50]

Kawakami thus exhorted historical materialists to acknowledge the natural laws governing human experience. Armed with an understanding of these laws, he argued, they could exercise a measure of control over the material world in which they lived. In answer to Seki's accusation that he had sacrificed his idealism in taking up the materialist cause, Kawakami protested that he had embraced an even more compelling form of idealism. By applying rigorous empirical standards to the study of human history, he maintained, Marx had unmasked the laws that animated it. This, in turn, had given Marx the "freedom"—that is, the intellectual clarity— necessary to project a practicable social vision for the future. Beyond the inevitable intensification of class conflict, continued Kawakami, Marx had envisioned a classless society in command of the material forces that had previously divided it. In Kawakami's view, this practical vision of "history in the future" made Marx a true idealist. And it was with this characterization in mind that Kawakami himself became a convert to historical materialism.

This lengthy rendition of Kawakami's rejoinder is significant not so much because Seki responded passionately to it but because the issues that they both confronted reveal the core of Japan's late Meiji debate over modernization. Seki challenged Kawakami's radical universalism on the same grounds as he had earlier attacked laissez-faireism: that it presumed a unilinear course of historical development. Although Marxists and laissez-faireists produced radically different accounts of the operation of natural law, they concurred in the view that nature dictated the course of social change. As Marxists portrayed it, history was the result of ineluctable laws that propelled humankind along a unilinear pathway of progress.

Seki rejected the deterministic universalism fundamental to both the Marxist and laissez-faireist notions of history for one simple reason: it denied human beings historical agency. While he readily acknowledged that material progress had led inexorably to the rise of industrial society, Seki attributed this development to human innovation. Against the laissez-faire view that natural law dictated the ultimate triumph of free enterprise and against the Marxist view that natural law dictated its inevitable demise, he promoted a notion of historical progress in which human beings were the active agents of their own destiny. Seki thus counseled the Japanese to look within themselves for the power to guide social and economic change.

Yet Seki did not make this plea with the sort of historical idealism that might tempt us to label him a "cultural exceptionalist." Though the Japanese had made their own distinct history, he argued, they had pursued material progress with the same sense of human purpose as the English or the French had. Similarly, they had accommodated material progress to the cultural traditions that distinguished their national history. Seki exhorted his countrymen, accordingly, to confront the disruptive social tensions that attended industrialization by invoking their collective capacity to channel change. Ridiculing Kawakami's Marxist assertion that class conflict was inevitable, he urged the Japanese to embrace self-determination *(jisei-jiritsu)* rather than "predetermination" *(yoketsu-sentei)* as the guiding principle of historical causation.[51]

Before he laid their debate to rest, Seki launched one final salvo in Kawakami's direction. Pointedly observing that economics was not geometry, he reiterated his complaint that Kawakami had confused social science with natural science. Seki suggested that Kawakami look to Max Weber for a more appropriately humanistic approach to the study of economics, noting that Weber had properly classified the discipline as a "cultural science" in recognition of the central role that human consciousness played in the enterprise of progress.[52] "The standpoint of *man* is decisive," Weber had written in 1898. "Economics is *not* a science of nature and its properties, but rather of man and his needs."[53] Taking this dictum to heart, Seki concluded his rejoinder to Kawakami with a cutting dismissal of his mindless materialism: "Making conscious beings into unconscious objects—to see something as nothing—does not constitute a scientific hypothesis, but a groundless fiction *(unbegründete Fiktion)*."[54]

As much as anything, it would seem, the debate with Kawakami in 1912 helped Seki to put Marxism in proper perspective. In 1910, he was decidedly ambivalent toward it—at once riveted by the Marxist class analysis of modern industrial society and appalled by the unfounded "catastrophism" *(saishū saiyaku ron: die Katastrophentheorie)* that Marxists had projected from it. In the coming years, as he domesticated Marxist class analysis, Seki steadily refined his critical perspective. Commonly referring to Marxism as scientific socialism, he noted that it differed significantly from other socialisms in two important respects: Marxism was not utopian *(kūsōteki)* but realist *(jitsuzaiteki)*, not rationalist *(gōriteki)* but historical *(rekishiteki)*.

Marxist historical materialism looked at history from a "natural sci-entific perspective," maintained Seki, but with a critical twist: It did not trace history to some "mysterious [first] cause in heaven" but to "mate-rialist processes of production on earth." But however impressed he was by Marxist historical realism, Seki could not abide its reductionism. He summarily rejected the Marxist assertion that historical change was dic-tated solely by changes in the means of production: "The fundamental deficiency of Marxism is its historical materialism. Marx's propositions are based on [the notion of] technological change. . . . [But] this cannot be con-sidered as the sole cause of the growth and advancement of social orga-nization. Changes in thought, as well as the growth and advancement of legal systems, customs, and morality, must [also] be taken into account."[55]

Noting that Marx had failed to grasp the interrelationship between technological and sociocultural change—that is, the mutually reflexive "cause[s] and effect[s]" *(inga kankei)* that these two vehicles of historical change set it motion—Seki complained that he had robbed human beings of their rightful place in the making of history. Seki dismissed the Marxist notion that all human history—"society, politics, and thought" included—owed to material change. Marxists, he wryly observed, were sustained by a single article of faith: that "social reality does not emanate from con-sciousness, but establishes consciousness."[56]

If Seki was disturbed by the uncompromising materialism of Marxism, he was distressed by its determinism. He ruthlessly attacked Marx's central assumption that history unfolded with fateful inevitability in accordance with "natural" economic laws. The "mechanistic fatalism" *(kikaiteki shu-kumeiron)* of the Marxist historical perspective, observed Seki, put hu-manity on a collision course with class conflict. Characterizing materialism as the "warp" of Marxism and revolutionism as its "woof," Seki upbraided Marxists for the hysterical "catastrophism" that defined their historical perspective.[57]

As we shall see, much more than a hint of historical idealism lurked between the lines of Seki's own rosy appraisal of early-twentieth-century industrial society. If he steadfastly refused to acknowledge the inevitability of social revolution *(kakumei)*, finding no historical basis for the predic-tion, he eagerly affirmed the equally debatable proposition that socio-economic evolution *(shinka)* had yet to run its course. Despite his idealistic enthusiasm for the sort of moderate social reformism that might accelerate this process of evolution, Seki continued to harbor the fear that class con-flict would one day worsen and lead to the class revolution that Marx had predicted. This apprehension explains, among other things, why he continued to interrogate the concept of surplus value and to test the soundness of Marxist wage theory.[58]

In the end, Seki was sustained as a social reformer by his faith in the nation as a social collectivity able to confront class conflict head on and thereby to erase the specter of class revolution. Unlike Kawakami, who encouraged the Japanese to transcend the "existential conflicts" of industrial society and to reach toward the classless paradise that awaited them in the future, Seki urged his countrymen to short-circuit these conflicts by fashioning a moral economy for the present. His immediate goal was "the elevation of workers" (rōdōsha no kōjō), his larger purpose the realization of social reform (shakai kairyō), and his ultimate objective the creation of a capitalist society that accommodated "the interests of the Japanese people as a whole" (kokumin zenpan no rigai). This was Marxian Listianism transposed in a Japanese key, and Seki enunciated it loudly and clearly in his nascent ideology of social reform.

THE MAKING OF A SOCIAL REFORMER

It is not sufficient to attribute Seki's nascent social reformism to his domestication of Marxist class analysis. Much as he had earlier followed the lead of Roscher and the older German historical school of political economy in humanizing his Listian model of the national economy, he now followed that of Schmoller and the younger German historical school in historicizing his Marxian model of class conflict within the people's national economy. Seki shared with this new generation of political economists, who included Brentano, Wagner, Sombart, and Weber, among others, the view that the industrial laborer question (Arbeiter-frage) was the central issue facing modern industrial economies.

By 1872, the younger German historical school of political economy, which built on the work of List and Roscher especially, had formed an association of like-minded reformers, the Verein für Sozialpolitik ([German] Association for Social Policy; hereafter, the Verein). At their first meeting, Schmoller spoke to the issues that would consume the membership in the coming years:

> [We are concerned] about the deep cleavage characteristic of our social conditions, the struggle between entrepreneurs and workers, between the propertied and non-propertied classes, and the distinct possibility of a social revolution in the far-distant future. . . . [Participants in the association] never regard the state, as does natural law and the Manchester School, as a necessary evil which should be restricted as much as

possible; for them the state is the greatest moral institution for the education of mankind. They are sincerely for the constitutional system, but they do not want an alternative class rule by the various antagonistic economic classes; they want a strong state which legislates above the egoistic class interests, administers with justice, protects the weak and elevates the lower classes.[59]

It goes without saying that Schmoller and his colleagues in the Verein were motivated by a strong desire to short-circuit the current of social revolution that surged through Europe in the 1870s. Their message was essentially conservative, in the sense that it tied reform to the maintenance of social order. Counseling prophylaxis, they urged European states to head off the impending clash of classes in industrial society by stepping in as social arbiters. As Kenneth Pyle has observed of Schmoller's position, "[He] urged integration of the lower classes into a national community and state intervention in behalf of their economic needs. To achieve this end, he placed his faith in an enlightened bureaucracy which, standing neutral above class interests, would act for the good of the whole, regulating economic conditions and reconciling opposing social forces."[60]

Although reformers like Schmoller were thus committed to state action in the interest of social order, they were by no means apologists for the status quo. To the contrary, in fact, they called on "enlightened" leaders to challenge the existing socioeconomic order. Promoting a popular concept of the nation that traced the authority of the state to the people, the Verein called on bureaucrats to step into the role of moral exemplars. Its membership urged state leaders to represent the public interest by transcending the private interests of industrialists and workers alike. Guided by a moral ideal of social order consistent with this principle, they contended, the state might begin at last to effect such far-reaching reforms as would head off class conflict and ensure national economic progress.[61]

Because the reformers of the Verein strove first and foremost to engineer the equitable distribution of wealth in Germany's rapidly industrializing economy, their cause was often confused with that of socialism. Contrary to their reputation as "academic socialists" *(Kathedersozialisten)*, however, Schmoller and his colleagues were no less wary of socialism than of laissez-faireism. Criticizing the latter for its inflexible resistance to state intervention in economics affairs, even as a means of protecting the interests of the poor, they criticized socialism for its misguided commitment to redistribute the profits of capitalist enterprise under the auspices of an omnipotent state. The political economists of the Verein promoted a reformist program that struck a balance between these extremist positions.

Aptly characterized by Ernest Notar as a "harmonic" view of capitalism,[62] their reformist agenda called for state-guided reforms conceived to relieve the social stress of industrialization without sacrificing the economic benefits of capitalism.

Many Japanese economists and bureaucrats in the late 1890s were drawn to the reformist position of the Verein, most obviously perhaps because it appeared to offer Japan a means of averting the nascent class conflict then threatening Europe. So impressed by the Verein were two young Tokyo Imperial University economists, Kanai Noboru and Kuwata Kumazō, that they founded its Japanese counterpart in 1896. Naming their organization the Nihon Shakai Seisaku Gakkai (Japan Association for Social Policy; hereafter, the Gakkai), they issued a declaration of principles in 1900 that affirmed the common purpose of German and Japanese reformers:

> Our country's industry has been making great strides and the national wealth is greatly increasing. Although we welcome this industrial progress we also realize that it is widening the gap between rich and poor and weakening social harmony. In particular, we see the beginning of clashes between capitalists and workers.
>
> We oppose laissez-faire because it creates extreme profit consciousness and unbridled competition, and aggravates the differences between rich and poor. We also oppose socialism because it would destroy the present private enterprise system. Within this framework we seek to prevent friction between classes through the power of government and through individual exertions and thereby to preserve social harmony.[63]

Like the Verein, the Gakkai was a professional association that drew its membership mainly from academia and government. Initially, it also attracted the participation of moderate socialists, labor organizers, and progressive businessmen representing a broad spectrum of ideologies ranging from the idealistic socialism of Katayama Sen to the pragmatic capitalism of Shibusawa Eiichi. As its declaration of principles suggests, however, the Gakkai eschewed extremism in all its guises. It is hardly surprising, therefore, that most of its more radical members ultimately resigned from the association.[64]

Those who remained active in the Gakkai were in agreement on one essential point: that Japan could best meet the challenge of progress by conjoining industrial policy *(kōgyō seisaku)* to social policy *(shakai seisaku)*.[65] As Notar has observed, "They realized that social and labor problems arose from economic issues, and felt that the key to their solution lay in economics rather than politics."[66] Accordingly, the members of the Gakkai conducted research into the causes and consequences of Japan's social and labor problems—research that they debated at conferences and presented as policy proposals to the government.

The Gakkai returned repeatedly to two critical issues in the early 1900s: industrial relations and labor protection.[67] Soeda Juichi, the Ministry of Finance official who wrote the foreword to Seki's first book, represented the moderately conservative perspective that held sway in the association. "It is my hope as a scholar that we shall be able to avoid repeating the mistakes of the advanced countries," wrote Soeda in 1896, "and gain the honor of finding a fine and complete solution to [the] problems in our country."[68]

Prior to the publication of *Shokkō jijō,* the Gakkai's leadership had great difficulty mustering sufficient concrete evidence of labor problems in Japan to mount a convincing case for labor-reform legislation, yet they were not deterred in their righteous cause. As Ikeda Makoto has astutely observed, it was the prospect of labor problems in Japan that motivated these reformers.[69] Armed with concrete evidence of a growing labor problem in Europe and equipped with the Verein's ideas for solving it, the Gakkai boldly projected a labor-reform program for Japan. Its members were emboldened by their unwavering faith in the natural law of universal progress. As one reform-minded official put it in 1896, "It is the advantage of the backward country that it can reflect on the history of the advanced countries and avoid their mistakes."[70]

Rather than being compelled to treat the symptoms of full-blown class conflict, as European labor reformers had been, the reformers of the Gakkai were challenged to prevent such conflict from developing into a "social problem" *(shakai mondai)* in the first place. Because Japanese factory workers *(shokkō)* had yet to form a full-fledged working class *(rōdōsha kaikyū),* the reformers maintained that the state could intervene in the process of "subjective [working]-class formation" by implementing a thoroughgoing program of "social reformism" *(shakai kairyō shugi).*

Members of the Gakkai disagreed considerably about the whys and hows of "subjective [working]-class formation" in Japan, but the tenor of the debate at the turn of the century was set by two of its leaders: Kanai Noboru and Kuwata Kumazō. Kanai, a Tokyo Imperial University professor, first confronted the labor problem in the early 1890s, when the government had begun to formulate factory-labor regulations. Observing that its proposals aimed mainly at increasing labor productivity, consistent with the official national objective of *shokusan kōgyō,* Kanai joined reform-minded government leaders such as Soeda Juichi and labor organizers such as Takano Fusatarō in calling for a sweeping labor law conceived, by contrast, to secure worker protection.[71]

As government leaders became increasingly aware of Japan's labor problems, including the scandalous abuse of women and children in the textile industry, many of them jumped on the reformist bandwagon. Acknowledging that factory owners and workers were no longer tied to each other by the "beautiful social customs" *(onjō bifū)* of old but instead were bound by strictly contractual wage relationships, they turned to reformers such as Kanai to advise them on the establishment of labor laws.

Two things, in particular, attracted government leaders to Kanai's perspective: first, his moderate view of the labor problem as a social problem essentially related to the economic inequities produced by industrial capitalism; and, second, his faith in an omnipotent state to mandate worker protection and thereby to legislate socioeconomic harmony. Tracing the authority of the Japanese state to the emperor and identifying it with "the ideal of righteous rulership," Kanai stressed the government's "obligation to protect the weak." He placed absolute faith in the state to rectify the labor problem, concluding that "the main purpose of the state . . . is to practice the politics of universal benevolence and to cultivate harmony in social life from above."[72]

Kuwata Kumazō, who had taken part in the labor surveys that resulted in *Shokkō jijō*, had a predictably different perspective on labor reform. While Kanai maintained that the labor problem was a reflection solely of objective circumstance—namely, the wide economic disparity between wealthy factory owners and poor factory workers—Kuwata maintained it was also a reflection of the workers' subjective perception of that objective reality. The labor problem had escalated into a social problem, he argued, because workers had rightly come to recognize their poverty as a symptom of the economic inequities that industrial capitalism had spawned.

If Kuwata expected the state to help rectify this social problem, he also expected the workers themselves to do their part. In keeping with his dualistic view of the nation-state as a civil society *(shimin shakai)* and a state *(kokka)* rolled into one, Kuwata called for a combination of individual and state action to alleviate the labor problem.[73] Despite his popular sympathies, Kuwata's loyalties ultimately lay with the state: this founding member of Japan's first labor union (the Yūaikai), who grew more disenchanted with unionism as workers grew more strident, ultimately became a director of the Kyōchōkai, a government-sponsored business circle formed, at least in part, for the purpose of eroding union influence.[74]

To read the work of historians of both the Verein and the Gakkai on the subject of their social reformism is to be left with the sneaking suspicion that the members were thinly disguised nationalists with statist instincts. Fritz Ringer suggests that the Verein was little more than a Bismarckian think tank.[75] Likewise, historians of the Gakkai have consistently highlighted its conservative socioeconomic agenda: Morris-Suzuki makes much of the Gakkai's state-centered vision of national "social welfare" and its resonance with the "pre-Meiji Japanese tradition of *keikoku saimin*" (administering the nation and relieving the sufferings of the people),[76] Notar stresses its predisposition to state "control" of laborers through a kind of "collective management,"[77] and Pyle characterizes its leaders as tutors of the "revisionist bureaucrats" who sought "a totalitarian solution to the social problem" of the 1930s.[78]

The older generation of the Gakkai may have fit these descriptions, but the younger generation did not. And it was this younger generation that quietly assumed leadership of the Gakkai during the heated, early-twentieth-century debate over labor reform. Despite the fact that these reformers prevented the association from veering to the right or simply collapsing into factionalism, historians have yet to tell their story.[79]

The younger generation of the Gakkai included high-profile scholars such as Takano Iwasaburō, a Tokyo Imperial University professor, who maintained that the solution to Japan's labor problem lay in the creation of strong labor unions,[80] and Fukuda Tokuzō, by then a Keiō University professor, who maintained that collective bargaining was an inalienable political right that should be written into the civil code.[81] Yet the younger generation was led by a less flashy group of political economists affiliated with the so-called practical-studies *(jitsugaku)* faction. These young turks, who included Seki Hajime and Tsumura Hidematsu, were decidedly less visible public figures than either the old guard of Kanai and Kuwata or the new one represented by Takano and Fukuda. If their predilection for practical research and their aversion to abstract theorizing tended to keep them out of the public eye, these traits also enabled them to exercise greater influence over their peers in officialdom.

In this connection, it is important to recall the newness of the Meiji state and its desperate need for expertise. Bernard Silberman has argued convincingly that the Meiji leaders had managed by 1900 to make the civil bureaucracy "the primary instrument of decision making and the primary structure of leadership selection."[82] Equally convincingly, Mark Ramseyer and Frances Rosenbluth have cast into doubt the autonomy of these bureaucrats, arguing that prewar politicians continued to exercise "effective, but invisible, control."[83] In at least one important respect, however, it makes precious little difference whether we cast our lot with the bureaucrats or the politicians in this leadership sweepstakes, for neither group had anything approaching a monopoly over expertise, and both therefore relied heavily on outside consultants.

In the arena of social policy, which was both new and alien to bureaucrats and politicians alike, the state was forced to rely heavily on outside expertise. Indeed, if Rodgers is correct, Japan was no different in this regard than Europe and the United States: " 'State-centered' analyses of social politics in this period have not adequately fathomed how indistinct the line between state and society remained throughout most of Europe and the United States, how thin the apparatus of state management was, and how reliant it was on temporary and borrowed expertise."[84] In Japan, not only guiding lights like Kuwata and Kanai wielded influence over bureaucratic and political policymakers but also research-minded experts such as Seki.

From around 1908, in the context of the Japanese debate over labor reform, the practical-studies faction rose to prominence as a contending ideological force. Arguably, their scholarship found favor with government bureaucrats such as Oka Minoru, the author of the Factory Law, because of its carefully wrought balance between positivist theory and empirical research. "Practical" to a fault, these young political economists produced the blueprints for a thoroughgoing program of labor reform in Japan. Tsumura Hidematsu identified their ideology as "social reformism" *(shakai kairyōshugi)* and characterized it as an ethical compromise between the extremes of individualism and socialism.[85] But this characterization does not do justice to the combination of theoretical sophistication and practical empiricism that exemplified their approach to labor reform.

It is important to note in this connection that the Gakkai's younger generation did not display the critical methodological weakness that has been attributed to their German mentors, the younger historical school. If Tribe is correct in his reading of the younger historical school's scholarship, and most especially that of Schmoller, it suffered from a fatal "lack of analysis and [surfeit of] eclecticism."[86] Tribe traces this weakness to the unthinking historicism of Roscher, Hildebrand, and Knies of the older historical school. Their wide-openness to "material from opposing theoretical camps," combined with their penchant for encyclopedic historical research, led them ultimately into abject methodological confusion.[87]

Although the practical-studies faction of the Gakkai did not display any such confusion, their historians most certainly have. The few who have endeavored to pin down the "practical studies" conducted by the practical-studies faction have been singularly unsuccessful in distinguishing their peculiar brand of social reformism from both the conservative reformist orthodoxy of the Gakkai's founders and the radical reformist heterodoxy of Japan's budding socialist movement.[88] Writing about the process through which Japan's first Factory Law was born, Sheldon Garon has drawn attention to the pressure exerted by "outsiders" who ran the gamut from muckrakers and socialists to organized labor.[89] Yet just as much of the pressure on government to initiate labor reforms took the form of "insider" criticism. Among the most influential such insiders were the members of the practical-studies faction, most prominently Seki Hajime.

At the time Seki took up the cause of labor reform, following the publication of *Shokkō jijō,* he had already established himself as one of the nation's most respected political economists—an impassioned promoter of the modern Japanese people's national economy. His credentials as a staunch supporter of *skokusan kōgyō* served him well in his new cause. Not only did the government's leaders listen attentively to his criticism of Japanese capitalism, but the reform-minded official charged with drafting Japan's first labor legislation took Seki's perspective to heart. Later, that same official, Oka Minoru, would praise Seki as the "benefactor" *(onjin)* of the Factory Law.[90]

In the early 1910s, Seki deconstructed Japanese industrial capitalism, breaking it down into its salient socioeconomic elements, and scrutinized the conflicting class interests that some argued were undermining the integrity of the nation/subject itself. Marx provided Seki with the inspiration for his anatomy of the modern social economy; the younger German historical school helped him to temper the Marxist model; and his own researches into labor relations in Europe and Japan enabled him to historicize and to domesticate Marxist class analysis.

Seki affirmed the Marxian proposition that property and occupation were the prime determinants of class and that the members of each class shared certain "specific economic rights and benefits." But he also made the altogether un-Marxian claim that other factors such as shared ideas *(shisō)* and ways of life *(seikatsu)* profoundly influenced the development of class consciousness. While Marx dismissed religious belief as a form of false consciousness, for example, Seki counted it among the many affective traits that defined different classes. Holding steadfastly to the un-Marxian position that class divisions were the result of a multitude of factors, he openly criticized Marxist reductionism: "Class divisions do not stem solely from inequalities in ownership [of property] and disparities in occupational status. They do not merely reflect the influence of economic and technological factors. It is important to note that class divisions are conditioned by historical and psychological factors as well."[91]

In Seki's distinctly non-Marxian definition of class, there was room for much more than the "propertied" and the "propertyless." While the propertied comprised several classes, including farmers, industrialists, small businessmen, and aristocrats, the propertyless comprised at least two, agricultural tenants and industrial laborers. Within each of these classes, members might enjoy relative equality, maintained Seki, but between them inequality was an inescapable reality. Observing that there was almost no common feeling *(dōjō)* or interchange *(kōtsū)* between classes, Seki noted that "the term 'class' invariably implied a confrontational relationship between at least two distinct groups." Then, adding a fascinating little twist to his new class-centered analysis of the people's national economy, Seki likened separate classes to distinct "national peoples" *(kokumin).*[92]

Contrary to Marx and his followers, Seki did not believe that class conflict was unavoidable: "Class conflict is not an inevitable consequence of class divisions. We need to acknowledge that the relationship between classes engenders both conflicts of interest and common benefits." Only "when two distinct classes are guided by mutually incompatible ideas and lead completely different ways of life," concluded Seki, does class conflict rear its ugly head.[93] Under these circumstances, the consequences could be disastrous: just as socioeconomic and ideological differences sparked wars between nations, suggested Seki, they could precipitate class conflict within nations.

Precisely this possibility drove Seki to militate for labor reform in Japan. Convinced that the class division between industrialists and workers had widened to the point that a "psychological revolution" was brewing in the hearts and minds of Japanese workers, Seki sounded the alarm in 1910. Farmers, aristocrats, and small businessmen might also have their differences, he declared, but they were mere spectators to the action in the center ring: "The clash of interests between industrialists and industrial workers is at the core of class conflict [in Japan]. It is linked to the most basic issue [that we face] today with respect to social organization. The social problem that social policy seeks to address is none other than the industrial-worker problem."[94]

Before Japan could even begin to address the industrial-worker problem, however, the nation's leaders would have to acknowledge its existence. What social reformers had identified as Japan's "worker problem" *(rōdōsha mondai)*, after all, the state still prosaically referred to as its "labor problem" *(rōdō mondai)*. Because state leaders remained fixated on the national goal of *shokusan kōgyō*, it would seem, they persisted in objectifying workers as extensions of the machines that they operated. Social reformers such as Seki strove mightily to dissuade them of this view. Subjectifying industrial workers as producers in their own right, they loudly acclaimed the historical agency of workers and unambiguously affirmed their co-starring role in the people's national economy. Rather than objectifying workers as interchangeable cogs in a national industrial machine or romanticizing them as the dutiful apprentices of benevolent factory owners in an industrial family economy, Seki urged the Japanese leadership to acknowledge them for what they were: an industrial proletariat, conscious of itself as such and fully aware of its exploitation at the hands of profit-hungry industrialists.

Although this same conflict in Europe had already ushered in the "age of class war" *(kaikyū sensō no jidai)*, Seki remained convinced that Japan could keep the class peace. He called on his countrymen to learn from the sad example of European industrial capitalism and to minimize class conflict before it escalated into class war. Observing that the European economies had spawned a militant industrial proletariat by ignoring the gross injustices and inequities of laissez-faire capitalism, he exhorted Japan to promote class peace by resisting the impulse to engage in "class politics" *(kaikyū seiji)* and by avoiding the social trap of class "isolation" *(koritsu)*.[95]

As a critical first step in thwarting the nascent class conflict that threatened to disrupt the Japanese people's national economy, Seki advocated state-mediated worker protection *(rōdōsha hogo)*. But he did not promote such protection as an end in itself. Worker protection, in his view, promised to level the playing field on which the proletariat and the bourgeoisie were playing out the conflict between their different economic interests, ideas, and ways of life. As society writ large, argued Seki, the state should properly serve as a moral arbiter between these two clashing classes. Much as he had earlier called on the state to protect entrepreneurs from "financiers" through antitrust legislation and the like, he now advised the state to protect industrial workers from industrialists through the establishment of "moral minimums." Seki bargained that, by guaranteeing workers decent working conditions, hours, and wages, among other benefits, the state could effectively thwart their exploitation.

While Seki called on the state to represent the overarching interest of the modern nation/subject by mediating the conflicting class interests of industrialists and industrial workers, he did not imagine that the state would or could eliminate the rivalry between them. He portrayed worker protection as a system of state-mediated checks and balances designed to stabilize the critical relationship between these classes and to prevent it from devolving into conflict.

Seki sought not to eliminate the class rivalry between industrialists and industrial workers entirely, then, but rather to forge a working partnership between these two groups in the larger interest of progress for the people's national economy. Paradoxically, he celebrated the coalescence of classes as a sure sign of national progress in the "age of classes." Even as Seki was encouraging industrial workers to form labor and consumer unions in affirmation of their common interests as an emerging class, he was encouraging industrialists to recommit their professional associations to economic and technological innovation rather than using them to thwart the interests of labor associations.

In the end, Seki committed himself to the articulation of a strategic model for the people's national economy, a model that would compel the rival classes whose energies propelled it to acknowledge their common interests as constituents of the nation/subject and to work together for the higher purpose of national progress. Given the extraordinary national character of the Japanese, Seki chauvinistically concluded, success was virtually assured:

> There is no doubt that the worker problem in a country like ours may be distinguished from the worker problem [as it manifests itself] in the advanced nations of the West—based on [differences in our] historical development, cultural character, and degree of industrial advancement. We have ample reason to be optimistic about the prospect [of solving] the social problems of our nation owing to the sublime national character of our country today. [Accordingly,] we should endeavor to promote unique policies designed to solve these problems.[96]

Toward the end of the Meiji period, as Japan's "worker problem" was worsening, Seki took it on himself to search out a lasting solution. In the process, as his scholarship shifted from political economics to social economics, Seki himself also underwent a critical change in identity. Simply put, he was steadily transformed into a social reformer.

4 Toward a Modern Moral Economy

The story of Japanese industrial development in the Meiji Era is well documented. While historians continue to debate the importance of proto-industrialization, government-owned enterprise, and social capitalism, among other issues, they at least offer a broad consensus about the pace of change: it was fast and furious. Working itself up to speed in the 1870s and 1880s, Japanese industry took off in the 1890s.[1]

As James Abegglen, Sheldon Garon, and countless others have emphasized, the results of Japan's industrial revolution were dramatic. This late-modernizing nation, whose working population had been overwhelmingly agricultural at the time of the Meiji Restoration in 1868, counted 450,000 factory workers by 1900.[2] By 1902, the number of workers had risen to 499,000, and the vast majority were employed by one of the approximately 7,200 companies (84 percent of the official count of 8,612) that had been founded since the Sino-Japanese War (1894–1895).

Before the machinery, tool-making, and chemical industries took off during the First World War, the textile industry dominated the industrial scene in Japan.[3] In 1902, approximately 269,000 of Japan's 499,000 industrial workers labored in textile mills, and, as Patricia Tsurumi has pointedly observed, the majority of these were women.[4] In 1909, such women constituted 62 percent of all factory laborers, and in 1930 they still represented an astonishing 52.6 percent.[5] That these women were young—most of them teenagers, and a fair proportion of these under the age of fourteen—at first raised the eyebrows, then later the hackles, of nascent labor reformers. Ultimately, as Garon aptly observes, "this preponderance of female workers aroused a particular set of concerns among Meiji-era social commentators and policymakers."[6] Most poignantly, it raised moral issues of vital concern to a nation that had portrayed itself as a family-state—

the very same issues, we might add, that concerned Seki Hajime as a self-appointed guardian of the people's national economy.

Given the rapidly increasing numbers of factory workers in Meiji Japan, not to mention the high proportion of those who could be thought of as potential mothers, we have to ask ourselves why labor protection was so slow in coming. Not until the turn of the twentieth century did labor reform begin to appear on the mental radar of Japanese leaders, and the toothless Factory Law they finally passed in 1911 did not go into effect until 1916. It was not so much that the state was blind to the social problems that attended Japan's rapid industrial expansion, I would argue, as that the state was myopically focused on "fostering industry and promoting enterprise" (shokusan kōgyō) in the interest of national power and prosperity.

Since the Ministry of Agriculture and Commerce (Nōshōmusho) was charged with the task of investigating labor legislation—and since this was the very same government ministry that had led the charge toward shokusan kōgyō—it is not altogether surprising that worker protection remained a low priority.[7] In the early 1890s, when the Ministry conducted consultations and surveys related to labor legislation, it simply treated industrial-labor policy as a subset of industrial-production policy. Whispering encouragement were Japanese industrialists, who repeatedly stressed that low wages and long working hours were Japan's economic aces in the hole where international competitiveness was concerned.[8]

Only one labor-related issue truly concerned the Meiji leaders through at least the early 1890s—the looming specter of labor unrest.[9] Even here, it is important to add, their concern was dictated not by misgivings about labor conditions but by anxiety about costly disruptions of industrial production. Thus, when government leaders first entertained the prospect of factory legislation, they spoke not in terms of a worker-protection law but of a worker-regulation law (shokkō torishimarihō).[10] When some early officials began to wonder aloud whether Japanese industry might spawn the same sorts of labor conflicts that had occurred in nineteenth-century Europe—a line of thought that even got some to consider the cause of these conflicts—Japanese industrialists hastened to reassure the nation that it was far "too early" even to begin worrying.[11]

Given the almost mesmerizing influence of the notion of unilinear progress in early Meiji Japan, it is not altogether surprising that government officials took industrialists at their word and basked blissfully in ignorance. From the late 1890s, however, government officials were no longer so sanguine about the slim prospect of labor unrest. Among other concerns, they had begun to witness serious labor unrest in their own backyard. While Tokyo experienced a mere 15 labor disputes between 1870 and 1896, it was witness to a whopping 151 such incidents between 1897 and 1917.[12] Elsewhere in Japan during these years, labor disputes involving tens of thousands of disgruntled workers rocked the nation, and this threat to social order arguably shook the Japanese leadership out of its complacency.[13]

The government responded initially by placing severe restrictions on union recruitment and public assembly under the Public Peace Police Law of 1900.[14] As many in government readily recognized, however, this law treated merely one obvious symptom of the "labor problem" without addressing its deeper causes. By the late 1890s, a "new breed of economic bureaucrats" (to use Sheldon Garon's term) confronted this dilemma. Not only did they readily acknowledge that it was no longer "too early" for Japan to confront the labor problem, they reconceived this problem as an endemic social problem. Rather than approaching labor disputes solely as breaches of social discipline and public order, they began to explore the deeper structural causes of labor conflict.

It was not long before change-minded bureaucrats had cleverly integrated labor reformism into the previously unquestioned state ideology of economic modernization, arguing forcefully that reforms would not stunt, but spur, economic growth. As Garon has observed of their emerging position, they linked industrial progress directly to labor reform and came out in favor of a factory law: "Though hardly hostile to the business community, these officials defined the state's interests in national industrial development as independent from those of individual entrepreneurs. Invoking the long-term interests of industry, they argued that a factory law would create a cooperative, healthy, and skilled work force. Good workers in turn meant increased productivity and 'the healthy development of industry.' "[15]

This argument loudly echoed the sentiments of social reformers such as Kanai Noboru and Kuwata Kumazō, who were already reconceptualizing the labor question (*rōdō mondai*) as the central social question (*shakai mondai*) facing Japan. As a member of the government council that proposed the introduction of factory legislation in the late 1890s, Kanai exercised considerable sway over the economic bureaucracy. Although he could not convince the Ministry of Agriculture and Commerce to widen its perspective on the labor question by consulting not only with industrialists but with laborers themselves, he did persuade its leadership to take worker protection (*rōdōsha hogo*) seriously.[16]

As more and more concerned officials jumped on the reformist band-wagon, observes Garon, the "bureaucratic proponents of factory legislation increasingly supplemented their productivist arguments with considerations of social policy."[17] Soeda Juichi, who was by then a high-ranking official in the Ministry of Finance, epitomized the position held by those within the government who finally put their political weight behind factory legislation:

> If the state does not intervene to some extent in relations between employers and employees, there will be no way to safeguard the interests of employees. . . . If we leave things as they are today, we will soon witness the onset of a virulent social disease of the type which befell England at the beginning of this century. . . . I fear that our country, too, will inevitably experience the problems associated with such social questions and social ills as strikes. . . . I sincerely hope we can solve these problems before they develop and save ourselves from the disease afflicting the advanced nations of Europe.[18]

Even as the publication of *Shokkō jijō* (1903) awakened Seki to the imperative of labor reform, it reconfirmed the commitment of reform-minded bureaucrats to a factory law. The survey's findings made it clear that the labor problems typical of Japanese factories were little different from those of their European counterparts. Since the evidence clearly indicated that Japanese industrialists were no less guilty of exploiting their workers than European industrialists were—that Japan had finally caught the dreaded capitalist "disease"—official support for factory legislation only grew.

Japanese industrialists closed ranks in the years that followed. Faced with a clear and present danger to the system of free enterprise that had served their interests so well, they set out to restore their credibility and to dampen the appeal of the proposed Factory Law. In place of their earlier claim that it was simply "too early" for the nation to formulate factory legislation—an argument that "presented Japan as a modernizing nation on a course no different from any other"—industrialists took a stunning new tack. As Andrew Gordon has observed, they argued compellingly that Japan's " 'beautiful [old] customs of paternalism' " obviated the need for all but the most basic factory regulations.[19]

One revealing example of the persuasiveness with which Japanese industrialists made their case is a position paper released by the Japanese Chamber of Commerce in 1902. Solicited in response to the government's proposal for factory legislation, this defense of industrialism was later cited by Seki as a shameless example of capitalist mumbo jumbo. From the outset, the Chamber took pains to recount the selfless commitment of Japanese industrialists to the "authority of progress" *(shinporyoku)*. It then worried aloud that factory legislation would weaken the relationship between capital and labor by displacing the moral restraints *(tokugi seisai)* that bound them together under the age-old Japanese employment system based on mutual obligation.[20]

Here and elsewhere, industrialists depicted their enterprises as bastions of traditional familism and portrayed themselves as selfless warriors for the national good. As Gordon points out, they successfully invented a tradition of labor relations that excepted Japan from the (Western) historical rule of escalating labor conflict and eventual class war. So persuasively did these wily industrialists argue their point that they managed to persuade many high-ranking bureaucrats that "this 'tradition' would be a key to heading off the social ills of industrialization before these erupted as a full-blown social disorder."[21]

Bureaucrats such as Soeda, who had once characterized paternalism as "a dying tradition, not a vibrant one," openly embraced this reassuring argument:[22] "The old, beautiful customs existing in Japan are concepts of mutual love and respect from employer and employee. This master-servant relationship is not an evil feudal remnant but a benefit gained from feudalism. Will not these beautiful customs, namely compassion from above for those below, and respect from below for those above, be greatly helpful in harmonizing labor-capital relations?"[23] By 1908, Soeda had made Japanese exceptionalism his mantra. "The capitalists of our country have a warm affection for their workers such as Europeans and Americans are incapable even of imagining," he wrote. "Nothing like these beautiful customs can be found within the capitalist system, or in the labor unions of Europe and America, which have developed from the ancient institution of slavery."[24] On this basis, writes Gordon, "most government leaders had modified the reasoning behind their support of the [factory] law. Rather than promoting the Factory Law as a substitute for Japan's 'traditional' paternalism, they now presented it as compatible with, or even inextricably linked to, the continued survival of such 'beautiful customs.' "[25]

Exactly why Soeda and others so readily endorsed this exceptionalist argument is not easy to fathom, especially given the compelling evidence of labor abuses documented in *Shokkō jijō*. On the one hand, such government leaders likely welcomed the comforting spin that industrialists put on Japan's unstable labor situation; on the other, they doubtless welcomed the suggestion made by industrialists that the laws of progress were not irreducibly unilinear—that Japan might carry forward critical elements of its own "feudal" past and use them to avert the labor problems suffered by the West.

Seki Hajime couldn't believe his ears when government officials began to parrot the paternalistic rhetoric of industrialists at this critical historical juncture. While he accepted the industrialists' argument that paternalism had once permeated the Japanese employment system and that this "beautiful social custom" had been good for its time, he pointedly identified it with Japan's feudal past. To drag this exceptionalist Japanese model of labor relations into the present, argued Seki, was to condemn Japan to backwardness.

Confronting Japanese officials with their own reactionary rhetoric, Seki incredulously recounted Soeda's misguided advice to the Gakkai on labor relations: "The beautiful social customs which exist in Japan are not evil remnants from [our] feudal past," Soeda had told his colleagues, "but benefits from it that are embodied in the employer-employee relationship."[26] What Soeda portrayed as a beneficial tradition, however, Seki put down to reactionary familism *(fukkoteki kazokushugi)*. Sternly admonishing "experts" such as Soeda against their misguided dream to resuscitate *(fukkatsu)* paternalism, he ominously predicted that their efforts would only result in the feudalization *(hōkenka)* of Japanese industry.[27]

"[Those who promote] paternalism have not even attempted to ascertain the facts surrounding the rise of the social problem," wrote Seki in 1910. "As such, they are just as utopian as the socialists in their proposals for solving it."[28] Once he himself had "ascertained the facts" about factory labor in Japan from *Shokkō jijō*, as we have already noted, Seki never looked back. Having been compelled to confront his own naivete concerning industrial labor relations in Japan, he now urged others to confront theirs: "On the question of whether or not a labor law is necessary, we must not allow doctrinaire free enterprise theorists to determine [our fate]. We should make our decision based on the realities of labor relations and working conditions."[29]

Seki did not object to the fact that industrialists put workers on time clocks, placed them under managerial supervision, or enforced work discipline in the factory. After all, these were the objective conditions of factory labor everywhere—conditions fixed by the demands of industrial production. What troubled Seki were the blatant abuses of factory labor bred by capitalist excess. Tragically, he observed, abysmal working conditions, poor wages, long hours, improper clothing, injury, sickness, and sometimes even death were the lot of Japanese industrial workers under the system of free enterprise.[30]

Noting that many industrialists were guilty of exploiting younger workers—laborers he characterized as "the ignorant and the unknowing" who lack the "power of self-control"—Seki reserved his harshest criticism for those who employed young women and children. Where do we find evidence of the vaunted "notion of benevolence" *(jinji no nen),* asked Seki, in textile factories that force impressionable young girls to do night work? Charging textile-factory owners with the worst sort of hypocrisy, he accused them of raising corporate benevolence as a smokescreen to mask their blatant profiteering: "They are incapable even of turning themselves around and taking notice of [the impact that night work has had on] the health and morals of scores of young girls who should [one day] become mothers of future Japanese citizens."[31] Here, suggested Seki, industrialists posed a clear and present danger to the social foundation of the people's national economy.

Bluntly asserting that no vestige of the paternalistic system of employment remained—that industrialists had long since forsaken their traditional obligation to guard the health and morals of their employees—Seki went on to observe that many industrialists claimed to provide social facilities *(shakaiteki shisetsu)* that they did not.[32] Seen in this light, industrialists were guilty not merely of myopia but of hypocrisy. Quick to illustrate the ethical shortcomings of Japanese industry, Seki came down hardest on industrial conglomerates, under whose influence workers had sunk into "a pitiful condition." He maintained that conglomerates had utterly dehumanized the industrial workforce: "People do not control machines in today's factories; machines control people. By speeding up their machines, [industrialists] can accelerate the pace of labor. [This] is the means by which they increase production."[33] Rather than cultivating the rise of warmly paternalistic companies, concluded Seki, conglomerates had spawned their antithesis: "parasitic industry" *(kiseiteki kōgyō).*[34]

For an economist who had so long championed the interests of Japan as a modernizing nation, it was doubtless disconcerting to discover that Japanese industrialists had become no less adept at the exploitation of factory labor than their Western cousins were. Earlier, as an advocate of tariffs designed to protect infant industry, Seki had been a tireless supporter of industrialists. Indeed, when the nation's future appeared to hang in the balance, he had suspended disbelief and portrayed industrialists as selfless "social capitalists" committed to the greater good. Not a decade earlier, in a powerfully sympathetic portrayal of industrialists, Seki had represented them as creative entrepreneurs besieged by bloodsucking capitalist financiers bent on undermining their autonomy and thus sapping their creativity. Now, faced with incontrovertible evidence of the social damage that industrialists themselves had wrought in their single-minded pursuit of profit, Seki was compelled to confront his own myopia. "The foundation of industry may be capital and labor," he wrote in 1910. "Yet, we Japanese, being gloomy over the lack of capital, soon neglect the worker problem."[35]

By the socioeconomic calculus that Seki had previously employed to assess progress in the people's national economy—the Roscheran "notion of value in use of the resources of the nation"—workers had hardly registered on his mental map. As one among many national resources whose husbandry was essential to the long-range goal of national economic progress, they had been objectified in his developmental scheme as elements of industrial production. *Shokkō jijō* shocked Seki into the recognition that workers were human resources whose continued exploitation augured disaster for the Japanese social economy.

What complicated Seki's assessment of this looming problem was that the dominant discourses on labor did not acknowledge industrial workers as a class. By depicting the plight of Japanese industry as a *labor* problem rather than as a *laborer* problem, state supporters of economic modernization managed to elide the subject position of the working class; by inventing the elaborate fiction of an exceptionalist Japanese framework of industrial familism, industrialists themselves denied the very existence of a working class. Alternately depicted as objective elements of national industrial production or as valued members of individual family enterprises, the industrial working class as such was effectively ignored.

Against these powerful discourses, both of which portrayed socioeconomic progress as a foregone conclusion under the Japanese system of free enterprise, even the most progressive bureaucrats sat in the wings as scholars like Seki confronted the issues.[36] In 1910, Seki witnessed his own conversion from economic nationalism to labor reformism. "No one can deny that the worker problem is the most pressing economic, social, and political issue [facing Japan] today," he declared. "It is a problem that concerns the rise and fall of civilization, the rise and fall of nations."[37]

Seki set the tone for his nascent labor reformism in the influential treatise *Rōdōsha hogo hō ron* (On a worker-protection law) (1910). At the outset, he produced a round of dueling quotations to place his argument in broad theoretical and historical perspective. Contrasting the laissez-faireism of Adam Smith and A. R. J. Turgot to the state interventionism of Wilhelm Roscher and Arnold Toynbee, Seki endorsed the Roscher-Toynbee ideology as a guiding principle of modern national development. What Roscher and Toynbee had most compellingly demonstrated, in his view, was the national imperative to regulate industrial enterprise. "The free-enterprise system may have brought about unprecedented increases in wealth for national peoples," observed Seki, "but [the world] has not seen such an unfair distribution of wealth or such pitiful conditions for workers since ancient times."[38]

Seki contextualized his new reformist perspective on industrial capitalism with the help of Roscher's massive study of modern society and Toynbee's movingly moral lectures on the industrial revolution.[39] But this was merely the tip of the scholarly iceberg: Seki was already steeped in the growing, and growingly critical, social-economic critique of industrial capitalism that had gripped Europe and North America. On his bookshelves were works by J. E. Cairnes, W. Stanley Jevons, Charles Gide, and other straight-shooting critics of free-enterprise theory and practice—the very same works being read by progressives in the West.[40] This literature, which testified to the "international disenchantment" with liberal economics,[41] reconfirmed Seki in his growing conviction that the socioeconomic inequities bred by the free-enterprise system posed a clear and present danger to the long-term goal of national social progress.

Forswearing his earlier, easy advocacy of *shokusan kōgyō*, Seki wrote a new agenda into his scheme for national economic prosperity: social and economic justice within the people's national economy. He theorized his nascent labor reformism with the help of two conceptual frameworks: Marxism and social reformism. Employing Marx's convincing symptomatology of class conflict to diagnose the hemorrhage that afflicted the Japanese social economy, Seki allowed the social reformers of the younger historical school to persuade him that the hemorrhage could be stanched by the state without sapping the energy of industrial capitalism. Calling on the state to stabilize Japan's bleeding social economy, Seki prescribed an initial course of treatment designed for this purpose: worker protection (*rōdōsha hogo*). But from what exactly did he wish to protect workers? In the following section, with this question in mind, I scrutinize Seki's diagnosis of the "worker problem" (*rōdōsha mondai*).

THE WORKER PROBLEM

What most late Meiji Japanese continued to characterize as Japan's labor problem Seki unequivocally identified as its laborer problem or worker problem. Observing that the confusion between the two terms could be traced back to Adam Smith, who had mistakenly conflated labor and production in his theory of free enterprise, Seki counseled his countrymen to avoid making the same mistake. Most important, however, he admonished them against the common tendency to treat workers as mere "elements of production." Dismissing Smith's functionalist definition of labor, Seki proffered a structuralist paradigm in its place. He argued that the industrial worker played an indispensable role in industrial production—a role no less critical to national economic progress than that of the industrialist himself—and urged the Japanese to assess the value of labor with this role in mind. "Industrial production does not derive simply from the division of labor," he succinctly observed. "Various producers and laborers cooperate to achieve this final objective."[42]

This argument obviously flew in the face of the nation's continuing obsession with *shokusan kōgyō*. Consequently, Seki took pains to establish its credibility. He began by tracing the historical roots of the industrial-worker problem, turning his attention to the pioneering industrial societies of Europe that had first experienced it. Seki argued that a volatile combination of objective *(kyakkanteki)* and subjective *(shukanteki)* historical factors had spawned the worker problem in Europe. He identified the objective source of the worker problem as the sharp division of labor under industrial capitalism, which had resulted in the formation of two distinct socioeconomic classes: the bourgeoisie and the proletariat. The subjective source of the worker problem he identified as the changes in culture and ideology that had accompanied the formation of these new social classes— especially the diffusion of new ideas such as freedom, equality, and individualism. Precisely because they had turned a blind eye to these objective and subjective changes in the modern social economy, maintained Seki, the European nations were now confronted with a worker problem of looming proportions.[43] With this formulation of the worker problem, of course, Seki at once witnessed his debt to Marx and began to distance himself from orthodox Marxism.

Looking first at the objective factors that had caused the worker problem in Europe, Seki located them in the transformative socioeconomic influence of industrialization. Rather than tracing the rise of industrial society to a strictly evolutionary process of social and economic change that proceeded from agriculture through cottage industry to the factory system, Seki attributed it to the revolutionary impact of mechanization during the Industrial Revolution: "The advent of machines caused a complete transformation of the organization of work. This, in turn, prompted the advancement of industrial production, which displaced the family economy previously characteristic [of society]."[44]

In his depiction of mechanization as a transformative influence, Seki drew a clear distinction between agrarian and industrial societies.[45] He portrayed industrial societies, in essence, as progressive societies liberated from the feudal restraints of the premodern family economy. Once the system of industrial production took root, contended Seki, work inevitably became more and more specialized. This process of specialization *(tokka)* affected every aspect of industrial production, including capital and technology. Most important, however, it determined the character of industrial organization. As technological innovations hastened the specialization of manufacturing, industrialists were compelled to introduce new systems of operation *(keiei seido)*. In the final analysis, wrote Seki, "these systems of operation determine[d] the organizational structure of industrial production."[46]

Rather than limiting his investigation of industrial specialization to the division of labor in factories, Seki scrutinized the sweeping socioeconomic transformation that it had triggered more generally in the "organizational structure" of the factory system: "[The term] occupational specialization has commonly been equated with the division of labor, . . . [but] it does not merely have to do with menial labor [of industrial workers]. The rise of the factory system has also stimulated specialization *between* industrialists and workers, giving rise to [various] 'social problems.'"[47] Noting that under capitalism the interests of industrialists and workers were naturally at odds, Seki traced the worker problem back to the phenomenon of occupational specialization. "The demise of the [reciprocal] relationship between employers and employees," he concluded paradoxically, "owes ultimately to the advancement of industrial organization."[48]

While evincing great concern over the social problems that plagued modern industry, Seki balked at the suggestion that the division of labor (i.e., occupational specialization) was at fault. Instead, he benignly characterized the division of labor as intrinsic to the factory system of operations: "The division of labor between capitalists and workers—between the leaders of industry and the obedient who follow their orders—is a necessary condition of capitalist enterprise. The formation of industry under the factory system demands workers whose livelihood depends on wages—that is, a 'proletariat' [*musan kaikyū*] that does not support itself based on [ownership of] property."[49]

Although the factory system of operations demanded a functional division of labor between capitalists and workers—one that sharply distinguished the propertied from the propertyless of society—it did not dictate any particular form of industrial organization. Indeed, argued Seki, industrial organization varied from nation to nation and reflected different "social structures, legal systems, customs, ethics, and technologies." In short, he concluded, industrial organization is "dictated by its relationship to the wider world outside [the factory]—that is, to the various economic and social conditions under which industrial production takes place."[50]

Having demonstrated that the industrial-worker problem was not irreducibly attributable to the sharp division of labor that characterized industrial operations, Seki strove to gain a wider perspective on its causes. Though class-centered conflicts of interest were an unavoidable by-product of the industrial division of labor, he contended, class conflict was not. Only when the division of labor escalated into the alienation of labor did the worker problem rear its ugly head.

Although Japan itself had yet to witness the alienation of industrial labor, Seki feared that it was on the brink of just such an eventuality. One specific subjective influence threatened to hasten the process of alienation: the application of laissez-faire economic principles to the province of labor relations. Although free-enterprise advocates had properly welcomed the division of labor as a sure sign of national progress, noted Seki, they had turned a blind eye to the problems it engendered. Allowed to extend their mistaken belief in "market principles" to the labor market, free-enterprise advocates would simply exacerbate the class tension between industrialists and workers: they did not seem to realize how easily class difference might escalate into class conflict.

Putting laissez-faireism in historical perspective, Seki traced the ideology back to its source: the European physiocrats who had first championed the cause of untrammeled personal freedom. Adapted to business, he observed, this idea gave birth to the free-enterprise system that had since enabled industrialized nations to record unprecedented increases in wealth. While the economic principle of free enterprise had helped to line the pockets of industrialists, it had also justified their extension of the profit motive to the labor market.

The exercise of laissez-faireism had produced a needlessly volatile situation, according to Seki, exacerbating the clash of interests between industrialists and workers: "The system of free enterprise has stimulated extraordinary increases in wealth among the peoples of various nations. Along with this, however, we have witnessed unprecedented unfairness in the distribution of that wealth and miserable conditions for workers." Attributing this *bunpai mondai* ("problem of the [unfair] distribution of wealth") directly to the self-aggrandizing laissez-faire practices of industrialists, Seki noted that they had enriched themselves at the workers' expense and thus hastened the appearance of the alienated class of wage-dependent laborers identified by Marx as the proletariat.[51]

While labor problems precipitated by the free-enterprise system could be traced back to the eighteenth century, contended Seki, "the issue assumed extraordinary significance as a result of the Industrial Revolution." Since then, wage labor had proliferated and labor conditions had deteriorated: "The extraordinary development of large enterprises since the eighteenth century has generated huge numbers of wage laborers. The lives they lead today both inside and outside the factory pose a manifold danger to national peoples—to health, public morals, education, and character."[52]

How and why the misguided ideology of free enterprise had been allowed to undermine the progressive historical force of industrialization was a matter of great interest and concern to Seki. In principle, the system of free enterprise was based on praiseworthy values such as human equality and personal freedom; in reality, however, it had witnessed their abuse. In theory, the free-enterprise system guaranteed occupational freedom to all, offering industrialists the opportunity to establish private businesses for profit and workers the right to seek labor consonant with their talents at wages commensurate with their skills. In reality, however, the free-enterprise system served the interests of industrialists alone. As owners of the means of production, always on the lookout for ways of lowering costs and maximizing profits, industrialists drove a hard-hearted bargain when it came to labor.

Citing Schmoller's research on the European economy, Seki noted that fewer than a third of industrial workers derived any benefit at all from the free-enterprise system. More often than not, he wryly added, the system worked *"contrary* to the benefit" *(furieki)* of workers: "The system of free enterprise leaves it up to the individual to make an employment contract. While the individual has no responsibility to work, neither does he have the right to work."[53]

Characterizing the free-contract *(jiyū keiyaku)* principle as a sham and castigating industrialists for their disingenuous justification of it, Seki urged his countrymen to see it for what it was:

> Those who plead [the cause of] freedom in labor contracts appear to think that workers are merely a kind of commodity. When they claim the freedom to buy and sell labor, they assert that employer and employee can stand equally before one another and that workers can receive just compensation for their labor. Yet, these advocates of laissez-faireism are actually opposed to the protection of laborers.

When we examine labor contracts in detail, we can see that their
position is hopelessly superficial. Freedom is not [the same as] equality.
While it is true that both employers and employees conclude contracts
of their own free will, we cannot escape the [fact of their] disparity
in status and note that this precludes the conclusion of contracts
on equal terms.[54]

For workers, concluded Seki, the Japanese system of free contracts had
virtually no redeeming value: "Since workers [must] sell their labor—and
since they are subject [in this] to the will of factory owners—they are
truly putting their lives on the line."[55]

To make matters worse, argued Seki, the same Japanese industrialists
who held workers captive to a completely disempowering system of labor
contraction then subjected them to utterly inhumane conditions within
their factories. Evincing little loyalty toward their employees—even toward those who served them well—Japanese industrialists had dehumanized the factory system. Not only did they hire heartless managers to do
their bidding, but they hired and fired workers as the "free market" demanded:[56]

With the invention of new technologies or the outbreak of a recession,
the employer lets large numbers of workers go at one time. Not
only do we see many unemployed workers, but we see many of sound
body who should rightly be engaged in labor. Today, under an
economic structure that permits untrammeled competition, this sort of
unemployed worker is steadily increasing in number. Among workers,
this [situation] has spawned what Sombart calls "the uncertainty of
social existence" [die Soziale Existenzunsicherheit]. Sacrificed to
the system of capitalist enterprise, tens of thousands of guiltless poor
have fallen into the miserable condition of hunger.[57]

In his assessment of the uncertainty of life for workers under the free-
enterprise system in Japan, Seki contrasted it in the first instance to the
security of life in preindustrial society. In the past, lamented Seki, masters
had offered their apprentices protection from the vicissitudes of human
existence. But this was no longer the case: "[Today,] the relationship of
employer to employee is no different from that between passers-by. The
ground has been swept bare of the kindliness and beautiful social customs
[onjō bifū] that bound master and servant together from ancient times."[58]

Tracing this seminal change in Japan's social economy to a new form of
social management (shakaiteki keiei)—one ostensibly introduced to satisfy
the operational demands of industrial production—Seki stripped it of its

pseudoscientific veneer. As occupational specialization became increasingly pronounced, he noted, industrialists had begun to divide the "manufacturing process into several different work levels and [attempted] to place the right worker at the right station." They and their managers thus distinguished "adult male workers from adolescent female and child labor, workers with heart from workers with [good] hands, skilled from unskilled laborers."[59]

If such "social management" helped to increase labor efficiency and to reduce production costs, thereby satisfying the purely economic concerns of the industrialist, it also hastened the alienation of labor: "As a result of this division of labor, industrial workers are denied the long-term expectation of [personal] independence that craftsmen of old once enjoyed. Day in, day out, they participate in highly specialized [forms of] labor, dedicating their bodies to the operation of one specific machine. This [system] hinders advancement, and the monotonous labor exerts a [deleterious] spiritual influence on workers." Observing that factory owners had perfected this dehumanizing system of social management, Seki railed against "cold-blooded industrialists who use machines as weapons to control their pitiful workers." At times, he noted sadly, they even put workers at the mercy of the machines they operated by "increasing drive rates" in an effort to "speed up" industrial operations.[60]

Reminding his countrymen that factory labor was strictly contractual wage labor, Seki urged them to call a spade a spade. Since "the foundation of these workers' lives is not to be found in income derived from property or customary practice," he noted matter-of-factly, "there is no injustice in calling them a proletariat [*musan kaikyū*]." Adding that most Japanese factory workers were barely able to make enough in wages to eke out a "base living" (*kokō*), Seki sadly traced their steady descent into social insecurity: "Since the demise of the paternalistic master-servant relationship, employers have felt less and less of an obligation to protect their employees, and industrial workers have experienced a [proportionate] rise in the level of anxiety in their lives."[61]

Seki extended his criticism of the factory system in Japan to the abstract ideology that its adherents employed to justify their labor practices, placing the principle of free enterprise under an ideological microscope. He objected most fervently to the unexamined assertion that free enterprise, no less than political freedom, was a natural right. Arguing to the contrary, that the system of free enterprise was the product of centuries of historical development, he chided its theorists for their blatant ahistoricism: "The political and economic freedoms that the people of advanced nations enjoy today are the result of thousands of years of cultural development. They are not the natural condition of humankind."[62]

Seki accused free-enterprise theorists of succumbing to a sort of self-imposed myopia. In portraying freedom and equality as inviolable natural rights—that is, in glorifying principles such as "absolute freedom" (zettai no jiyū) and "[absolute] equality under the law" (hōritsujō no byōdō)—they had presented a spurious defense of the free-enterprise system that entirely ignored the interests of the industrial working class: "[These theorists] do not acknowledge the exploitation of workers caused by the profit impulse nor the pitiful condition of the propertyless classes born of the unfair distribution of wealth." Such insensitivity to the plight of workers, concluded Seki, had blinded these theorists to the very nature of the labor problem: "When [such theorists] interpret the problem of wages, they consider only material capital [yūeiteki shihon], not the relationship between . . . labor and wages. Because they view this social problem as a simple matter concerning [the] mouths and stomachs [of workers]—and refuse to recognize it as a cultural problem—they have yet to find the right means of solving it."[63] Only "by acknowledging the injustice of employer-employee relationships, which are [presently] fixed by the industrialists' unilateral [exercise of] free will," continued Seki, "can we [begin to] alleviate the abuses born of untrammeled competition in the marketplace."[64]

Whereas free-enterprise-minded industrialists stressed the formal equality of employers and employees before the law, Seki noted the actual disparity in their socioeconomic status: "Under the law, workers may have rights equal to those of industrialists, but, in the factory, they not only are tied to a work discipline fixed at the discretion of the industrialist but must also follow the orders of managers who receive a fixed salary from him. In [today's] factories, which employ hundreds, even thousands, of workers, workers do not even have a direct relationship to the industrialist."[65] Placing the lion's share of the blame for this situation on industrialists themselves, Seki castigated them for their utter social blindness. "Capitalists look on workers as commodities or as machines, refusing to acknowledge their humanity. Ignoring the fact that individual equality is the result of several thousand years of human development, they identify their class alone as indispensable to the elevation and advancement of society."[66]

The failure of the capitalist class to grasp the concept of social responsibility (jita kyōeki) compelled Seki to conclude that society and the state would have to force "capitalists and industrialists to acknowledge the humanity of workers and to put a stop to their inhumane exploitation of workers."[67] What rendered this social imperative the more urgent, from Seki's perspective, was that Japanese industrial workers were awakening at last to the stark reality of their condition. Long held at the mercy of industrialists, in a social economy precariously tilted toward the interests of the property-owning classes, workers had fallen steadily into a condition of status anxiety (chii fuan).

The promise of freedom and equal rights for workers had proven empty, declared Seki, and this broken promise had provoked a crisis of consciousness: "What has caused the worker problem to spread is the self-consciousness of workers. As the gap between the wealthy and the poor has widened, . . . workers have experienced [increasing] status anxiety."[68] In short, Seki identified workers' self- consciousness (rōdōsha no jikaku)— that is, their collective awakening to the realities of social injustice—as the trigger of a societywide crisis traceable to the worker problem.

In an effort to impress on Japanese the gravity of this national social problem, Seki first chronicled the rise of worker consciousness in other industrial societies. Often, he observed, it began simply with suspicion and envy (saigi shitto) of the wealthy and the powerful. Soon, however, it developed into disillusionment (kakusei). Given the demeaning status of workers under the capitalist system, this development was hardly surprising. After all, "as disillusioned workers were demanding a satisfying daily life [in the nineteenth century], the leaders of society were fretting over whether they should accord workers a life worthy of human beings." In the end, noted Seki, the European working classes were deprived of property, education, family, and religion. After falling into an abyss (fuchi), the growing proletariat found itself increasingly isolated. Is it any wonder, asked Seki, that workers finally forged the class consciousness necessary to extricate themselves from poverty and injustice?[69]

Having alerted his countrymen to the dangers inherent in isolating the proletariat and thus triggering class conflict, Seki reminded them that Japan had yet to reach the point of no return. Reassuringly, he noted, Japanese workers were not clamoring for rights but for status. What this "new class of [industrial] workers" was striving for was "their rightful status [chii] within Japan's time-honored state and social structure."[70] Among other things, Seki here demonstrated his appreciation of the critical distinction between rights and status made by industrial workers themselves in late Meiji. Ironically, this distinction was later lost on historians of Japanese labor.[71]

As to why Japanese workers were seeking status rather than rights, Seki offered a deceptively simple explanation: They had yet to develop individual character *(kojinsei)*. Once they did, he warned, full-blown class conflict might well be the result. Seki's pessimism in this regard had to do with his fear that Japanese industrial workers were rapidly approaching a critical fork in the road in their evolution as a class. Chiding his countrymen for their complacency regarding the appalling conditions under which factory workers labored, he warned that it was simply a matter of time before workers would refuse to "defer to the absolute authority of the industrialist." Seki predicted that Japanese workers would soon begin to develop "individual character" on their own, and when they did, they would certainly follow the lead of industrialists themselves and manifest it as possessive individualism. Thus raising the specter of full-blown class conflict, Seki warned his readers that Japanese workers were but a hair's breadth away from revolt.[72]

Although Seki feared that the increasing class consciousness of Japanese factory workers might lead to class conflict, he summarily rejected the proposition that class conflict was inevitable. Only when society utterly obviated its responsibility to workers, sending them over the proverbial edge, would workers be driven to the extreme of class conflict. Arguing that a moral society would step in to "elevate" the status of workers, properly enabling them to assert their civil rights, Seki held that society might thereby thwart the rise of class conflict.[73] Seki found ample reason for optimism in the attitudes expressed by workers themselves: "Workers today are not asking for an expression of mercy regarding their condition, nor are they begging for sympathy. What they demand of us has nothing to do with feelings [*kanjō*]; it has to do with issues of reason [*risei*], rights [*kenri*], and obligation [*gimu*]."[74] Attributing to workers a fundamental understanding of the concept of "rights and obligations," he gave the Japanese hope of reaching a peaceful solution to the nascent conflict between industrialists and workers.

In the end, suggested Seki, Japanese workers were not seeking the demise of capitalism but the creation of a capitalist moral economy that would guarantee them human dignity. As T. C. Smith has expressed their motives, "In demanding higher status and improved treatment, the workers were, of course, seeking more than higher pay and better working conditions: they were also seeking recognition of their human worth from those with the power and the reputation to confer it."[75]

Ultimately, Seki identified the worker problem as a cultural problem of consequence to the nation as a whole.[76] This problem could decidedly not be resolved simply by ameliorating the working and living conditions of industrial workers. As a problem that instead demanded attention to workers' anxieties about their daily lives, status, and social existence, the worker problem raised fundamental questions about the ethical foundations of Japanese society.[77]

Observing that the Japanese had yet to develop a "new system of morality" *(shin dōtoku shin seido)* capable of redressing this looming cultural problem, Seki noted that "none of the ideas of social responsibility advanced by any class meets the demands of the new age." Because he worried that it might soon be too late, Seki strongly urged industrialists and workers to recognize their common interest in "social peace." In an effort to draw their mutual attention to this critical challenge, he solemnly projected the cost of failure: "When classes no longer acknowledge their common interests, we witness the collapse of society."[78]

Seki placed his faith in social reformism *(shakai kairyōshugi)*, claiming that it alone would help Japan avert this bleak fate by harmonizing the distinct interests of industrialists and workers. After all, social reformers did not seek "to eliminate differences in material lifestyles or to achieve uniform equality" but to temper the individual urge to selfishness *(rikoshin)* by invoking the social ideal of collectivism *(kyōdōshin).*[79] With the help of the state—that is, through the agency of society writ large—Seki contended that the Japanese might translate social reformism into social policy, thus propelling Japan toward social progress.

In this view, Seki witnessed his kinship with the diverse group of European and American progressives who stood behind what James Kloppenberg terms the "economic theory of social democracy."[80] These ideologues, whose works on the subject filled Seki's bookcases, included a host of German social economists led by Gustav Schmoller, Adolf Wagner, Adolf Weber, F. A. Lange, and Heinrich Herkner, the "evolutionary socialist" Eduard Bernstein, the British Fabians Beatrice and Sidney Webb, and the American economist Richard Ely, among others. As Kloppenberg summarizes their common message:

> All of these theorists . . . discerned in the logic of capitalist development a progression toward prosperity, stability, and a wider diffusion of property, and they saw in those tendencies cause for optimism rather than despair. As workers were freed from the bondage of poverty through the unwitting efforts of capitalists pushing to increase production, they were being prepared for citizenship in the cooperative societies of the future. . . . As industrial capitalism matured, people

became more interdependent in fact; the task of social democracy consisted of transferring that interdependence from a competitive to a cooperative basis.[81]

As his own nation rapidly transformed itself into a modern industrial power at the end of the Meiji Era, Seki embraced just such a set of beliefs. Exhorting the state to seize the opportunity for sweeping social-economic reform, he urged it to place worker protection at the top of its emerging agenda for the reform of industrial capitalism.

FROM SOCIAL REFORM TO SOCIAL POLICY

In his search for a solution to the worker problem in Japan, Seki strove to articulate a reformist strategy that would enable Japan to sustain economic growth without undermining social stability. However, while he took special pains to distinguish his position from that of laissez-faireism, with its misguided belief in inviolable "natural rights," he made certain as well to dispatch the arguments of other contending ideologies:

> If we wish to solve the social problem, we cannot use the individualist argument, which prohibits state intervention and stresses individual self-help. Neither can we embrace the socialist method, dreaming of an ideal society where all evils may be removed by collectivizing ownership of the means of production. Nor can we endorse the familistic method of reviving the class system of the past and sacrificing the [social] equality that has resulted from several thousand years of cultural development. In place of these currents of thought, all three of which are utopian [in character], I propose to proceed according to [the principles of] social reformism.[82]

Citing public order, good morals, and the public benefit as his ethical standards for social reform, Seki criticized the industrial agents of capitalist society for their antisocial predilection to selfishness and profiteering. "For my part," he declared, "I despise selfishness and prize public spirit."[83] While he went on idealistically to stress the importance of justice, social responsibility, peaceful tolerance, and social education,[84] Seki had no illusions about the practical challenges that lay before social reformers such as himself. In answer to the challenge of creating a moral order equal to the task of both protecting and elevating the industrial working class, he called for clear thinking on a national scale.

Seki encouraged the Japanese to think of themselves first as citizens of a unified nation, rather than as members of its distinct classes, sternly admonishing them to avoid the ideological myopia that classist thinking could create: "The classes do not live on separate planets, as widely separated groups with no mutual relationship to one another. They belong to the same society and accordingly should seek to enhance their common interests."[85] In an effort to identify social policies *(shakai seisaku)* appropriate to the specific problems facing Japan, Seki conducted extensive comparative research. Most significantly, he surveyed the pioneering social legislation coming out of England. While the exercise alerted him to the need for careful deliberation, it also filled him with enthusiasm for the socialist idealism of the Fabians.[86]

After warning the Japanese against the temptation to try to "solve [Japan's] social problems in a night and a day," Seki set out to "discover the [most] reliable means of solving [Japan's] social problems."[87] This was the central purpose of the two major works he completed between 1910 and 1913: *On a Worker-Protection Law* and *Industrial Policy*. In these books, Seki elucidated the connection between social reformism and social policy. As he expressed that distinction in the second volume of *Industrial Policy,* "Social policy aims to [secure] the benefit of society as a whole by conciliating the conflicts of interest between classes. By awarding status to each class, according to its abilities and accomplishments, social policy promises to achieve [a single overarching] objective: alleviation of the evils produced by class conflict."[88]

Although Seki believed that social policymakers should promote mutual understanding through social education,[89] he was not so naive as to believe that such education alone would place Japan on the road toward meaningful social reform. He recognized that the looming social problems facing Japan would have to be aggressively redressed through the agency of the state and, in particular, through the promulgation of laws. Characterizing law as the clearest expression of a society's values—as the codification of its common convictions *(kannen)*[90]—Seki maintained that law drew societies and their states together in a "reflexively hierarchical relationship" *(sōgō ni jōge no kankei)*:

> The established legal order of the state has a crucial relationship to the structure of society. It is no exaggeration to say that society operates within the limits of the law. At the same time, changes and advances in the life of the nation, especially those in the law, are based largely on the unique [social] organization and [political] control exhibited by each society. There is no question that the state and society exhibit a reflexively hierarchical relationship to one another.[91]

Going on to characterize the state as "society in its most organized [form]," Seki argued that truly modern states do not need to resort to coercive control precisely because they operate according to rules of law stipulated by the societies that sanction their authority. Believing, as he did, that the social life of the nation was the source of state authority—and that civil-law codes were an expression of national values—Seki predictably urged government leaders to promulgate new laws conceived in this spirit. His argument for state-mediated worker protection was little different, in this respect, than his earlier argument for trade laws, banking legislation, and securities regulation. Whether protecting industrialists from financiers or workers from industrialists, he maintained that the state had an obligation to act in the collective interest of the Japanese people.

Where worker protection was concerned, Seki exhorted the Japanese leadership to fashion a social-reformist agenda designed to redress the socioeconomic injustices suffered by the industrial working class:

> Social-policy theorists . . . anticipate the development of a society of freely united individuals. Aiming to preserve the order of society and to avoid the obstacles to progress born of class conflict, they acknowledge the structural deficiencies of the capitalist system. . . . Though they [mean to] put limits on untrammeled competition, they also stress the importance of a society structured on the basis of private property and individual responsibility. Accordingly, social-policy advocates seek to temper the unrestrained power of wealth, to protect proletarian workers, and to prevent destruction of the [existing] social structure.[92]

In the belief that "true individual progress and development" would require "the existence of a stable society," Seki broadly identified social policy with the pursuit of human welfare.[93]

But how exactly did Seki propose to project ethics into social policy? And how did he propose to balance the rights of the individual against the welfare of society? His answer to these searching questions was as simple as his characterization of social policy was complex: He would pressure the state to concern itself less with the rights of individuals than with those of the collectivity. Asserting that private rights should not "contravene morality and justice," Seki held that "the enjoyment of these rights [was] conditional on their not endangering social progress."[94]

If Seki counseled the Meiji leaders to implement social policies designed to restrict the possessive individualism of industrialists, he did not regard social policy as a challenge to individualism per se. Concerned specifically with the possessive individualism of profit-hungry capitalists, Seki concluded paradoxically that true social policy "anticipates the perfection of individualism." In thus repudiating the behavior of industrialists, he also signaled his rejection of the abstract philosophical ideals of absolute freedom and equality. Rather than measuring economic freedom against a formal, philosophical standard derived from natural-rights theory, Seki held it to a practical historical standard based on empirical research. Accordingly, he spoke of "real freedoms" *(jissaijō no jiyū)* grounded in a considered commitment to social justice rather than of "absolute freedoms" *(zettai no jiyū)* tied to the concept of inalienable individual rights. In this spirit he enunciated a national ethical imperative to secure socioeconomic justice for all Japanese: "[True] economic freedom is not the absolute, passive freedom to pursue self-interest, [for] society is not an assemblage of self-indulgent individuals; it is an organic structure tied together by morality, customs, law and the [political] system. The individual preserves his independence through freedom, but, at the same time, he cannot be allowed to impede the [ongoing] struggle for social development."[95]

Developing this position with explicit reference to his new and improved definition of society, Seki noted that the individual stood in a subordinate position to society as a whole:

> The individual has an autonomous existence and possesses an independent will, but he is also a member of society. Thus, the will of the individual, on its face, is actually a product of society. Because individual improvement is integrally related to the social system in which the individual lives, we must acknowledge from the outset that the development of national economic life is integrally related to the phenomenon of mutual action which [governs the lives both] of individuals and of society.[96]

Having established the superordinate position of society vis-à-vis the individual, Seki redefined the concept of individual freedom, rendering it as a social prerogative rather than a natural right. True freedom, he declared, is "freedom consistent with ethical and moral ideas"; it is "freedom under a particular authority."[97] Thus drawing a clear distinction between freedom and license, Seki imposed clear ethical limits on socioeconomic behavior. Here, his views closely paralleled those expressed by the Webbs in their epoch-making tome *Industrial Democracy.*[98]

By restricting the industrialists' unilateral freedom to dictate the conditions of factory labor, Seki argued that Japan might secure workers' freedom from exploitation. In a nutshell, Seki placed the rights of society before those of the individual, substituting the ideal of civil rights for that of natural rights. Putting a positive spin on this whole argument in the end, Seki counseled the state to restrict the freedom of the industrialist in affirmation of "the worker's right to a decent life as well as his/her right to work."[99]

Having recast freedom as a social concept, Seki subjected equality to the same sort of reconceptualization. Against the abstract standard of "absolute, uniform, formal equality" invoked by free-enterprise theorists, he proposed a realistic standard of "relative, relational, substantive equality." As with freedom, so also with equality, Seki advocated the introduction of explicit ethical guidelines for national social behavior. "We [social reformers] acknowledge the importance of living by ethical convictions based on the interests of society as a whole," he declared. "[Accordingly,] we seek a standard of equality based on [the realities of] human social life that will compel people to make [proper] value judgements where [the cause of social] equality is concerned."[100]

Rather than relying exclusively on the state to protect the weak, in the manner of conservative social reformers such as Kanai, Seki exhorted the weak to make themselves strong. Once the state had implemented factory legislation, leveling the playing field of labor relations and thus neutralizing the inordinate power of industrialists over workers, Seki maintained that workers would at last be in a position to secure their proper place in society. Specifically, he encouraged workers to become agents of their own destiny by acting collectively, as a class, to rectify the socioeconomic inequities of industrial capitalism.

But where did state authority end and individual responsibility begin? Instead of stressing the coercive, universal, and imperative qualities of state authority, Seki seized on its nurturing, directive, and educational capacities. He proposed specific limits to the scope of state power, indexing these to the "level of social consciousness" *(shakaiteki jikakushin no teido)* exhibited by the people in any given society. Offering compulsory education as an example of properly administered social policy, Seki declared that all "state action taken in the name of social policy embraces as its ultimate purpose the spiritual development of the individual."[101]

By calling on the state primarily to establish a legal framework designed to protect the civil rights of workers, Seki deliberately consigned the state to a circumscribed role in the pursuit of social reform. If he did so to reinforce its status as the servant of society, he also did so to leave workers the room to act as agents of their own destiny. Convinced that individual self-help *(kojin no jijō)* was no less essential to properly conceived social policy than state facilitation *(kokka no shisetsu)*, Seki made the case for broad-based individual action as an indispensable element of social reform.[102]

While Kanai, Kuwata, and the Gakkai in general similarly proposed "to avoid class friction and to occasion social harmony through individual action and national authority,"[103] Seki shifted the balance between individual action and state action. Not only did he lay greater emphasis on worker self-help as a vehicle of reform, but he called on society as a whole to stand behind the labor unions that represented this ideal: "Social reformism does not merely make state intervention and worker self-help essential to the achievement of its objectives. It anticipates the cooperation of industrialists, philanthropists, priests, and educators."[104]

In keeping with this ethic of national cooperation, Seki called on industrialists especially to embrace the overarching ideal of social responsibility by negotiating good-faith labor contracts and by submitting to binding labor arbitration. Encouraging them as well to be proactively responsible employers, he exhorted them to provide residential, educational, health, savings, and recreational facilities for their wage laborers.[105]

While Seki hoped that industrialists might put their power and prestige behind the transcendent national goal of labor reform and work with the state to achieve worker protection, he also expected workers to act decisively on their own behalf by forming labor unions and consumer cooperatives committed to the "spirit of fraternity and mutual aid." Likening labor unions to trade associations as vehicles of collective self-help *(dantaiteki jijō)*, Seki argued that workers might legitimately use them to "strengthen their resistance to outside pressure."[106]

Because workers as a class were otherwise powerless before the collective might of industrialists, Seki was not the least averse to the idea of bending labor unions to this political purpose. He maintained that unions exemplified the righteous ideal of collective self-help and might therefore be employed to help secure workers their rightful social status vis-à-vis industrialists. By empowering workers to organize on their own behalf and to engage collectively in labor negotiations, maintained Seki, labor unions promised to help "eliminate the inequality between employers and employees and [thereby] to occasion the perfection of the capitalist economic system."[107]

Aside from heralding labor unions as a central element of labor reform, Seki identified them as a key element of the larger national goal of socioeconomic progress. "By placing restrictions on harmful forms of competition in our national economy," he insisted, "labor unions stimulate increased industrial production." Adding that "unions set norms for the relationship between employers and employees," he contended that they thereby "provided support [for] and [the] elevation [of workers], [helping Japan to] prevent reductions in labor efficiency and to avoid worker dismissals."[108]

Given the central role that Seki accorded labor unions in Japan's economic future, it is hardly surprising that he was also prepared to afford them considerable latitude in their activities, including the right to strike.[109] While he was ardently opposed to labor syndicalism on the grounds that it perversely pitted workers against industrialists, this view did not diminish his commitment to working-class solidarity or his support for the principle of collective action. In the end, Seki defended strikes as a perfectly legitimate means of addressing socioeconomic injustice.[110]

This sketch of Seki's social reformism has traced the sea change in his perspective of the Japanese people's national economy. As a member of the younger generation of Meiji who had grown up with his young nation, Seki continued to dream the dreams of his youth. He was a man on a mission, in this sense, who fully expected Japan to seize the reins of destiny and to transform itself into a modern capitalist society. Despite the nagging problems that sometimes caused the nation to veer from this course, Seki remained convinced that Japan was tracing a developmental trajectory that held out the promise of unprecedented national power and prosperity. Unlike Thorstein Veblen, who spoke of "Japan's opportunity" to avoid the social costs of industrialization by borrowing Western technology while retaining Japanese social traditions,[111] Seki believed that the challenge was not to freeze social change, but to channel it. Here, he loudly affirmed Japan's kinship with the modern nations of the world and boldly witnessed his own kinship with social progressivism. This unshakable belief in Japan's ability to make good on the promise of social progress informed Seki's steadfast commitment to worker protection and fueled his ardent enthusiasm for the passage of an epoch-making factory law.

THE FACTORY LAW AND WORKER PROTECTION

As Gordon and others have aptly observed, the "concern for social order, narrowly and broadly conceived, lay at the heart of the bureaucratic push for a [labor] law."[112] Yet not all labor reformers who promoted labor legislation toward the end of the Meiji Era turned reflexively to tried and true, putatively traditional models of social order for inspiration. Seki, for one, boldly anticipated the formation of a new social order that would enable Japan to perfect modern industrial capitalism.

Oka Minoru, the forward-looking bureaucrat who shepherded the Factory Law through special committee and on to the Diet, was a great admirer of Seki's boldly progressive vision of labor reform. Of the four works cited by Oka in 1913 as seminal influences on the debate over labor legislation, two were written by Seki: *On a Worker-Protection Law* and *Industrial Policy*.[113] The other two books on Oka's list, Kuwata Kumazō's *Kōjōhō to rōdō hoken* (The Factory Law and labor insurance) and Toda Kaiichi's *Nihon no shakai* (Japanese society), were simply not cut from the same cloth as Seki's pioneering volumes. The social reformer Kuwata Kumazō had usefully disjoined the labor question *(rōdō mondai)* from the poverty question *(kyūmin mondai)* in his tome, distinguishing productive workers from the endemically poor and thus assuaging the government's fear that a labor insurance clause in the Factory Law might be used by the shiftless as a convenient social refuge.[114] The social thinker Toda Kaiichi had crafted a sweeping study of Japanese society that tellingly distinguished its structure and problems from those of Western societies, a study that apparently reassured the government that the Japanese national character *(kokuminsei)* would prevent class conflict from devolving into class war.[115] Only Seki, however, took a broad perspective of the Factory Law conceived to compel its advocates and critics alike to draft meaningful labor legislation.

Seki began to investigate labor legislation in 1907. Soon after that year's meeting of the Gakkai, whose theme was "The Factory Law and the Labor Problem," he published a blow-by-blow critique of the proceedings.[116] Seki was shocked to learn that many objected to the Factory Law on the grounds that it would encourage farmers to leave the country for the city, and he was dismayed to discover that industrialists continued to oppose the law on the grounds that it would stunt national economic growth.[117]

Prompted to do some research of his own, Seki published an article on the Factory Law in 1909 that brought his readers up to date on the status of the Japanese debate over labor legislation.[118] After discovering how misinformed and misguided many of the law's critics were, he altered his research agenda to confront the issues head on. Wading into the fray in 1909, Seki discreetly framed his own perspective as a personal view *(kanken)* of the Factory Law, but proceeded immediately to pigeonhole the law's detractors and to dispatch their arguments.[119] Dividing the law's most vociferous critics into two basic groups, the laissez-faire theorists and industrialists, Seki accused the laissez-faire theorists of ideological shortsightedness and the industrialists of smug reactionaryism.[120]

After spending some three years researching labor legislation in the West and surveying factory conditions in Japan, Seki produced his masterwork on worker protection. *On a Worker-Protection Law* was his first attempt to address the worker problem as an issue of tantamount concern to the nation. If he drew inspiration for these laws from European and American labor legislation, he also drew the line at analogy.[121] On the volatile issue of international legislation, he professed to profound skepticism based on the significant differences that divided nations on everything from climate and customs to education and factory organization.[122] Counseling state leaders to immediately initiate sweeping and appropriate labor legislation, Seki urged them to focus on seven issues of vital public concern: working conditions, wages, hours, worker self-help (unionization), unemployment, labor recruitment, and home life.

With respect to working conditions, Seki initiated his critique with a scathing indictment of the widespread employment of children in Japan. Characterizing the use of child labor as a barbaric practice that threatened the very foundation of the family system, he went on to associate it with a second, even more widespread, labor problem: the exploitation of young women by textile manufacturers. In addition to proposing a minimum-age requirement for youthful workers (equivalent to compulsory education) and placing restrictions on night work for young women, Seki advocated the institution of a variety of other workplace-related regulations. He called for the elimination of dangerous factory work, and he championed a worker-protection law designed to deal specifically with issues such as safety, health, and morality.[123]

Regarding wages, Seki immediately distinguished himself from most other labor reformers. While Kanai and Kuwata remained transfixed by the economic question of just distribution, Seki went one critical step further to articulate a model system of wage determination. Characterizing the wage issue as one that straddled the line between social and industrial policy, Seki pronounced its critical importance. "Not only is the wage issue profoundly related to the mutual [concerns of] workers and industrialists," he declared, "it is the most pressing problem facing our national economy."[124]

Seki endorsed a new wage model premised on what he termed "social wage determination" *(shakaiteki chingin kettei)*—a model clearly based on the Fabian concept of the civil minimum. Projecting the establishment of entirely new procedures for the assignment of wages, he called on the state to intervene in the process of labor contraction in order to ensure the equitable distribution of industrial profits. In place of the laissez-faire practice of "relatively free [labor] contraction," Seki advocated a new system of joint contraction. Such a system would not merely enable workers to obtain their rightful share of industrial profits in the form of a just wage, he argued, but would foster a spirit of cooperation between employers and employees.[125]

By setting a legal standard of social wage determination, Seki contended that Japan might simultaneously restore dignity to the social economy of the industrial workplace and stimulate industrial productivity. He railed against the inhumanity of wage systems that "determine[d] wage levels based solely on [labor] supply and demand" and called instead for the implementation of a standard of "wage determination based on the fruits of [industrial] labor." Specifically, Seki proposed to index the wages of workers to labor efficiency. "We must not forget that increased labor efficiency is both the cause and the effect of rising wages. It is only natural that we first see increasing labor efficiency when we increase wages, for it [directly] reflects the physical and spiritual betterment of workers."[126]

Aside from fostering a system of social wage determination based on joint contraction, Seki also supported the establishment of a minimum wage. In this, he acknowledged the influence of English socialists such as Sidney Webb, applauding their efforts to discredit the bare-subsistence ethic and to secure workers the right to a living wage *(seikatsu chingin)*. Proposing the introduction of a moral minimum wage *(dōtokuteki saitei chingin)* conceived to guarantee workers a decent livelihood *(sōtōnaru seikatsu)*, Seki reaffirmed his commitment to the elevation of their social status.[127]

In an effort to derive an appropriate socioeconomic calculus for the minimum wage—a standard tailored specifically to the character and the needs of the Japanese people's national economy—Seki surveyed a number of theoretical models and policy initiatives from the West. After reviewing everything from David Ricardo's subsistence ethic to a U.S. proposal that the minimum wage be indexed to workers in small towns, he elected to follow the lead of Schmoller. Seki reiterated Schmoller's argument that wages, standard of living, and labor efficiency were integrally related, and he rejected the socialist position that all workers have the right to a living wage. Arguing rather that workers were morally entitled *(dōtoku no yokkyū)* to wages commensurate with their productivity, Seki went on to express his basic agreement with the famous principle articulated by Henry George: "a fair day's wage for a fair day's work."[128] Not surprisingly, Seki concluded that Japan should calculate a national minimum wage.[129]

In answer to Japanese industrialists, who feared that such a wage system would be manipulated by the proletariat out of their desire for the good life, Seki proposed that all demands based solely on desire be dismissed out of hand.[130] He championed the principle of remuneration for results, characterizing it as a standard calculated to meet the social demand for justice and morality *(seigi dōtoku)*:

> We simply cannot, as a general rule of economic organization today, abandon the principle of setting wages in accordance with the results of labor. . . . In other words, we [must] acknowledge the minimum-

wage [principle] as a necessary element of social policy, for, by assessing
the value of labor, we will be able to eliminate the unjust reduction
of wages by employer fiat and thereby purge free competition of
evil.[131]

In addition to social wage determination and a minimum wage, a third
labor issue that commanded Seki's attention was the excessive number of
hours put in daily by factory workers. Determined here as well to dispatch
the objections of industrialists, especially those who denied the relationship between decent labor hours and labor efficiency (rōdō kōtei), Seki
offered concrete evidence of the deleterious effects of overwork.[132] Aside
from inducing physical and mental fatigue, excessive working hours also
had harmful social consequences. Workers who were overworked, maintained Seki, simply could not be good citizens, and this result in turn had
a negative influence on a nation's "level of cultural progress."[133]

Seki argued that shorter labor hours would increase productivity by
enhancing workers' physical ability to labor efficiently and by increasing
their desire to work; and increased productivity would help raise the working-class "standard of living."[134] Laboring fewer hours in the factory,
workers would have more time to spend with their families. This result,
argued Seki, would be of tremendous value to the nation. Making his
appeal for shorter labor hours on vaguely patriotic grounds, Seki contended that it was imperative for Japan "to favor the lower classes with
the benefits of civilization, to firmly set the foundation of [the] family
system, and [thus] to cultivate [a nation of] great and loyal people under
[the] constitutional government."[135] Under such a system, he anticipated
that workers would take pains to improve themselves and their families,
thereby earning the "right to political participation" and moving Japan
toward the ultimate political objective of all civilized nations, universal
suffrage. We must reduce labor hours, concluded Seki, to permit workers
the time to acquire "political wisdom."[136]

Faced with the challenge of establishing a national standard, Seki urged
the state to stipulate the optimal number of labor hours for the average
Japanese worker according to a calculus devised by Lujo Brentano. Brentano's formula indexed labor hours to certain specific cultural and economic
variables: the level of production technology, the structure of industrial
operations, the knowledge of workers, morality, hygiene, and national
character. For his own model, Seki divided these variables into two major
categories: "the level of national culture" and "the level and structure of
industrial production." Based on his analysis of these variables, he concluded that the Japanese working day should be shortened to ten hours.[137]

While there was a relatively broad consensus among Japanese labor reformers about the desirability of better working conditions, higher wages, and shorter hours, there was no such clear consensus about the final two issues that Seki took up: worker self-help and unionization. His strident support for worker self-help and unionization issued from the conviction that workers had been unfairly and unwisely objectified as elements of industrial production. Admonishing the Japanese against the attendant tendency to confuse worker protection with labor pacification, he insisted that "any plan to mitigate the clash between classes must [be based on the realization that] each class must have a mutual understanding of the other."[138]

Along with Fukuda Tokuzō and several other like-minded labor reformers, Seki counseled Japan to formulate an entirely new understanding of the relationship between labor and capital.[139] As I suggested previously, Seki had long been a strident supporter of "corporate self-help"—that is, of labor unions. Now, during the debate over the Factory Law, he would couple that agenda with the demand for labor mediation and arbitration.

In making the argument for unionization, Seki stressed its complementary relationship to state-initiated labor reform: "While worker-protection laws mandate certain specific labor conditions by authority of the state, labor unions prohibit certain labor conditions through the strength of the group. Thus, they reach the same objective but by different means." Commonly characterized as contentious organizations bent solely on extracting concessions from industrialists, labor unions were looked on with considerable suspicion. Seki strove to correct this misimpression: "Going to the essence of labor unions, [we must understand that they] do not only enable workers to organize permanent groups for the purpose of securing improvements in labor conditions. Workers organize unions for mutual aid, to help one another out when work-related calamities—sickness, disability, old age, or unemployment—befall them."[140]

By likening labor unions to such voluntary associations as consumer unions and trade associations, Seki aimed to alter the image of unions as militant, strike-prone working-class gangs.[141] At one point, he went so far as to draw a parallel to trusts and cartels: "Just as employers employ cartels and trusts to maintain reasonable industrial profits, to set prices, and to avoid suicidal competition, workers form groups to maintain a decent consumption level for their own social class."[142]

As for the positive role labor unions promised to play in the Japanese people's national economy, Seki emphasized their capacity to minimize harmful competition and to instigate increased production: Whenever and wherever labor unions succeeded in improving employment and working conditions, he observed, they would indirectly be promoting increased labor efficiency and thus fueling economic development. In addition, argued Seki, unions promised to serve a critical "social and political function." By addressing the needs of an alienated (and isolated) working class, they would help educate workers about their rights and responsibilities as Japanese citizens. Indeed, Seki added wryly, "if we [truly] wish to halt the propagation of socialist ideas, then the best policy to adopt would be the advancement of labor unions."[143]

Seki pressured Japan's leaders not only to encourage unionization but to sanction peaceful methods of conflict resolution such as labor conciliation and arbitration instead of compelling workers to fight tooth and nail against injustice *(fusei)* and social inequality *(fukōhei)*.[144] Otherwise, warned Seki, workers would be left with no other choice but to go on strike. Observing that Japan's rapacious industrialists, with their powerful trade associations, continued to place factory workers in an impossibly disadvantageous position *(furi no chii)*,[145] Seki was compelled to conclude that "labor strikes are an evil which . . . we cannot avoid in today's social economy."[146]

Seki's support of trade unionism and his tolerance of strikes set him apart from most other labor reformers of the day. Though he was harshly critical of "emotional" strikes, such as those engineered by the copper miners at Ashio and the railway workers of Tokyo Densha, Seki sanctioned "combative" strikes on the grounds that workers were merely responding in kind to the harsh conditions imposed on them by monopoly capitalists.[147] He asked only that labor unions consider the consequences of their own actions, approaching strikes "gradually" and "in an orderly fashion."[148] Not too surprisingly, Seki's support for labor unions did not go unnoticed by the labor community. He was placed on the advisory board of Japan's first bona-fide labor union, the Yūaikai.[149]

Among the other thorny issues that Seki addressed as a labor reformer were recruitment practices, workmen's compensation, and unemployment. With respect to labor recruitment, Seki was harshly critical of current practice. Condemning especially the tactics employed by labor recruiters to lure young girls into textile factories,[150] he proposed the establishment of public labor exchanges *(kōkyōteki rōdō shōkaijō)* designed to mitigate the abuses endemic to Japan's disorderly labor market.[151] Rather than looking to the West, where labor exchanges were designed primarily to deal with the problem of unemployment, Seki advised Japan to form labor exchanges designed specifically to address the problem of recruitment.

Calling for the creation of a system of labor registration, as well as one of labor introduction *(rōdō shōkai)*, he strove to convince the state to adapt its labor program to the nation's specific needs.[152] As Seki saw it, such public labor exchanges promised at once to serve as a clearinghouse for industrial labor by bringing "suppliers and demanders together" and to enhance the spirit of cooperation between employers and employees.[153]

Equally concerned about the controversial issue of workmen's compensation, Seki implored the Japanese not to view efficient labor recruitment as a convenient excuse simply to discard workers injured on the job. Urging the state once again to institute a policy tailored to Japan's particular needs, he proposed a program of accident insurance *(saiyaku hoken)* designed to deal with job-related injuries caused by overwork. While he also advocated the initiation of a comprehensive program of compulsory insurance *(kyōsei hoken)*, he counseled the government to wait until such time as the nation could afford to underwrite it.[154]

With respect to the issue of workmen's compensation, as with labor recruitment, Seki stressed the state's role as a mediator and conciliator. He ardently defended the workmen's compensation system as an institutional means of promoting public spirit, justice, and social responsibility—ethical qualities that promised to help Japan realize the overarching national goals of peaceful tolerance and social enlightenment.[155]

Yet Seki also recognized limits to what the state could and should do for the industrial working class. If he expected it to set "moral minimums" for working conditions, hours, and wages—as well as to help people find work, then help them to recover from job-related injuries in order to return to work—Seki was profoundly ambivalent about the unemployed. In this ambivalence he was not different from the social progressives of Europe and the United States. As Rodgers has observed of Americans, they found it intensely difficult to reconcile social policy with social welfare and found it virtually impossible to identify with the endemically poor: "To most [such] middle-class social reformers, including most of those groping toward new forms of social policy, the poor were citizens of a distant country, socially and psychically apart from the nation transatlantic progressives had in mind."[156]

For his part, Seki professed to believe that unemployment was unavoidable—that it was "not the fault of the unemployed themselves but result[ed] from deficiencies in economic organization." Indeed, he traced the common tendency to blame workers for unemployment to incomplete and often skewed labor statistics. Yet even after reciting the litany of possible explanations for unemployment—seasonal labor, market fluctuations, technological obsolescence, inadequate labor recruitment—he could not escape the suspicion that there were shirkers about as well. Reluctantly acknowledging that Japan possessed more than its share of the unemployable *(rōdō nōryoku no ketsubōsha)*, Seki despaired of effectively distinguishing them from the unemployed *(shitsugyōsha)*.[157]

Characterizing unemployment as a "sickness of today's social economy," Seki reluctantly conceded that the state could not and should not unilaterally initiate a program of unemployment relief. His position had everything to do with his overarching commitment to the productivity of the people's national economy: He feared that a state-run unemployment-relief program would encourage otherwise productive workers to mistakenly equate the right to work *(rōdō no kenri)* with the right to a living *(seikatsu no kenri)*. In other words, he feared that such a program would encourage workers to view labor as an inalienable right rather than as a social responsibility, a view that would ultimately reduce their will to work and might trigger reduced productivity.[158]

Despite his misgivings about sweeping national unemployment relief, Seki deemed it the state's obligation to ensure workers the opportunity to work when work was available and to guarantee them some form of unemployment relief when it was not. As the elimination of unemployment was no more than a pipe dream, he called on the state, industrialists, and workers together to take a synergistic approach toward unemployment relief. Industrialists could do their share by reducing surplus production; workers could do their share through labor unions by helping to rationalize the labor market; and the state could do its share by employing more workers during slack periods.[159]

Seki made this suggestion not in hope of eliminating unemployment entirely but of "reducing [it] just enough to eradicate the evils [attendant to it]." Given his hostility to the socialist system of state-supported universal employment, which he considered a "suicidal remedy" guaranteed to rob industrialists and workers alike of their incentive to work, it would seem that the "evil" Seki feared most was enervation of the people's national economy.[160] As long as work remained central to people lives—and as long as industrialists, workers, and the state conspired to keep it that way—unemployment would be the least of Japan's concerns.

As Seki formulated his multifaceted program of worker protection, he was carefully monitoring Japan's progress toward the passage of a factory law. Thus, when he reached the last chapter of his masterwork, *On a Worker-Protection Law,* he was eager to bring his readers up to date. After producing an annotated version of the official proposals that had already been generated,[161] Seki wrote a final note on the morning of February 27, 1910. With palpable optimism, he noted that draft legislation had reached the Upper House of the Diet; but, with equally obvious disappointment, he reported that it remained stalled there in special committee. According to the morning paper, wrote Seki, the powerful Seiyū-kai Party was still debating certain provisions in the law and planned, one last time, to recirculate the legislation through the government. Seki's patience was wearing thin. "As for myself," he wrote that morning, "I feel only one thing: the pressing need to proclaim the growing importance of worker protection."[162]

It would be a year before the Factory Law reached the Diet and another five before it went into effect. To make matters worse, the Factory Law that was promulgated in 1911 bore little resemblance to the worker-protection law that Seki had envisioned. It was so toothless a piece of legislation that the embattled Oka Minoru, the Factory Law's official godfather, admitted to a critic in the Diet that it was not something "that, *vis-à-vis* the advanced nations, we can *be proud of.*"[163]

In the coming years, as his perspective on worker protection broadened, Seki became even more convinced that Japan's Factory Law was little more than a stop-gap measure. "If we truly wish to achieve the objective of worker protection," he wrote, "we cannot restrict ourselves to the sphere of factory workers." Calling for the establishment of a worker-protection law that would cover mining, home industry, handicrafts, commerce, and transportation, Seki evinced his support for sweeping labor legislation that crossed sectoral lines.[164] In addition, however, Seki steadily deepened his notion of the guarantees worker protection should entail and of its ultimate purpose. In the belief that worker protection should guard the nation and its future, he concluded that it was all about cultivating good citizens and solid families. "If we wish to resolve social policy in the broadest sense, we must favor the lower classes with the benefits of culture [*bunka*]," he counseled. "This will enable us to forge a solid foundation for the family system and to cultivate a great and loyal people under [our] constitutional government."[165]

Seki was able to make the leap from worker protection to the family system and good citizenship because he was convinced that workers required protection beyond the workplace as well. This consideration worked its way into his vision of worker protection as a legislative agenda, much as it had already worked its way into his ever-widening concern with social reform. Soon, as I shall illustrate, worker protection came to assume central importance in his work and in his life.

FROM FACTORY TO FAMILY

Even as he labored toward the passage of the Factory Law, Seki was refining his understanding of the worker problem. Most important, he had come to believe that it not only involved abuses in the workplace but encompassed abuses of the home as well. In the most basic sense, Seki saw this as an inevitable, if also paradoxical, consequence of progress. In his view, the urban residential problem *(jūkyo mondai)*, no less than the worker problem, was an unavoidable by-product of industrialization: Seki traced its origins straight to the separation of work and residence that the factory system had produced.

Seki's analysis of the residential problems that had resulted from the introduction of the factory system hinged on the historicist argument that industrial workers no longer had the family economy to fall back on. Whereas preindustrial workers in the handicraft and wholesaling businesses had been treated like members of the family by their employers, he contended, industrial workers were no more than wage-earning employees. Thus, although Seki concurred with industrialists in the belief that Japan could proudly lay claim to a distinguished tradition of peaceful employer-employee relations, he rejected the industrialists' argument that the "beautiful social customs" embodied therein had been reproduced within the modern factory system. Quite to the contrary, he insisted, such social traditions were a thing of the past.[166]

Just as the factory system had produced a division of labor that placed the interests of industrialists and workers in conflict, argued Seki, it also had precipitated a separation of work from residence that accentuated the emerging class distinctions between the two groups. As if this separation were not enough to create a rift between the classes, industrialists and workers had taken up residence in separate neighborhoods. The resulting pattern of urban residential segregation reproduced the socioeconomic divisions created by the factory system, driving the classes even further apart. Not only did industrialists and workers now live in separate social and economic universes, observed Seki, but they had begun to forge such mutually exclusive value systems and ways of life that class conflict was looking not only possible but probable.[167]

While Seki heaped a great deal of the blame for class conflict on industrialists and the urban bourgeoisie, whose acquisitive instincts had driven a wedge between the propertied and unpropertied classes, he maintained that the rise of monopoly capitalism had immeasurably exacerbated the social dilemma that Japan now faced. Seki called attention to the growth of urban industrial conglomerates in particular. Based on their size and location, Seki sanguinely characterized these huge companies as the functional equivalent of regional communities. He went on to argue that, indeed, industrial conglomerates should be held no less responsible for the welfare of employees and their dependents than local governments were held responsible for the welfare of their citizens:

> [Considering the fact] that large industries employ between a thousand and a hundred thousand workers each, we are [actually] talking about the fate of millions of people when we include their families. Since their fate rests squarely on the shoulders of industrialists, who hold within their grasp [the equivalent of] a city, a region, or a prefecture, we might [justifiably] look on these industries as huge organizations that have assumed a semipublic status.[168]

Because of his belief that the sheer size of Japan's industrial conglomerates justified treating them as semipublic institutions, Seki had few qualms about advocating state intervention in their affairs. Indeed, he noted ominously that the concentration of factories in certain districts of Japan's largest cities had produced regional industrial agglomerations *(dai shūdan)* whose local influence had seriously undermined the social and political integrity of the urban jurisdictions in which they were located.[169] Characterizing these agglomerations as factory-centered fiefdoms bankrolled by profit-hungry investors and run by miserly industrialists,[170] Seki counseled the government to take serious note of their growing local influence. Since there was still no factory law to chasten industry and to hold it to "moral minimum" standards for wages, working conditions, and hours, hundreds of thousands of industrial workers found themselves essentially at the mercy of the captains of industry within urban regions over which they exerted unitary control.

The mistreatment and indignity suffered by laborers employed by the conglomerates, observed Seki, had had a horrific impact on their home lives. In big cities most especially, where Japan's industrial conglomerates were concentrated, workers and their families led a miserable existence:

> The rapid growth of industry has paved the way for a trend toward greater population density in [Japanese] cities. The damage to health and morals wrought by [the resulting] residential overcrowding has become a part of urban life, destroying that which should be the foundation of morals and culture: the household. Workers who have discharged their excessive day-long labor duties, and who should be able to rest when they return home, find they have no households.

So instead they gather in sake shops, where they become intoxicated on strong drink. We can find none of the charm of a family circle in this.[171]

If workers watched helplessly as their households disintegrated, then tragically exacerbated the problem by drinking their cares away, their families were arguably the biggest losers. Seki identified the root causes of their misery as deficient housing, high rents, and residential overcrowding—in a word, the conditions of "slum life." He lamented (paraphrasing Werner Sombart) that in industrial cities children live the bleakest of lives: "[They] cannot hear the birds, don't know the beauty of flowers in the meadow, and are utterly isolated from nature in crumbling tenements."[172]

Because both parents in many worker households were required to work long hours, continued Seki, family life had deteriorated into an intolerable condition. Already divorced from their native places, such worker families were left utterly bereft in the big city as part of a growing urban proletariat whose existence was tragically defined by isolation *(koritsu):* "Separated from nature, from family, and from home, propertyless workers live in isolation until finally they lose their constancy [*kōshin*]. The only things that connect them to other people are wages and material relationships."[173]

Paradoxically, then, the very same things that had secured the "progress of civilization" *(bunmei no shinpo)*—the formation of large factories, the utilization of machines, the division of labor, urbanization—were also the undoing of the industrial working class. This, concluded Seki, was the "dark side" *(ankokumen)* of the Industrial Revolution: industrial workers were effectively "martyred" *(gisei to nari)* for the capitalist cause.[174] Left unaddressed, he went on, the grievous dissatisfaction of the working class threatened to develop into "disillusionment" *(kakusei).*[175] Characterizing industrial laborers and their families as the "most pitiful victims of capitalism," Seki predicted that they would not much longer submissively accept their plight: "Having grasped the ideas of freedom and equality, workers in their attic rooms harbor [serious] discontent. They are intent on securing far better quarters and will demand the places refused them by that class which now monopolizes decent housing. Here is a source of 'class conflict.'"[176]

The more concerned Seki became about the plight of laborers beyond the confines of the workplace—as an ever more isolated social class within an increasingly class-contentious national collectivity—the more attention he paid to the environment in which laborers worked and lived. As he thus began to shift his attention toward cities, he began as well to reconceptualize the worker problem/social problem as an urban problem.

In this reconceptualization of cities as social subjects, Seki was hardly alone. But, initially at least, few who shared his views were to be found in Japan. Although a vocal minority of social reformers had begun to turn their attention to Japan's urban social problems, they were swimming against a strong ideological current that continued to treat cities primarily as economic objects. From this perspective, which was powerfully represented by Listian political economists, cities were central nodes of the modern exchange economy and were thus associated first and foremost with the accumulation of wealth. While social economists had gone a long way toward altering this perspective by reconceiving cities as social organisms, this message was slow to penetrate public policymaking—perhaps most importantly because the Japanese leadership remained preoccupied with the mechanics of economic growth for their late-modernizing nation.

Seki, however, came easily to this shift in perspective. Indeed, even as a young political economist, he had been sympathetic to the social-economic critique of modern capitalist cities. As early as 1903, in *Commercial Economic Policy*, he had remarked in the Japanese context on an issue that was known to have obsessed his German intellectual mentor, Adolf Wagner: the socially predatory practices of urban landowners. Observing that real estate speculators in Tokyo and other cities had produced the same residential problems for the working poor of Japan as had their counterparts in Europe, Seki foreshadowed his concern with an urban social problem that would later consume him as a city official of Osaka.[177]

Seki brought to Japan's urban problems a social-economic perspective seeded by the reformist ideas of Schmoller, Wagner, and Brentano, then cultivated by the ethical sensibility of the social reformer Charles Booth, the Fabian Socialists Sidney and Beatrice Webb, and the evolutionary socialist Eduard Bernstein. By the mid-1910s the branches of his perspective, in full bloom, extended to a diverse range of urban visionaries, including the philanthropist George Cadbury, the social thinker Ebenezer Howard, and the urban planner Joseph Stübben. He was attracted to these critics of modern cities, though not necessarily to their prescriptions for change, by their shared conception of cities as complex social organisms that could grow and change.

Coming from the intellectual tradition that he did, Seki saw modern cities as an evolutionary by-product of national economic progress. Noting that Japan was growing steadily more urban *(tokaiteki)*—and that the nation's great cities represented the "core of national culture" *(kokumin bunka no chūshin)*—he urged his countrymen to draw a lesson from the experience of the West.[178] Having long ignored the growing problem of urban overcrowding—a social problem that struck at the very foundation of the national social economy, the home—the Western nations were now playing a desperate game of catch-up. Japan, warned Seki, was on the brink of a similar disaster.[179]

Thus galvanized in his conviction that Japan's urban social problems, and most especially its housing problem *(jūtaku mondai)*, demanded immediate attention, Seki hastened to focus his attention on urban life. Unbeknown to him at the time, he would soon be confronting Japan's urban problems not just as a scholar but as a policymaker.

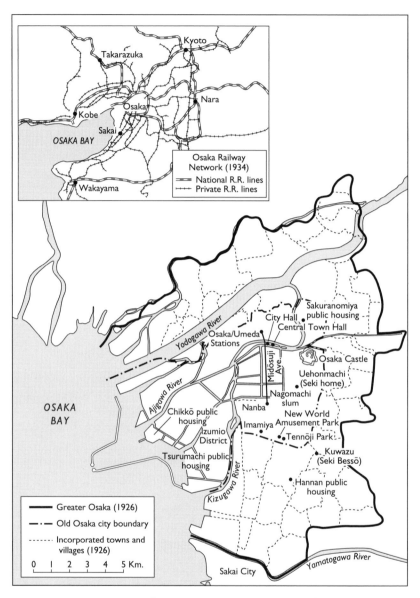

Map 1. Greater Osaka (Dai Ōsaka). Information drawn from Ōsaka Shiyakusho, *Jūshūnen kinen Dai Ōsaka shiiki kakuchō shi* [Tenth-anniversary commemorative history of the urban expansion of Greater Osaka] (Osaka: Ōsaka Shiyakusho, 1935); and Hara Takeshi, *"Minto" Ōsaka tai "teito" Tōkyō: shisō toshite no Kansai shitetsu* ["The people's capital" Osaka versus "the imperial capital" Tokyo: the Kansai private railways as an idea] (Kyoto: Shibunkaku Shuppan, 1997).

5   A New Urbanism

On New Year's Day 1914, Seki Hajime resolved to confound the fates. Astrologically speaking, he faced the prospect of an "unlucky year" (*yak-udoshi*), and this possibility put him in an introspective frame of mind. In his daily diary, where he normally recorded his comings and goings, Seki waxed unusually philosophical. He recalled Tokugawa Ieyasu's defiance of the fates at the battle of Sekigahara, where the great lord had quelled the fears of a skeptical aide with the wise observation that "an unlucky day is also an unlucky day for one's enemies."[1] Truth be told, Seki had every reason to dread the coming year: He and his colleagues at the Tokyo Commercial College had become embroiled in yet another bitter dispute with the Ministry of Education.

The controversy erupted in July 1913, when the Ministry proposed that the College be absorbed into the School of Economics at Tokyo Imperial University. In November, as Seki shuttled between Hitotsubashi and the Ministry of Education, he resolved to throw down the gauntlet. Remarking fatalistically that "the inevitable course of events [would] demand a martyr," he decided to confront the Ministry with his uncensored opinion of the ill-conceived scheme. Seki took heart from the example of his late brother, whose diary overflowed with admonitions always to act "in the interest of people and the interest of society," and he took strength from the support of Shibusawa Eiichi, who had urged the Minister of Education to reconsider the proposal.[2]

Under similar circumstances barely four years earlier, Seki had been forced to tender his resignation before the Ministry backed down. The Tokyo Commercial College faculty had rewarded his leadership with trust and mounted a campaign to appoint him headmaster. According to his friend and confidant Tsumura Hidematsu, Seki nipped their initiative in the bud. Publicly reaffirming his fundamental commitment to research, he privately characterized "cultural administrators" as "one part petty official, one part man of affairs." Seki chose, as he put it, to remain on a "wider stage" in a "rather more luminescent life."[3]

Putting his scholarly ambitions aside once again—this time to spearhead the college's counterattack against the Ministry of Education—Seki witnessed his deep commitment to the Tokyo Commercial College and its national mission as a business school. He was compelled to contend not only with a maddeningly equivocal headmaster but also with a contentious lot of colleagues whose attitudes ranged from "obstinacy" to "reticence."[4] The selfless abandon with which Seki threw himself into the ensuing melodrama confirms what we can surmise from his diary entries: that this was a man who longed to get on with the real business of life. Tsumura insists that Seki was never merely the "bookish man" that everyone took him to be; he was always a "natural leader."[5] Even as he demonstrated just this quality in his handling of the Hitotsubashi affair, successfully introducing a counterinitiative to accredit the college as a full-fledged university, he had already begun to disengage from the academic world he was trying to preserve.

As early as October 1913, public rumors began to circulate that Seki would soon be nominated for the post of senior deputy mayor of Osaka.[6] How the city's new mayor, Ikegami Shirō, settled on Seki as his prime candidate remains a minor mystery. As the most convincing story goes, Ikegami wished to appoint a research scholar to the post and sought the advice of Toda Kaiichi, the Kyoto Imperial University professor whose inspirational work on labor reform was outlined in the previous chapter. In mid-1913, Toda reportedly recommended Seki to Mayor Ikegami.

Before contacting Seki directly, the mayor quietly cleared the nomination with the Osaka City Council.[7] When exactly Seki first learned of the nomination, not to mention when and how he confirmed his candidacy, is unclear. The fact that his diary does not mention the decision compels us to speculate. Perhaps the most persuasive explanation of this lacuna is that Seki took some time to weigh the offer in the knowledge that accepting it would carry him off in a completely new professional direction. It stands to reason, moreover, that the continuing chaos at the college behooved him to keep the nomination discreetly under wraps.

Seki first confided his interest in the deputy mayorship in mid-January 1914, when Mayor Ikegami and the Osaka City Council initiated formal negotiations. Koyama Kenzō, the one-time Tokyo Commercial College headmaster who had appointed Seki to the faculty and had since become a powerful Osaka banker, conveyed the mayor's interest in his candidacy.[8] Seki could not have asked for a better go-between than Koyama, who had continued to support him throughout his career as a political economist. As Seki struggled with his impending decision to leave higher education for municipal government, Koyama reportedly stepped up his role as a mentor.

Three days after receiving word of the city's nomination, Seki began gathering the supporting materials the mayor had requested. When he turned these materials over to Koyama for delivery to the mayor's office, Seki tells us in his diary, he finally confirmed his reasons for pursuing the position: "Today, rather than remaining content in my current position [as a professor at Hitotsubashi], I am opening myself up to a different universe of action. Isn't this because I refuse to squander my life and choose to devote myself instead to an enterprise more suitable to a man [such as myself]?" Adding that he did not in the least "aspire to the status accorded deputy mayors," Seki insisted that he was attracted primarily to the professional challenges that the position posed: "Despite the [glowing] circumstances of Osaka's past, I cannot help but believe that I might realize some of my [own lofty] aspirations there."[9]

Not long after Seki penned this entry in his diary, he made a rare visit to his birthplace.[10] One may wonder whether he did so both to announce the decision to his ancestors and to remind himself of his own humble beginnings. No sooner did Seki return to Tokyo in early February than Koyama conveyed Mayor Ikegami's desire to discuss the nomination in person. The meeting between Seki and the mayor took place the following month in Kyoto. According to Seki, Ikegami stressed Osaka's pressing need, as a growing city, for new urban "facilities" (shisetsu). Told that he would be responsible for surveying the city's needs and determining which facilities to facilitate, Seki agreed in principle to accept the position.[11]

Anxious perhaps to confirm what he had been told by the mayor that day, Seki arranged to meet Professor Toda the following morning. His recommender provided just the right sort of reassurance, conveying his own deep-seated conviction that municipal administration should not be left to politicians. Like Ikegami, Toda expected social scientists such as Seki to help Osaka set a forward-looking urban agenda.[12] Apparently, Seki left this meeting ready and willing to accept just that responsibility. Asking only that he be permitted to delay the appointment until July, when the college's academic term ended, he submitted his formal acceptance nine days later in a letter sent to the mayor via Koyama.[13]

When Seki's intentions were made public in April 1914, he was confronted almost immediately by a fellow professor at the college, who had read the news in an Osaka daily. According to Seki, his incredulous colleague demanded to know whether the story was true or false.[14] It seems, indeed, that the news took all but Seki's closest friends by surprise. A week after the story broke, the headmaster called him to his home for a private meeting, apparently in hope of forcing him to reconsider his decision to leave the college.[15]

If Seki entertained any second thoughts about his decision, they evaporated the following day. After enduring yet another frustrating and fruitless meeting at the Ministry of Education over the accreditation of the college's program in economics, Seki bitterly acknowledged the futility of his efforts to save the program. He confided to his diary that he could not wait to begin his new career: "The ways I might serve my nation are by no means to be found solely in the little world of Hitotsubashi. Whether I choose to realize my personal ambitions in the realm of local government or that of business, I can still say that I am fulfilling my duty to the nation."[16]

No sooner did Seki go public with his decision than a number of his longtime supporters also urged him to reconsider. Shibusawa Eiichi, a longtime supporter of the college and a loyal ally of Seki himself, called Seki to a private conference at his residence. Recalling his own bittersweet experience with government service, Shibusawa characterized it as a thankless job. Even the good deeds of the Meiji oligarchs *(genrō)*, he told Seki, had been greeted with impassivity *(reigan)* by the Japanese people. While Seki listened politely to Shibusawa, he simply did not buy the argument. In the end, he tells us, he was entirely unmoved: "The Baron's point meant next to nothing to me."[17]

If Seki faced stiff criticism from movers and shakers such as Shibusawa, he met open resistance from the educational establishment. Through May and June, the administration of the Tokyo Commercial College and the Ministry of Education apparently conspired to sabotage his appointment. For three long hours at the beginning of May, soon after he submitted his formal resignation, Seki was subjected to "pointless grumbling" from his headmaster.[18] The Ministry of Education, for its part, began a long delaying action. After the Ministry refused time and again to take action on Seki's resignation from Hitotsubashi, Mayor Ikegami himself was compelled to intervene.

Two weeks of excruciating negotiations followed. Unwilling to release Seki from his teaching position, the Ministry suggested that Ikegami hire him as a consultant *(komon)*.[19] Seki's own students got into the act at this point, mounting a campaign to keep him at the college. By one account, he convinced them to give up the fight by confiding that he longed to make policy not merely to teach it.[20] When the students abandoned their effort a week later, Seki wondered why the Ministry of Education refused to do the same.[21] Ultimately, he became so frustrated with the government's "unbending" position that he considered a truly radical course of action: "What if I were simply to make a plan to resign from both positions?"[22]

Amid continuing controversy, which included a public allegation attributed to Shibusawa that Seki was interested primarily in securing a higher salary, Mayor Ikegami finally prevailed on the Ministry of Education to affirm the Osaka City Council's endorsement of the appointment.[23] When the Osaka Municipal Assembly voted unanimously to appoint Seki deputy mayor on July 9, the Ministry of Education finally caved in.[24]

Three short weeks later, on July 30, Seki boarded the night train for Osaka. Seen off at the Tokyo station by his wife and several colleagues, he was joined along the way by Osaka's head clerk and a throng of newspapers reporters, who boarded the train at Yonehara. They briefed and debriefed the new deputy mayor for three full hours, until the train finally pulled in to Osaka Station at 8:07 A.M. on July 31. There to meet Seki were Koyama and Ikegami, the old mentor and the new boss. The mayor lost no time in putting Seki to work. Permitting him a quick change of clothes in the back of a nearby flower shop, he trotted Seki off to City Hall, then hustled him over to the Osaka Prefectural Office. Later that same day, this former professor of economics from the Tokyo Commercial College was formally instated as deputy mayor of the City of Osaka.[25]

In his short inaugural address to the Osaka Municipal Assembly on September 3, 1914, Seki affirmed Osaka's famed reputation as the Manchester of the Orient *(Tōyō no Manchiesutā)*. "With its forest of smokestacks," he declared, "Osaka may certainly be compared to Manchester." Rather than advising Osakans to rest on their laurels, however, he exhorted them to new heights. "Osaka," he added dramatically, "should also rank with Manchester as a center of economic power—indeed, it must."[26]

It is hard to say what Seki intended with this acceptance speech, which marked the beginning of a twenty-year-long career in Osaka municipal government, during which he rose to become the mayor of Japan's largest and most populous city. In all likelihood, he told the assembled municipal assemblymen just what they expected to hear: that this was a municipal official who would help make their renowned commercial city into a pulsing industrial metropolis.

Following his speech, Seki fielded questions about a municipal waterway initiative. Somewhat incredulously, he described the exchange as "nothing special" and went on to characterize the assembly meeting as "completely uneventful."[27] One senses that Seki liked it this way for the moment, as he was getting to know the city he had vowed to serve. There would be ample opportunity for him to stand on principle, to press his urban agenda, and to answer his inquisitors. This was his time to determine what the city was all about, to see whether his reformism accorded with reality, and to transform himself from a college professor into a public policymaker. Before moving forward to assess Seki's agenda as deputy mayor, however, I propose to examine and contextualize the ideas that he brought to his new job.

THE URBAN PROBLEM AS A SOCIAL PROBLEM

In 1909, at the annual meeting of the Gakkai, Seki spoke passionately about his new interest in urban social reform. His address on urban transport and residential life reads like an extended editorial on the urban social problem. Seki's old rival, Kawakami Hajime, seems to have provided the impetus. Upon hearing Kawakami suggest that the solution to Japan's urban residential problems was to evacuate cities, Seki openly accused him of antiurbanism:

> The expansion of cities, which is a modern phenomenon common to all advanced national peoples, is inevitable. If you want Japan to remain beneath the advanced nations of the world, then continue to press [for a return to the land]. But if you believe, [as I do,] that it is imperative for Japan to stand alongside the advanced nations of the world, then it makes no sense to urge people to return to the countryside.[28]

Seki went on to encourage Japan's leaders to confront rather than to evade the urban problems that had come to plague the country. "Looking at this [issue] from the perspective of the people's national economy," he wrote, "the proper course of action clearly is to come up with laws specifically devised to reform residential [conditions] in the urban community."[29]

When he referred to "the city" at this early juncture, Seki pointedly employed the term *tokai* (urban communities). Unlike the more common term *toshi* (literally, urban markets), with its overtly economic connotation, *tokai* eloquently conveyed Seki's deep-seated conviction that cities were not inanimate objects but social subjects.[30] This characterization of cities as social communities marked the apex of Seki's steady subjectivization of the people's national economy. Earlier, as a young political economist interested mainly in railway development, he had treated cities as focal points of commercial exchange and industrial production—that is, as abstract spaces. Not only had he since breathed life into cities, locating Japanese cities at "the core of national culture," but he had gone on to assert the transnational significance of cities to the "collective benefit of world civilization."[31] In this assertion, he and other progressives the world over were of one mind: that if "Coketown" was the first "defining element" of the "new world [of] industrial capitalism," as Rodgers has put it, then the "great city" ran a close second.[32]

For all his enthusiasm about the transnational significance of urban development, however, Seki's gaze remained fixed on the nation-state. Over the course of his career as a political economist, he had drawn portraits, one by one, of the modern figures who composed the people's national economy. Wholesalers, retailers, bankers, financiers, industrialists, industrial workers, farmers, shopkeepers, public policymakers, families, and a host of others found their way into his work. Once he was able to visualize these figures collectively as the composite parts of a socioeconomic whole—and thus was able to conjure up an image of the people's national economy as a living, breathing entity—Seki also found himself reconceptualizing the socioeconomic communities in which they lived and worked.

At the top of Seki's list were the focal points of national economic activity: cities. Whereas he had previously seen cities as points and lines on maps, the location of markets and factories as well as the railroads, waterways, and streetcar lines that served as conduits between them, he now began to see cities as animate socioeconomic entities. Pursuing this analogy even further, he identified cities as the vital organs of that complex organism he had long been calling the people's national economy.

No sooner did Seki come to this understanding than he proceeded to elaborate a biological metaphor to capture his new perspective. He contended that the Japanese people's national economy had witnessed a natural process of development in the modern era that was akin to the "evolution of living things" *(seibutsu no shinka).* Its cities, maintained Seki, had undergone a process of change roughly equivalent to natural selection. In the face of a rapidly changing domestic and international economic environment, after all, modern Japanese cities had readily adapted themselves to new challenges. These dynamic urban communities had capitalized on the combination of improved transport facilities and fluid labor migration to transform themselves into centers not just of exchange but of production and consumption as well.[33]

The evolutionary adaptation of modern cities, according to Seki, could be seen clearly in the emergence of distinct urban districts (financial, wholesaling, entertainment, residential), "each of which had a special function [in the urban body] just like the different parts of the human body."[34] Seki maintained that Japan's highly evolved cities had guided the development of the people's national economy, with industrialists and workers playing a starring role. Eventually, argued Seki, these dynamic communities called cities had come to "structure the whole."[35] Not unlike urban progressives in Great Britain especially, Seki thus evidenced an implicit belief in the Darwinian notion that "man's well being was largely determined by his environment."[36]

At the time he made this argument, Seki was already swimming upstream against two distinct countercurrents of public opinion and official policy in Japan. First, the legendary Japanese ambivalence toward city life had long since worked its way into state policy toward cities. This sentiment first crystallized as an ideology amid the urban growth and change that overtook castle towns during the Pax Tokugawa, finding expression in a succession of vaguely antiurban movements that called for a "return to the land." Second, a new state agenda of urban modernization had taken root during the Meiji drive toward national economic progress. While its advocates tended to support urban containment—for reasons that echoed those of the aforementioned antiurban ideologues—they otherwise enthusiastically acclaimed cities as focal points of modern commercial exchange and industrial production.[37]

The legendary ambivalence of modern Japanese leaders toward city life was rooted in the neo-Confucian uneasiness of their Tokugawa predecessors with the explosive growth of castle towns as vibrant sites of commerce and consumption rather than as stable sites of production. Historians have routinely accused these ideologues of antiurbanism. But as Henry Smith has astutely observed, official Tokugawa attitudes toward cities were rarely so cut and dried. Even doctrinaire return-to-the-land *(dochaku)* advocates such as Kumazawa Banzan and Ogyū Sorai, who worriedly likened city life to "living in an inn," were not actually antiurban: "Sorai did *not* propose . . . to eliminate the city; on the contrary he affirmed it for its bureaucratic functions. With Sorai as with all of the many *dochaku* advocates who followed him, cities were undesirable largely to the extent that they produced change: if consumption was maintained at modest and fixed levels, cities were happily tolerated if never morally affirmed."[38] Not so much antiurban as anti–urban change, then, Ogyū epitomized the deep ambivalence that many Japanese leaders would continue to feel toward cities even in the modern era.

Come Meiji, such sentiments were ritually reiterated by the new national leaders, some of whom expressed the same visceral fear of urban change as their Tokugawa predecessors. The Meiji oligarch Ōkuma Shigenobu, for example, reflexively identified cities with social and moral dissipation. "Put man in cities," he warned, "and the city will become a graveyard, where natural regenerative processes are closed off."[39] More than anything, Ōkuma's outspoken antiurbanism was a reflection of his fear that village Japan, the foundation of national unity and tradition, would become infected with urban viruses such as sloth and profligacy. As is well known, this fear was later transformed into rabid antiurbanism by reactionary Agrarianists in the 1930s.[40] But, as I shall soon demonstrate, it earlier worked its way into the Local Improvement Movement of the 1910s, where it was manifested as vigilance against the moral turpitude supposedly bred by urban life.

While the central government was not openly hostile toward cities in its urban policy, its leaders nonetheless exhibited profound ambivalence toward urban life. In the course of the Meiji Era, as Japan passionately pursued modernization, this ambivalence only grew. Torn between two conflicting sentiments—their moralistic suspicion of the corrupting influence of city life on Japan's urban inhabitants and their pragmatic recognition of the functional importance of cities to the overarching goal of national progress—the early Meiji leaders managed neither to resolve nor to transcend their misgivings about cities. Instead, most of them publicly embraced urban change but privately shuddered at the prospect of urban disorder. Thus, the central government insistently asserted administrative control over cities, retaining authority over their finances and planning, among other things, even as it was introducing a confusing series of stillborn and unfinished schemes to reinvent the Japanese city.[41]

As capital of the modern Japanese nation-state, Tokyo was subjected to an excruciating series of half-baked urban experiments during the Meiji Era. Since Tokyo was commonly viewed as the Japanese city writ large during the early Meiji enthusiasm for "civilization and enlightenment," the Meiji leaders blithely generalized from its experience when they generated urban policy elsewhere. This pronounced tendency toward Tokyo centrism, combined with the state's closely guarded control over regional urban administration, produced such a high degree of uniformity in urban thought and policy that we can readily extrapolate a national pattern from Tokyo's urban experience.

In their enthusiasm for *bunmei-kaika* (civilization and enlightenment) at the beginning of Meiji, Japan's new leaders masterminded the construction of a model urban neighborhood known as Ginza Brick Town (Ginza Renga-gai). This neighborhood, which was built on the ashes from a devastating downtown fire in 1872, was designed by the British architect Thomas J. Waters and was composed of some thousand "fireproof" brick structures. With its rectangular blocks, tree-lined avenues, and gas lampposts, Ginza Brick Town looked every bit the "civilized" Western-style urban neighborhood it was intended to represent.[42] The Meiji leaders apparently hoped that it would serve as a model for homeowners and landlords and that Tokyo might realize residential modernization by a process of cultural osmosis. But they guessed wrong. Precious few brick houses were built anywhere in Tokyo, no less elsewhere in urban Japan, and the residents of the Ginza systematically altered their "civilized" residences to make them feel livable.[43]

This attempt to put a modern face on Tokyo evidenced the facile logic of urban modernization invoked by the early Meiji leaders. Equally facile in its way was the other angle worked by state leaders in the 1880s. Their new idea for Tokyo, which involved its reinvention as an imperial capital *(teito)* to rival Paris or Berlin, apparently germinated during the Iwakura Mission to the West in the early 1870s. Utterly bewitched by the French capital, Iwakura Tomomi himself wrote enthusiastically about its rational districting, monumental public architecture, triumphal arches, and grand, tree-lined boulevards: This was a city that exuded authority, and Iwakura envisioned Tokyo as its equal.[44]

Iwakura's sentiments were echoed by other Meiji leaders who, in the well-chosen words of one, considered "the face of Tokyo the face of our nation."[45] In the mid-1880s, under the Westernizing oligarch Inoue Kaoru, the Meiji leaders sanctioned an ambitious capital plan *(shuto keikaku)* to give Tokyo a massive makeover.[46] Two German architects, Hermann Ende and Wilhelm Böckmann, were hired to design a monumental, Western-style "capital district" of state offices adjacent to the imperial palace.[47] In the end, after scrapping several sets of plans, the Meiji leaders elected to erect only two of the buildings.[48] It was one thing to imagine Tokyo as a Paris of the East, it seems, and quite another to face up to (and to finance) the creative destruction necessary to achieve such a revolutionary objective.[49]

Not easily discouraged, the Meiji leaders soon adopted yet another version of capital planning. Rather than concerning themselves primarily with image making, as they had in the case of both Ginza Brick Town and the Ende-Böckmann plan, they embraced physical planning as the key to Tokyo's modern transformation in the late 1880s. Inspired by Fukuzawa Yukichi, Taguchi Ukichi, and other Westernizers associated with the so-called Enlightenment Faction (Kaimei-ha), some among the Meiji leaders began to envision Tokyo as a manifest symbol of progress. To them, this vision meant roads, railways, ports, and such other infrastructural improvements as promised to make Tokyo "civilized" *(bunmeiteki)*—in the materialistic sense that this term was most commonly used at the time. Henry Smith has called these new capital planners "urban modernizers" and has aptly characterized their perspective as a *"mechanical* view of the city."[50]

This new version of capital planning was premised on the ideal of rational urban spatial order. Yoshikawa Aramasa, Tokyo's prefectural governor in the late 1880s, championed the approach. Pursuant to the Tokyo City Improvement Ordinance of 1888, he endeavored not merely to change the way Tokyo looked but to change the way it functioned. Conducting urban modernization under the rubric of "city improvement" *(shiku kaisei)*, Yoshikawa called for a massive infrastructural renovation of the Japanese capital. He proposed first to make revolutionary changes in urban transport (new and resurfaced roads, improved canals, and new bridges), then to provide new urban facilities designed to promote health and hygiene (a new housing system, water lines, sewers, and parks), and finally to produce the sort of monumental public architecture that would witness Japanese national progress (chambers of commerce, a stock exchange, and public markets).[51] In Yoshikawa's own words, these projects promised "to secure national strength forever and to achieve prosperity for the imperial capital."[52] Yet if Yoshikawa and other like-minded urban modernizers projected a bracing urban vision of Tokyo, they failed even to come close to realizing it.

By the 1890s, the Meiji leaders faced a new urban challenge in Tokyo. Driven by the engine of urban industrialization, the city had begun to spill beyond its boundaries. The urban space that the Meiji leaders once comfortingly imagined as a bounded world suddenly appeared boundless. Reluctantly acknowledging the impact of urbanization *(toshika)*—that is, the operation of a kinetic process of spatial and demographic expansion—a new breed of urban modernizer appeared on the scene. These men identified cities both literally and figuratively as vehicles of progress.

Promoting a dynamic, economic model of capital planning conceived to enhance the efficiency of urban and interurban transport, these moderniz-

ers produced proposals that paralleled the government's growing commitment to *shokusan kōgyō*. Much like their predecessors, on the one hand,
they viewed the city as an inanimate object; completely unlike them, on
the other, they celebrated the growth of cities into metropolises. As they
plotted points and lines on their maps of Greater Tokyo, they envisioned
the avenues, railways, and streetcar lines that would one day carry raw
materials, finished goods, and labor in and out of the metropolis.

The primary objective of these urban modernizers was to grease the
wheels of commerce and industry, and they linked this objective directly
to the state's road- and rail-centered city-improvement agenda. When city
improvement was extended beyond Tokyo to other Japanese cities in
1899—then again when city improvement was superseded by full-fledged
urban planning *(toshi keikaku)* in 1919—urban modernizers continued to
hold the day. Backed by a state committed wholeheartedly to robust national economic development, they had little trouble convincing their fellow leaders to associate cities with economic growth and thus to identify
cities primarily as instruments of progress and prosperity.

When city improvement was first extended to Osaka, under the provisions of the Tokyo City Improvement Ordinance of 1888, the Osaka City
Council hatched a plan for infrastructural improvements that recalled Governor Yoshikawa's vision for Tokyo. Calling for the construction of new
roads and bridges to facilitate commerce and industry, they anticipated the
impending expansion of their growing industrial city from fifteen to fifty-
six square kilometers. No sooner were the city limits expanded in 1897
than the central government sent in a hand-picked planner to reinvent
Osaka.[53] A Paris-trained urbanist who had taken a course of study that
included architecture, engineering, and economics, Yamaguchi Hanroku
concocted an avenue-centered city-improvement plan for Osaka that projected the construction of 212 new roads, 20 canals, 29 parks, and a raft of
port improvements.[54]

Yamaguchi's plan for Osaka, which celebrated the city's identity as Japan's commercial capital *(shōto)*, was a composite expression of Meiji-style
urban modernism; it combined the two different trends that Seki later
referred to derisively as "city beautiful-ism" *(toshi bikanshugi)* and "avenue-ism" *(gairoshugi)*. Predictably, given Yamaguchi's Paris training and
the facile modernist proclivities of his Meiji bosses, the *pièce de résistance*
of the urban plan was a shrub-lined strolling circuit.[55] Like the ambitious
plans that urban modernizers had previously promoted for Tokyo, however, this avenue-centered scheme to enhance the efficiency and the glitter

of Osaka came to naught. Only isolated elements of the plan ever reached fruition; the most conspicuous of these was a broad avenue, completed for the Fifth Industrial Exposition in 1903, that connected Osaka's new wharf to the city's main railway terminal and boasted the city's first streetcar line.[56] Until the promulgation of Japan's Urban Planning Law in 1919, urban planning in Osaka continued to be identified almost exclusively with roads and streetcar lines.

In Osaka, as in Tokyo, then, Meiji urban policymakers—impelled by a baldly instrumentalist equation of modernization with Westernization—objectified the city as an abstract space. While some of these urban modernizers associated modern cities with monumental architecture, and others associated them with transport infrastructure, both groups identified modern cities with modern material civilization and patterned their development after Paris, Berlin, London, and New York. Entranced by these spectacular examples of modern, Western, urban civilization—and armed with a facile explanation of progress that attributed their accomplishments to the operation of universal historical laws—Japanese urban modernizers anticipated the imminent rise of Japan's cities to a comparable level of development.

Lost on Meiji urban policymakers, understandably perhaps, was the human element of urban identity. Only when they belatedly acknowledged the operation of a social economy beneath the political economy that had commanded their blind attention did urban policymakers finally begin to change their tune. What first prompted them to see cities as peopled places rather than abstract spaces was the jarring evidence from Tokyo, Osaka, and other growing cities that material progress did not necessarily engender social progress. By the mid-1880s, after wistfully embellishing their portraits of Western cities in the service of a wild-eyed developmental ideal for Japanese cities, the Meiji leaders came down from the clouds.

One of the first to make the plunge was Maeda Masana, a prominent official of the modernization-mad Ministry of Agriculture and Commerce. Charged with the responsibility of investigating industrial affairs, Maeda produced a study of industrial labor in the mid-1880s that opened his eyes not merely to the horrible working conditions of urban factory laborers but to their miserable living conditions as well. His exposé demonstrated that over half Japan's city-dwellers lived in "inferior conditions," and he compellingly presented their situation as a signal of the serious social problems that loomed on the horizon. Calling on the state to guarantee the urban poor "a base minimum of routine living with the household maintained intact,"[57] Maeda represented the problem as an issue of family welfare in Japan's family-state and thus shocked a number of state leaders out of their complacency.

Outside of government, in the coming years, a chorus of urban critics chimed in, chiding the authorities for their failure to take Japan's urban social problems seriously. Muckraking journalists were the first to pick up the story: Their shocking exposés of tenement life were especially effective in dramatizing the issue of urban poverty.[58] In Osaka, Suzuki Umeshirō, a young reporter for the newspaper *Jiji shinpō*, surveyed conditions in the notorious slum of Nagomachi in the late 1880s. Nagomachi, located in the Nipponbashi neighborhood near what was then the southern boundary of Osaka, was the modern incarnation of a Tokugawa tenement district known as Nagamachi. The slum had originally grown up around an agricultural village, but both were enveloped by the city well before the Meiji Restoration.[59]

Suzuki crafted his exposé of tenement life in Nagomachi to draw attention to an issue that Seki would later highlight in his diagnosis of Osaka's looming social problems: the immigration of urban labor. Writing in the 1880s, Suzuki captured this phenomenon early on—at a point when Osaka had just begun to transform itself into a modern industrial city. While he professed to be dismayed by the poverty that he encountered in Nagomachi, he was truly shocked by the sharp disparity between the wealthy and the poor. "The central districts [of the city] are lined with great homes and high buildings. The ceaseless horse and vehicular traffic, accompanied by the bustle of splendidly attired men and women rushing here and there, is simply dazzling to the eye," wrote Suzuki. "Yet, when one ventures off the beaten path, toward rear tenements on the outskirts of the city, one encounters people turned toward the posts of [the] crumbling walls [of their dwellings], crying aloud from hunger and cold."[60]

Placing the problems of Nagomachi in historical perspective, Suzuki noted that the area had long since been pegged as a place where newcomers could alight. Osaka officials had erected inns here during the Tokugawa Era, and as sake-brewing, rice-polishing, and oil-pressing businesses had opened in the vicinity, Nagomachi's landowners had erected cheap lodging houses *(kitchin yado)* and back-alley tenements *(uragnagaya)*.[61] Eventually, reported Suzuki, the slum had attracted beggars and outcasts from the nearby temple district of Tennōji as well as an irascible criminal element. Without directly indicting the local authorities, Suzuki made it clear that Nagomachi continued to suffer from benign neglect. It was governed, he observed, by innkeepers and landlords who were known to conceal criminals in the tenements they operated.[62]

While muckrakers such as Suzuki dramatically redefined cities as "urban communities" *(tokai)*, they tended to be long on social criticism and short on social action. Not surprisingly, the Meiji officials who heeded their reports were equally clueless when it came to solving the urban social problems that had finally been brought to their attention. In Osaka, local authorities loudly proclaimed their intent to eradicate tenement housing, but they immediately evidenced their indifference to its causes. Determined to eliminate what they recognized as a blight on Osaka's increasingly modern urban environment, city officials began by focusing their attention on the poor urban *buraku* (outcast neighborhood) of Nishihama. In 1887, they embarked on a plan to clear cheap lodging houses from the area. Soon after the city demolished these lodging houses, however, they were replaced by some 270 tenement apartments.[63]

Out of sight, out of mind seems to have been the mind-set of city officials in the late 1880s. However aware they were of the urban social problems that tenement neighborhoods evidenced, the local authorities were less interested in getting at their root causes than they were in erasing their most obvious symptoms. Soon, in fact, Osaka graduated from benign neglect to social cynicism: a central element of the city's cosmetic makeover for the Fifth Industrial Exposition of 1903 was the demolition of slums near the site. Making much locally of their commitment to social reform— reform of the very same Nagomachi neighborhood, coincidentally, that Suzuki had exposed fifteen years earlier—city leaders instead accomplished a kind of slum clearance that might best be described as removal of the poor.[64] Highlighting this official indifference to Japan's urban social problems, the Osaka historian Tamaki Toyojirō has characterized this era as "the Dark Ages of Meiji Urban Policy."[65]

Toward the turn of the century, one small group of urban critics proposed a drastic course of treatment for Japan's urban social problems. These were the advocates of municipal socialism *(toshi shakaishugi)*, most notably Katayama Sen and Abe Isoo. Active from the turn of the century, these radical critics of Japanese urban policy bemoaned the central government's tendency to dehumanize cities by treating them merely as the mechanical means to national economic development. Katayama, who pioneered this Western-inspired movement in Japan, called on the Meiji state to redefine cities as the "homes of their citizens." In this spirit, he championed a revolution in "urban management" conceived to shift authority over urban planning and city finance from the national government to municipal governments.[66] Much that Katayama and Abe had to say about the importance of municipal political autonomy and the wisdom of municipal ownership of city utilities and facilities was later echoed by other Taisho urban reformers. But their dogmatism grated against the practical reformist sensibilities of progressives such as Seki. Although many embraced the principle of municipal enterprise, none did so unconditionally.

Though they had little sympathy for municipal socialism and other utopian solutions to Japan's urban problems, ranging from anarchosyndicalism to Christian socialism, the late Meiji leadership was hardly oblivious to the social issues that inspired such radicalism. Many were awakened during the painful economic recession that followed the Russo-Japanese War. As the blush wore off the rose of urban industrialization, the nation's leaders found themselves compelled to acknowledge the deleterious social impact of unchecked urban expansion on city life.

Even under these urgent conditions, however, the Meiji leaders proved incapable of fashioning a direct and proactive response to Japan's urban social problems. Rather than confronting these problems head on and in the process acknowledging the looming significance of cities to the nation's future, they sidestepped the issue of urban social change by electing instead to confront the exodus from the countryside that seemed to have triggered it. Exhibiting profound ambivalence toward urban life, the late Meiji leaders deflected national attention from the root problem of urban immigration by drawing attention to the causes rather than the effects of what was then called "city fever" *(tokai netsu)*. "As more rural Japanese succumbed to this fever," Carol Gluck tells us, "the ideological concern for the countryside mounted."[67] Rather than treating the urban social dislocation caused by "city fever" as a problem in its own right, the Meiji leadership tended to identify it as a symptom of the more looming problem of the destabilization of rural social tradition. Paradoxically, they responded to the urban social problem by mounting a rural retrenchment campaign known as the Local Improvement Movement (Chihō Kairyō Undō).[68]

The Local Improvement Movement, which publicly promoted local administrative reform and civic action in the name of nationalism, called on rural Japanese to reinforce the "traditional" cultural identification between their villages and the nation.[69] Yet this nationwide program had an unspoken, unofficial purpose as well: it aimed to inoculate village Japan against city fever. As portrayed by the chief of the Home Ministry's Bureau of Local Affairs, the Local Improvement Movement was a preventative program designed to fortify the nation's traditional rural foundation against the corrupting cultural influence of its modern urban superstructure: "The city *(tokai)* is the first to feel the various social stimuli: it is the first to receive both the blessings and the baneful influences of civilization. In contrast, the countryside *(chihō)* is slow to receive these influences; and it has the function of slowly absorbing them and shaping them to our national temperament. Promotion of a strong, and spartan national spirit depends above all on the countryside."[70]

As Kenneth Pyle has convincingly characterized the Local Improvement Movement, it offered a prophylactic for Japan's urban social problems. In lieu of a proactive program of urban social reform, its advocates aimed to protect Japan against the debilitating effects of urbanization: "The best prophylactic for social tensions, they believed, was a deliberate program to strengthen the cohesion of local communities where the great majority of people lived."[71] Paradoxically, then, Japanese state leaders initially responded to the social problems attendant on urban expansion by calling for the creation of model villages *(mohan mura)*.[72] Apparently, they hoped to deploy traditional villages as a kind of counterweight to modern urban society and thereby make it possible for Japan to reap the economic benefits of urban industrialization without paying too heavy a social price.

Even as the Meiji leaders thus continued to evade the looming imperative of urban social reform, a select group of erstwhile progressives had begun to bend their ears on the subject. The first to make a concrete proposal was the Gakkai's renowned labor reformer Kuwata Kumazō. In an essay on urban social policy written in 1900, Kuwata pressed for the establishment of "urban social facilities" designed to meet the pressing needs of the urban poor. Especially concerned with the increasing disparity between rich and poor in Japanese cities, Kuwata urged the Japanese leadership to treat this social problem as a subset of the labor problem. Calling for the introduction of a sweeping urban social policy, which he characterized as the local counterpart of state social policies such as factory reform, he encouraged municipal officials to transform their cities into decent places to live by modernizing urban transport, opening parks, and laying sewer and water lines.[73] Predictably, however, Kuwata stopped here. As with labor policy, he ultimately regarded urban social policy as a prophylactic administered by the state to thwart worker unrest.

Within the government itself, the influential Home Ministry official Inoue Tomoichi hammered home a similar message. Like Kuwata, Inoue stressed the importance of municipal activism and counseled city officials specifically to pursue "[social] relief" and thus to propagate "public spirit."[74] Rejecting municipal socialism and other similarly radical responses to Japan's urban problems, he settled squarely on urban social reform as the only viable and ethical alternative. As Inoue envisioned it, urban social reform would engender a comprehensive program of moral reform to include job training, poor relief, sanitation, and residential improvement—that is, reforms conceived fundamentally to improve the lot of the lower classes.[75]

While Inoue firmly maintained that cities should broker these reforms, he envisioned cities as being in a strictly hierarchical relationship with the state: "By reviving the autonomy of cities, [we mean to make] cities serve the state, for it is the state that guides cities by granting them autonomy [in the first place]." Going on to place urban society in this same hierarchical position—at the bottom of the heap, beneath state government and municipal government—Inoue betrayed the larger purpose behind his support of urban social reform. He, like Kuwata, was interested first and foremost in social control. His state-directed program of moral reform through urban relief, whose stated goal was to promote public morality, was conceived primarily to bring the lower classes into a more intimate relationship with the state.[76] By eliciting what might be called civic patriotism, Inoue hoped to quash a potential threat to social order.[77]

In brief, the Meiji state's response to Japan's worsening urban social problems was a double-edged strategy of denial and evasion. In cities, urban modernizers promoted virtually peopleless "city improvement," placing in the foreground a host of urban initiatives designed to promote infrastructural efficiency and pushing into the background a handful conceived to achieve livability.[78] In villages, Local Improvers cultivated the institutional strength and spiritual resolve of rural Japan in an effort to thwart the corrupting influence of urban life. And in the hallowed halls of the Home Ministry in Tokyo, well-meaning social bureaucrats prattled on patriotically about the responsibility of local leaders to administer relief to the poor and thus to revive public spirit. In short, the late Meiji state acknowledged the existence of looming urban social problems only to ignore the imperative of proactive urban social reform.

If the Meiji leaders awakened excruciatingly slowly to the gravity of the urban social problems facing Japan, some finally began to show subtle signs of recognition following the Russo-Japanese War. One poignant anecdotal illustration is the quasi-official endorsement of Miyake Iwao's pioneering 1908 tome on urban reform, *Toshi no kenkyū* (Researches of the city). In this path-breaking work, which called for comprehensive urban deployment *(toshi sankai)* in the face of urban social problems that threatened the very "order and tranquility of [Japanese] society," the author called on his countrymen to acknowledge cities as "the entryway to and the nucleus of national culture." In making his point, Miyake cleverly turned the antiurbanism of Ōkuma Shigenobu on its head. He observed that what truly threatened to turn cities into "the people's graveyards" was not the act of "put[ting] man in cities," as Ōkuma had suggested, but rather the nation's failure to "improve urban life."[79] Three prominent Meiji officials wrote prefaces to Miyake's book, and all three praised the author for his attention to urban social concerns. Two bear mention here: Ōkuma Shigenobu and Inoue Tomoichi.[80]

That Miyake was able to obtain the endorsement of these particular national officials—the first a national leader with a history of visceral antiurbanism, the second one with a history of hollow urban idealism—suggests just how large Japan's urban social problems now loomed on the mental radar of the Meiji leadership. Their new-found enthusiasm for sweeping urban social reform was expressed most poignantly in the official buzz sparked by the introduction of Ebenezer Howard's urban utopian vision of the garden city.[81] Jumping on an already international bandwagon, with progressives in France, Germany, Italy, Belgium, Poland, Spain, Russia, and the United States rushing to form garden-city societies, the Home Ministry soon released Howard's book *Garden Cities of To-morrow* in translation as *Den'en Toshi* (literally, field and garden cities).[82] Emblematic of the creative tension between internationalism and nationalism that informed global progressivism at the turn of the century, the universal figure of the garden city was now variously rendered as *den'en toshi, cité-jardin, Gartenstadt, ciudad-jardin,* and *Tuinstadt.*

A self-styled urban social visionary, the British author of *Garden Cities of To-morrow* deplored the overcrowding of London and bemoaned the fact that "people should continue to stream into the already over-crowded cities, and should thus further deplete the country districts."[83] Proposing the creation of self-sufficient satellite cities where there would be a carefully contrived balance between industry and agriculture, Howard made his case for urban reform with utopian fervor. "Town and country must be married," he proclaimed passionately, "and out of this joyous union will spring a new hope, a new life, a new civilisation."[84] The planned communities Howard projected, as described by one author, provided a "blueprint for the resocialized city."[85]

While this "social experiment" echoed earlier urban utopian proposals—most conspicuously those of utopian socialists such as Claude Henri Saint-Simon, Charles Fourier, Étienne Cabet, and Robert Owen—Howard claimed that most such models of urban community had been constructed piecemeal.[86] The garden city, as he and his supporters both emphasized, expressed a powerful "unity of design and purpose."[87] Howard himself projected this unitary vision as follows:

> I will undertake, then, to show how in "Town-country" equal, nay
> better, opportunities of social intercourse may be enjoyed than are
> enjoyed in any crowded city, while yet the beauties of nature may
> encompass and enfold each dweller therein; how higher wages are
> compatible with reduced rates and rents; how abundant opportunities
> for employment and bright prospects of advancement may be secured
> for all; how capital may be attracted and wealth created; how the
> most admirable sanitary conditions may be ensured; how beautiful
> homes and gardens may be seen on every hand; how the bounds
> of freedom may be widened, and yet all the best results of concert and
> co-operation gathered in by a happy people.[88]

If the progressive Home Ministry bureaucrats who commissioned the translation of *Garden Cities of To-morrow* were enthusiastic about Howard's revolutionary urban vision, they were also primed from the outset to adopt and adapt his garden-city model to their own, specifically Japanese, concerns. Thus proposing an alternate translation of garden cities—*kaen toshi*, or flower-garden cities, in place of *den'en toshi*, or field and garden cities—the Home Ministry editors of Howard's work subtly altered his vision.[89] In a grandiose epilogue that linked "labor protection and labor relief" to urban resettlement, they evinced a broad-gauged understanding of Japan's urban social problems but a hopelessly escapist vision of urban social reform.[90]

Behind the social idealism that Howard's ideas inspired in progressive bureaucrats lay a hopelessly utopian aspiration: to find a unitary means of achieving both urban improvement *(toshi kairyō)* and village renewal *(nōson kōshin)*. With this in mind, the Home Ministry editors of Howard's work reinvented his garden-city idea, portraying it as a method of producing new cities and new villages in one neat package. Garden cities, they submitted, should be designed to embody "the best in the city and the best in the village."[91]

While the enthusiasm of reform-minded state bureaucrats for the garden-city ideal illustrates that Japan's leaders were prepared in principle to acknowledge cities as social communities, it also suggests that they were unwilling in reality to acknowledge them on their own terms. Instead of facing up to the social ills that afflicted city life, Japanese leaders dreamt aloud of inventing happy new cities and leaving the unhappy old ones behind.

In the pivotal 1909 address to the Gakkai to which we have already traced Seki's nascent concern with the urban problem, he raised this very issue with the champions of the garden-city ideal. After diplomatically applauding their commitment to urban social reform in Japan, Seki roundly criticized their approach to it. He argued that their ideal, which was premised on the idea of abandoning big cities, was no less escapist in the end than Kawakami Hajime's suggestion that urbanites abandon the city for the village. Counseling Japanese city-dwellers against panic, Seki encouraged them to "stay put in the city" and to confront its problems head on. "There's bound to be a way to right its wrongs," he assured them.[92]

When Seki made this passionate plea for urban social reform in 1909, he professed to know exactly what was at stake. But his uncharacteristic inability to proffer a practical solution suggests that he had only begun to engage the weighty issues involved. What began as an intellectual tickle soon became an ideological itch. After reading Yanagita Kunio's famous work on the city and the country, in which Yanagita characterized Japanese urban neighborhoods as villages writ large, Seki wrote a review that politely challenged the cultural essentialism implicit in the proposition. Specifically, he questioned Yanagita's conclusion that the similarities of urban and rural life suggested the operation of a uniquely Japanese process of socialization. Seki asked whether it might not be appropriate first to explore the "development of Western cities" before rushing to the hasty conclusion that the cities of Japan and thus also the Japanese pattern of urbanization were unique.[93]

Noting elsewhere that Westerners had repeatedly observed of Tokyo that it had the feel neither of a city nor of a village, Seki offered a simple explanation: the urban space of Tokyo did not yet exhibit "the pronounced functional differentiation of Western cities." While Yanagita attributed the unique feel of Japanese cities to the cultural idiosyncrasies of Japanese society as a whole, Seki attributed it by contrast to late modernization. Simply put, Japanese cities had yet to reach the level of modern development achieved by their Western counterparts. It was only a matter of time, Seki went on to argue, before these Japanese urban organisms would evolve to a comparable level of functional differentiation and spatial rationalization.[94]

By the beginning of the Taisho Era, just prior to his appointment as deputy mayor of Osaka in 1914, Seki was no longer just dabbling in urban studies but was devoting his undivided attention to the challenge of urban social reform in Japan. At first bemused, then later alarmed, by the fact that the once-growing national interest in genuine urban social reform seemed to have been supplanted by a burgeoning enthusiasm for vacuous urban utopianism, Seki hammered home a point that he had made before and would repeatedly recite during his twenty-one-year tenure as a city official: that the garden-city movement was both misguided and impracticable. In an article on the subject written in 1913, he openly criticized the movement as a "back-to-the-land movement" that struck at the very foundation of industrial progress. After all, Seki mused, the champions of flower-garden cities *(kaen toshi)* were calling for the invention of new cities *(shin toshi)* whose very name betrayed their utopian aspiration to flee Japan's problem-ridden metropolises and to fashion urban Gardens of Eden in their place.[95]

Expressing equal skepticism about the garden-city movement in Europe, which had already spawned the pilot projects of Letchworth and Welwyn in England and whose advocates in Germany, France, and the United States were promoting similar developments,[96] Seki gently chided the Japanese scholars and officials who had cavalierly jumped on the bandwagon. He encouraged the movement's cheerleaders to abandon their garden-city pipe dream, challenging them instead to face up to the pressing urban problems that they were now conspicuously ignoring. Rather than plotting the imminent evacuation of big cities in favor of urban utopias, argued Seki, Japanese urban social reformers would do better to confront the culprit: unchecked and irresponsible real estate development perpetrated by land speculators *(tochi tōkisha)* on the outskirts of big cities *(dai toshi kinkō)*.[97]

Here, Seki raised an issue that had seemingly been on his mind since he attended Adolf Wagner's lectures in Berlin at the turn of the century: urban property rights. No less destructive of the national social economy than the unchecked profiteering of industrial capitalists, he maintained, freewheeling landed capitalism struck at the very foundation of urban society. Seki solemnly noted that urban real estate speculators had blithely erected disorderly and deficient housing, thoughtlessly developed land in a haphazard and self-serving manner, and wantonly destroyed historical landmarks. Accusing them of utterly ignoring the public benefit *(kōkyōteki rieki)* and amassing obscene profits in the process,[98] he reserved his most damning criticism for last: that they were slumlords who leased ramshackle housing at exorbitant rents to the working-class urban families who represented the social bedrock of the industrial metropolis.

Waxing just a bit rhetorical on the subject, Seki suggested that the growing slums *(hyakken nagaya)* on the ragged urban edge of Japan's biggest cities posed an imminent danger to the health of the national body as a whole:

> The living conditions of the urban poor in what we can simply call slums . . . have harmed their education, morality, and health. This, in turn, is destroying the family system, which should be the foundation of [Japan's] social structure; is eating away at the spirit of loyalty and patriotism which should serve as the basis of nation building; and is responsible for the rise in infant mortality that has stunted the nation's population growth. In truth, slums harbor the worst illnesses of modern civilization.[99]

The gravity of this problem notwithstanding, Seki failed to find sufficient reason to flee the city for new, self-contained towns. To the contrary, in fact, he insisted that the problem highlighted the need for thoroughgoing urban reform. The time had come, he argued, for Japan to begin conducting "orderly planning on the outskirts of [its] big cities" in an effort to assert control over the "haphazard process of citification [*shigaika*]" that was sweeping the nation.[100]

Unlike the one-dimensional urban thinkers and policymakers we have described thus far, Seki came at the problem of the city from several different directions at once. Conducting the same sort of comparative research as had characterized his earlier work on Japan's political and social economy, Seki now looked to the advanced Western nations for models of urban social reform that might be adopted and adapted by Japan. Based on a broad comparison of urban conditions in Tokyo and New York, he began sketching out a reformist agenda. These early researches, as we shall see, ultimately helped Seki articulate a pioneering ideology of urban social reform.

In his address to the Gakkai in 1909, where Seki began to spin out the ideas that would later coalesce as a paradigm of urban reform *(toshi kairyō)*, he compared and contrasted Japan's great capital, Tokyo, to one of the world's most venerated metropolises, New York. Applauding the people-moving efficiency of New York's elevated trains, Seki contrasted it to the traffic-bound inefficiency of Tokyo's streetcar system. Praising New York for the impressive network of affordable suburban commuter trains that had enabled it to relieve the problem of residential overcrowding, he criticized Tokyo for its failure to regulate fares on suburban train lines and for the attendant aggravation of residential overcrowding. Holding up New York as a model of progressive urban renewal—for eliminating many of its slums by buying up tenement properties and redeveloping them as worker housing projects—Seki chided Tokyo officials for their regressive slum-clearance policies.[101] By every measure of urban reform he came up with, Tokyo lagged behind New York.

In the years that followed this first foray into the field of urban social reform, Seki worked several comparative angles of the issue that had been suggested to him by this survey of Tokyo and New York. Less insistently Tokyo-centered in these later comparisons, he made the pleasantly surprising discovery that one Japanese city repeatedly measured up to the more "highly evolved" cities of the West: the industrial metropolis of Osaka.

Looking first at the pressing issue of intraurban transit, Seki noted that Tokyo had missed out early on when it permitted private companies to develop the city's streetcar lines. By contrast, he observed, Osaka had created an affordable and profitable municipal streetcar system that served the public both by relieving residential overcrowding and by producing public income.[102] To Seki, the lesson was obvious: "those with a direct interest in [riding] streetcars—[namely,] urban citizens—should retain direct control over their operation."[103]

In 1912, Seki extended his investigation to interurban transit. Here again, he praised Osaka as a pioneer, noting that railway developers in the city had linked Osaka to Kobe and Kyoto with trains, thus creating a regional urban network.[104] Impressed as well with the public-private collaborations that Osaka had nurtured on a number of municipal projects, Seki seemed well on his way toward singling the city out as the exception to Japan's sorry urban rule—a city willing and able to take the problem of urban social reform by the horns.[105]

The urban investigations that Seki conducted between 1909 and 1914— of municipal enterprise, urban transit, garden cities, suburban real estate speculation, and urban planning, among other topics—were designed to cast light on discrete elements of Japan's urban social problems. Indeed, he seems to have regarded these investigations as interlocking pieces of an urban jigsaw puzzle. As the shape of that puzzle gradually emerged—that is, as he thought through Japan's urban social problems—he finally envisioned the contours of the whole and gradually came up with a strategy for thoroughgoing reform.

Reiterating his contention that the central problem facing modern Japanese cities was residential overcrowding on the urban periphery—because of which working-class families found themselves victimized by landed capitalists—Seki proposed a four-pronged response. He called first for new transit facilities to connect the city *(shichī)* to the urban edge *(basue);*

second, for town planning *(toshi sekkei)* in anticipation of expanded city limits; third, for tax and planning incentives designed to stimulate new-housing construction; and fourth, for the joint introduction of a property-tax assessment system and a property-appreciation tax *(tochi zōkazei)* conceived to discourage owners from deliberately leaving prime urban real estate undeveloped until its value rose precipitously.[106]

Aside from puzzling through and prioritizing the urban social problems that plagued Japanese cities, then coming up with a plan to eradicate the most troublesome among them, Seki proposed a radically new model of urban policymaking. Much as the social economist in him could not help but see cities primarily as social places rather than as economic spaces, the social democrat in him could not help but regard local authorities as the proper source of urban policy.[107] Rather than yielding to the longstanding Japanese tradition of state paternalism *(fuseishugi)* with regard to urban affairs, Seki exhorted local authorities *(jichitai)* to seize control of their own destiny by invoking the principle of public benefit *(kōeki)* and expanding the scope of municipal enterprise *(shiei jigyō)*.[108]

Thus galvanized by his new-found commitment to urban social reform, Seki could not have come to Osaka at a more fortuitous moment in his scholarly career. Not surprisingly, he quickly established himself as the mayor's right-hand man.[109] Between 1914 and 1923, as Osaka's senior deputy mayor, he spearheaded several critical municipal initiatives, including the expansion of Osaka's city limits, the abolition of its elitist school-districting system, the establishment of critical social facilities, the implementation of a social-survey system, the initiation of urban planning, the modernization of intraurban and interurban transit, and the municipalization of electricity. Singing Seki's praises, a fellow deputy mayor would later describe him as the municipal leader who transformed Osaka into a metropolis.[110] In the following section, I suggest how he placed himself in a position to do so.

POVERTY IN THE CAPITAL OF WEALTH

Seki spent his first days on the job as deputy mayor of Osaka familiarizing himself with the city he had sworn to serve. Koyama Kenzō, his old mentor, introduced Seki to Osaka's movers and shakers, while Mayor Ikegami, his new boss, introduced him to its public officials. A former police official for the Prefecture of Osaka, the mayor was reputedly recruited to cleanse Osaka's municipal government of the corruption and incompetence that had weakened it under previous administrations.[111] In this spirit, apparently, Ikegami had warned the city's Tammany-like political bosses to steer clear of municipal administration. Introducing a new quasi-scientific model of urban management *(toshi keiei)*, he actively recruited highly skilled scholars such as Seki and lined up an army of more narrowly trained technocrats to serve them.[112]

Ikegami inherited leadership in a rapidly growing industrial city with a powerful capitalist elite—a city that would be riding even higher once industrial production picked up during the First World War. As if to set an example of social responsibility for the *narikin* (newly rich), whose wheeling and dealing over industrial properties and streetcar routes had brought down two previous municipal administrations, Ikegami traveled everywhere he could by public transport. In blatant contradistinction to the many capitalists who ran businesses in Osaka but had avoided taxes by taking up residence in suburbs toward Kobe,[113] Ikegami registered his own domicile within the city limits.[114]

Given tremendous latitude by this public-spirited municipal leader to fashion his own urban agenda, Seki began by inspecting the locale. One of his first stops was Osaka's port, which remained heavily in the throes of expansion. There, Seki tells us, he discussed "town planning" with the port director.[115] A week into his tenure as deputy mayor, Seki chartered a small steam-powered launch and made a wide-ranging inspection tour of the city's river and canal projects.[116] If he spent many hours on the job familiarizing himself with the city's political and physical infrastructure, he spent nearly as many as a private citizen sampling its cultural amenities. From his new home near Tennōji on the southern boundary of Osaka, he took his family on evening walks in Tennōji Park, on weekend excursions to the bayside resort of Hamadera in the nearby city of Sakai, on recreational outings to the New World (Shin Sekai) amusement park on the city's southern boundary, and on shopping trips to Osaka's multistory department stores.

The networking, inspecting, and touring with which Seki filled his time worked a powerful personal and professional influence on him. Among other things, it brought him into intimate contact with the multifaceted urban world that he had been hired not merely to survey but to manage. By virtue of its vibrant identity as a port city during the Tokugawa Era, Osaka had long been known as the Capital of Water (Mizu no Miyako). But during the late Meiji Era, as it steadily industrialized, the city had come to be called the Capital of Smoke (Kemuri no Miyako). Eventually, schoolchildren throughout Japan sang Osaka's praises as they read the following passage in their elementary school primers:

It is only natural that Osaka should be called the Capital of Smoke. Even on a fair day, the sky grows dull as you approach Osaka station by train, making the city appear overcast. There are over eight thousand factories here, large and small. Lined up one after another like trees in a forest, their chimneys belch smoke incessantly. With its diversity of flourishing industries, Osaka is truly Japan's greatest industrial city.[117]

A city of roughly 1.4 million at the time Seki arrived, Osaka had recovered from a frightening post-Restoration decline to transform itself from a commercial port into an industrial metropolis. Osaka made its reputation as an industrial city in the textile business and was so successful that it earned yet another sobriquet: the Manchester of the Orient (Tōyō no Manchesutā). During the First World War, however, the industrial picture changed. Apparently in response to regional and global demand, local Osaka entrepreneurs went into heavy industry: mainly dyeing and weaving, chemicals, metalworking, shipbuilding, and machine manufacturing. The result was stunning. Between 1914 and 1919, nearly one thousand new factories opened, increasing the total to roughly three thousand. During this same period, there was also a flood of immigrant labor: The numbers of industrial workers nearly doubled, reaching 215,000. The vast majority of Osaka's new factories, as well as the laborers they employed, were ensconced on the north, west, and southwest edges of the city in heavily polluted industrial districts packed with the sort of ramshackle housing that Seki had long since condemned.

In one of his first official acts as a municipal administrator, Seki was brought face to face with the social and political realities of life on the edge of the industrial metropolis. His charge was to convince local landowners in the harbor-lying Izumio district to cede strips of paddy land and marshland to the city for the construction of access roads to a peripheral site slated for municipal housing. As Seki soon discovered, this was easier said than done. Haggling with him over the width of the proposed roads, the landowners stubbornly held out for ten *ken* against the municipal standard of fifteen. The exasperated deputy mayor asked himself a rhetorical question at the end of the day: "Should the municipal administration allow its long-term plans to be derailed by such petty issues?"[118]

Seki answered his own question a year later. In a paper delivered to the Kobe Economics Association, he declared that Japan was faced with an urban crisis that demanded a visionary solution. Its modern cities, like those of the Western nations, had witnessed an unprecedented influx of working-class immigrants from the countryside. In 1895, just over 6 percent of Japan's total population lived in cities of one hundred thousand or more; by 1908, the figure had risen to 10 percent. Among the so-called six metropolises (roku daitoshi), all of which had experienced dramatic growth, Seki singled out Osaka. With a population of only 332,425 in 1882, it had grown to 758,285 by 1898, then ballooned to 1,388,909 by 1913. This population explosion, observed Seki, had given rise to various problems, but none more pressing than those related to "disorderly [new] construction on the outskirts of the metropolis." He noted that the new arrivals (gairaisha) who had flocked to Osaka in search of financial and recreational opportunities had been confronted instead with living conditions so poor that they posed a perilous threat to public morals (fūkyō). Cast into a kind of residential purgatory—into haphazardly constructed and hopelessly overcrowded housing developments—these urban immigrants bore witness to the rise of a "special sort of residential problem."[119]

Seki attributed this new residential problem to the greed of local landowners. In the knowledge that urbanization was rapidly driving up land values and housing rents, these landed capitalists had happily jumped on the bandwagon, becoming rapacious slumlords. "In the interest of making a quick profit, without a thought for the future, [they] have confusedly erected housing and thus plunged residential life into an increasingly disorderly condition." Seki's criticism of these slumlords was reminiscent of his earlier criticism of greedy industrialists. Much as industrialists adhered to the creed of free enterprise, these slumlords clung to the principle of private property. "Local landowners place no limits on the property rights they claim," observed Seki. "As land values and housing rents rise, they construct [new] housing as they see fit."[120]

Narrowing his spatial focus to Osaka's Nishi-ku—to the very same urban ward whose propertied elites he had wrangled with a year earlier—Seki broadened his thematic focus to the larger issue of town planning. "Close to two-thirds of Nishi-ku is paddy land today," he observed, "but it is clear that [all] this will soon revert to residential use." In anticipation of this development, the municipal administration proposed to lay out a network of new roads. Yet because it was deprived of a "suitable legal foundation" to establish eminent domain, the city found itself instead "looking on as landlords put in roads at their own discretion."[121] None too subtly, Seki berated the landowners of Nishi-ku for their profiteering and myopia. Not only had they held the city captive by demanding exorbitant sums of money for slender slivers of land, but they had defied all rational standards of spatial planning within their private domains.

Although Seki laid Osaka's residential problems at the feet of local landowners, he did not look to them for solutions. Convinced that landowners, no less than industrialists, were driven primarily by greed, he placed his faith in government alone to curb it. He observed that the national government had long since acknowledged this responsibility when it introduced the Tokyo City Improvement Ordinance in 1888. Yet the most practical provisions of this law had never been extended to the nation's other cities. Thus, when cities such as Osaka exercised the public prerogative of eminent domain, their purchases remained subject to the nation's private-property laws. Held captive to the capitalist whims of local landowners—to what Seki described as their instinct to "line their own pockets"—local authorities found themselves between a rock and a hard place. Either they coughed up the exorbitant asking price for the lands they needed, or they abandoned their plans for rational urban development.[122]

Profoundly disillusioned with this state of affairs and acutely agitated by the experience that brought it into focus, Seki invited Japan to entertain the prospect of sweeping new urban legislation. Specifically, he urged his countrymen to follow the legal lead of the Western nations. Among those who had recently put teeth into their urban-planning laws, Seki singled out the British for praise. Britain's Town Planning Act (1909), which was conceived mainly to eradicate that nation's urban residential problems, included a pivotal provision enabling local authorities to set the planning priorities and financial terms of eminent domain. Seki quoted this provision in its entirety, identifying it as the centerpiece of Britain's model legislation. Then, as if to distinguish this forward-looking urban-planning law from Japan's antiquated Tokyo City Improvement Ordinance, he went on to self-consciously invoke the English term *town planning* in his own proposal.[123]

Seki's proposal for urban-planning legislation in Japan highlighted the residential problems of its largest cities, rendering the city primarily as a social organism rather than an economic entity. In keeping with the urban-planning agenda set in Brussels at the International Planning Conference of 1913, however, Seki also acknowledged the functional diversity of modern cities: "The primary purpose of urban planning is to promote the diverse functions of cities, large and small, by identifying [functional] districts and plotting the arrangement of roads and other means of transport. [Only] when this has been accomplished should construction begin, and then in keeping with [each city's] actual topography."[124]

The international zoning model produced in Brussels identified five functionally distinct urban districts: administration, business, shopping, residential (subdivided into upper/middle-class and working-class enclaves), and manufacturing. Applying this model to Japan, Seki noted "the particular importance of circumscribing factory quarters." Here, his social definition of the city came explicitly into play. Particularly concerned with the deleterious effects of industrial air pollution, Seki toyed with the idea of transplanting the most egregious perpetrators. Recognizing this as little more than a pipe dream, however, he recommended a practicable compromise: "to delineate [the boundaries of existing] factory quarters and, at the very least, to restrict [the number of] smokestacks in residential quarters." As a model, Seki cited the English garden city *(den'en toshi)* of Letchworth. There, in an effort to reduce the impact of smoke and smog on urban life, planners had sited the city's residential districts upwind of its factory quarters.[125]

Notwithstanding his overriding concern with urban residential problems, Seki was careful to cast urban planning as a multipurpose enterprise. If public-health concerns demanded that cities circumscribe factory districts, for example, their ghettoization in industrial zones would also make it easier for local authorities to provide transport facilities and to expedite production. Likewise, the designation of special residential districts for the working classes—with structural and infrastructural features designed to fit their means as well as their needs—represented a critical first step toward the social rationalization of urban space. "When the local authorities [begin to] divide cities into distinct [residential] quarters and to stipulate the size of each [different] quarter's 'city blocks' [*burokku*]," argued Seki, "[local authorities] will no longer find it necessary to adhere to a uniform citywide building code. Instead, they will be free to construct buildings appropriate to each different quarter."[126] To Seki, in other words, it was not merely the introduction of urban zoning—and under this rubric the designation of residential zones—that mattered. Going one step further, he maintained that cities could and should make class-based distinctions between residential zones and thus begin transforming Japanese cities from melting pots into truly modern communities.

Completing his first foray into the field of urban planning with a selective comparison of German, French, and Belgian town-planning provisions, Seki hammered home his central point: it was time for Japan, as an equally civilized nation, to make its cities modern. He praised the Europeans for their strict adherence to modern building codes and their equally strict application of the principle of eminent domain. Seizing on what he took to be the most visionary element of their town-planning laws—the incorporation of neighboring towns and villages into the administrative jurisdiction of large cities—he made the case for expanding city boundaries in anticipation of future urban development: "When we leave large cities and their neighboring towns and villages under different administrative jurisdictions, we run the risk of creating an invidious distinction between them and depriving the latter of numerous conveniences. For this reason, it is essential to incorporate neighboring towns and villages and to plan 'greater metropolitan areas [*ichi daitoshi*].' "[127]

Noting that university research teams in Germany and England had made urban boundary expansion an urgent priority, Seki predicted that there would soon be a Greater Berlin with an urban administrative radius of fifteen miles. "In Japan as well," he concluded, "it is essential that we introduce legislation for urban planning of the future."[128]

By 1916, Seki had begun to anticipate the creation of a Greater Osaka to rival Greater Berlin. First, however, he felt the need to identify the local enemies of incorporation. In an extended meditation on the challenge of urban planning, he put the final touches to his criticism of landlordism in Osaka. He portrayed the original, grid-lined city as a masterpiece of urban planning and its ever-expanding edges as an abomination. Blaming local landowners for the spatial disorder that had come to define Osaka's urban periphery, he castigated these lords of the urban manor for condemning working-class Osakans to a kind of residential purgatory.

Interwar Osaka was ringed by slums, most of them adjacent to the many factories that had been erected near the harbor and along the rivers of the city. Arguably worst hit were the unincorporated districts of Nishinari-gun and Higashinari-gun. Both areas were flush with factories, and both experienced a huge influx of industrial labor during the economic boom of the First World War. Nishinari-gun reported a 47 percent increase in total population, jumping from 170,000 to 250,000, while Higashinari-gun reported a 43 percent increase, expanding from 140,000 to 200,000.[129] The Nishinari-gun neighborhood of Sagisu and the Higashinari-gun neighborhood of Tsuruhashi virtually exploded demographically, reporting respective population increases of 81 and 78 percent. Given that demographic growth within the city limits tallied a paltry 11 percent during the same period, it would appear that Seki's worries about unchecked urban expansion on Osaka's periphery were more than justified.[130]

For the poor workers who flowed into Osaka during the industrial boom years of the First World War, this residential purgatory came to look a lot like hell. In 1917, a journalist for the *Ōsaka Mainichi Shinbun* produced a gripping ethnographic exposé of slum life on the southern edge of Osaka in the Kamagasaki area near Imamiya—a place that to this day remains a magnet for transient day labor. In his introduction, Murashima Motoyuki revealed the tragic paradox of life in Osaka: here, in a city so prosperous some called it the Capital of Wealth (Tomi no Miyako), 140,000 of the 1,500,000 residents were desperately poor.[131] (See figure 10.)

In Seki's preface to the work, which identified him not as deputy mayor of Osaka but simply as a doctor of law, he rubbed salt into the wound that Murashima had inflicted. He drew attention to the disparity in living conditions between Osaka's "upper crust" *(jōryū shakai)* and its "lower classes" *(kasōmin)*, and he encouraged Osakans obsessed with industrial production and moneymaking to put their materialism in social perspective:

> Of course it is important to protect the dye industry, and of course iron production and shipbuilding have a crucial relationship to [Osaka's] future. Although we often look upward to count [the city's] smokestacks, however, we also need to look downward to examine the living conditions of lower-class workers. Stretched out at the base of the [so-called] industrial-production problem [*sangyō mondai*] is [another] problem: [that of] distribution and consumption [*bunpai shōhi*]. [What we loosely call] economic problems are [ultimately] the problems of those people who find themselves in desperation [*kyūkyokujin*].[132]

It is worth reemphasizing that this harsh criticism of the city's greedy capitalist classes came from the deputy mayor they had helped put in office. Apparently unmoved by this fact himself—indeed, moved conversely to diminish the influence of Osaka's capitalist elite—Seki made the leap from talk to action in the summer of 1918.

SUMMER IN THE CITY

At the end of the First World War, when Japan went into a serious economic recession, the nation was wracked with popular protests that came to be known collectively as the Rice Riots (Kome Sōdō). While these riots were triggered by rapidly rising rice prices, to their participants they represented something much larger than mere consumer anxiety. As portrayed by Michael Lewis, these violent popular protests signaled the people's anger at a critical violation of the domestic moral economy.[133] By allowing the cost of Japan's most basic staple to rise beyond the means of the average household, the state, as guardian of the family-state, had violated its implicit commitment to benevolent rule. Not only did the rioters feel justified in attacking "market profiteers and hoarders," they felt righteously indignant about it. As Lewis aptly observes, their activism ultimately took on much greater significance than they themselves ever imag-

Figure 10. Slum life on the edge of Greater Osaka. From Ōsaka Shi Shakaibu, "Furyō jūtaku chiku zushū" [Collected illustrations of tenement housing], *Shakaibu hōkoku*, no. 236 (June 1938).

ined: "They turned tradition on its head by seeking political and economic rights suitable to the place of the citizen or the worker in a newly emerging urban and industrial society."[134]

When rice prices began to rise during the summer of 1918, Osaka was already in the grip of a series of worrisome industrial strikes—largely over wages. Since the beginning of the year, the umbrella, dye, textile, brush, and shipbuilding industries had been hit with crippling work stoppages. For working-class families who already felt their backs to the wall, the steady rise in rice prices could not have come at a worse time. As Inoue Kiyoshi and Watanabe Tōru have eloquently illustrated, the crisis hit workers in their heads and their hearts as well as in their stomachs. First, poorer workers found their meals reduced from three to two a day. Next, they began to pawn clothing in order to buy rice but found they could not amass the cash to buy it back. Finally, workers took on second jobs, and, in many working families, the proud housewives known in local neighborhoods as "moms on patrol" *(junsa no okusan)* were forced to take paying jobs.[135]

As the crisis deepened in August 1918, workers wrote heart-wrenching letters to the local newspapers dramatizing their plight.[136] Then, on August 9, all hell broke loose. In the notorious day-laborer quarter of Imamiya, which a year earlier had been exposed as a horrific slum by the newspaperman Murashima Motoyuki, several hundred people gathered outside the shop of a local rice dealer. Brandishing sticks and stones, they used their geta to pound on the doors as they demanded rice at one-third the going price. That evening, five thousand people gathered at a town meeting hall in nearby Tennōji Park. When a youth was arrested after the meeting and placed on a streetcar for the trip to jail, the crowd freed him, then trashed the next few streetcars that came along. Over the next week, an estimated 232,000 people rioted in the Osaka region. Mayor Ikegami, who immediately called in troops to restore order, cut off streetcar service each evening at seven o'clock, severely restricted public assembly after dark, and censored newspaper reports of the rioting.[137]

To Mayor Ikegami, the former prefectural police chief, the Rice Riots represented a clear and present threat to social order. But to Deputy Mayor Seki, the labor reformer turned urban reformer, they represented clear and indisputable evidence of the need for far-reaching urban social reform. To his credit, Mayor Ikegami seems to have appreciated the difference between himself and Seki and seems to have understood the importance of building urban order on a foundation of municipal social responsibility rather than on the power of a national police force. Accordingly, in the wake of the Rice Riots, Mayor Ikegami issued his deputy mayor a new assignment: to initiate a proactive process of urban social reform at the municipal level.[138]

Osaka's Rice Riots were a watershed experience for Seki, but not in the conventional sense. In essence, they confirmed ideas and convictions about urban social reform that had been percolating in him for nearly a decade. Long concerned about the cost of living, for example, Seki had brought the issue before the Osaka Municipal Assembly in February 1918. Resolving to "supply food affordably" to Osaka's poorer citizens,[139] whose cost of living had roughly tripled since 1914, he made good on his promise by the spring, bringing consumers and producers together at four public retail markets.[140]

If the Rice Riots triggered a national change in "the public concept of social welfare," as Lewis has observed,[141] the change was felt less keenly in Osaka than elsewhere. Largely because of Seki's influence on social policy in the city, the critical distinction between social relief (kyūsai) and social policy (shakai seisaku) had long since been introduced into the Osaka municipal vocabulary.[142] While central government officials may have had to overcome their nervous reaction to the term society (shakai)— a reaction that has been attributed to their fear of socialism—Seki never harbored any such irrational anxiety.[143] Not only had social reform (shakai kairyō) long since become a key phrase in his vocabulary, but it had become the key concept behind his vision for Osaka.

Seki was not the only one who brought a vision of social reform to the post–Rice Riot world of Osaka, however: Japan's national leaders invoked an equally new, but also profoundly different, model of urban social reform. Under the direction of the social bureaucrat Ogawa Shigejirō, Osaka Prefecture set up a district-commissioner system *(hōmen iin seido)* that employed local elites as reformist leaders.[144] As described by Sheldon Garon, this system pivoted on middle-class volunteers "deputized" by the state as "people of virtue" *(toshika)*.[145] Even more to point, as David Ambaras has since refined our understanding of the system, these volunteers came largely from a so-called old middle class with deeply rooted local business and landed interests.[146]

Under Ogawa's direction, the prefecture strove to transform Osaka's old middle class into a kind of social priesthood dedicated to elevating the living standard of the supposedly spendthrift working classes by raising their moral consciousness.[147] District commissioners in Osaka thus worked tirelessly for the public benefit *(kōeki)* by pressuring local factory owners to offer their workers social assistance and by forming neighborhood residential associations.[148] Yet however well-meaning, these middle-class district commissioners indulged a classist conceit that did less to help the poor improve their lives than it did to help the state reinforce urban social order.[149]

The Osaka municipal program of social reform was vastly different in substance and in spirit from this prefectural initiative. From 1918, largely under Seki's guidance, the City of Osaka erected an elaborate apparatus for the establishment of an entirely new set of social programs. Not only did it establish a Social Bureau (Shakai-bu) to administer its new social facilities *(shakai jigyō)*, but it set up a special Labor Survey Unit (Rōdō Chōsa-ka) to investigate the conditions under which Osaka's working classes labored and lived.[150] Both these institutions were path-breaking additions to Japan's municipal administrative repertoire: the Social Bureau, which was dedicated exclusively to the creation and administration of social facilities, was the first department of its kind in any Japanese city; and the equally pioneering social-survey system set up by the Labor Survey Unit set a new standard for the social-scientific investigation of social problems.[151]

On the cutting edge of urban social policymaking in Japan, the City of Osaka put together an impressive array of social facilities in the late 1910s and early 1920s. The most important of these facilities were municipally run retail markets, a central wholesale market, employment offices, pawnshops, lunch counters, public baths, technical schools, maternity hospitals, nurseries, day-care centers, hospitals, and municipal housing. The concept behind these programs was proactive social reform: They were social services conceived specifically to enable the working poor to achieve a just "civil minimum" in living conditions.

The brains behind Osaka's pioneering social policymaking was Seki Hajime, and, significantly, he had already established the foundation for its programs by the time the Rice Riots broke out. Invited to address the Social Relief Research Association (Kyūsai Kenkyūkai) on the topic of urban social policy *(toshi shakai seisaku)* in May 1918, just months before the Rice Riots, Seki began his talk by challenging a doubtlessly skeptical audience to acknowledge the critical distinction between the welfare problem *(kyūsai mondai)* and the social problem *(shakai mondai)*.[152]

Whereas the welfare problem affected the endemically poor and was properly addressed through social relief, argued Seki, the social problem affected the working poor and was properly addressed through social policy.[153] This critical distinction in policymaking reflected a social perspective toward poverty shared by progressives worldwide at the turn of the century. Rodgers observes the following of their common attitude toward the indigent:

> The very poor were another nation: outsiders, to one degree or another, in the social reformers' imaginations. Social politics did not start with them. . . . The crucial class in that debate was the working class, suspended above [Charles] Booth's poverty line by fragile economic threads. As progressives saw it, their task was not to abolish poverty but to diminish the likelihood that the many standing at poverty's brink would be pushed in by an ill turn of fortune.[154]

While the endemically poor and the working poor of Osaka shared the same standard of living, according to Seki, they were radically different in one critical respect: the distinct psychologies *(shinri jōtai)* that they exhibited toward the act of labor. While the endemically poor were routinely unemployable, the working poor were simply temporarily unemployed.[155]

Seki maintained that urban social policy should be designed to give the working poor the opportunities they deserved, including gainful employment, and he provided several examples of the ways in which municipal governments might accomplish this objective: by providing referral services for the unemployed, by subsidizing unemployment-insurance programs administered by labor unions, and by mandating uniform hours of retail operation to protect shop employees from overwork. But while Seki firmly supported such municipal initiatives and put his weight behind them when Osaka set up its pioneering social facilities in the late 1910s, he placed special emphasis from the outset on one critical and unresolved social issue: the residential problem *(jūkyo mondai)*.[156]

Seki was prompted to highlight the residential problem by his heightened appreciation of the dimensions and the significance of this issue for the working poor of Osaka. From the mid-1910s, as he discovered in his new capacity as deputy mayor, working-class families in Osaka faced an increasingly desperate housing situation. As more and more factory laborers immigrated to the city, attracted by the booming wartime economy, the housing market became progressively tighter. In 1914, the residential vacancy rate in Osaka was 8.36 percent. It fell to 5.47 percent in 1915, to 5.29 percent in 1916, then to 0.26 percent in 1917. When the bottom dropped out of the wartime economy in 1918 and many workers relocated, the vacancy rate rose again to 5.41 percent, but it promptly fell to 0.15 percent in 1919.[157] With an estimated 998 of every 1,000 units occupied that year, industrial workers and their families commonly found themselves consigned to scandalously substandard rental housing[158]—tenements whose rents had increased one and a half times between 1914 and 1919.[159]

In a 1919 expose of slum life on Osaka's periphery, one local journalist lamented that "one first feels the lack of [open] space and the dearth of [single-family] homes. [Then,] inside dwellings, one notices the lack of air and light as well as the absence of plumbing. One also feels the want of parks, playgrounds, and trains." This is an "overcrowded life," he concluded, and one defined by inadequacy *(busoku seikatsu)* in every respect.[160]

It has been estimated that the average worker in Osaka before the First World War occupied about the same amount of living space as a Japanese sailor aboard ship. In the rapidly urbanizing villages surrounding the city, workers and their families were restricted on average to 2 mats per person (each mat measuring roughly 3 feet by 6 feet), and in districts on the urban edge the figure dropped to 1.8. According to a survey conducted by the city in 1918, the average member of a slum household in the downtown Nipponbashi area occupied the equivalent of 1.03 tatami of living space.[161] Even for these abysmal quarters, Osaka's working-class tenants were subjected to a threefold increase in rents between 1910 and 1922.[162]

The social costs of urban industrialization in the Capital of Smoke, then, were frighteningly high. Blanketed with acrid smoke from the factories surrounding their cramped tenement apartments, workers and their families were the victims of capitalist greed and government neglect. Place bound, in most cases, they could not have moved even if they had wanted to. According to a city survey conducted much later, in 1930, despite the cost and inconvenience of commuting, workers still did not relocate. Of those surveyed, 50 percent walked to work, 13 percent went by bicycle, 15 percent boarded streetcars, and only 7 percent commuted by suburban railway.[163] Unlike white-collar workers, who had become suburban commuters starting in the mid-1910s, Osaka's industrial workers tended to stay wherever they first landed. And where they stayed was anything but pleasant. In the words of a city housing report from 1925, the working-class poor were subjected to physical and spiritual hardships that "damaged their health and threw them into moral confusion."[164]

Well before the residential situation of workers reached this crisis point, to his credit Mayor Ikegami formed a municipal commission to investigate living conditions in the city and to come up with a viable scheme for urban reform *(toshi kairyō)*.[165] Not surprisingly, he named his principal deputy mayor, Seki Hajime, to its chairmanship. The members of Osaka's new Urban Reform Association set explicit priorities. At the top of their list lay zoning (commercial, industrial, and residential), building codes, and housing for industrial laborers. Drawing particular attention to the residential dimension of urban life in the expanding industrial metropolis, the Association later exerted a powerful influence on the national commission that drew up Japan's first urban-planning law.[166]

On the heels of his appointment as chair of this important local commission, Seki began to press the limits of his argument for urban residential reform. Taking the position that rising rents were of even greater import than the rising cost of living, he set out a comprehensive agenda focused on three related imperatives: slum clearance, reasonably priced new housing, and the eradication of parasitic landlordism. Most important, however, he urged the audience to rethink the purposes of urban planning. Rather than continuing to employ urban planning solely as a means of greasing the wheels of commerce and industry, Seki encouraged his countrymen to reconceive it as a social enterprise designed to enhance the public welfare. Once they did he so, he assured them, they would come to recognize housing as the most urgent demand on the modern urban-planning agenda.[167]

While crafting the Osaka Urban Reform Association's revolutionary proposal for metropolitan regional planning focused on residential development, Seki was slowly refining his reformist agenda. In 1919, he penned an article that proclaimed housing policy *(jūtaku seisaku)* the most pressing challenge facing the nation. Exhorting the public to endorse a sweeping program of residential reform, including building codes, rental regulations, and other critical urban legislation, Seki called most loudly for public action to increase the housing supply:

> [Residential reform] is not simply about regulating abuses. It is about looking toward the future—to the residences that low wage earners *should* possess from the perspectives of health, public morality, and social policy. As citizens of an advanced nation, we must somehow find a way of providing proper housing. And we must supply that housing cheaply. Beyond eliminating the abuses that exist at present through the passive device of a housing law, we must move positively to enrich the housing supply.[168]

In Seki's view, the establishment of urban housing policy was not just a public challenge but a public responsibility. Using the very same language he had earlier used to promote labor reform—moral minimums for the working class—Seki now put his political weight behind residential reform. The nation, argued Seki, faced the "[moral] demand [to set] a minimal [housing] standard."[169] Lending the issue even greater poignancy, as he saw it, was the fact that residential reform was not just about workers but about working families. "The advancement of a healthy citizenry," he concluded, "can be achieved only in healthy homes."[170] Initially projecting a sweeping agenda of residential reform designed to provide working-class families with decent housing in a livable environment, Seki ultimately went even further to promote a program under which industrial workers might buy homes of their own. By thus deproletarianizing this volatile class, he hoped to propel Japan toward a higher level of capitalist development.

Loathe to entrust the state and its central urban-planning apparatus with the task of implementing this reform program, Seki called on the nation's leadership to expand the jurisdiction of municipal government. In defense of this radical proposal for a shift from central to local jurisdiction over the urban-planning enterprise and over urban social reform more generally, Seki referred back to the defining experience of the Rice Riots, which had both broadened and deepened his perspective on the urban social problem and on its eradication.[171] His experience suggested that the strategic position municipal governments occupied as "public bodies" *(kōkyō dantai)* located between the state *(kokka)* and the individual *(kojin)* recommended them as effective social policymakers. "Whether we are talking about the people [in their capacity] as national citizens or [in their role] as municipal citizens," he reminded the authorities in Tokyo, "the days are past when the people would simply await orders from above."[172]

In extending this general argument about urban social policymaking to urban planning, Seki maintained that municipal authorities alone possessed the local knowledge, authority, and commitment to formulate and implement the sort of comprehensive urban plans that would relieve residential overcrowding *(misshūteki jūkyo)* and create livable cities in the process. Toward this end, he encouraged municipal governments to project a positive future for their respective cities by plotting transport networks designed to carry commuters to new exurban residential enclaves, by planning livable space in these new residential developments, and by putting up model housing and offering it to the working poor—whether for sale or for rent—at reasonable prices.[173]

Although Seki had his *idée fixe* by the early 1920s, he had yet to spin out its implications or to work out its kinks. This project would require two different methodologies: following one he would work from the general to the particular, and for the other he would do the opposite. Particularly comfortable with working from the general to the particular, as a scholar trained to think and work comparatively, Seki immersed himself immediately in the relevant European and North American literature on urban planning and residential reform. His job was made easier because he remained on the same reformist wavelength as the transnational progressive fellowship with which he had shared ideas and convictions since he was a young scholar in Europe.

As he had done in his early incarnations as a political and social economist, Seki premised his comparative studies on the conviction that Japan continued to lag behind the Europeans and Americans in its march toward social progress. Not only did he propose to use the teleological insight intrinsic in this comparative perspective to spot nascent urban problems, but he also proposed to use it as a means of identifying potentially ironclad prophylactic measures designed to nip those same problems in the bud. Armed with this modus operandi, Seki steeped himself in the rapidly growing European and North American literature on the modern city. Initially at least, he read in the work of a hodgepodge of scholars, muckrakers, philosophers, and policymakers including, but hardly limited to, George Cadbury, Patrick Geddes, Percy A. Harris, Werner Hegemann, Peter Kropotkin, Nelson P. Lewis, William Bennett Munro, John Nolen, A. C. Pigou, B. Seebohm Rowntree, Raymond Unwin, Lawrence Veiller, and Adolf Weber.[174] Seki was clearly attracted to these writers in particular—and to the exclusion of many others—because of their common concern with urban social reform.

Yet for all his abstract scholarly zeal, Seki was also seized by a keen sense of practical purpose. While he was eager to reflect on the urban social problems that plagued other modern cities and to assess their relevance to the problems that faced Osaka, he was even more eager to come up with lasting solutions. By the early 1920s, Seki had identified what he believed to be the proper parameters of urban social reform; he had also projected a vision of proper policymaking that promised success. Only when his progressivism was put to the practical test, however, would he discover whether his ideals might be lastingly inscribed on the lives of working-class Osakans.

6 The Livable City

In the mid-1910s, Seki Hajime sketched the parameters of an urban plan conceived to bring sweeping social reform to Osaka. Speaking to a group of economists in Kobe, he noted that Osaka had been the fortunate beneficiary of a "grand [urban] plan" *(endai no keikaku)* in the seventeenth century but that its leadership had since allowed the "[outer] environs of the city" to lapse into "disorder." Then he threw down the gauntlet.

Seki noted that the Tokugawa leadership had effected a dramatic spatial overhaul of Osaka. Not only had they relocated the city's temples to a designated temple district (Teramachi) on the southern boundary, but they had designated the downtown districts of Senba and Shimanouchi as Osaka's commercial center and had "taken decisive action to plot [a network] of city streets." Compared to the "extreme disorder" of peripheral districts that had been incorporated into the city in 1897, he wryly observed, the old grid-planned city with its uniform blocks was a vision of "systematic zoning." As if to sweeten this bitter pill just a bit, Seki added that Tokyo was no different than Osaka in this critical respect. In both cases, he concluded, the modern urban dilemma owed to the unfortunate combination of haphazard development by greedy landlords wedded passionately to the principle of private property and toothless town planning administered autocratically by myopic state officials sequestered in Tokyo.[1]

While Seki was concerned specifically with the Japanese version of this modern urban dilemma, he understood it as a variation on urban problems that affected all modern nations. Surveying these problems as they had been manifested in Europe and the United States, Seki concluded that modern European cities especially were subject to pressures similar to those that had hamstrung Japanese cities—pressures exerted simultaneously from within and without on local governments that were eager solely to secure the public welfare. His description of these pressures and their impact on policymaking in European and Japanese cities closely parallels Rodgers's description of the situation faced by European and American cities: "Challenged from without by the centralizing appetites of the nation-states, and hollowed out from within by demands for an ever-widening sphere for entrepreneurial liberty, the economic functions of cities shrank down to a much more limited compass."[2]

By the early 1920s, Seki had fashioned a sweeping policy proposal that addressed the modern social dilemma of urban sprawl. He urged the central government to empower the municipal authorities of Japan's largest cities to employ urban planning as a vehicle of social reform. By extending urban planning to the undeveloped land beyond the urbanized periphery and by expanding its scope to include working-class housing, argued Seki, municipal authorities might put an end to sprawl and the social problems traceable to it. Seki's reconceptualization of urban planning was path-breaking in several respects: first, in its redirection of planners' attention from the urban center to the urban periphery and, more specifically, to the undefined space between city and country; second, in its redefinition of urban planning as a housing-centered, rather than a road-centered, enterprise; and third, in its insistence that urban planning properly belonged under the control of local governments rather than of the central government.

In its focus on planning on the urban periphery, Seki's proposal arguably carried within it the seeds of an utterly new Japanese concept of space and place. After all, the land from which Seki proposed to carve sub-urban residential enclaves on the urban periphery remained nebulous and undefined. Once completely rural, it was gradually being engulfed by the city. Even as Seki was fixing his gaze on the urban hinterlands outside of Osaka, some local landowners were selling their property to industrial concerns, others were preparing plots for working-class tenement developments, and still others were selling off contiguous plots to regional land companies engaged in real estate consolidation schemes. Rather than allow landed capitalists thus to determine the direction of urbanization, developing their properties as they saw fit, Seki urged the Japanese leadership to confront the looming challenge of haphazard urbanization by empowering municipal leaders to guide suburban development through the application of urban planning.

Needless to say, this was easier said than done. Among other problems, as Henry Smith has astutely observed, "there was no conception of a settled zone between city and country which might provide the basis for a 'middle landscape ideal.' "[3] Hobbled by the same ambivalence toward cities that had crippled their Tokugawa predecessors, modern urban policymakers so routinely dichotomized the city and the country that they were hard-pressed even to imagine an alternative. Rather than standing paralyzed, an anxious spectator to creeping urbanization in Osaka, Seki resolved to take preemptive action. He crafted a proposal designed to rescue open land on the outskirts from exurban purgatory—that is, to prevent it from being swallowed up by the profit-driven hell that had already engulfed Osaka's periphery. Hoping to snatch the nebulous exurbs from the jaws of this fate, Seki proposed that they be transformed into a residential oasis of garden suburbs *(den'en kōgai)*.[4] But before he could even begin to hope for success, Seki knew that he would have to help his countrymen overcome the paralyzing dogmatism that bound them blindly to the city-country binary.

At the time Seki began to hatch his path-breaking garden-suburb proposal in the mid-1910s, most other urban policymakers remained ambivalent not only toward urban life but toward urbanization as well. Rather than confronting the realities of modern urban expansion, they pursued a policy of urban containment. Their modus operandi, such as it was, was to incorporate newly urbanized districts into the metropolitan jurisdictions of the cities they surrounded. Thus, each time the planning authorities in Tokyo authorized the expansion of Japan's largest cities, they only extended the new boundaries to the (already) urbanized edge.

In thus turning a blind eye to the process of urbanization until urban sprawl was a *fait accompli,* modern urban policymakers proved themselves incapable of fathoming, no less solving, the pressing urban problems facing the nation. It is hardly surprising that these same myopic policymakers left lands on the urban periphery undefined and left the "improvement" of these lands almost exclusively to private developers. This was the sorry legacy of Meiji urban policymaking: ostrichlike indifference to the nation's looming urban problems. In the end, it is fair to say, the Japanese leadership forfeited control over urbanization.

On the urban periphery of Osaka, as Seki discovered during his first years as deputy mayor, the combination of benign neglect on the part of urban officials and aggressive investment on the part of local landlords and real estate speculators had resulted in haphazard urban growth. As land was steadily commodified under the influence of capitalism—that is, as the principles and the practices of private property firmly took root in the Meiji Era—landowners strove to maximize the value of their real estate. By the mid-1910s, as industry and industrial laborers headed for Osaka's undeveloped exurbs, landlords went into a frenzy of haphazard residential development while land companies *(tochi gaisha)* played the real estate market, selling off some properties and sitting on others.

The undeveloped real estate that these private landlords and investors controlled on the periphery of Osaka came in various forms, including marshland, landfill, dry fields, and paddy land. Paddy land was especially plentiful on the outskirts of Osaka, where agriculture had flourished during the Tokugawa Era. For the landlords and land companies who had exercised virtually monopolistic control over many of these properties from late Meiji, industrialization represented an extraordinary business opportunity. Unrestricted by zoning requirements or building codes, these landed capitalists had gradually transformed Osaka's once-productive agricultural outskirts into a jumble of fields, farmhouses, factories, slums, and undeveloped tracts of land. Neither urban nor rural in the end, these haphazardly developing settlements on the urban periphery represented little more than the ragged urban edge *(machi hazure)* of the city.

When in the 1910s Seki began to focus his attention on Osaka's ragged urban edge, as I have suggested, he recognized the worrisome symptoms of a growing social problem. Identifying the haphazard development on Osaka's periphery as urban sprawl and associating that sprawl most explicitly with ever-worsening residential problems, he went one critical step further than any other Japanese urban policymaker of his day to sketch out a preventive solution. Looking beyond the urban periphery to the nebulous space between city and country—to what most other urban policymakers continued to regard as a kind of buffer zone between two completely distinct, and distinctly settled, communities—Seki envisioned a new manner of place. Here, he believed, progressive urban policymakers might produce space, carving out residential oases conceived at once to relieve metropolitan overcrowding and to hasten the evolution of modern urban society.

Paradoxically, Seki's garden-suburb model has been condemned by some historians as an attack on the integrity of the indigenous "urban communal order" *(toshi naibu no kyōdōtaiteki chitsujō)* and by others as an assault on the integrity of the countryside *(inaka).*[5] Unlike these blindly dogmatic critics, who have tendentiously depicted Seki as a capitalist lackey intent on eradicating tradition—urban or rural, take your pick—I will argue that the garden-suburb ideal was Seki's attempt to invent a new social tradition: working-class suburbanism. While his plans entailed the conversion of agricultural lands to housing, and although they anticipated the relocation of working-class families from urban slums to new suburban neighborhoods, what his plans threatened most, in both instances, was the hegemony of landed capitalist elites.

Those who have criticized Seki as either antirural or antiurban have tended to base their arguments on the same dangerously fallacious assumption: that the much-vaunted social traditions of rural village communalism *(mura kyōdōtai)* and urban neighborhood communalism *(machi kyōdōtai)* describe Japanese tradition with a capital T. As any number of historians and ethnographers have demonstrated, however, rural villages and urban neighborhoods were never the timeless founts of communal solidarity that so many critics have imagined.[6]

In proposing the creation of residential oases between city and country, Seki meant to introduce a new spatial ideal consonant with the overarching goal of social progress. As he saw it, this was a liberating agenda. Specifically, by asserting municipal jurisdiction over exurban real estate, Seki hoped to prevent greedy landlords and rapacious land developers from further reproducing the urban sprawl that had condemned working-class families to ghettoes on the urban periphery.

In order to pave the way for his garden-suburb idea, Seki first had to convince other urban policymakers that he had properly diagnosed urban sprawl as a social problem. He did so by putting a familiar ethical spin on the pattern of land development that had reduced the periphery of Japan's largest cities to a ragged urban edge. As we have already noted, Seki identified landlords and real estate speculators as landed capitalists bound and determined to maximize profits in the booming exurban real estate market. Much as industrialists and financiers had once projected their laissez-faire values onto Japanese factories, without so much as a peep from the authorities until the early 1900s, landlords and real estate speculators were now projecting theirs with equal impunity into unzoned, unplanned, mixed-use land development just beyond the urban periphery. The wanton, market-driven mentality of landed capitalists grated on Seki's ethical sensibilities: it was the same relentless possessive individualism that was embraced by financiers and industrialists.

As Seki saw it, urban sprawl was the spatial and architectural manifestation of the laissez-faire values that continued to dominate Japanese capitalism. Accordingly, he expressed special concern about the social irresponsibility evinced by profit-driven landowners who were willy-nilly erecting tenement housing next door to smoke-belching factories constructed by profit-hungry industrialists. In the knowledge that Japan was about to implement its new Factory Law in 1916—thus putting a brake on unchecked industrial development by introducing needed labor reform—Seki turned his attention toward the parallel imperative of residential reform for working-class families trapped in tenement neighborhoods in the shadow of polluting factories where substandard housing, inadequate infrastructure, and exorbitant rents were the rule.[7]

While a number of social reformers had similarly seized on the urban housing problem as the next great social challenge facing Japan, Seki was the first to seek the solution in urban planning. At a time when most other urban social reformers continued to treat the symptoms rather than the cause of the problem, Seki advocated prophylaxis. At a time when residential reform took the form of slum-clearance projects that amounted essentially to removal of the poor—and at a point when most urban planners remained myopically committed to the Meiji ideal of urban modernization through road building and rail laying—Seki reconceptualized urban planning as the key to urban social reform and identified working-class garden suburbs as its ideal expression. Calling on the nation's leadership to empower local municipal authorities to implement this scheme and thus secure the public welfare, Seki unwittingly set himself on a collision course with a state that may have been vaguely aware of cities as social places but that continued to treat them fundamentally as economic spaces.

TOWARD A SOCIAL ETHIC OF URBAN PLANNING

At the time Seki began to reconceptualize urban social reform in this way, the urban-planning profession in Japan was still in its infancy. Not all its practitioners were oblivious to the social applications of planning, but most remained mesmerized by the modern planning paradigms that reigned in the West—idealistic schemes that represented cities as imaginary points and lines on visionary maps, schemes that in the end reduced cities to abstract spaces. For them, the most famous models of Western urban planning were the grand designs of Paris, Vienna, Berlin, and Washington, D.C., where glorified geometers had ripped through the social fabric of existing cities.

Modern Western planners of this ilk were endeavoring to express a spatial quality described by the urbanist Kevin Lynch as "imageability": by laying grand boulevards and erecting monumental buildings defined by their visual "legibility" or "apparency," planners could create urban spaces with the sort of "visibility" that promised to enhance the exalted status of modern capital cities.[8] When successful in giving these cities appropriate legibility, as in the case of Georges Haussmann's Paris, the effect was dramatic. To quote T. J. Clark on the subject, "Part of Haussmann's purpose was to give modernity a shape, and he seemed at the time to have a measure of success in doing so; he built a set of forms in which the city appeared to be visible, even intelligible: Paris, to repeat the formula, was becoming a spectacle."[9]

While many Meiji urban planners were drawn to this visual ideal of legibility and thus endorsed projects such as the 1880s' capital plan outlined in the previous chapter, most of their Taisho successors were gripped by a different, more utilitarian version of urban modernity. Whereas the urban planners of Meiji Tokyo invoked a visual geometry that dramatized the symbolic function of the city as *teito* (the imperial capital), to borrow Henry Smith's formulation, Taisho urban planners adopted one that stressed the socioeconomic function of the city as *taito* (the great capital).[10] Thus in 1921 Fukuda Shigeyoshi, a Tokyo city engineer, could produce a functionalist fantasy of the "New Tokyo" that later served as the model for urban reconstruction following the Great Kanto Earthquake of 1923. Fukuda's map of the expanded city featured a network of new roads and intersections; he visualized the city as a nautilus-shaped entity whose roads, rails, intersections, and terminals formed concentric circles, radiating lines, and strategic points, all ostensibly designed to mimic the functional complexity of nature itself.[11]

If most urban planners remained wedded to functionalist fantasies of the city such as this one, some were beginning to awaken to the looming social import of the enterprise of urban planning. Miyake Iwao, whose ideas were introduced in the previous chapter, was one of the first to do so. His emphasis on urban deployment *(toshi sankai)* as the key to urban reform—namely, the sequential establishment of zones, transport networks, and social facilities, including housing—anticipated Seki's visionary working-class garden-suburb proposal.[12]

Yet social thinkers such as Miyake, as well as the urban-planning neophytes who had found their way into central and municipal government, were slow to translate their recognition of the social dimension of planning into a practical agenda. While their eyes were open to the social problems that plagued modern cities and though they had come to recognize that misguided urban planning had exacerbated many of these problems, Japanese urban planners rarely took that next step of advocating proactive solutions. Unlike their urban modernizing predecessors just a decade earlier, the state and municipal planning officials who made site visits to Europe and North America in the 1910s were no longer bewitched by the mere sight of Paris or New York. By the same token, however, they had not quite figured out how to assess the urban problems that lurked behind the resplendent facades of these great metropolises.

One such visitor to the West in 1911, the urban planner Yamazaki Rintarō, found himself scandalized, rather than amazed, by the ubiquity of high-rise housing in U.S. cities. Apparently alarmed at the prospect of copy-cat development in Japan, he voiced his concern that comparably dense, high-rise residential neighborhoods would spring up in Japanese cities and would seriously undermine public morality *(fūkyō)*. Yamazaki's argument, which issued from a sort of cookie-cutter cultural nationalism, raised the specter of urban alienation from traditional values. Noting ominously that the residents of high-rise housing would be physically distant from the land, Yamazaki argued that they would thus be equally distant from the social fabric of the urban community. Because the basic values of cooperation and group harmony emanated essentially from the Japanese attachment to the soil, he insisted, high-rise living posed a real and present danger to love of country *(aikokushin)* itself. While Yamazaki was quick to dismiss misguided schemes of urban development, he was slow to identify desirable ones. In the end, he did little more than suggest that the authorities disperse the urban population by means of effective transit planning.[13]

In the early 1910s, urban planners were sufficiently sanguine about the nascent urban problem *(toshi mondai)* in Japan to self-confidently predict its prevention. Their self-confidence was born of much the same myopia that had earlier enabled state officials to dismiss the urgency of the labor problem. Having acknowledged the mistakes made in Western cities, they believed, officials in Japanese cities might short-circuit the urban problem. By the late 1910s, fortunately, many Japanese urban planners had come to recognize their earlier self-confidence for what it was: hubris. They were shocked out of their smug complacency by one simple fact of Japanese urban life: the looming specter of crippling social problems.

Many of the urban planners who reluctantly acknowledged the existence of an urban problem at this juncture began to look at the planning enterprise through new eyes. Introducing social reform into the equation, they altered the key concept around which urban planning had revolved. In place of urban economic efficiency, they began to speak of urban social reform. Accordingly, they also articulated a new ideal: urban reform *(toshi kairyō)*. One self-styled urban reformer, the planner Nakagawa Masajirō, produced a wish list of urban infrastructural changes in 1914. These included paved streets, sewers, waterlines, garbage collection, parks, libraries, public halls, and museums. Convinced that Japan had entered "the revolutionary age of the city," Nakagawa was eager to bring its cities up to code. He articulated a baldly nationalistic justification for urban reform, maintaining that cities should set a national cultural standard *(ikkoku bunka no hyōchū)*. Appealing in the end to the chauvinistic impulses of his countrymen, Nakagawa reminded them that foreigners were so openly contemptuous of Japanese cities that they saw only "houses like pigsties and muddy oceans for streets."[14]

By the mid-1910s, mainstream urban planners such as Ikeda Hiroshi and Kataoka Yasushi began to articulate a more sophisticated social ideology of urban planning. Ikeda, who was named head of the Home Ministry's newly formed City Planning Section in 1918, came out strongly in support of residential reform as the crux of urban reform. Observing that city dwellers were the palpable force behind urban progress, he linked economic advancement directly to social reform. "Urban planning [should] fortify the foundation of urban prosperity," argued Ikeda, "by advancing a systematic plan to place urban collective life in an orderly spatial framework."[15]

As chairman of the national commission charged with drafting Japan's first urban-planning law, Ikeda wielded considerable influence within the emerging planning establishment.[16] And he used this influence to promote a distinctly social agenda. Although he was joined on the commission by like-minded reformers such as Iinuma Kazumi and Seki himself, Ikeda faced an uphill battle. As Iinuma would later observe, socially minded planners met resistance from all sides. Not only did the Construction Section of the Home Ministry claim jurisdiction over urban-planning projects, but officials within the Agriculture and Commerce and Finance Ministries resisted the very enterprise of urban planning.[17]

In his opening remarks to the commission, Ikeda spoke of the Urban Planning Law as a sweeping social measure. He cited the need for zoning, transport networks, building codes, health regulations, and public facilities. "City planning is thinking about the future conditions of development in [our] important cities," insisted Ikeda, "and about how we should conduct urban management."[18] Writing in 1919, he stressed the special importance of incorporating surrounding villages into the metropolis so that urban planners might at last project a comprehensive land policy *(tochi seisaku)*. Toward this end, Ikeda encouraged urban planners to begin with regional land surveys and to use them to devise plans that designated distinct urban-planning districts *(toshi keikaku kuiki)*.[19]

Only after scrutinizing land-survey maps and thus familiarizing themselves with the functional and spatial characteristics of the specific cities under consideration, maintained Ikeda, could urban planners effectively plot future development. Wary of the predilection among urban planners to rely so heavily on maps that they read the life out of city space, he urged them to remind themselves that they were ultimately in the business of rescuing people from the hazards of urban industrialization.

Ikeda's sense of social purpose found expression in the Urban Planning Law itself, which was finally promulgated in 1919. Its opening clause set the tone of urban planning as a forward-looking social enterprise: "This law states that we must carry out plans to preserve public peace and to advance social welfare in perpetuity through urban planning, by which we mean necessary facilities in such areas as transportation, health, security, and the economy."[20] Consistent with this emphasis, Ikeda introduced a social agenda for urban planning that included zoning, park construction, and fire districting.[21] Yet, in many respects, Ikeda still remained tied to the conventional categories of urban planning. Paradoxically, residential reform figured prominently in his urban-planning program, but people did not. When Ikeda spoke of overcrowding, he spoke of it in abstract spatial terms, portraying urban planning as a means of dispersing an anonymous urban population and "occasioning the consolidation of urban life."[22]

While Ikeda succeeded in lending urban planning a sociospatial focus, Kataoka Yasushi managed to place people in the picture as well. This Osaka-based architect was the first urban-planning professional to lend social depth to the Japanese planning agenda. Like Seki, Kataoka was fascinated by Ebenezer Howard's concept of garden cities. Moved by the idealism of Western garden-city theorists and practitioners alike, who had endeavored to help "workers surmount [the problem of] low wages" by providing them with affordable housing in a livable environment, Kataoka resolved to adopt and adapt the idea to Japan.[23]

Rather than attempting to transplant garden cities to Japan, Kataoka gleaned ideas from the garden-city experience in England for a model of urban housing policy *(toshi kaya seisaku)* adapted to local conditions. After making a detailed study of living conditions in the English garden city of Letchworth, Kataoka concluded that the main beneficiaries of garden-city development were working-class commuters who had been afforded an "ideal way of life in the urban domain." He was especially impressed by the provisions that had been made for inexpensive housing in Letchworth, noting happily that these provisions had stimulated the construction of model municipal housing elsewhere in England.[24]

Turning his attention to Japan, Kataoka lamented the lack of "systematic [urban] site planning" and extracted from the garden-city model a potential solution to the residential problems plaguing big cities. Rather than exhorting planners to develop self-sufficient garden cities beyond metropolises, as garden-city devotees had, Kataoka encouraged them to plant garden suburbs around them. He echoed Seki's thoughts on the same subject and, writing at roughly the same time, envisioned a transformation of the nebulous space between city and country. Advocating the production of a livable human environment and, more specifically, residential enclaves for the industrial working class, Kataoka floated the concept of suburban garden cities (kinkō den'en toshi). In such places, he argued, the poor might be afforded decent, inexpensive housing in a healthy atmosphere of light, air, and open space.[25]

As he refined his concept of suburban garden cities in the early 1920s, Kataoka wrote effusively of the need to employ urban planning in the service of a sweeping social ideal: "happy urban life." Here, he went well beyond Ikeda's abstract vision of urban planning as a means of achieving the spatial dispersion of city dwellers, poignantly portraying such planning instead as the "skeleton" of the urban social body. Kataoka thus added a dimension to urban planning that was conspicuously absent from Ikeda's approach: the pulse of human life. While Ikeda viewed urban planning as the technical means of dispersing a faceless population, Kataoka viewed it as the social key to "elevating cultural life."[26]

Kataoka's new approach to the enterprise of urban planning promised, most importantly, to liberate it from the map-bound, two-dimensional straitjacket of city improvement (shiku kaisei). Earlier, city-improvement advocates such as Yamaguchi Hanroku in Osaka had reflexively flattened urban space, relying on grid maps to plot new roads and rails across the peopleless space of the city-as-object. While more sophisticated urban planners such as Ikeda Hiroshi remapped the urban grid, designating residential zones as well as economic conduits, they continued to render the city as an abstract urban landscape. In his reconceptualization of the enterprise of urban planning, by contrast, Kataoka not only brought people into the picture but drew an animated, three-dimensional portrait of the residential enclaves in which they might one day live.

Trained not as a planner but as an architect, Kataoka naturally depicted the built environment in three dimensions. But, driven increasingly by the impulse toward urban social reform, he depicted the suburban garden cities central to his urban vision as animated human settlements. Inexorably drawn to a new paradigm of urban planning that focused on residential reform, Kataoka was impelled to integrate land (tochi), buildings *(kenbutsu),* and people *(hito)* into his site designs. If this integration lent social and spatial depth to his plans, ultimately his urban planning gained social meaning because of the ethical ideal injected into the whole. In designing suburban garden cities as havens from the manifold social problems of big-city life, Kataoka voiced his firm commitment to the preservation of Japanese family life.[27]

Given his bracing urban vision, it is not surprising that Kataoka became one of Osaka's leading urban planners in the Taisho period. Nor is it surprising that he worked closely with Seki Hajime to transform the industrial metropolis of Osaka into a livable city.[28] At roughly the same historical moment in the mid-1910s, these like-minded urban reformers began working from different directions toward what would turn out to be remarkably similar visions of urban residential reform along garden-suburb lines: Seki building urban planning into his urban social reformism, Kataoka building urban social reformism into his urban planning.

Owing to their innovative thinking, Kataoka and Seki soon found themselves at the forefront of a growing national movement within the nascent planning establishment to identify a sociospatial solution to urban sprawl. In the 1920s, urban planners emerged to sing the praises of urban planning as a social enterprise. One such enthusiast was Miyao Shunji, who in 1921 challenged urban planners to alter their ideological priorities. Decrying the influence of bourgeois utilitarianism, Miyao observed that Japanese urban planners had typically held up Paris as a model. To the degree that they had thereby identified convenience and beauty *(benri to bikan)* as their objectives, however, they had ignored the rightful beneficiaries of urban planning: "To the extent that the pride of cities has increased, the welfare of people as a whole has been diminished. To the extent that streets have been widened, residences have been reduced to tenements. And to the extent that central neighborhoods have been beautified, the back streets and edges of the city have been divided."[29]

In defense of his radical reconceptualization of urban planning as a social enterprise, Miyao poignantly observed that Paris had more parks than any other city in the world but that it also had the world's most crowded living conditions. Pointing out that urban planners in the West had already transcended the limitations of the Parisian model, Miyao called on their Japanese counterparts to do the same. He urged them specifically to engage in urban planning as social policymaking. "Urban planning," concluded Miyao, "means making cities healthy, convenient, safe, economical, and pleasant."[30]

As urban planners became increasingly aware of their social mission, they began to elaborate notions of the city that echoed ideas Seki had casually introduced as early 1909. Depicting the city as a living organism, Kishi Kazuta went so far as to characterize urban planners as sociospatial chiropractors. In the end, he argued, they needed to "tune the urban form and its various functions according to biological principles."[31]

While few urbanists adhered to such literalistic interpretations of the city as a social subject, many employed organic concepts of the city to promote a new environmentalist perspective. The journalist Tochiuchi Yoshitane, for example, urged planners to "create an ideal environment in cities of the future that would harmonize the whole."[32] Characterizing contemporary cities as artificial environments hostile to nature, Tochiuchi complained that city dwellers themselves had introduced problems such as residential overcrowding and atmospheric pollution into urban life. In the process, he noted sadly, they had sapped the human spirit of its energy. Accordingly, Tochiuchi encouraged urban planners to restore the environmental balance by transforming Japan's sprawling cities into organic bodies *(yūkutai)*. Once they had restored order to the artificial infrastructure of Japanese cities—to the railroads, streets, sewers, wires, and other accouterments of modern urban life—Tochiuchi encouraged urban planners to bring nature back into the urban environment in the form of parks. Only then, he insisted, would they finally secure the welfare of city dwellers.[33]

By the 1920s, Japanese urban planners were mesmerized by such environmentalist perspectives of urban planning. Firmly convinced that Japan's urban problems were primarily social in nature and that the solution to these problems lay in the (re)creation of livable cities, many felt compelled to identify a sociospatial paradigm equal to the looming urban challenges that clearly lay ahead. Casting about for ideas, many planners latched onto the garden-city model and dressed it up in Japanese garb. One youth group in Nagoya, for example, introduced a wild new adaptation of Howard's utopian idea. Deeming urban (over)crowding *(toshi shūchū)* the greatest source of social distress in big cities, they encouraged Japanese to abandon the idea of urban renovation and instead to seek the creation of "ideal cities" *(risō toshi)*. Cleverly adapting the garden-city ideal to the realities of heavy land use (and high land values) in urban Japan, these young visionaries proposed to create "mountain forest cities" *(sanrin toshi)* on the underutilized hillsides of the Japanese uplands.[34]

Yūge Shichirō cast his plea for garden cities in the form of a mock dialogue:

A: We don't have them [garden cities] in Japan yet, do we?

B: Well, there are places that look like them. But, in every case, companies have set them up simply to provide their employees with housing. And they're only operated for [the company's] convenience anyway. In their appearance and in their [actual] facilities, such as running water and sewers, these [places] are exceedingly puerile. You really can't go so far as to call them garden cities.[35]

While Yūge and others heaped criticism on the so-called garden cities that had been constructed by private developers in Japan, several of which are examined in the final section of this chapter, Kōno Makoto hoped nonetheless to sell the idea as a model of popular urban planning *(minshū no toshi keikaku)*. He praised garden cities as ideal places that combined the "convenience of the city" with the "livability of the countryside." Characterizing the garden-city cause as a revolutionary movement, Kōno proposed to find a way of adapting its ideals to the needs of the Japanese metropolis. Like Seki, he considered cities "centers of contemporary civilization" and was firmly committed to their reinvention.[36]

In his visionary proposal, Kōno advocated both the greening *(den'enka)* of the city and the citification *(toshika)* of the countryside. Calling for the establishment of city parks and the "liberation of private gardens," on the one hand, he championed the creation of satellite cities *(eisei toshi)* on the other. Against the myopia of those plodding urban planners who continued to work at reorganizing the old city rather than planning the new one, Kōno envisioned the creation of satellite cities that might serve as residential havens for the poor and that might become humane places in the process. Like Seki, he was dubious of the "aristocratic" and "capitalistic" forms of urban planning previously practiced in Japan.[37] His was a supremely organic vision of the city as a home.

While Kōno was a bold urban visionary, he was an utterly impractical social reformer. Rather than producing an analytical justification for his radical position, he provided a poetic evocation of it. Likening cities to the human body at one point, he waxed wildly philosophical about their common anatomy:

The city is just like a living organism
Transport facilities are its hands and legs
Telegrams and telephones are its nervous system
Railroad stations are its mouth
Public services are its heart

Roads are its skeleton
Houses are its joints
City Hall is its brain

Well said!
Truly, the city is alive
And it has been organically unified
Just as Tolstoy once proclaimed
Man lives by love
Yes, yes, a thousand times yes!

But how does the city stay alive?
This is an interesting problem
It is [also] a deep mystery[38]

In the same book, Kōno wrote an equally enigmatic prose poem evoking the deficiencies of Japanese cities:

In Japanese cities
There are passageways but no streets
There are means of shipping but not of transport
There are wide open spaces but no parks
There is land but no residential space
There is expansion but no growth[39]

If the dreamer in Kōno thus enabled him to embrace a powerful vision of the city of the future, the poet in him left that vision immersed in riddles and platitudes.

Like Kōno, Seki was driven by a bold vision of the metropolis that ultimately came to include the creation of satellite cities. Yet unlike Kōno, Seki was able to distinguish between utopianism and idealism. He demonstrated this distinction most convincingly in his critique of the popular garden-city idea. Revisiting many of the criticisms that he had first offered in the early 1910s, Seki made them more emphatically and also more provocatively in the 1920s. This time, when he branded the garden-city idea an example of backward-looking utopianism, he traced its roots directly to the utopian socialist Edward Bellamy. While Seki applauded the commitment to urban reconstruction *(toshi kaizō)* and social reconstruction *(shakai kaizō)* that had impelled Howard to envision the creation of self-contained, self-sufficient, owner-occupied towns, he also bemoaned Howard's utter lack of realism.[40]

Harshly criticizing Howard for "deny[ing] the necessity of the metropolis,"[41] Seki endeavored to put the story of big cities back where it belonged: at the center of the modern narrative of national progress. He argued, as he had many times before, that big cities represented the fulfillment of Japan's promise as a modern industrial nation. Contrasting these dynamic urban communities to the anemic rural towns with which Howard proposed to replace them, Seki saw simply no comparison. Not only were garden cities undesirable substitutes for big cities, he insisted, they were economically infeasible as well.[42]

Here, Seki placed himself in the center of a stream of thought about great cities and progress that flowed across continents in the early twentieth century. Not only did the transnational fellowship of progressives share his belief that cities were at the heart of industrial capitalism—and that, as Rodgers puts it, "the capitalist city manifested everywhere its family resemblances"[43]—but they shared his ambivalence toward modern urbanization. If the modern city generated show-stopping innovations and untold wealth, after all, in the process it also sowed the seeds of social discord. Thus, the modern city was both a showcase of progress and a cauldron of cultural conflict. As a social entity, it was difficult even to grasp: "Though a place of fractures and fragments," Rodgers reminds us, "the city was at the same time an enormous collectivity."[44]

Like many other progressives of his day, Seki embraced the social complexities of the modern city. While he was aware that industrial metropolises such as Osaka were hothouses of class abrasion—and learned firsthand from his experience during the Rice Riots of 1918 that it did not take much in the close quarters of the crowded metropolis to ignite class conflict—he also identified such cities with social progress. From this perspective, Howard's ideal of the garden city looked regressive rather than progressive.

If Seki was harshly critical of Howard's garden-city idea, he was even more critical of those in Japan who had appropriated it and marketed it for profit. He noted paradoxically that the term *garden city* had been adopted by real estate concerns whose objectives were utterly antithetical to those articulated by Howard. These "Garden City companies," as they often called themselves, were interested not in creating self-sufficient, publicly owned cities but in promoting suburban, middle-class developments where rising real estate values and well-heeled clients would ensure them huge profits.[45]

Despite his misgivings, Seki was not inclined to throw the baby out with the bathwater. While wandering about in the confusing conceptual space between Howard's utopian idea and the cynical cast put on it by Japanese real estate concerns, he experienced something approaching a revelation. His hybrid idea, which sprang from a deep-seated desire to thwart urban sprawl, resonated at once with the garden suburbanism of the British urban planner Raymond Unwin, the industrial suburbanism of the U.S. regional planner Graham Romeyn Taylor, and the urban evolutionism of the Scottish social thinker Patrick Geddes.[46] Out of this congeries of ideas and influences sprang a visionary concept: working-class garden suburbs.

Seki credited Howard with the insight that impelled him to abandon the city-country dichotomy that was once a commandment of his progressive creed. Catching the American-spawned new wave of regional planning that had recently made a splash in Japan, he opened himself up to a new perspective on metropolitan progress.[47] Rather than building self-contained, self-sufficient garden cities designed expressly to defy change, as Howard had urged, Seki encouraged his countrymen to celebrate urban growth (seichō).

Even as he repudiated Howard's ahistoricism, he was searching out new models of urban progress. In the spirit of historical idealism, he encouraged Japanese urban planners to invoke sweeping ideals (risō) and to articulate cogent guiding principles (shidō genri) capable of guiding them toward the realization of a forward-looking model of urban planning in the service of urban social reform. Equally important, he called on urban policymakers to seize the reins of reformist leadership by fashioning innovative proposals "generated from the ideas of great men and [based on] contemporary ideological currents."[48]

Seki professed to have developed in precisely this way his own approach to urban planning—an approach that he now characterized as "housing-centered pragmatism" (jūtaku hon'i jitsuyōshugi). Distinguishing this approach both from the "avenue-centered aestheticism" of the urban planning establishment and from the "utopianism" of garden-city theorists,[49] Seki called for "urban planning along garden-city lines" (den'en tōryū no toshi keikaku). By creating satellite cities (eisei toshi) and garden suburbs (den'en kōgai) on the outskirts of the metropolis, he maintained, Japan might be able at last to humanize the city.[50] Focusing his attention on the "cities where we lead our daily lives" (wareware no seikatsu suru toshi) and declaring it his primary purpose to transform them into livable cities (sumigokochiyoki toshi),[51] Seki identified urban planning as the key to success.

Here, he made an explicit distinction between urban construction (toshi kōchiku) and urban planning (toshi keikaku). Urban construction, observed Seki, had constituted urban planning under the old Meiji rubric of city improvement, in which cities consisted of roads, streetcar lines, and canals. But this "anachronistic, French-influenced" model of urban planning had hopelessly confused means and ends. Contending that true urban planning was not merely about constructing public works *(kō no shisetsu)* but also about regulating the uses of private property under the legal and administrative umbrellas of zoning regulations *(yōto chiiki no kitei)* and building codes *(kenchikubutsu hō)*, Seki declared that urban planning in the future would need to merge *(kondō)* urban construction with these basic considerations. Once urban policymakers learned to distinguish the fundamental objectives *(mokuteki)* of urban planning from its practical substance *(hontai)*, he concluded, they would have no trouble maintaining the integrity of the enterprise. Pragmatically speaking, this plan meant producing the material, legal, and administrative infrastructure for livable cities.[52]

In the early 1920s, as he detailed his new urban planning agenda of housing-centered pragmatism, Seki was often compelled to convert other urban policymakers to the cause. Rather than eliding their concerns and simply proclaiming his own, he took to task the old Meiji paradigm of city improvement. Seizing first on the controversial issue of urban renewal, an enterprise that doubtless made Meiji urban modernizers feel like social reformers, Seki took pains to demonstrate that slum clearance was an ineffectual strategy for residential reform. While it eradicated old slums, he observed, it simply sent residents scurrying to find cheap housing elsewhere and thus effectively created new slums. Rather than simply ripping down tenement housing, urban policymakers, according to Seki, should provide new housing as well and should set "minimal standard requirements" for its design and construction.[53] In this and in other aspects of his new urban-planning ideology, Seki urged urban policymakers to strike a balance between the treatment and the prevention of urban social problems.[54]

In casting residential reform as an essential element of urban planning, Seki knew that he would have to overcome the objections of conservatives within the urban-planning establishment. Pulling out the stops, he scrutinized the French conventions that had worked their way into Japanese urban planning. He reminded urban planners that the highly vaunted French aestheticism was actually rooted in nationalism, noting that Haussmann's majestic plan for Paris had issued from his desire to create a capital city symbolic of imperial authority.[55] The visitor to Paris, asserted Seki, is bound to be impressed by its wide, tree-lined avenues, its parks, plazas, and grand architecture. But, describing this effect as superficial rather than practical, Seki posed a gnawing question: Where in this majestic metropolis does the city dweller fit?[56]

Having conjured up a Parisian image of broad avenues flanked by monumental buildings, Seki reminded his readers that the poor could be found behind these majestic landmarks in squalid tenements. He questioned the value of an urban aesthetic that served the interests only of rulers and aristocrats, and he questioned as well the Parisian tendency to restrict planning to the urban core. Urging Japanese urban planners to relinquish French-influenced aestheticism and avenue-ism in favor of British-influenced residentialism and pragmatism, Seki called for the introduction of a popular urban-planning aesthetic premised on the interests of the social collectivity.[57]

Knowing that many socially conscious Japanese urban planners already shared his reservations about French aestheticism and avenue-ism, Seki encouraged them to remain skeptical as well of the highly vaunted British alternative of housing-centered planning.[58] If there was much to be praised in the British example, he argued, there was also much to criticize. Seki expressed admiration for British urban policymakers who had successfully employed urban planning "to induce the construction of decent, healthy housing," and he praised them more generally for rejecting French concentrationism (shūchūshugi) in favor of British dispersionism (bunsanshugi) and committing themselves to the creation of a livable suburban residential environment. But he hastened as well to remind Japanese urban policymakers that, just as French planners ignored the suburbs, British planners ignored the urban core.[59] By relegating urban planning to site planning, insisted Seki, the English had substituted disunity for centralism.[60]

Seki used these French and English examples of urban planning to illustrate the dangers of dogmatism. Counseling Japanese urban policymakers to learn from the mistakes of their European counterparts, he left them with a deceptively difficult assignment. "We must survey the contemporary situation in Japan," Seki insisted, "and move forward with plans appropriate to it."[61] He meant, of course, that urban policymakers had spent far too long modeling Japanese policies on those of the West. It had come time, he believed, for Japan to confront its urban problems on its own terms.

Seki's challenge to Japanese urban policymakers—that they begin producing policies of their own rather than reflexively domesticating those generated by their Western counterparts—resonated with a task he had clearly set himself. He was no longer the neophyte who engaged the urban question in 1909 by counting the ways that New York was superior to Tokyo; he was a deputy mayor of Osaka committed to transforming the Capital of Smoke into a livable city.

While Seki continued to learn from the West, he no longer reflexively objectified the Western experience as the embodiment of progress. Perhaps because he was no longer a scholar/consultant but a policymaker in his own right, Seki suddenly found himself at a critical methodological crossroads: particularizing from the general, as he always had, but now generalizing from the particular as well. As he was increasingly sensitized to the stark realities of the urban experience in Japan, it would seem, Seki awakened to his own intellectual naivete. While he had once generated reform platforms through a relatively straightforward process of cultural borrowing, Seki now approached the process more subtly and deliberately in appreciation of Osaka's dynamism as a complex and often contentious urban community. His tumultuous experience as deputy mayor surely accentuated this impression, and his public responsibility to make practical policy lent the position even greater gravity. Here at last was the chance that Seki claimed to have been waiting for when he signed on as deputy mayor of Osaka—a golden opportunity to change the world—and yet he often found himself overwhelmed.

One further reason for Seki's change of heart with respect to cultural borrowing bears mentioning: the shock of the so-called Great War in Europe. Not unlike U.S. intellectuals, many Japanese were at once disillusioned and energized by the Great War. On the one hand, it compelled them to reevaluate the universal doctrine of progress that had pointed for so long to Western Europe as the fount of modern civilization. On the other hand, it offered both the United States and Japan a remarkable opportunity to reap the profits of industrial innovation and production. As early as November 1914, Seki spoke of the grave responsibility faced by the people of Japan *(kokumin)* to seize their own destiny by making a hundred-year plan.[62] In the years that followed, as he continued to cultivate his own unique brand of urban progressivism with Japan's glorious future in mind, he looked more and more to U.S. cities and American urban theorists for inspiration.

For all the idealism, perspicacity, and enthusiasm that Seki invoked in the cause of urban social reform, he was forced to acknowledge that his little piece of the world remained remarkably intractable. Transforming the Capital of Smoke into a livable city proved to be a far greater challenge than he ever imagined. In this very real world, change was hard won. As Seki pursued his dream for Osaka in the early 1920s, the quest found him traveling to Tokyo on a regular basis for urban-planning commission meetings and for audiences with the Home Ministry and Finance Ministry officials who wielded central authority over local urban planning. In Osaka, it found him justifying plans before the Municipal Assembly, negotiating with landowners over easements and eminent domain, and debating the merits of urban incorporation with local elites in the exurbs. In other words, although Seki found himself on the wider stage of action that he had coveted on the eve of his appointment, it remained to be seen whether his presence would make a difference.

THE CREATION OF GREATER OSAKA

Ultimately, behind the garden suburb/satellite city proposal that Seki generated in the early 1920s lay a conviction he had held for nearly a decade: that slum life was one of "the greatest illnesses of modern civilization."[63] While he bemoaned the plight of all slum dwellers, he was scandalized by the experience of the working poor. As productive members of a modern industrial society whose potential was limitless, the working classes, Seki maintained, were entitled not merely to their fair share of the profits but to the decent lives that this share should rightly secure for them. Instead, however, they were subjected at work and at home to injustices that threatened the very foundation of public morality *(fūkyō).*[64]

The home lives of working-class families were disrupted most, maintained Seki, by the disorderliness, overcrowding, and exorbitance of their slum neighborhoods. Rather than clearing these slums and fueling a working-class diaspora, however, he proposed to right the social wrongs that had reduced the working classes to penury and misery. Most urban social reformers were eager primarily to provide worker households with decent homes conducive to family life, but Seki upped the social ante considerably. Consistent with his long-held belief that class differences should be celebrated as a sign of continuing social progress rather than mourned as a signal of impending social warfare, he set out to ensure that Japan would realize its social promise. If this policy meant stipulating a "civil minimum" and thus guaranteeing the working classes their due, the civil minimum that Seki endorsed was considerably less minimal than one might imagine. Simply put, Seki called for the deproletarianization of the urban proletariat.

In practical terms, Seki proposed offering the working classes decent housing at an affordable price—ideally, housing for purchase that would transform them from hapless tenants into proud homeowners.[65] If Seki ultimately came to advocate the creation of garden suburbs as residential havens for the working poor, he worked his way there from one basic insight: that residential dispersion was the key to thoroughgoing housing reform.[66] From the moment that he articulated this *idée fixe* in the early 1910s, Seki saw cities through new eyes; and, from the moment he entered Osaka, these new eyes began sizing up the exurban landscape for its residential promise.

By Seki's lights, Osaka possessed the potential to help "perfect" modern Japanese society by literally producing a place where the working classes might realize their destiny. Just as Napoleon III had projected his imperial values into urban space when he commissioned his majestic plan for Paris,[67] and just as Austrian liberals had projected their bourgeois values into the public center of *fin-de-siècle* Vienna,[68] Seki yearned to project his working-class values into the "empty" exurban space on the outskirts of Osaka.

Such a vision required a plan, of course, and Seki worked tirelessly in the early 1920s to generate one. As deputy mayor of Osaka, he knew the distinct advantage of working with a municipal assembly that had gone on record by the late 1880s as an ardent advocate of rational urban planning. By 1916, several local newspapers had added their support, declaring urban planning the foundation of urban improvement and residential reform its handmaiden.[69] By 1918, Seki was riding the crest of a popular wave of support for innovative solutions to the social problems spawned by urban sprawl.

As Seki soon discovered, however, municipal policymakers faced a wide variety of political, financial, and technical obstacles. Challenged to generate a comprehensive urban plan capable of fulfilling Osaka's immediate and future needs, he finally found a practical application for his scholarly expertise in railway transit. Seki was given responsibility for the expansion of Osaka's already-extensive streetcar network, and he took this opportunity to refine and to humanize the *Verkehrswirtschaftlicht* perspective on national progress that he had embraced as a young economist. Injecting the pulse of urban life into his assessment of urban transit and linking this agenda to his sociospatial objective of residential dispersion, Seki ultimately crafted a multifaceted intraurban and interurban transit model for Osaka that was fundamentally designed to shuttle commuters between work and home.[70]

From 1917, as Japan prepared to draft its first urban-planning legislation, Seki was given the opportunity to help set the national agenda. Appointed chairman of Osaka's newly formed Survey Association for Urban Reform Planning (Toshi Kairyō Keikaku Chōsakai), he was appointed the following year to the Home Ministry's Urban Planning Survey Commission. As chairman of the Association, Seki spent over a year setting the agenda and laying the groundwork for Osaka's first modern urban plan.[71] Aside from meeting regularly with the Association's membership to develop the plan, he consulted frequently with local businessmen and technical advisors to ascertain its viability.[72] By 1918, Seki had guided a provisional proposal past the Osaka City Council.[73]

Representing Osaka on the national Urban Planning Survey Commission, Seki was offered the opportunity to actively promote his social perspective on urban planning.[74] By the time he left for the Commission's initial meeting in June 1918, he was clearly eager to promote his new agenda. He confided to his diary that the proceedings began on a sour note, as the members were regaled with "empty theory" at the morning session. Not until an engineer from the Tokyo city government arrived in the afternoon to discuss technical issues related to site planning was Seki assuaged.[75]

In the Commission meetings that followed, Seki spearheaded discussion of three important issues directly related to his particular urban-planning agenda: land readjustment *(kukaku seiri)* in the exurbs, public-funding models, and the sequence of project implementation. Land readjustment, which involved the spatial rationalization of undeveloped and partially developed lands, mainly in districts on the periphery, was vital to Seki's plan. This was the legal mechanism by which planning officials could mandate the reorganization of land to correct existing problems and to prevent future ones. Since it was under the rubric of land readjustment that planning officials laid out residential grids, for example, it should come as no surprise that Seki raised the question of jurisdiction at the first Commission meeting.[76]

Equally important to Seki's urban-planning agenda for Osaka was the issue of funding. Although the central government continued to consider urban planning a vital national concern and planned to keep administration highly centralized, its representatives on the Commission hoped nonetheless to shift most of the financial burden to local authorities. Inoue Tomoichi raised the issue indirectly at the Commission's first meeting by suggesting that "funding issues were [a reflection of the larger] financing issue." During that convocation, Seki voiced his agreement with Inoue about the importance of the issue of finance.[77]

When the issue came up for serious discussion during the Commission's second set of meetings, however, Seki took a relatively hard line. As deputy mayor of Osaka, he was understandably wary of the central government's intention to retain administrative authority over local planning projects and yet to shift the financial burden to municipal governments. Speaking diplomatically to the issue, he asked the Commission's members to consider it from the perspective of the local authorities. Seki proposed a balanced strategy of local financing and national subsidies, making his point poignantly by proposing a critical change in terminology. Rather than calling on the state to provide financial supplements *(hojū)*, he urged the Commission to call for state subsidies *(hojō)*. The distinction was important: While a system of supplements promised to take the central government completely off the financial hook, even as it wielded autocratic authority over the planning enterprise, subsidies carried the strong connotation of state responsibility in the form of regular and proportionate contributions.[78]

Finally, Seki addressed the important issue of sequence in the implementation of urban plans, fully aware that this sequence often reflected the priorities of policymakers. Observing at the outset that "designated [planning] districts" *(yotei chiiki)* were not the same as zones *(zōn)*—that designated planning districts were locations designated for surveying and development, while zones were the blocks and grids of neighborhoods—he counseled the members of the Commission to consider the order and process of planning. The most rational sequence, insisted Seki, was first to designate and survey planning districts, second to plot transit networks, and third to lay out zones—that is, blocks and neighborhoods.[79]

As a draft of the Urban Planning Law neared completion in July 1918, Seki proposed that special committees be formed to consult with experts about its provisions. At this same meeting, he was delegated to conduct a comprehensive review of the draft legislation and to investigate the process of enactment.[80] This special assignment suggests that Seki had assumed some prominence within the Commission, and other evidence points to the same conclusion. If Watanabe Shun'ichi is correct in tracing the social agenda of the Urban Planning Law directly to Osaka's Survey Association for Urban Reform Planning, then we might confidently conclude that Seki was one of its intellectual godfathers, for, as mentioned earlier, Seki chaired that important local commission.[81] While we can only guess at what marginalia Seki produced in the legal critique that he sent to the national commission's chair, Ikeda Hiroshi, at the end of July 1918, it is reasonable to assume that he massaged the language of the law yet one more time in an effort to address the ethical and practical concerns that motivated him as an Osaka urban policymaker.

Back in Osaka, where he could exert greater control over the spirit and the letter of urban planning, Seki was much more explicit in promoting his particular ideological agenda. In a public address delivered on the eve of his appointment to Osaka's Survey Association for Urban Reform Planning, he detailed his views on the subject. Noting that Japan had a long history of urban planning, he made polite reference to Kyoto's heralded grid and to castle-town districting in the Tokugawa Era. Not surprisingly, however, he reserved his greatest praise for Osaka. Here, in the seventeenth century, Seki recalled, the lord Matsudaira Tadaaki had been sanctioned by the shogun to create a vast commercial capital. Working from the compact grid laid out by Toyotomi Hideyoshi's surveyors in 1583, Matsudaira redrew city blocks, widened streets, and developed a new temple district. In Seki's words, he implemented an "imposingly uniform urban plan under which city districts were properly laid out."[82]

Paradoxically, continued Seki, this splendid example of seventeenth-century urban planning fell victim to economic progress. While newly urbanized districts (shinchi) had been carefully laid out and brought within the city limits in the Tokugawa Era, they had been left to languish in the Meiji Era. "The districts carved out by people in the past were carefully divided on a checkerboard basis," he lamented. "But in recent years those areas on the outskirts [to which urbanization] has spread have not been planned at all." While the steady development of early modern cities had been carefully monitored by the authorities, concluded Seki, the explosive growth of their modern incarnations had gone unchecked and unplanned.[83]

Historically speaking, Seki traced this disturbing pattern of urbanization to the baneful influence of modern values such as individualism and laissez-faireism. Noting that the story of Western cities was similarly tragic, he pointedly recalled the impact of the French Enlightenment on the Industrial Revolution. If modernity had sprung from the dual impact of technological advancement and occupational freedom, argued Seki, so too had urban sprawl.[84] In Western cities a century before, as in Osaka right then, these modern forces had combined to produce a massive influx of industry and workers.

The most disturbing aspect of this emerging phenomenon of urban sprawl, according to Seki, was the victimization of urban newcomers (shinraisha). He portrayed the plight of this growing urban proletariat (mushisan kaikyū) as the dark side (ankokumen) of modern urban life. Repeating his common refrain that the unrestrained laissez-faireism and individualism of landowners on the outskirts of town had led inevitably to the rise of residential problems in growing slums, Seki traced the looming social problems of Japanese cities to unregulated land use. "Individualism and laissez-faire may have caused commerce and industry to advance and may have prompted the expansion of cities," he declared, "but because this has not been accompanied by any regulation of land use, great violence has been done to the metropolis." Contrasting Osaka's orderly core to its ragged periphery, he bemoaned the "formless confusion" of land development on the outskirts of Osaka. The edge of Osaka, observed Seki, had come to resemble a "tattered rag."[85]

After diagnosing the problems faced by Osaka, Seki spelled out the solution: a course of urban planning that called for expansion of the city's boundaries, enforcement of new building codes, implementation of land-use zoning, and establishment of infrastructural improvement fees.[86] Most striking about this urban planning model is that it only gestured toward the treatment of existing urban problems and aimed straight at the prevention of future ones. As Seki saw it, urban planning was mainly about creating the new metropolis and only secondarily about renovating the old city: " 'Urban planning' asks how best we can design the city. It asks how we can eliminate inconvenient transportation, threats to health, and social abuses. It asks how best we can *form* [*kōsei*] the city as a whole in order to fulfill the needs of commerce and industry. . . . As cities expand, it becomes extremely uneconomical and irrational to carve out new urban neighborhoods without a plan."[87]

The moment it became clear that Japan would soon have an urban-planning law and that he might be able to craft at least some of its provisions to pave the way for such formative urban planning, Seki set the wheels of Osaka's municipal government in motion. After reporting on the national commission's initial resolutions in 1918, he set about forming a local committee to direct Osaka's planning effort.[88] Seki personally conducted a site inspection of outlying areas to the south and the east of the city proper that promised to figure prominently in Osaka's anticipated expansion.[89] By July 1918, he had directed the new Urban Planning Section in City Hall to draw up a "provisional urban plan," had conferred with officials in the Osaka Prefectural Office about the selection of planning districts, and had written an urban-planning white paper for the Commission in Tokyo.[90]

In 1919, when the Urban Planning Law was finally promulgated, Seki was virtually dividing his time between Tokyo and Osaka. In Tokyo, he attended the Commission's meetings and met regularly with officials in the Home Ministry and the Finance Ministry. Over the course of this busy year, as Seki lobbied for Osaka in the capital, three things became clear: that the central government intended to hold his city and others to an urban-planning standard that reflected Tokyo's unique needs, that Osaka would be denied sufficient administrative and financial autonomy to advance a comprehensive urban plan, and that most other cities had become so caught up in similarly practical problems *(jissai mondai)* that they had lost sight of the larger purpose of urban planning.[91]

In hope of helping Osaka overcome these obstacles, Seki militated tirelessly for a comprehensive urban plan. He gave press interviews on the residential problem, conducted site inspections for visiting dignitaries, conferred with prefectural officials about technical and financial issues, and attended urban-planning conferences. All the while, it should be added, he continued to deepen his understanding of modern urban problems by reading as widely as he could in the Japanese and Western literature on the subject. Both literally and figuratively, as we shall see, the road toward forward-looking urban planning in Japan proved not to be paved with gold but mired in mud.

By 1920, the Home Ministry had made it abundantly clear that it had no intention of sanctioning so comprehensive an urban plan as Osaka sought. When the city announced its intention to plot a broad network of roads beyond the old town *(kyūshi)*, the Home Ministry immediately quashed its proposal. Ueki Rintarō, then head of Osaka's Urban Planning Section, reported to the Municipal Assembly that the issue of extending roads to the suburbs had elicited skepticism from officials in Tokyo.[92] Some years later, along this same story line, Seki fondly recalled the municipal assemblyman who had shocked a group of Home Ministry officials. Asked sarcastically whether Osaka "could really build the big roads" central to its comprehensive plan, the representative replied without hesitation, "Easily!"[93]

Such blustery shows of official confidence notwithstanding, local Osaka reporters sadly observed in 1920 and 1921 that the city's provisional urban plan did not appear to address the need for comprehensive planning on the outskirts nor the ideal of residential reform.[94] At nearly the same time, indeed, the Municipal Assembly began to complain ever more vociferously that its proposals were being subjected to a tedious and time-consuming process of central administrative review and revision.[95]

The fears, suspicions, and frustrations of these local advocates of urban planning proved to be more than justified in the end. Osaka's First Urban Plan (Dai Ichiji Toshi Keikaku), which Prime Minister Hara Kei signed into law in 1921, was but a ghost of the proposal advanced by the city three years earlier. Seki's grand vision of a Greater Osaka (Dai Ōsaka) was ultimately whittled down to little more than a network of modern roads and bridges at the city's core.[96] In the coming years, Osaka managed to widen forty thoroughfares and to modernize eighty-one bridges.[97] But as

Seki noted of these accomplishments some years later, they ultimately witnessed the Plan's misguided emphasis on urban reconstruction *(toshi kaizō)* at the city's core rather than urban construction *(toshi kensetsu)* on its outskirts.[98]

However important roads and bridges were to the reconstruction of "old-town" Osaka, they did not come close to satisfying Osaka's pressing need for urban construction in "new town." As Seki poignantly recalled the stark reality of Osaka's road-centered First Urban Plan, thoroughfares ostensibly designed to ease the flow of traffic created as many problems as they solved. Since the new roads were widened only to the city limits, where they joined unimproved roads on the ragged edge of the metropolis, future traffic congestion was virtually guaranteed.[99]

The truncated plan approved by the Home Ministry restricted the boundaries of Osaka's planning area to the city proper, calling in effect for what Seki described as "urban planning with the old town at the center."[100] Rather than projecting a plan that would go beyond the city limits into the urban hinterland, in other words, the Home Ministry focused myopically on built-up areas of the metropolis. According to Seki, it did so for two main reasons: first, because it was constrained by the financial conservatism of the post–World War I state, and it thus balked at the costliness of urban planning; second, because it was afflicted by the conceptual conservatism that had long blinded Japan's central leaders both to the problems and to the promise of urban expansion. Together, these tendencies conspired to render the Home Ministry skeptical of Osaka's grand plan. Over the vociferous objections of the national commission members from Osaka, according to Seki, the Home Ministry proceeded to strip the city's plan of projects it deemed superfluous to the central mission of urban planning. And since that mission consisted primarily in the "correction of [past] errors," Osaka found itself picking up the pieces.[101]

To make matters worse, the central government scoffed at Osaka's objection to this truncated version of its once-grand urban plan. When the Osaka Municipal Assembly threatened to table a special city budget for planning projects, for example, Home Minister Yamagata Aritomo blithely dismissed the gesture with one simple, sobering observation: "If the Osaka Municipal Assembly rejects the urban-planning projects for a given year, it will be exceeding its authority. The mayor has the prerogative to execute the proposal anyway."[102]

While it might seem reasonable at this point to conclude that an autocratic state run by overzealous bureaucrats simply torpedoed Seki's grand plan for a Greater Osaka, Seki's own testimony compels us to fashion a rather more nuanced narrative. Later recalling his role in implementing Osaka's First Urban Plan, he attested to his own myopia. Although the national commission emasculated the city's bold plan, conceded Seki, he himself had been complicit in promoting the road-centered plan that took its place. Seki attributed his mistake to a combination of weak-willed idealism and misguided pragmatism. Lacking confidence in the new urban-planning paradigm that he had generated, and persuaded by Home Ministry bureaucrats that some planning was better than none, he put as positive a spin on the inevitable as he could. Noting that city beautification and city sophistication were central to the Home Ministry's plan, Seki took comfort in the knowledge that Osaka would leastwise be blessed with an infrastructure "appropriate to the new [modern] age."[103]

As Seki tells the story at least, the shock of recognition that gripped him when he finally saw the light was enough to trigger an epiphany. Once he understood how misguided Osaka's First Urban Plan was, recounts Seki, he redoubled his commitment to its mirror opposite. Recalling the experience ten years later, Seki described his change of heart:

> My way of thinking about urban planning changed significantly. I began to wonder how we might go about constructing "a city with decent residential neighborhoods" rather than making "city beautiful(ism)" central to our task—[rather, that is, than] prizing only the beauty of cities as had been the rule since antiquity. Accordingly, I came to believe that we should set up a central city surrounded by smaller cities, rather than a big city [extending to Sakai]. Using our galaxy as a model, [I saw] a sun in the center surrounded by numerous satellites.[104]

According to Seki, this sudden revelation set him on a new course. Whether envisioning Greater Osaka as a sun surrounded by satellites or as a grand organism *(taisana yūkitai)*, he openly embraced the concept of metropolis.[105]

From this point forward in the early 1920s, Seki endeavored to articulate the proper priorities of urban planning. While he did not deny the importance of seeking improvements in the old city and vowed, among other things, to continue widening narrow streets, Seki exhorted urban planners to develop the new city by formulating an integrated plan *(sōgō keikaku)* to construct new roads, sewers, parks, and cemeteries on the outskirts of Osaka. Only then would the city be "complete." While urban planners should always be concerned at the outset to "correct [past] errors" *(gobyū no teisei)* and thus to bring cities up to a modern standard commensurate with "the new age" *(shin jidai)*, argued Seki, they also had an obligation to keep their eye on the prize: developing new land *(atarashii tochi [no] kaihatsu)* for the metropolises of the future.[106]

By the mid-1920s, Seki had begun to cast this looming challenge in the most explicit historical and ethical terms:

> The big cities of the present day were formed spontaneously. Big cities and metropolises were not built by design under the direction of powerful men, but issued from material, spiritual, economic, and cultural forces propagated in the course of [urban] development. Although these big cities are symbols of each nation's economic and cultural progress, and constitute [manifest] expressions of it as well, they have come to threaten the very lives of their citizens. Once people began thinking of cities as "tombs of the people," they came up with two ideas for defense of the [urban] public: first, the correction of [past] errors through the renovation of previously built-up districts; second, the exercise of public control over undeveloped areas that represent the cities of the future. The former requires treatment, the latter demands prevention.[107]

As he was helping to introduce such ideas into the Japanese urban-planning vocabulary in the late 1910s, Seki was also debating them diplomatically with the members of the national Urban Planning Survey Commission and other urban policymakers. But the stark reality of Osaka's truncated First Urban Plan changed both his mind-set and his modus operandi. If it cast his convictions into high relief, as I have already indicated, it also politicized his perspective of urban planning and urban reform. Seki began to show the first telltale signs of disillusionment in 1921. After yet one more fruitless meeting with Home Ministry officials, where he once again watched them drag their feet, he conceded that he was feeling increasingly pessimistic about implementation of the Urban Planning Law.[108] Later that same year, Seki found himself describing the same sorry state of affairs in the Diet, where political leaders had incredulously dismissed urban planning as premature *(shōsō)*.[109]

Ultimately convinced that the central government's financial, political, and conceptual conservatism had come to border on reactionary obscurantism, Seki counseled his countrymen to radically rethink the larger purpose of urban planning with a practical eye toward rewriting the nation's urban legislation: "One important reason for [crafting] an urban-planning law focused on [future] city development is to help establish organically structured socioeconomic urban regions," asserted Seki. "We can ensure the future [only] by promoting this [objective] under the law and thus giving official force to our resolve."[110]

Seki made his plea for metropolitan urban planning at a crucial juncture in the history of urban reform in Japan. Many others in high city office—most famously, Gotō Shimpei, then mayor of Tokyo—had begun to militate for a thoroughgoing overhaul of city government in Japan. In 1922, Gotō brought the renowned American urbanist Charles Beard to Tokyo in an effort to set that city on the proper course of reform.[111] Publishing his findings in 1923, Beard drew the controversial conclusion that municipal rather than central-government officials should be placed in charge of Japanese urban policymaking:

> At the end of six months' hard work I became convinced that the difficulties of Tokyo do not lie in any lack of knowledge about local needs or about modern methods of meeting those needs. The difficulties do lie in the lack of adequate financial and legal powers, occasionally in the lack of actual experience in putting technical theories into practice, and fundamentally, here as elsewhere, in the absence of an adequate public spirit to support intelligent and enthusiastic municipal leaders.[112]

Gotō, or "Big Talker," as he was popularly known, used the occasion of Beard's visit to advance his own political agenda. This slick political operator, who in 1921 had attempted to float the notorious 800,000,000 Yen Plan to modernize Tokyo, proclaimed October 1, 1922, Popular Self-Government Commemoration Day (Shimin Jichi Kinen no Hi).[113] An ardent supporter of both technocratic and citizen involvement in urban reform, Gotō had been instrumental in bringing Japan's urban problems into public view. He was markedly less successful, however, in implementing urban reform. Despite the support of such powerful men as the industrialist Yasuda Zenjirō and the oligarch Ōkuma Shigenobu, Gotō saw his ambitious plans for the renovation of Tokyo torpedoed by the central government on financial grounds.[114]

Ultimately, it took a natural disaster to awaken Japan's central government to the pressing imperative of urban reform. Disaster struck at 11:58 A.M. on September 1, 1923. Devastated by a massive earthquake, Tokyo and Yokohama were shaken to their cores. Raging fires punctuated by cyclonic firestorms ravaged Tokyo for three days, setting nearly half the city ablaze. When the smoke cleared and government officials assessed the damage, they were awestruck. Nearly 3,500 hectares of the city had been laid waste; some 310,000 dwellings had been destroyed; over 1.3 million people, 58 percent of the city's population, had been left homeless; and in Tokyo, Yokohama, and other affected areas an estimated 140,000 people had died. The Great Kanto Earthquake, as this disaster came to be called, inflicted nearly unimaginable human suffering. In a single rogue firestorm, which swept down on a mass of refugees who had taken shelter in the compound of a military-uniform depot, over forty thousand people were incinerated in an instant.

As modern Japan's imperial capital and its greatest metropolis, Tokyo had long loomed large in the lives and imaginations of the Japanese people. It is hardly surprising, therefore, that the nation was thrown into shock by the lurid news that leaked slowly from their crippled capital of a seemingly apocalyptic event.[115] This disaster shocked Japan's leaders at last into taking urban problems seriously. While they rather disingenuously characterized the earthquake as a natural disaster, thus denying public responsibility for death and destruction that had arguably been caused by their earlier failure to implement building codes and land-use plans, they were awakened nonetheless to the lurking danger of urban overcrowding. For a fleeting moment, it appeared as if urban planning might undergo a pivotal conversion to the social ideology that Seki and a few other urban reformers had been promoting for the previous decade.

In wake of the Great Kanto Earthquake, a spate of new works appeared on urban planning, virtually all of them devoted to the dream of creating new cities. Ikeda Hiroshi led the way, proclaiming it a national imperative to respond promptly to future urban demands.[116] One by one, urban planners met Ikeda's challenge. Uchida Toshikazu wrote of creating "complete" and "perfect" cities by introducing a forward-looking model of popular urban planning *(minponteki toshi keikaku)*,[117] while Takahashi Usaburō urged his countrymen to adopt some version of the garden-suburb model as part of the "movement to build new cities" *(shin toshi kensetsu undō)*.[118] Nakagawa Nozomu encouraged the Japanese to explore the character of their cities and thereby "fulfill the mission of the metropolis,"[119] and Hashimoto Seinōsuke heralded the cause of city expansion, anticipating the creation of "tomorrow's cities" *(asu no toshi)*.[120]

Crystallizing these disparate projections into a compelling proposal suggestively entitled *Tsukurarubeki Tōkyō* (The Tokyo we should build), the urban planner Tagawa Daikichirō urged Japan to seize the moment and to reinvent Tokyo as a true *teito* (imperial capital): "Tokyo is no longer Japan's city alone. Because of worldwide sympathy, it has become the central wonder of the world. It is a city of the world, and must be redesigned as such."[121] In short, the destruction of Tokyo lent a new sense of urgency to the enterprise of urban planning. Not only did it serve as a poignant reminder of the shortcomings of simple city improvement, but it acted as a positive stimulus of new paradigms of urban planning.

For Seki, who had left Tokyo for Osaka the evening before the earth-quake struck, the frenzy of post-earthquake ideologizing and rebuilding was alternately energizing and enervating. Filled at first with hope that the reconstruction of Tokyo would finally witness Japan's acknowledgment of the importance of forward-looking, socially conscious urban planning, Seki gradually grew more and more skeptical of the prospect. Toward the end of 1923, as an appointee to the newly formed Reconstruction Bureau, Seki got to experience the issues firsthand and found himself working closely with central and municipal officials such as Gotō Shimpei and Ikeda Hiroshi.

No sooner did he arrive in Tokyo than Seki found himself increasingly troubled by the direction reconstruction was taking. Although he had been called to Tokyo to address urban policymakers on land readjustment and the residential problem, Seki saw little evidence that such ideas were being taken seriously.[122] After a site visit to the old book quarter of Jinbōchō, where he surveyed new "barrack" housing that sadly reproduced the "old state of affairs" (kyūtai), Seki registered palpable dismay at its shocking inadequacy (hinjaku).[123] In the end, despite all their talk about land read-justment and residential reform, the urban planners and policymakers who reconstructed Tokyo in the aftermath of the Great Kanto Earthquake priv-ileged pavement over people.[124]

In a speech delivered toward the end of 1923, just prior to his promotion from deputy mayor to mayor of Osaka, Seki spoke bluntly about the valu-able lesson he had learned from Tokyo's destruction. He characterized this brutal event as a tragic indication that the "brilliance of Meiji civilization," ostensibly represented by the capital itself, was actually a "fraud." Girded by this understanding, he urged his countrymen to transcend the super-ficial approach to modernization represented by their ill-fated capital and instead to intensify industrial production (sangyō no kōdo ka) in the in-terest of establishing supremacy in international economic competition. Observing that this industrial build-up would require a massive social re-construction (shakai kaizō) to parallel the material reconstruction of the Japanese capital, Seki insisted that such a change could be achieved only by affirming the "self-consciousness and spontaneity" (jikaku-jihatsu) of the Japanese people themselves and thus putting the state in its proper place.[125]

Taking heed of this advice to Tokyoites, Seki endeavored to reinvent Osaka according to a developmental paradigm that projected the public welfare as its main focus. From the beginning of 1924, following his ap-pointment as mayor at the end of 1923, Seki finally possessed the political authority to set his own reform agenda for the city.[126] He came to power on the heels of a hard-earned and important municipal victory—the municipalization of Osaka Light and Power after a decade-long battle—and was thus galvanized for the critical challenge that awaited him. No sooner did he assume office than the central government took up an issue that loomed large on his own urban agenda: new provisions to Japan's Urban Planning Law.

Seki immediately convened a subcommittee of the Osaka Municipal Assembly,[127] and his contribution to the proceedings tells us just how eager he was to reinvent urban planning in Japan. He so single-mindedly pursued the goal of urban expansion for Osaka that a member of the committee pointedly asked whether he was in search of "political fame."[128] Telling the speaker that he would not grace the question with an answer, Seki instead steamed ahead to defend the merits of his proposal. He criticized those who would continue to view urban planning solely as a means of renovating the city. "No matter how much money we put into existing slums," insisted Seki, "the results will not be satisfactory." Going on to observe that a significant proportion of Osaka's population was already clustered on the outskirts and that land development there had been conducted haphazardly, he encouraged his fellow committee members to recognize the wisdom in using planning funds to prevent the growth of new slums in the future.[129]

Not a year passed before Seki succeeded in achieving his objective. On April 1, 1925, Osaka officially became Greater Osaka (Dai Ōsaka). Under this urban expansion, the city's area was increased from 56 to 181 square kilometers, and its population was thereby boosted from 1,430,000 to 2,210,000.[130] It is important to recall, however, that this dramatic result came only after intense political and bureaucratic maneuvering. Among other requirements, the expansion demanded the willing cooperation of local leaders from villages on the outskirts of the city. Much has been made of this process by Kawase Mitsuyoshi, who argues that Seki considered the urban hinterlands just so much vacant space and jammed the deal down the throats of villagers in a fit of urban centrism (*toshi chūshinshugi*).[131] Indeed, according to one apocryphal account, Seki ultimately persuaded local priests to intercede on the city's behalf.[132]

The real story, as it were, is much more complicated. Seki himself later acknowledged that the expansion had precipitated collisions of interest between the city and outlying villages, and he professed to believe at the time that Osaka's future was at stake.[133] While he fully intended to integrate villagers on the periphery of Osaka into the life of the city, and though he expected the city to purchase their fields for residential and recreational development, Seki's ultimate objective in pursuing urban expansion was not to demonstrate the superiority of the city but to short-circuit the pattern of haphazard urbanization that had previously characterized development on the urban periphery.

At the moment of village incorporation, significantly, local village officials themselves acknowledged that their villages had already metamorphosed into towns (shigaichi), and they welcomed the development for at least two reasons: first, because the city would extend its modern urban infrastructure into their towns and second because it would help restrict future development.[134] It is important to remember as well that local landlords and regional land companies had already made heavy real estate investments in the urban hinterlands.[135] Finally, as Seki indicated in his public justification of the expansion, he did not propose to overrun the countryside but to defend the countryside and the city alike from haphazard development: "We must resolve to free our eyes to scrutinize the posture of urban development as a whole, considering the mission of cities in the domestic economy. Urban planning is not merely planning seen from [the perspective of] the city. We must resolve seriously to consider the relationship of the city to the countryside."[136]

Seki's own characterization of the relationship was quite revealing. At a reception in 1925 for local leaders of Higashinari-gun, one of the outlying districts that Osaka was about to incorporate, he likened the new relationship to a marriage. Far from laying claim to the "virgin soil" (shojochi) of Osaka's urban hinterlands like some urban imperialist, then, Seki saw himself as a kind of go-between appointed to help the extended urban family of Greater Osaka develop a collective identity. In this spirit, he counseled the citizens of Greater Osaka to decide collectively "what sort of place the city of Osaka should be" before even putting a spade to the newly incorporated districts.[137]

While urban planning had previously entailed acts of renovation, observed Seki, it would now engender acts of creation (sōsaku) as well.[138] In a rambling meditation entered into his diary on New Year's Eve 1924, Seki witnessed the deep-seated convictions that were propelling him forward:

> The advancement of Greater Osaka, at present and in the future, does not simply await a demonstration of political acumen and moral spirit on the part of the people, it awaits a show of responsibility on the part of the mayor to defend the people from political decay. . . . In this transitional period, then, a new and integrative social and political force promises to emerge, and it will certainly form the structure of a

new age. Behind this sociopolitical energy lie economic and political forces. While Osaka should tap the energy of [the] economic force [it possesses], it must not fall into the habit of repressing moral impulses. About this, we must be vigilant. The balance of these two forces is a necessary condition of future urban development, and it is the most vital condition of Osaka's advancement.[139]

To read this passage is to understand that Seki was not simply playing at municipal politics but attempting to forge the basis for lasting urban change.

The city expansion of 1925 inaugurated a new phase of urban planning in Osaka. Tanaka Kiyo, the city architect who in 1925 published a highly acclaimed book on the city's new plan, promoted a grand new image of metropolitan Osaka.[140] His map of the Proposed Plan for Greater Osaka depicted a network of rational grids extending from city center to the boundaries of the new metropolis. Significantly, however, Tanaka's map featured the blocks of Greater Osaka's proposed land-readjustment districts. In this respect, it was virtually a photo negative of the Reconstruction Plan of Tokyo produced in 1924. Whereas Tokyo remained mired in the road-centered urban planning of the past, Osaka was about to introduce the neighborhood-centered urban planning of the future. (See figures 11 and 12.)

At the very beginning of his book, Tanaka offered two visual emblems of Osaka's planning objectives: a drawing of the reflecting pool and radiating avenues designed by Pierre L'Enfant for Washington, D.C., and an aerial photograph of George Cadbury's garden city at Bournville, England.[141] Tanaka meant to convey with these images the ethos of Osaka's new urban plan: a conflation of the grand urban-design principles of the past with the intimate site-planning regimen of the present.

In his preface to Tanaka's book, the urban planner Ueki Rintarō seized on a theme that resonated powerfully with Seki's views on urban planning. He asserted that the purpose of urban planning was not treatment but prevention, not renovation but creation. In his own account, Tanaka drew even closer to Seki's synthesis of these two elements of urban planning, finding a place for both in the repertoire of the urban planner. "The essence of urban planning," he wrote, "is to project both rational renovations and ideal development." Equally important, Tanaka endorsed Seki's social perspective of the planning enterprise, citing as its ultimate objectives the preservation of "public tranquility forever" and the "pursuit of [public] welfare."[142]

Seki hammered home this same theme in 1925, claiming that the

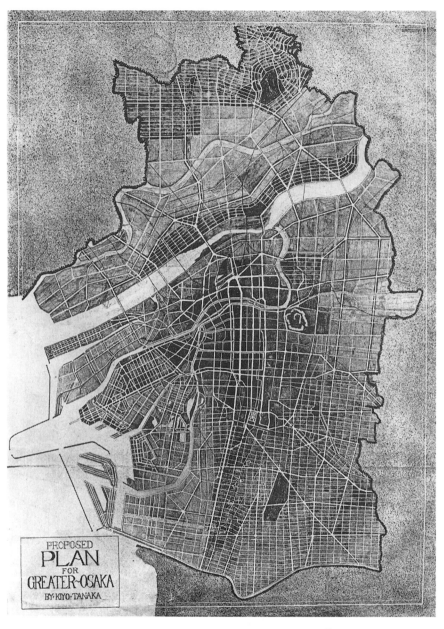

Figure 11. Proposed Plan for Greater Osaka. From Tanaka Kiyo, *Ōsaka no toshi keikaku* (Osaka: Hinoshita Wagakujiya, 1925).

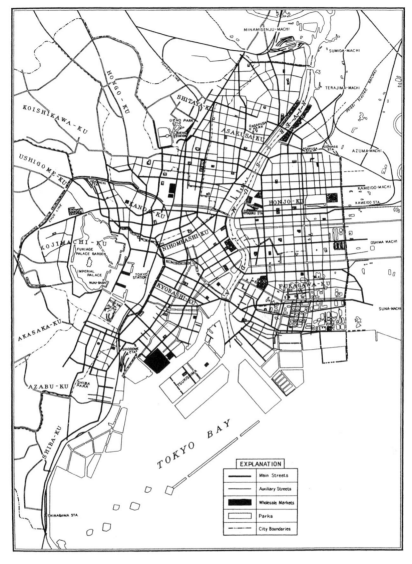

Figure 12.   Reconstruction Plan for Tokyo. From the Tokyo Municipal Office,
The Reconstruction of Tokyo (Tokyo, 1933).

expansion of Osaka would at last allow municipal leaders to promote the "prosperity of the city" and the "welfare of its citizens."[143] The new plan that Seki introduced designated turning radii, vehicle weight, and speed for roads; designed sewers to achieve "sewer water purification"; called for fire-proof construction in some areas and fire-resistant construction in others; and introduced zoning (residential, commercial, and industrial).[144] As Tanaka and others made clear, Osaka's urban planners were also prepared to resolve a whole host of social concerns by properly plotting residential lots; reducing land prices; providing public works (water, sewer, gas, electric); designing well-built dwellings intended to reduce disease and mortality rates by ensuring adequate drainage, light, and ventilation; designing streets to facilitate the flow of traffic, prevent accidents, and intersect with major arteries; and laying out districts with an eye toward public security and ease of movement in the event of earthquakes or fires.[145]

Reiterating his belief that new construction should be severely restricted, Seki was now able to offer Osakans a compelling reason for doing so. "It would be a big mistake to consider completing Greater Osaka by precipitating the emergence of a sea of roofs over its sixty square miles," he insisted. "The new trend in urban planning is to secure the future welfare of the people by preserving greenbelts."[146] Reminding Osakans of the obvious—that urban planning was no longer simply about roads, railways, and canals—Seki asked them to help redefine its scope by thinking through its larger purpose: "The first issue facing the increasing number of Osakans is how to use the eighteen thousand hectares (eleven square miles) of land [that the city has gained]. If urban planning is not used to regulate the relationship between people and land, nothing but problems for people will result."[147]

With this concern foremost in his mind, Seki proceeded to outline the long-range objectives of forward-looking urban planning in Osaka. He argued that land within the city's new planning wards should be placed in two distinct categories, "land with buildings" and "open space." These distinct areas, continued Seki, ought then to be divided into four different categories, according to land-use standards: (1) commercial, industrial, and administrative zones, (2) areas containing residential housing, schools, libraries, hospitals, and markets, (3) greenbelts with parks, playgrounds, playing fields, gardens, cemeteries, and airports, and (4) land reserved for roads, tramways, railroads, canals, harbors, storehouses, and parking lots.[148]

When Osaka finally received central-government approval for its proposal to move into a second phase of urban planning based on its expansion, Seki went out of his way to distinguish this Second Urban Plan from the first. Whereas the First Urban Plan of 1921 consisted essentially of urban-reconstruction projects, the Second Urban Plan was focused instead on urban construction. Characterizing the new plan as a "first work"— that is, as an example of the production not the renovation of space—Seki maintained that it would make urban planning into a genuinely creative enterprise. He noted proudly that Osaka was at the forefront of this revolutionary movement and challenged Osakans to set a new standard *(kijun)* of urban planning in Japan by creating new "neighborhoods designed [to set] a healthy [standard of] living for the people."[149]

After over a decade of militating for the sort of urban planning that would enable Osaka to transform itself from the Capital of Smoke into the Livable City (Sumigokochiyoki Toshi), Seki stood on the brink of success. Significantly, however, he proceeded cautiously in order to set an appropriate developmental agenda:

> Before putting a single line on paper, we must generate a fitting sketch of the whole. In order to create a plan for the future, we must [first] possess an ideal that goes to the core of the plan as a whole. . . . We should draw pictures inside our heads of the city of tomorrow, the city of the future, fifty years hence, and make these the basis for a plan.[150]

To his credit, Seki took his own advice to heart and began sketching a visionary portrait of Greater Osaka. He even went so far as to submit a design-and-build timetable: thirty years from start to finish.[151] Applying his knowledge and experience to the exercise, he ran through the structural elements essential to his regional plan: zoning, land readjustment, "urban greening," housing.[152] In this exercise, it appears, he adopted and adapted planning principles with worldwide popularity: most important, the U.S. model of regional planning. The root concept of this new planning emphasis in the United States, as described by Christine Boyer, was to reorganize "metropolitan agglomerations" according to "planning standards that set limits to their growth into surrounding regions and forced them to decentralize their industrial and commercial activities into autonomous functional subunits."[153] In Japan, as in the United States, maintained Seki, the greatest challenge faced by planners was to disperse the dense population of big cities and yet to find ways of harmonizing urban life *(toshi seikatsu)* and rural life *(inaka seikatsu)* within the regional areas where that dispersion was engineered.[154]

In the end, however, Seki allowed his imagination to take over. Conjuring up a complex image of Greater Osaka that affirmed its economic functions but celebrated its social identity, he projected a vision of the future metropolis as a "grand organism" *(taisana yūkitai)* divided into distinct use zones *(yōto chiiki)* conceived to preserve the integrity of the whole. The zone that truly captured his imagination, however, was the band of undeveloped land on the outskirts, where urban visionaries such as himself could produce new spaces and thereby create new places. Significantly, Seki did not envision this new space as either urban or rural but, to use Henry Smith's term, as a kind of hybrid "middle landscape."

Calling for half of the newly incorporated area to be left without buildings,[155] Seki proposed to preserve open land *(jiyū kūchi)* for parks, playgrounds, athletic grounds, gardens, and the like.[156] For the other half—that is, the fields, marshlands, landfill, and scattered settlements of what had once been Osaka's hinterlands—Seki conjured an image of garden suburbs inhabited by working-class homeowners. Properly planned and produced with orderly neighborhoods, efficient rail service, decent roads, piped water, sewers, municipal electric and gas service, parks, playgrounds, gardens, and decent, affordable housing, these working-class garden suburbs promised to accomplish the strategic residential dispersion that Seki had long considered essential to the survival of cities as urban communities. Indeed, as he saw it, these new residential enclaves represented the key to urban progress. For they promised to "perfect" the class system whose stability was imperative to the continued evolution of capitalist society.

Even as Seki was elaborating his visionary plan for working-class garden suburbs, however, he was also preparing to go to battle for it, for he was not the only one making plans for the "virgin soil" of Osaka's urban hinterlands. As he well knew, local landlords and regional land companies had capitalist visions of their own.

GARDEN SUBURBS FOR THE CAPITAL OF SMOKE

In 1919, in no uncertain terms, Seki affirmed the intimate connection between urban planning and residential reform. "The purpose of urban planning is residential improvement," he argued bluntly, "and this is its most important focus as well."[157] Later placing this basic principle in broad practical perspective, Seki memorably evoked the challenge that lay before Osaka: "Since the purpose of urban planning is to make the cities in which we reside 'livable cities' [*sumigokochiyoki toshi*], our plans for urban renovation must be inextricably connected, in substance and reality, to [the search for solutions to] the residential problem."[158]

When Seki projected this combination of urban planning and residential improvement as the key to urban social reform in Japan, his was a lonely progressive voice in the prewar bureaucratic wilderness of Japanese urban policymaking. Yet he drew hope and inspiration from the healthy urban progressive fellowship that continued to gather strength in Europe and North America. While Seki could not attend the international planning and housing conferences where his fellow progressives compared notes and hammered out global agendas, such as the famous International Town Planning Conference in Amsterdam (1924) that formally endorsed garden cities, he later pored over the proceedings in search of ideas. And although he did not go on the grand European tour of model communities such as Letchworth and Essen that once "drew social reformers like magnets," according to one historian,[159] he conducted a virtual tour of his own through the progressive treatises, handbooks, and reports that lined his bookshelves.

In *Jūtaku mondai to toshi keikaku* (The housing problem and urban planning, 1923), where he finally put flesh on the bones of his *idée fixe*, Seki provides us with a vivid illustration of the painstaking research, analytical perspicacity, and progressivist passion that he applied to the challenge of urban social reform in Osaka. After deconstructing the urban-planning histories of France, Germany, and England in an effort to identify their defining characteristics, he strove to assess the applicability of different planning models to Japan.

Much less wildly eclectic than before in the intellectual influences he entertained, Seki came back repeatedly to the same sources of inspiration: among others, the British journalist William Dawson, whose passion for the Verein had impelled him, among other things, to write extensively on German urban progressivism;[160] the American urban engineer Nelson P. Lewis, who helped to scientize the planning profession;[161] the German polymath Werner Hegemann, who spearheaded the Gross-Berlin initiative and later became a globetrotting advocate of metropolitan regional planning;[162] the American urban planner John Nolen, whose advocacy of elaborate planning maps was happily combined with a passion for housing reform;[163] and the German economist Rudolf Eberstadt, who denied the economic necessity of Berlin's ubiquitous *Mietskaserne* (huge apartment complexes) and, in the name of health and economy, called for the construction of single-family houses.[164] If Seki associated each of these writers with a specific piece of his own emerging model of urban social reform, he also identified them together as fellow progressives.

Yet, again, Seki was not interested in grafting Western social theory onto Japanese urban practice. While he recognized broad parallels between Western and Japanese experience, his deep-seated empirical instincts kept his abstract imagination in check. Thus, Seki began and ended his quest for a viable model of urban social reform in Japan.

Seki's quest began soon after the Rice Riots subsided. Sensitized to Osaka's social problems, and with a heightened awareness of the looming importance of its housing problem in particular, he readily identified residential reform as the central imperative of urban social reform. Thereafter, he was arguably drawn into the enterprise of residential policymaking by a combination of conviction and circumstance. Toward the end of September 1919, as he watched the working classes struggle to get by in the recessionary postwar economy, Seki jotted a cynical note in his diary: "There is still no [real] labor problem in Japan, only hard living, yet no one seems prepared to take responsibility for [addressing] the latter."[165] A week later, amid labor strikes for higher wages and a lower cost of living, Seki found himself asking when the authorities would finally begin regulating prices *(bukka chōsetsu)* and providing "relief from daily distress" *(seikatsunan kyūsai)*.[166] When Osaka's municipal streetcar employees went on strike that same month, Seki found the answer to his question in himself: he would address the problem in his capacity as deputy mayor of Japan's second largest city.

Spearheading a searching municipal response to the rising cost of living, which had driven the working classes in Osaka to the brink of despair, Seki set up the city's Social Bureau and expanded its public services to include housing reform. Even before the labor strikes of October 1919, reportedly under Seki's direction, the city had constructed 389 units of desperately needed public housing. In the wake of the strikes, Seki apparently had little trouble convincing Mayor Ikegami and the Municipal Assembly to expand Osaka's new public-housing program. By 1920, 650 new homes had been constructed at Tsurumachi[167]—a significant portion of them earmarked for the streetcar employees whose strike had propelled Seki into action a year before.[168]

Seki committed himself to a sweeping program of residential reform centrally conceived to "supply housing to low-income earners," and the municipal housing he helped produce in 1919 met that objective: it was designed specifically to set a decent standard for worker dwellings.[169] The sketches provided in Seki's timely article on the subject, written for the prestigious architectural journal *Kenchiku zasshi* (Architecture Magazine), represented Osaka's new public-housing developments as residential refuges from the hazards and the anonymity of modern urban life. (See figures 13 and 14.)

The communal lodging houses planned in the day-laborer district of Imamiya were designed to provide every occupant with a single room in a compound ranged around an interior garden. Likewise, the municipal multiplexes and communal lodging houses slated for construction near Chikkō, Osaka's port project, were planned as a single complex and were focused on two interior parks. The same basic plan was applied at Sakuranomiya, where two clusters of municipal *nagaya* (row houses) were sited on either side of substantial parks.[170] Like oases in an urban desert, these inwardly oriented municipal housing projects stood in stark contrast to the sprawling metropolis that continued to grow like a field of weeds around them. In 1921, when his deputy mayoral counterpart from Tokyo made a visit to Osaka, Seki made certain to arrange a guided tour of the public housing constructed for Osaka's once-obstreperous streetcar conductors. Here, in his eyes, was a concrete example of what municipal governments could do to better the lives of working-class families.[171]

The construction of municipal public housing in 1919 carried Seki one step closer to his dream of creating a livable city. But ultimately he was able to advance his more radical scheme for the production of an entirely new residential space on the outskirts of Osaka because of the worsening of Osaka's residential problems in the 1920s. Thrown into desperation by their intolerable living conditions, working-class tenants had held a huge renters' rally *(shakkajin taiki)* in 1921. Out of it emerged the Osaka Renters' Alliance (Ōsaka Shakkajin Dōmeikai), which staged a series of increasingly militant tenant protests.[172] Although there were only 75 recorded incidents in 1922, the police reported 599 renters' strikes and related disturbances the following year.[173]

These acts of desperation were triggered by the proliferation of substandard, exorbitantly priced rental housing as well as a continuing housing shortage. In 1921, the residential vacancy rate in and around Osaka stood at 0.79 percent. That same year, the city conducted a sweeping survey of residential problems. The report painted a dismal picture of crowded tenement housing throughout Osaka. With none of the beauty, health, convenience, and comfort offered by the suburbs, observed the writers, life at the core and on the margins of Osaka was perilously poor. This report identified industrial workers *(shokkō)* as the most conspicuous victims of Osaka's housing crisis. Not only did they face an acute shortage of housing, but they were compelled to live in poorly lit, poorly ventilated

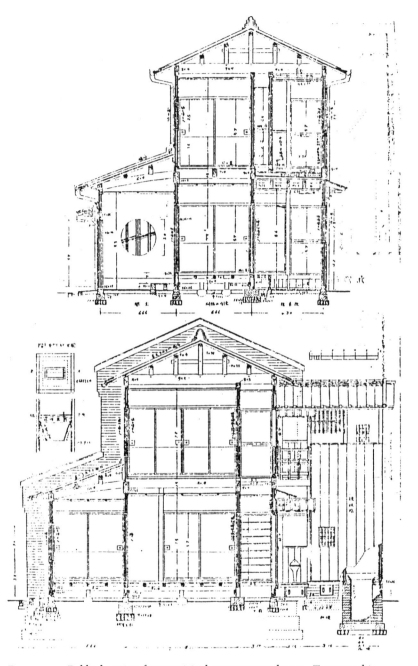

Figure 13. Public housing for municipal streetcar employees, Tsurumachi.
From Seki Hajime, "Toshi jūtaku seisaku," *Kenchiku zasshi* 33, no. 391 (1919).

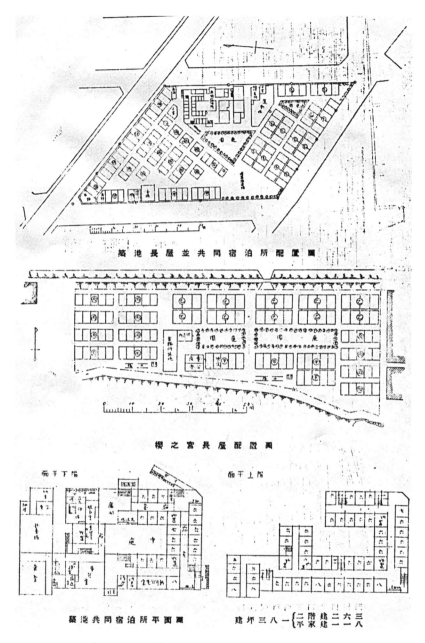

Figure 14. Osaka municipal housing. *Top to bottom:* Chikkō *nagaya* (row houses), Sakuranomiya *nagaya,* Chikkō boarding house. From Seki Hajime, "Toshi jūtaku seisaku," *Kenchiku zasshi* 33, no. 391 (1919).

firetraps along narrow lanes—when they were lucky enough, that is, to find any housing at all.[174]

The report also revealed, tragically, that worker households were compelled to deal with a variety of inconveniences and injustices. Often, tenants were forced to negotiate with "unfair" real estate brokers, to pay exorbitant deposits, and to absorb escalating rents—all this for housing that often lacked private kitchens and toilets.[175] The report concluded that scandalously inadequate housing had become a basic reality of worker life in Osaka.

In his own investigation of Osaka's residential problems at this critical juncture—when the rallying cries of "landlord fighting" (yanushi kōgeki) and "landlord extermination" (yanushi seibatsu) seemed to be on everyone's lips—Seki probed the source of popular discontent.[176] He seized the opportunity to address the public on this controversial topic in 1921. In a formal Citizens' Address, given at the Central Town Hall, he began by recording his intellectual indebtedness to the London housing reformer Octavia Hill, then proceeded to sketch the contours of Osaka's gathering residential crisis. Observing that the city faced an acute housing shortage of some twenty thousand dwellings, he noted grimly that one unfortunate result was an inordinate rise in rents. Given that working-class families now expended as much as 70 to 85 percent of their income on rent, Seki added dryly, it was no wonder that the relationship between landlords and tenants had become tense.[177]

Yet Seki went on to identify Osaka's "housing problem" as much more than a dispute over accommodations and leases. At root, he argued, the housing problem was seriously disrupting the cultural life (bunka seikatsu) of the metropolis. Urging Osakans to grasp the relationship between residence and culture—that is, "to examine the relationship of housing to the lives of individuals, and to [the goal of] social progress"—Seki characterized the housing problem as a matter of the greatest import to the life of the region as well as that of the nation. Looking out over the public gathering, Seki went straight to the ethical issue at the core of his residential concerns. He noted parenthetically that the English term economy was derived from the combination of oikos (household) and nomos (norm)—thus cleverly suggesting to his fellow citizens that this most basic aspect of human life was associated fundamentally with the home (hōmu). Then, he made his pitch: "The advancement of a healthy national people can be achieved only in healthy housing."[178]

Seki traced the roots of the urban residential problem as a cultural problem to the combination of overhousing and overcrowding that typified modern cities, associating overhousing with external, and overcrowding with internal, space.[179] With respect to overhousing, he stressed the deleterious social influence of the lack of open space. "We cannot ignore the fact that environmental conditions related to housing have an influence on the residents," he contended. "We cannot overlook the fact that the individual residence is intimately related to its surroundings—to neighboring houses, streets, and open spaces. We must not shut our eyes when it comes to asking how these [factors] affect residence."[180]

In answer to this challenge, Seki encouraged Osakans to create an entirely new residential space/place on the margins of the city: a sub-urban space between city and country where working-class families might experience the civil minimum due them as productive citizens of the nation. Once these working-class garden suburbs were in place and once they were linked by intraurban and interurban transit both to Osaka's urban core and to the wider region beyond the metropolis, Seki predicted that they would transform Osaka into one great regional organism.[181]

Seki first offered working-class garden suburbs as the ultimate solution to Japan's urban problems following the city's expansion in 1925. While he called loudly for land readjustment in the haphazardly developed districts on the city's northern and southern periphery, in what he himself considered a largely futile attempt to treat existing urban problems, his eyes grew much larger when he surveyed the open spaces of Osaka's hinterlands. Here Seki hoped to make his mark as a residential reformer by laying out entirely new neighborhoods with orderly and systematic block divisions.[182] Once such rational residential grids were plotted, in blocks and lots with properly shaped, rectilinear contours, Seki believed that Osaka might finally transform itself into a "fine city."[183]

Having addressed the issue of overhousing, Seki turned to his second major concern: overcrowding within tenement housing. Identifying overcrowding as a serious threat to the health, morals, and public discipline of city dwellers, Seki went on to condemn it as a national abomination.[184] "The housing issue is not about houses; it is about people and where they live," he asserted. "In every respect, it is a social issue." Drawing an implicit parallel between decent housing and decent working conditions, Seki portrayed housing policy as a way of "rais[ing] people up."[185] He called specifically for the enactment of public housing policies (jūtaku seisaku) conceived to ensure the construction of new housing. "As citizens of an advanced nation," he concluded, "we must find a means of supplying proper housing."[186]

Seki wasted little time in identifying a housing model for his garden suburbs. He enumerated the obvious deficiencies of "tenement duplexes," which he compared to the barrack housing of European slums, and attempted to come up with housing designs appropriate to Japanese society.[187] Rejecting the high-rise apartment buildings *(kōsō jūtaku)* so popular in Germany and the United States,[188] Seki maintained that they were inimical to the goals of housing reform in Japan. In support of this view, he related the experience of a Japanese friend who had lived in such a complex: "I asked a friend who recently returned from the United States about the advantages of apartment living. He said they have all the [necessary] facilities, but that it is difficult to rid oneself of a certain feeling of fatigue. As a result, many [residents] feel the need to escape, and go off to the country on weekends."[189]

Seki wove this story into a didactic critique of high-rise apartments, noting ominously that they might have a deleterious effect on Japanese children. Forced by circumstance to play indoors, children would be denied the "physical education necessary to their future well-being," he wrote, "and since these children will, in the future, become citizens of our nation, . . . we must not hesitate to declare this [sort of housing] a [potential] cause of many grave problems for the future of our citizenry." Seki concluded that high-rise living would seriously discourage the social harmony *(shakaiteki chōwa)* on which community life rested.[190]

In the end, Seki advocated a residential ideal that pivoted on the construction of "small houses" *(kojūtaku)*—that is, single-family homes—in orderly neighborhoods on the outskirts of Osaka. These were to be his garden suburbs, and he expected them to humanize the metropolis by providing working-class families with a livable environment and thus integrating them into the larger metropolitan community. By thus projecting his values into space and architecture, to borrow Carl Schorske's colorful imagery, Seki gave manifest expression to his convictions about urban social reform.[191]

Urban planning and housing policy together, as Seki visualized them, promised to transform Osaka into a regional metropolis for the future. Bringing this point home by way of a biological metaphor that he was fond of invoking in a variety of different contexts—cities as social bodies—Seki identified planning as the "skeleton" and housing as the "meat" of a new metropolitan regional organism.[192]

By appropriating this biological metaphor—and using it instead to visualize the human anatomy of Seki's "new metropolitan regional organism"—we can take an early snapshot of the spatial figure of social progress that Osaka promised to cut. This city of the future would consist of an administrative core, a commercial center, and an industrial periphery. Ranged around these core elements of its dynamic exchange economy, like planets around the sun, would be the separate garden suburbs of the working classes and the middle classes. At last, the contentious classes of modern society might move into their respective neighborhoods, make homes out of their new houses, and in the process create that perfect place of class harmony that was synonymous with social progress. Or so it must have seemed to the idealist in Seki.

It was as a realist, however, that Seki was compelled to pursue his dream. Despite his enthusiasm for residential reform through the building of working-class garden suburbs on the outskirts of Osaka—and his conviction that this project would produce lasting social peace—he harbored no illusions about the immensity of the task that lay before him. As mayor of Osaka, he set a thirty-year term for the creation of his livable city[193]—a term determined in the first instance by the daunting exigencies of the enterprise. Since this plan involves "the dispersion of people and [the apportionment] of land," he explained, "drawing up the plans for distribution will require a host of historical, geographical, social, and technical surveys." Given the ever-changing reality of the metropolis, he knew this would not be easy. "Unlike building a house," he warned, "we are handling a living city [which is] always moving and changing."[194] In the bittersweet years that lay ahead, Seki would find out just how right he was.

THE UNDOING OF URBAN PROGRESSIVISM

In the late 1920s, Seki called on Greater Osaka's planners to map out his working-class garden suburbs. Instructing them to plot orderly blocks, to plan rational road networks, and to lay proper sewer lines and waterlines, he ordered them as well to "preserve open spaces" for parks, playgrounds, gardens, and athletic fields.[195] Such spaces, insisted Seki, were indispensable to the physical and mental health of city dwellers. Citing their special importance to the physical education of children, who needed places to run and play, Seki linked them to the mental health of adults as well, who needed relief from the pressures of urban life.[196]

As Seki moved deliberately toward the creation of working-class garden suburbs on the outskirts of Osaka, he laid out a comprehensive urban plan involving land readjustment, zoning, and residential improvement. By 1926, he had carved out his first working-class residential oasis: 104 single-family homes in a neighborhood of grid-planned blocks at Hannan-chō.[197] Bordered by wide streets and laid out over modern sewer lines and water-

Figure 15. Public housing, single-family homes, Hannan-chō. Photo by the author.

lines, this development served as a model for those that followed.[198] (See figure 15.)

Over the next two years, the city put up similar housing in four different locations—a total of 354 houses in all—and offered homes for sale to working-class families for a down payment of four hundred yen and monthly installments of thirty-two yen. These two-story wooden homes came complete with tatami and fixtures, fenced-in entryways, water and electric hookups, and private baths. Moreover, nearly 42 percent of the land dedicated to these residential developments was reserved for parks and playgrounds.[199] By 1929, the City of Osaka had developed twenty-one different public-housing developments, ranging from private homes to communal lodging houses.[200]

Well aware that the city alone could not bear the expense of such an extensive scheme, Seki appealed to the local landlords, regional land companies, and railway companies that owned most of the land on the outskirts of Osaka to create housing developments on the municipal model.[201] This plan would never get off the ground. While Seki had apparently hoped to entice private developers to emulate the public developments—and had hoped to sweeten the deal with property-tax incentives—his plan soon fell victim to a combination of capitalist greed and bureaucratic caprice.

As one might expect, Osaka's landed capitalists had designs of their own on the open spaces that Seki envisioned for his working-class garden suburbs. Local landlords continued to put up the same ramshackle rental housing they had in the past; and when regional land companies weren't doing the same thing, they simply left their land undeveloped and contentedly watched it rise in value as the city engulfed the countryside.

The region's railway companies were a horse of yet a different color. Taking a page from Seki's garden-suburb book, they actively promoted suburban residential development. To the north, west, and south, Osaka was soon surrounded by newly planned residential communities.[202] But the ten or so privately developed garden suburbs along the Hankyū, Hanshin, Keihan, Kintetsu, and Nankai lines had nothing to do with the deproletarianization of Osaka's working classes and everything to do with the comfort of the middle classes. These were the Japanese equivalent of the comfortable British and North American middle-class suburbs that Robert Fishman has evocatively called "bourgeois utopias."[203] Planting department stores at one end of the line and recreational facilities at the other, railway companies such as Hankyū discovered that they could corner a lucrative consumer market by placing middle-class suburbs between them.[204]

Seki resolved to fight the forces of landed capitalism with every weapon he could—stricter building codes, property-appreciation taxes on undeveloped property, even moral suasion—but he was engaged from the start in a losing battle. After all, he was up against not only powerful local landed capitalists but also a state that stubbornly refused to take action against them. Although the central government had sanctioned the expansion of Osaka, this hardly meant that it had converted to Seki's working-class garden suburbanism. To Seki's dismay, the city expansion of 1925 had a negligible impact on Osaka's ability to actively promote urban planning in its undeveloped exurbs. Failing to secure jurisdiction over urban planning from the central government, the city remained unable to implement Seki's grand plan. In this sense, as Seki himself cynically observed, the expansion had accomplished little more than a "redrawing of the city's physical contours."[205]

Despite repeated entreaties from Osaka's leadership for greater municipal autonomy, noted Seki in 1925, Tokyo had yet to even draft a proposal.[206] This meant not only that the Home Ministry continued to wield autocratic authority over urban planning in Osaka but that the Construction Section and the Finance Ministry continued to take their ounce of flesh as well. Given that 67 percent of the taxes collected from Osakans by the central government remained in Tokyo and only 16.5 percent was invested in the city, Mayor Seki found himself with little power and even less money to pursue his dream of urban social progress.[207]

To make matters worse, the central government was hopelessly passive aggressive in its relationship to the city. As lamented by Seki, it had encouraged jurisdictional competition between the prefectural and municipal authorities over social work *(shakai jigyō);* overridden the municipal government's social-planning priorities and used locally collected taxes to build new roads instead; and urged the municipal government to open a public wholesale market only to award the prefectural government with licensing power.[208]

Thus ignored by landed capitalists and hamstrung by the central government, Seki was forced to put his grand plan for Osaka on the back burner. In the coming years, this irrepressible progressive shifted his attention from the socioeconomic ends to the political means of urban social progress. Spearheading a national movement for metropolitan autonomy *(daitoshi jichi),* he galvanized the support of big-city mayors from all over Japan to form a National Mayoral Commission (Zenkoku Shichō Kaigi). Together, they went to battle against the top-heavy political and financial system that continued to deprive Japan's urban communities of meaningful control over their own destinies.[209]

Paradoxically, Japan's national government deprived municipal authorities of precisely the prerogative they were best qualified to exercise: fulfillment of the public welfare. As Rodgers has compellingly expressed the fundamental difference between modern national and local interests, "Where the primary business of nation-states was with armies and empires, public welfare lay in the domain of local government."[210]

Even as Seki was pulling together his reformist coalition of big-city mayors and helping them to produce concrete proposals such as the metropolitan policy proposal *(tosei-an)* of 1932,[211] he was working on a number of other different fronts to promote the interests of his own metropolitan constituency. When he was unable to extract more tax revenue from Tokyo for municipal projects, he searched the world for innovative fiscal schemes that might take up some of the slack. He learned how to float municipal bonds effectively,[212] how to subsidize infrastructural improvements with public-use assessments *(jūekisha futankin),*[213] and how to increase the efficiency and profitability of Osaka's extensive system of municipal enterprise.[214]

Yet while these innovative ideas arguably brought Seki one step closer to a substantial measure of de facto metropolitan autonomy, they did little to advance his dream of reinventing Osaka's urban hinterlands as working-class garden suburbs. By the time Seki had truly begun to rationalize municipal administration in Osaka and to get the business of city government running smoothly, the "moving and changing" he had earlier cited as a fact of urban life had made a dead letter of his grand plan for social progress. Drawn in by Osaka's sustained economic growth, urban immigrants continued to flood into the metropolitan region. And, as they did, Greater Osaka underwent an almost unabated housing-construction boom.

Between 1925 and 1941, according to one estimate, Osaka's newly incorporated districts witnessed the construction of ten thousand new units of housing per year.[215] Of this new housing, the preponderance was aimed at the rental market. By 1930, city officials estimated that 90 percent of Osaka's dwellings were tenant-occupied,[216] and it classed roughly half of these as tenement housing.[217] Without light and ventilation, not to mention running water and sewer pipes, this new housing was no better than the slum housing that Seki and others had been criticizing since the turn of the century.[218]

In 1930, as urban sprawl overwhelmed Osaka, Seki was forced to concede that his once-bracing vision of a metropolitan organism had been rendered an anachronism. It had been barely five years since the boundaries of the city had been expanded, creating Greater Osaka, but in that time the hinterlands had filled up and filled out. Having spent most of the previous five years doing battle with Tokyo over the issue of metropolitan autonomy—that is, over the prerogative of municipal officials to exercise primary jurisdiction over public policymaking in Osaka—Seki had been distracted from his other, local battle with landed capitalists over unregulated residential development in the exurbs.

In 1930, Seki awoke to the harsh reality of sweeping change. Even in the short time that had transpired since Osaka's expansion in 1925, the city had changed dramatically. It was no longer just a big city (*daitoshi*), he marveled, but a "super city" (*chōtoshi*).[219] No sooner did Seki come to the realization that Greater Osaka had become Super Osaka than he reassessed its circumstances and rethought its future. As he scanned the planned middle-class residential communities that had been developed by suburban railway companies along the lines that fanned out around Osaka—expansive garden suburbs such as Ōmino on the Nankai line and Ikeda Muromachi on the Hankyū line—he was awestruck. Appearing before his very eyes were some of the satellite cities that he had envisioned years before, but they were sadly devoid of working-class character.

Perhaps feeling outdone and outmatched by Osaka's landed capitalists, the once-implacable urban progressive retreated at this point from his tire-

Figure 16. Midōsuji Avenue under construction (mid-1930s). Ōsaka Shiritsu Hakubut-sukan, *Utsusareta Ōsaka: Kindai 100 nen no ayumi* [Osaka photographed: A stroll through a hundred years of the modern age] (Osaka: Ōsaka Shiritsu Hakubutsukan, 1998).

less advocacy of garden suburbs for working-class families. Suddenly seized with the desire to perfect Greater Osaka's burgeoning *Verkehrswirt-schaft,* he hatched a grandiose scheme to connect the far-flung communities that composed the Osaka metropolitan region. The key to his pioneering plan was a futuristic subway system that promised not only to reinvent travel at the urban core but ultimately to intersect suburban railway lines, forming an elaborate metropolitan transit network.

In 1933, Seki celebrated the completion of Osaka's first subway line: a two-mile stretch of track, called the Midōsuji line, that ran down the spine of the city between the northern subcenter of Umeda and the southern subcenter of Shinsaibashi. Above it, the city put in a broad boulevard that has since come to be known as Osaka's Champs-Élysées. Coming in as it did at a whopping thirty-four million yen—and having ripped through the fabric of several old urban neighborhoods—the project and its prime mover earned more than their share of critics. (See figure 16.)

The most vociferous among Seki's detractors, ironically, were those who represented the interests of Osaka's working poor. Complaining bitterly about the extravagant investment, municipal assemblymen from the left-leaning Reformist Faction (Kaishintō) openly accused the mayor of neglecting the poor in order to convenience the rich.[220] This stinging criticism of the city official who had devoted his entire career to working-class causes apparently hit its mark. According to at least one firsthand account of a heated assembly meeting, Seki's face shone a bright red when his priorities were thus challenged. Literally rising to his own defense, the mayor reportedly responded, "If [this project] will make the lives of Osaka's citizens even a little bit better, then I have no choice but to stand by it strongly, even if I am digging my own grave."[221]

In explaining his passionate commitment to the Midōsuji project, on the occasion of its completion in 1933, Seki did little to quiet his social critics. As he had before, again he highlighted his vision of an interconnected metropolitan region, but with a distinctly political-economic twist that recalled his early emphasis on cities as central nodes of activity and exchange in the people's national economy: "Residential districts and business districts are separate from each other [today], and the distance between them is widening. Now that Osaka has expanded, incorporating [outlying] districts into the city, we should figure out how to connect them to each other. We need to make a serious effort in the future to forge a hundred-year plan for the city of Osaka that places high-speed train [lines] in operation."[222] Although he didn't say so at the time, Seki was surely thinking in the familiar terms of his favorite biological metaphor: the urban social body. His projected network of high-speed trains was nothing other than the arteries and the veins of that giant metropolitan organism, the Super City, conveying producers and consumers into and out of its commercial/industrial aorta.

Whether Seki intended Midōsuji as a monument to his mayorship remains an open question, but today Osakans remember him almost exclusively for this. When one reads back over the exchanges between Seki and his Reformist Faction antagonists in the municipal assembly, it becomes crystal clear that, at least in their left-leaning eyes, he was becoming little more than a "servant of the bourgeoisie."[223] It is instructive to point out that, on a personal level, Seki led a thoroughly middle-class—some might even say upper-class—life. As the highest-paid municipal official in Japan, at twenty-five thousand yen per year, he was able to buy a *bessō* (country home) of sorts at Kuwazu, in the hinterlands south of Osaka, not far from Tennōji. On Sundays and holidays, when he and his family were not off to Kuwazu for rest and recreation, they could be found in the same places as other middle-class Osakans: on sightseeing trips to Nara or Kyoto, on excursions to the Takarazuka Spa at the end of the Hankyū line or to the

Figure 17.   Seki family excursion to an Osaka department store. Courtesy of the Seki family and the Osaka City History Archive.

suburban seaside resort of Hamadera, or on downtown shopping trips to the Mitsukoshi, Sogō, and Daimaru department stores.[224] Known to have frequented the Yamatoya and Maruya drinking establishments—and to have relished the release from formal banquets into "democratic sake" shops[225]—Seki also appears to have enjoyed an occasional night out on the town.[226] In short, we might reasonably surmise that he identified personally with the bourgeois aspirations of the so-called new middle class and shared their affinity for the creature comforts of modern urban life. (See figure 17.)

There is ample evidence, moreover, that Seki's social sympathies and priorities were gradually changing. Never comfortable dealing with the endemically poor, he came to identify them reflexively with the intractable slums of Osaka's downtown districts. "No matter how much money we put into existing slums," he told the Municipal Assembly in 1924, "the results are never satisfactory."[227] The fact is: Seki progressively lost patience with the panacea of poor relief supported by the Reformist Faction. Not only can we read creeping contempt in his antipathy for the place-bound poor—who, in Osaka, included ample numbers of outcasts (burakumin), Koreans, and Okinawans[228]—but we can also arguably read the writing on the wall where the working poor were concerned. By 1933, after successfully indulging his impulse to "creative destruction" by cutting a clean swath through the urban neighborhoods along Midōsuji, Seki may well have acquired a taste for this more draconian approach to social change.[229]

Ultimately, it seems, Seki's passionate progressivist pursuit of social prosperity as mayor of Osaka impelled him to confuse ends and means. Whether or not he intended to continue carving out garden suburbs for working-class families in the hinterlands of his Super City, he clearly felt ethically justified in arrogating the authority, when necessary, to propel this metropolitan organism toward maturity. In the priorities he set during the latter years of his mayorship, at least, one can see traces of what Scott calls "authoritarian high modernism."[230] Indeed, Seki appears to have gone out of his way to acquire the work of four of the central exponents of this new autocratic approach to progress: Walther Rathenau, Frederick Taylor, Gustave Le Bon, and Le Corbusier.[231] These ardent disciples of technocracy, scientific management, social control, and total city planning, respectively, aimed to take the confusion and guesswork out of the quest for social and material progress. Like Seki, they had visualized that better life and were bound and determined to inscribe its elements onto the modern world and thus to insinuate its influence into modern lives.

In the end, ironically enough, Seki's progressivism was undone by nature itself. Following the devastating Murōto Typhoon of September 1934, which triggered a one-hundred-year flood, Seki could not help but recall his one-hundred-year plan. Worry not, he hollowly exhorted the weary citizens of his city; we will rise from adversity and "push on to perfect the metropolis of Osaka."[232] Thus reduced to empty rhetoric and pushed to exhaustion by overwork, Seki succumbed to typhoid fever on January 26, 1935.

Sadly, Seki left a mixed legacy of social reform and social control. Had he succeeded in erecting working-class garden suburbs around Osaka, undeniably he would have accomplished meaningful social reform. But, by promoting social reform in this particular way—that is, by creating a class-segregated residential quarter—he also stood to achieve a significant measure of social control. In the last analysis, I would argue, Seki's garden suburbs were gilded cages, designed quite literally to put the working classes in their proper place.

While some readers will certainly be tempted to read Seki's slippage from social reform into social control as a sign of the times—a signal of the authoritarian turn that Japan was making in the 1930s—I find myself hard-pressed to simply write Seki off as a lapsed progressive primed for conversion to ultranationalism. This was a man, after all, who continued to struggle mightily with many of the same issues that had engaged him as a young economist.

When his college-aged son Hideo was arrested as a communist sympathizer in 1933, Seki the father penned a moving testimonial to Japanese nationalism *(kokutairon)* that seems to have played an important part in his son's later renunciation of his newfound internationalist faith. Interestingly, Seki framed his argument in familiar terms that recall his theorizing as a young political economist. He urged his son to acknowledge the reality *(genjitsu)* of Japan's "three-thousand-year history" and to affirm the "unified ethnic consciousness" *(toitsu minzoku ishiki)* of its national people.[233] No sooner did Seki deliver this ethnic nationalist sermon than it came back to haunt him. Sent on an official tour of Japanese-occupied Manchuria, he confronted a class/ethnic issue that vividly recalled a thorny social problem *(shakai mondai)* he had ignored at home. The sight of "coolies" *(kūrii)* at work in Manchuria awakened Seki at last to the sorry state of Korean immigrant labor in Osaka.[234]

At a time when rumors of one-party rule *(ikkoku-ittō)* hung in the air and the specter of Japanese ethnic nationalism loomed large in his mind,[235] Seki took a moment to reflect on the rapidly changing state of the world. In 1934, he hazarded a guess at what the future might bring. "Nationalism and internationalism, individualism and totalitarianism: even though these ideas remain mutually repellent, aren't they likely [to be reconciled] in the next great [ideological] accord?"[236] One cannot help but wonder what Seki was thinking—whether he was simply lamenting the failure of social progressives to save the world from itself or whether he was preparing to take a stand at what appeared to be a critical social turning point *(shakai tenkanki)* in modern history. Endorsing the sentiments expressed by his old friend Minobe Tatsukichi in a political editorial written in January 1934, Seki declared his support for a strong government *(kyōryoku seifu)* that commanded expertise *(senmon chishiki)* and thus promoted responsible governance *(sekinin seiji)*. In the margins of that same diary entry, he then scribbled a cryptic note: "The same thing applies to city government."[237] Given the paternalistic turn that his progressivism had taken—the father/mayor of Osaka presiding resolutely over his boisterous urban branch of the Japanese family-nation—Seki had to have been hatching a plan to guide the metropolis through the coming storm of social change and into a new age of social reconciliation. As a true believer in progressivism, how could he possibly have done otherwise?

Notes

INTRODUCTION

1. For details, see the special issue of Osaka's municipal journal put together in commemoration of the mayor's achievements: *Dai Ōsaka* 11, no. 2 (February 1935), pp. 108–117.

2. Daniel T. Rodgers, *Atlantic Crossings: Social Politics in a Progressive Age* (Cambridge, Mass.: Harvard University Press, 1998), p. 33.

3. Ibid., pp. 33–34.

4. Ibid., pp. 34, 1–2.

5. Given the interest of other non-Europeans—such as the Peruvian Haya de la Torre—in this reformist message, it is tempting at least to daydream about an emerging global progressive fellowship around the turn of the century. See Fredrick B. Pike, *The Politics of the Miraculous in Peru: Haya de la Torre and the Spiritualist Tradition* (Lincoln: University of Nebraska Press, 1986), pp. 94–95.

6. Beard, as I indicate in chapter 6, was twice invited to Japan by Tokyo municipal officials.

7. Charles A. Beard, *The Administration and Politics of Tokyo: A Survey and Opinions* (New York: Macmillan, 1923), p. 11.

8. Rodgers, *Atlantic Crossings*, pp. 33–34.

9. Ibid., p. 30.

10. Andrew E. Barshay, *State and Intellectual in Imperial Japan: The Public Man in Crisis* (Berkeley: Univesity of California Press, 1988), p. 4.

11. On the progressivist slide into scientism and social control in the United States, see Dorothy Ross, "American Social Science and the Idea of Progress," in *The Authority of Experts: Studies in History and Theory*, edited by Thomas L. Haskell (Bloomington: Indiana University Press, 1984), pp. 161–171.

CHAPTER 1. A PORTRAIT OF THE
ECONOMIST AS A YOUNG MAN

1. Shibamura Atsuki, *Seki Hajime: Toshi shisō no paioniā* [Seki Hajime: Pioneer of urban thought] (Kyoto: Shōriaisha, 1989), p. 22.

2. Kawabata Naomasa, *Seki shichō shōden* [A brief biography of Mayor Seki] (Osaka: Ko Ōsaka Shichō Seki Hajime Hakase Itoku Kenshō Iinkai, 1956); Shibamura, *Seki Hajime*.

3. Pierre Bourdieu, with Luc Boltanski, *Photography: A Middle-Brow Art*, trans. Shaun Whiteside (Stanford, Calif.: Stanford University Press, 1990), pp. 30–31.

4. Susan Sontag, *On Photography* (New York: Dell, 1977), p. 154.

5. John Berger, "Uses of Photography," in *About Looking* (New York: Vintage Books, 1991), p. 55.

6. Ibid., p. 65.

7. Yamaori Tetsuo, *Nihonjin no kao: Zuzō kara bunka o yomu* [The face(s) of Japanese: Reading culture from icons] (Tokyo: NHK Bukkusu, 1995), p. 215.

8. John Dower, "Ways of Seeing, Ways of Remembering: The Photography of Prewar Japan," in *A Century of Japanese Photography*, ed. Japan Photographers Association (New York: Pantheon Books, 1980), pp. 9–10.

9. Julia Hirsch, *Family Photographs: Content, Meaning, and Effect* (New York: Oxford University Press, 1981), p. 70.

10. Dower, "Ways of Seeing," p. 10.

11. Ibid., pp. 5–6.

12. On early Meiji *shashinshi*, see especially Kinoshita Naoyuki, *Shashinga ron: Shashin to kaiga no kekkon* [On photographic pictures: The marriage of photographs and pictures] (Tokyo: Iwanami Shoten, 1996), and Tokyo Metropolitan Museum of Photography and Hakodate Museum of Art, Hokkaido, eds., *The Advent of Photography in Japan* (Tokyo: Tokyo Metropolitan Museum of Photography, 1997).

13. For an interesting account of Western photography in Meiji Japan, see Hugh Cortazzi and Terry Bennett, *Japan: Caught in Time* (New York and Tokyo: Weatherhill, 1995).

14. See, for example, the portrait of the last shogun, Tokugawa Yoshinobu, reproduced in Masao Miyoshi, *As We Saw Them: The First Japanese Embassy to the United States (1860)* (Berkeley: University of California Press, 1979), p. 153.

15. Dower, "Ways of Seeing," p. 9.

16. Ibid., p. 10.

17. Hirsch, *Family Photographs*, p. 77.

18. Dower, "Ways of Seeing," pp. 9–10.

19. Kumamoto Kenritsu Bijutsukan, ed., *Tomishige Shashinjo no 130 nen* [130 years of the Tomishige Photographic Studio] (Kumamoto: Kumamoto Kenritsu Bijutsukan, 1993), p. 162.

20. Suren Lalvani, *Photography, Vision, and the Production of Modern Bodies* (Albany: State University of New York Press, 1996), pp. 66 and 68. See Kumamoto Kenritsu Bijutsukan, *Tomishige Shashinjo*, pp. 161–162, for the floor plan of a large Meiji photographic studio.

21. Lalvani, *Photography*, p. 68.

22. Kumamoto Kenritsu Bijutsukan, *Tomishige Shashinjo*, passim.

23. For a fascinating glimpse into the artifice of Victorian photographic portraiture, see Audrey Linkman, *The Victorians: Photographic Portraits* (London: Tauris Parke Books, 1993).

24. Hirsch, *Family Photographs*, p. 70.

25. Shirley Teresa Wajda, "The Artistic Portrait Photograph," in *The Arts and the American Home, 1890–1930*, ed. Jessica H. Foy and Karal Ann Marling (Knoxville: University of Tennessee Press, 1994), pp. 165–182.

26. Wilbur M. Fridell, "Government Ethics Textbooks in Late Meiji Japan," *Journal of Asian Studies* 29, no. 3 (August 1970), p. 829.

27. Quoted in Ueno Chizuko, *Kindai kazoku no seiritsu to shūen* [The formation and the demise of the modern family] (Tokyo: Iwanami Shoten, 1994), p. 71.

28. T. Fujitani, *Splendid Monarchy: Power and Pageantry in Modern Japan* (Berkeley: University of California Press, 1996), pp. 190–191. Embedded quote is from an unnamed primary-school ethics textbook written by Higashikuze Michitomi in 1890.

29. See especially Sally A. Hastings, "The Empress' New Clothes and Japanese Women, 1868–1912," *Historian* 55, no. 4 (Summer 1993), passim.

30. Quoted in Fridell, "Government Ethics Textbooks in Late Meiji Japan," p. 831.

31. Illustrated in Muta Kazue, *Senryaku toshite no kazoku: Kindai Nihon no kokumin kokka keisei to josei* [The family as a strategy: Women and the formation of the modern Japanese family state] (Tokyo: Shinyōsha, 1996), pp. 94–99.

32. Ibid., pp. 35 and 55–56.

33. Muta Kazue, "Images of the Family in Meiji Periodicals: The Paradox Underlying the Emergence of the 'Home,'" *U.S.-Japan Women's Journal English Supplement* 7 (1994), p. 54.

34. Quoted in Carol Gluck, *Japan's Modern Myths: Ideology in the Late Meiji Period* (Princeton, N.J.: Princeton University Press, 1985), p. 189. On the home and the invented tradition of "Japanese domesticity," see Jordan Sand, "At Home in the Meiji Period: Inventing Japanese Domesticity," in *Mirror of Modernity: Invented Traditions of Modern Japan*, ed. Stephen Vlastos (Berkeley: University of California Press, 1998), pp. 191–207.

35. Gluck, *Japan's Modern Myths*, pp. 187–189.

36. Not that it was ever relaxing to have a studio portrait taken. As Nakano Makiko recounts in her Kyoto diary of 1910, "Posing for photographs made me nervous. I felt my body stiffen, but at the moment the photographer said, 'Now, please hold still,' it was all over." Nakano Makiko, *Makiko's Diary: A*

Merchant Wife in 1910 Kyoto. Trans. Kazuko Smith (Stanford, Calif.: Stanford University Press, 1995), p. 70.

37. Perhaps the most difficult "illusion" for the photographer to create was that of Meiji motherhood. As a working mother who could no longer devote most of her time to child rearing, Yoshi was quite explicitly at odds with the state-sponsored ideal. See Muta, "Images of the Family in Meiji Periodicals," p. 66.

38. Kawabata, *Seki shichō shōden*, p. 20.

39. On the "residential geography" of Japan's modern aristocracy, see Takie Sugiyama Lebra, *Above the Clouds: Status Culture of the Modern Japanese Nobility* (Berkeley: University of California Press, 1993), pp. 148–155.

40. Sontag, *On Photography*, p. 38.

41. Ibid., pp. 37–38.

42. Tsumura Hidematsu, "Waga hansei no tomo o kataru" [About my lifelong friend], *Dai Ōsaka* 11, no. 2 (1935), p. 13.

43. Kawashima Yasuyoshi, *Fujin/kateiran koto hajime* [The advent of the women's/home-life page] (Tokyo: Seiabō, 1996), pp. 51–71.

44. On *ryōsai kenbo* and its limitations as an ideological model in Meiji, see Kathleen S. Uno, *Passages to Modernity: Motherhood, Childhood, and Social Reform in Early Twentieth Century Japan* (Honolulu: University of Hawai'i Press, 1999), pp. 44–45.

45. Byron K. Marshall, *Learning to Be Modern: Japanese Political Discourse on Education* (Boulder, Colo.: Westview Press, 1994), pp. 69–71.

46. During his tenure as Japan's first official ambassador to the United States, Mori saw fit to canvass leading Americans on the educational challenges facing his nation. He asked them specifically to assess the "effect of education" on five areas of national concern: material prosperity; commerce; agricultural and industrial interests; the social, moral, and physical condition of the people; and laws and government. Their replies, as vetted by the economic historians Chūhei Sugiyama and Tamotsu Nishizawa, affirmed the looming importance of business education; Chūhei Sugiyama and Tamotsu Nishizawa, "'Captain of Industry': Tokyo Commercial School at Hitotsubashi," in *Enlightenment and Beyond: Political Economy Comes to Japan*, ed. Chūhei Sugiyama and Hiroshi Mizuta (Tokyo: University of Tokyo Press, 1988), pp. 152–154.

47. Quoted in ibid., p. 156.

48. Ibid., pp. 160–161.

49. Donald Roden, *Schooldays in Imperial Japan: A Study in the Culture of a Student Elite* (Berkeley: University of California Press, 1980), p. 123.

50. Sugiyama and Nishizawa, "'Captain of Industry,'" p. 161.

51. Ibid., p. 164.

52. Quoted in Hidaka Kisaburō, "Kōfūkai to bōto no omoide" [A recollection of the Kōfūkai and rowing], *Dai Ōsaka* 11, no. 2 (1935), pp. 15–16.

53. Sugiyama and Nishizawa, "'Captain of Industry,'" p. 164.

54. Koyama Kenzō, *Koyama Kenzō den* [Biography of Koyama Kenzō] (Osaka: Sanjūyon Ginkō, 1930), p. 380.

55. Shibamura, *Seki Hajime*, p. 24.

56. Kenneth B. Pyle, *The New Generation in Meiji Japan: Problems of Cultural Identity, 1885–1895* (Stanford, Calif.: Stanford University Press, 1969).

57. Ibid., pp. 10–21.

58. Quoted in Kawabata, *Seki shichō shōden*, p. 25.

59. Earl H. Kinmonth, *The Self-Made Man in Meiji Japanese Thought: From Samurai to Salary Man* (Berkeley: University of California Press, 1981), pp. 157–158.

60. Sugiyama and Nishizawa, "'Captain of Industry,'" pp. 164–165.

61. Seki Hajime, *Shōgyō keizai taii* [An outline of commercial economics] (Tokyo: Dōbunkan, 1898).

62. Ibid., foreword.

63. Seki Hajime, "Testudō gakkō" [The railroad school] (1899–1900), Osaka City History Archive.

64. Michel Laffut, "Belgium," in *Railways and the Economic Development of Western Europe, 1830–1914,* ed. Patrick O'Brien (New York: St. Martin's Press, 1983), p. 203.

65. Sugiyama and Nishizawa, "'Captain of Industry,'" p. 162.

66. Seki Hajime, "*Anmelds Buch*" [Class record] (October 23, 1900), Osaka City History Archive.

67. V. R. Berghahn, *Imperial Germany, 1871–1914: Economy, Society, Culture, and Politics* (Providence, R.I.: Berghahn Books, 1994), p. 182.

68. Daniel T. Rodgers, *Atlantic Crossings: Social Politics in a Progressive Age* (Cambridge, Mass.: Harvard University Press, 1998), pp. 89–97.

69. Ibid., p. 90.

70. Ibid., p. 91.

71. Tsumura, "Waga hansei no tomo o kataru," pp. 10–11.

72. Quoted in Richard D. Mandell, *Paris 1900: The Great World's Fair* (Toronto: University of Toronto Press, 1967), pp. x–xi.

73. Quoted in Yoshimi Shunya, *Hakurankai no seiji gaku: Manazashi no kindai* [The politics of exhibitions: The modern gaze] (Tokyo: Chūkō Shinsho, 1992), p. 83.

74. Rodgers, *Atlantic Crossings*, p. 10.

75. Mandell, *Paris 1900*, p. 56.

76. Quoted in ibid., p. 56.

77. Ibid., p. 84. For a photograph of the Japanese pavilion, see Yoshida Mitsukuni et al., eds., *Zusetsu bankoku hakurankai shi, 1851–1942* [An illustrated history of international expositions, 1851–1942] (Kyoto: Shibunkaku Shuppan, 1985), p. 164.

78. Quoted in Shibamura, *Seki Hajime*, p. 34.

79. Rodgers, *Atlantic Crossings*, p. 11.

80. Ibid., p. 12.

81. Ibid., p. 90.

82. Horst Matzerath, "Berlin, 1890–1940," in *Metropolis 1890–1940*, ed. Anthony Sutcliffe (Chicago: University of Chicago Press, 1984), p. 291.

83. Peter Fritzsche, *Reading Berlin 1900* (Cambridge, Mass.: Harvard University Press, 1996), p. 30.

84. Ibid., p. 29.

85. Quoted in Rodgers, *Atlantic Crossings*, p. 90.

86. Fritzsche, *Reading Berlin*, p. 33.

87. Shibamura, *Seki Hajime*, pp. 34–35. Rodgers notes that the Krupp worker community was one of several European sites that had become "show-places of pre–World War I city planning"; Rodgers, *Atlantic Crossings*, p. 163.

88. Shibamura, *Seki Hajime*, pp. 32–33.

89. Rodgers, *Atlantic Crossings*, pp. 76–111.

90. In his memoirs, Burgess proclaims Roscher as "almost the founder of the science of national economy," noting that "his lecture room was the best attended one in the whole university, and his books were the most widely read"; John W. Burgess, *Reminiscences of an American Scholar* (New York: Columbia University Press, 1934), p. 109.

91. Rodgers, *Atlantic Crossings*, pp. 101–103.

92. Quoted in Shibamura, *Seki Hajime*, p. 35.

93. To get a feel for the development of New York as a modern metropolis, see Edwin G. Burrows and Mike Wallace, *Gotham: A History of New York City to 1898* (New York: Oxford University Press, 1999), pp. 1041–1246. And, for a portrait of New York at the turn of the century, see David C. Hammack, *Power and Society: Greater New York at the Turn of the Century* (New York: Russell Sage Foundation, 1982), passim.

94. Shibamura, *Seki Hajime*, p. 35.

95. Quoted in Hammack, *Power and Society*, p. 237.

96. Burrows and Wallace, *Gotham*, pp. 1059–1070.

97. Quoted in Shibamura, *Seki Hajime*, p. 35.

98. Dreiser quoted in Hammack, *Power and Society*, p. 61.

99. Quoted in Shibamura, *Seki Hajime*, p. 35.

100. Quoted in ibid., p. 35.

101. Quoted in William Cronon, *Nature's Metropolis: Chicago and the Great West* (New York: Norton, 1991), p. 366.

102. Seki Hajime, "Tabi nikki" [Travel diary] (1900), Osaka City History Archive.

103. Rodgers, *Atlantic Crossings*, p. 368.

104. Kawabata, *Seki shichō shōden*, p. 27. The Tokyo Commercial College was frequently referred to simply as Hitotsubashi, after its location.

105. Ibid., p. 28.

106. Seki, *Shōgyō keizai taii*, preface.

107. Sano Zensaku, "Tokyo kōshō kyōju jidai no Seki hakase" [Dr. Seki

during his days as a Tokyo Commercial College professor], *Dai Ōsaka* 11, no. 2 (1935), p. 20.

108. Kawabata, *Seki shichō shōden*, p. 29.

109. Tsumura, "Waga hansei no tomo o kataru," p. 13.

110. Tessa Morris-Suzuki, *A History of Japanese Economic Thought* (London: Routledge, 1989), pp. 13–14.

111. Seki Hajime, *Shōgyō keizai seisaku* [Commercial economic policy] (Tokyo: Ōkura Shoten, 1903), p. 67.

112. Ibid., p. 293.

113. Ibid., p. 60.

114. For a stimulating discussion of Japanese ethnic nationalism, see Kevin M. Doak, "What Is a Nation and Who Belongs? National Narratives and the Ethnic Imagination in Twentieth-Century Japan," *American Historical Review* 102, no. 2 (April 1997), pp. 283–309.

115. Frank O. Miller, *Minobe Tatsukichi: Interpreter of Constitutionalism in Japan* (Berkeley: University of California Press, 1965), p. 59.

116. Seki Hajime, *Shōkō seisaku kōryō* [Essential principles of commercial and industrial policy] (Tokyo: Dōbunkan, 1909), p. 69.

117. Seki Hajime, *Rōdōsha hogo hō ron* [On a worker-protection law] (Tokyo: Ryūbunkan, 1910), p. 46.

118. Seki Hajime Kenkyūkai, ed., *Seki Hajime nikki: Taishō Shōwa Shoki no Ōsaka shisei* [Seki Hajime diary: Taisho–Early Showa Osaka municipal government] (Tokyo: Tokyo Daigaku Shuppankai, 1986), passim.

119. Unpublished testimonial dated April 1932, Osaka City History Archive.

CHAPTER 2. THE PEOPLE'S NATIONAL ECONOMY

1. Quoted in Shibamura Atsuki, *Seki Hajime: Toshi shisō no paioniā* (Kyoto: Shōraisha, 1989), p. 36.

2. Fritz K. Ringer, *Max Weber's Methodology: The Unification of the Cultural and Social Sciences* (Cambridge, Mass.: Harvard University Press, 1997), pp. 12–13.

3. Keith Tribe, *Strategies of Economic Order: German Economic Discourse, 1750–1950* (Cambridge: Cambridge University Press, 1995), p. 71.

4. Ibid., p. 73.

5. Ibid., pp. 72–73.

6. Henri Lefebvre, *The Production of Space*, trans. Donald Nicholson-Smith (Oxford: Blackwell, 1991).

7. Shibamura Atsuki, "Seki Hajime to sono jidai (I): Shisei tantō izen no shiseki to shisō" [Seki Hajime and his era: Historical landmarks and ideas prior to becoming a municipal manager], *Shisei kenkyū* 56 (July 1982), p. 4.

8. Paradoxically, as Brophy has observed, List had difficulty convincing the economically reform-minded Prussian bureaucracy of the value of railways.

Dropping the ball on this important initiative, the state instead left early railway development to enterprising entrepreneurs; James P. Brophy, *Capitalism, Politics, and Railroads in Prussia, 1830–1870* (Columbus: Ohio State University Press, 1998), pp. 22–23.

9. Tribe, *Strategies of Economic Order*, pp. 63 and 64.

10. On the early Meiji debate between railway and waterway advocates, see Matsuura Shigeki, *Meiji no kokudo kaihatsu shi: Kindai doboku gijutsu no ishizue* [A history of national land development in Meiji: The foundation of modern construction technology] (Tokyo: Kajima Shuppankai, 1992), pp. 28–46.

11. Seki Hajime, *Koruson-shi kōtsū seisaku* [C. Colson on transportation policy] (Tokyo: Dōbunkan, 1903), p. 1.

12. Wolfgang Schivelbusch, *The Railway Journey: The Industrialization of Time and Space in the 19th Century* (Berkeley: University of California Press, 1986), p. 45.

13. Tribe, *Strategies of Economic Order*, p. 63.

14. Seki Hajime, "Kangyō tetsudō no keizai shugi" [The economics of state-run railways], *Kokumin keizai zasshi* 1, no. 1 (June 1906), p. 1.

15. Stephen J. Ericson, *The Sound of the Whistle: Railroads and the State in Meiji Japan* (Cambridge, Mass.: Harvard University Press, 1996), p. 376.

16. Ibid., p. 256.

17. Jeffrey E. Hanes, "Contesting Centralization? Space, Time, and Hegemony in Meiji Japan," in *New Directions in the Study of Meiji Japan*, ed. Helen Hardacre and Adam L. Kern (Leiden: Brill, 1997), pp. 491–492.

18. Here, I am using Tribe's terms, as he applies them to List; Tribe, *Strategies of Economic Order*, p. 63.

19. Seki Hajime, "Chihō tetsudō ron, I" [On local railways, I], *Kokumin keizai zasshi* 1, no. 7 (December 1906), pp. 51–52.

20. Ibid., pp. 55–59.

21. Seki Hajime, "Chihō tetsudō ron, II" [On local railways, II], *Kokumin keizai zasshi* 2, no. 1 (January 1907), pp. 74, 75, and 84.

22. Ericson, *Sound of the Whistle*, p. 375.

23. Seki Hajime, "Berugi chōson tetsudō no kinkyō" [Recent conditions of Belgium's local railways], *Kokumin keizai zasshi* 2, no. 6 (June 1907).

24. See especially Seki Hajime, "Unchin ron" [On fares], *Kokka gakkai zasshi* 19, no. 11 (November 1905), and Seki Hajime, "Tetsudō keizai ni kansuru shinsho" [New works concerning railway economics], *Kokumin keizai zasshi* 1, no. 5 (October 1906).

25. Seki, "Unchin ron," passim.

26. Seki Hajime, "Tōshin tetsudō no shūeki ryoku" [Earning power of the railways of eastern China], *Kokumin keizai zasshi* 1, no. 3 (August 1906).

27. Quoted in Tribe, *Strategies of Economic Order*, p. 63.

28. Seki Hajime, "Toshi kōtsū kikan no hattatsu to kyojū kankei" [The development of urban transit facilities and their relationship to residence], in *Shakai Seisaku Gakkai ronsō: Kanzei mondai to shakai seisaku*, 2 [Treatises

of the Japan Association for Social Policy: The tariff issue and social policy, 2], ed. Shakai Seisaku Gakkai (Tokyo: Dōbunkan, 1909), p. 173.

29. Ibid.

30. Bai Gao, *Economic Ideology and Japanese Industrial Policy: Developmentalism from 1931 to 1965* (New York: Cambridge University Press, 1997), p. 61.

31. Seki Hajime, *Shōgyō keizai taii* (Tokyo: Dōbunkan, 1898), preface.

32. Akira Iriye, "Japan's Drive to Great-Power Status," in *The Cambridge History of Japan*, vol. 5: *The Nineteenth Century*, ed. Marius B. Jansen (New York: Cambridge University Press, 1989), p. 765.

33. Kenneth B. Pyle, *The New Generation in Meiji Japan: Problems of Cultural Identity, 1885–1895* (Stanford, Calif.: Stanford University Press, 1969), p. 4.

34. Quoted in ibid., p. 180.

35. Tessa Morris-Suzuki, *A History of Japanese Economic Thought* (London: Routledge, 1989), pp. 13–14.

36. Quoted in Kenneth B. Pyle, "Meiji Conservatism," in *The Cambridge History of Japan*, vol. 5: *The Nineteenth Century*, ed. Marius B. Jansen (New York: Cambridge University Press, 1989), p. 677.

37. Morris-Suzuki, *A History of Japanese Economic Thought*, p. 58. For an overview of liberal economic thought in Meiji Japan, see pp. 49–58.

38. For a brief review of the liberal economic response to protectionism early on, see Chūhei Sugiyama, *Origins of Economic Thought in Modern Japan* (London: Routledge, 1994), pp. 7–8.

39. Quoted in ibid., pp. 8–9.

40. The guiding lights of the German historical school itself were Wilhelm Roscher, Adam Müller, Karl Knies, Johannes Konrad, Bruno Hildebrand, and Adolf Held.

41. Paraphrased in Morris-Suzuki, *A History of Japanese Economic Thought*, p. 60.

42. David Williams, *Japan: Beyond the End of History* (London: Routledge, 1994), p. 120.

43. Friedrich List, *The National System of Political Economy*, trans. Sampson S. Lloyd (New York: Longmans, Green, 1904), pp. 99–100.

44. Ibid., pp. 102–103.

45. Ibid., p. 103.

46. Ibid., p. 103.

47. Morris-Suzuki, *A History of Japanese Economic Thought*, pp. 60–61.

48. Tribe, *Strategies of Economic Order*, p. 71.

49. Drawing attention to this parallel and its continuing resonance, Williams has observed that "German and Japanese economic nationalists have been consistently alive to the fact that the greatest proponents of free trade have tended, during the past two centuries, also to be spokesmen of the world's dominant economic power"; Williams, *Japan*, p. 121.

50. Morris-Suzuki, *A History of Japanese Economic Thought*, p. 62.

51. Richard J. Samuels, *"Rich Nation, Strong Army": National Security and the Technological Transformation of Japan* (Ithaca, N.Y.: Cornell University Press, 1994), p. 56.

52. As Inukai put the issue in 1880, "National economy is different from 'cosmopolite economy' and so it is from 'private economy.' As all nations are not alike in race, language, custom, institution, law, and civilization, so they cannot help differing in their interests. What is harmful or beneficial to one nation is not necessarily so to another." Quoted in Sugiyama, *Origins of Economic Thought in Modern Japan*, pp. 10–11.

53. Quoted in Morris-Suzuki, *A History of Japanese Economic Thought*, p. 61.

54. See Williams, *Japan*, pp. 83–84, and Samuels, *"Rich Nation, Strong Army,"* p. 56.

55. Tribe, *Strategies of Economic Order*, p. 94.

56. Ringer, *Max Weber's Methodology*, p. 14.

57. William Roscher, *Principles of Political Economy*, trans. John J. Lalor (Chicago: Callaghan, 1882), p. 84.

58. Ibid.

59. Ibid., pp. 387–388.

60. Ibid., p. 84.

61. Ibid., p. 114.

62. Ibid., p. 80.

63. Ibid., pp. 246 and 258.

64. Ibid., pp. 70–73.

65. Seki, *Shōgyō keizai taii*, pp. 281–282.

66. Ibid., passim.

67. Ibid., pp. 37–38.

68. Samuels, *"Rich Nation, Strong Army,"* p. 6.

69. Williams, *Japan*, p. 121.

70. Christopher Howe, *The Origins of Japanese Trade Supremacy: Development and Technology in Asia from 1540 to the Pacific War* (Hong Kong: University of Chicago Press, 1996), pp. 135–136.

71. Seki Hajime and Fukuda Tokuzō, eds. and trans., *Saikin shōsei keizai ron* [On the economics of contemporary commercial politics] (Tokyo: Ōkura Shoten, 1902). On the ins and outs of the larger German controversy over industrialism that framed this debate over foreign trade, see Kenneth D. Barkin, *The Controversy over German Industrialization, 1890–1902* (Chicago: University of Chicago Press, 1970).

72. Seki and Fukuda, *Saikin shōsei*, pp. 128–129. Seki would hammer this methodological point home some years later in a debate over Marxist determinism with Kawakami Hajime. This debate is the focus of chapter 3.

73. Ibid., p. 109.

74. Seki, *Shōgyō keizai taii*, pp. 281–282.

75. Ippei Yamazawa, *Economic Development and International Trade: The*

Japanese Model (Honolulu: East-West Center Resource Systems Institute, 1990), p. 141.

76. Taketoshi Ito, *The Japanese Economy* (Cambridge, Mass.: MIT Press, 1992), p. 27.

77. Kent E. Calder, *Strategic Capitalism: Private Business and Public Purpose in Japanese Industrial Finance* (Ithaca, N.Y.: Cornell University Press, 1994), p. 16.

78. One contemporary argument for the gold standard went as follows: "The civilisation of a country may be gauged in many ways and by many standards. But one of the surest ways of gauging it is by the standard of money used. The passing from copper to silver marks one stage. The passing from silver to gold marks a more perfect stage in the progress of civilisation." Quoted in Howe, *Origins of Japanese Trade Supremacy*, p. 147.

79. Fuji Bank, Research Division, *Banking in Modern Japan* (Tokyo: Fuji Bank, 1967), pp. 37–38.

80. Ibid., p. 41.

81. Ibid., pp. 41–43.

82. See Calder, *Strategic Capitalism*, p. 24, and Yamazawa, *Economic Development and International Trade*, pp. 141–142.

83. Seki Hajime, *Shōgyō keizai seisaku* (Tokyo: Ōkura Shoten, 1903), p. 63.

84. Seki and Fukuda, *Saikin shōsei*, p. 109.

85. Ibid., p. 111.

86. Soon, indeed, Seki would steep himself in the literature of a diverse range of European and American intellectuals who fit this general description, including the Fabian socialists Sidney and Beatrice Webb, the "evolutionary socialist" Eduard Bernstein, and the political economist Richard Ely. On the transatlantic roots of social-democratic thought, see James T. Kloppenberg, *Uncertain Victory: Social Democracy and Progressivism in European and American Thought, 1870–1920* (New York: Oxford University Press, 1986), pp. 5–11.

87. Seki, *Shōgyō keizai seisaku*, p. 59.

88. Ibid., preface.

89. Seki and Fukuda, *Saikin shōsei*, p. 111. Although Seki thereby distinguished "backward" nations from "progressive" ones, he did not argue the issue from a unilinear historical perspective. Even as he acknowledged Japan's "relative backwardness," to use a term later popularized by Gerschenkron, he celebrated its emergence into modernity; Alexander Gerschenkron, *Economic Backwardness in Historical Perspective* (Cambridge, Mass.: Harvard University Press, 1962).

90. Seki, *Shōgyō keizai seisaku*, pp. 1 and 2.

91. Ibid., pp. 2–3.

92. Ibid., p. 6.

93. Ibid., pp. 6–7.

94. Ibid., pp. 16–18.

95. Ibid., p. 19.

96. Ibid., p. 7.

97. On the importance of "analogies" to economists influenced by the German historical school, see Ringer, *Max Weber's Methodology*, p. 14.

98. Toby has since demonstrated that *sakoku* was a chimera; Ronald P. Toby, *State and Diplomacy in Early Modern Japan: Asia in the Development of the Tokugawa Bakufu* (Princeton, N.J.: Princeton University Press, 1984).

99. Seki Hajime, *Shōkō seisaku kōryō* (Tokyo: Dōbunkan, 1909), p. 5.

100. Ibid.

101. Samir Amin, *Unequal Development: An Essay on the Social Formations of Peripheral Capitalism* (New York: Monthly Review Press, 1976), 369.

102. On the complicated relationship between the United States and Europe, see Daniel T. Rodgers, *Atlantic Crossings: Social Politics in a Progressive Age* (Cambridge, Mass.: Harvard University Press, 1998), p. 1.

103. Seki, *Shōkō seisaku kōryō*, pp. 64–67.

104. Seki Hajime, "Gaikoku shōsei gairon, I" [An introduction to foreign commercial policy, I], *Kokumin keizai zasshi* 2, no. 6 (June 1907), p. 90.

105. Seki, *Shōgyō keizai seisaku*, pp. 292–293. With this thinly veiled reference to the government's increasing support of *shokusan kōgyō*, Seki first put himself on record as a critic of monopoly capitalism.

106. Ibid., pp. 292–293.

107. Seki Hajime, "Tsūshō jōyaku ron, I" [On commercial treaties, I], *Kokumin keizai zasshi* 5, no. 3 (September 1908), pp. 10 and 29.

108. Seki Hajime, "Tsūshō jōyaku ron, II" [On commercial treaties, II], *Kokumin keizai zasshi* 5, no. 4 (October 1908), p. 86. The specific "national advantage" that Seki aimed to protect was Japan's burgeoning industrial economy. Fully cognizant of the fact that Western investors held half the war bonds that Japan had floated to finance its conflict with Russia—a war that had cost Japan seven times more than the Sino-Japanese War had—he knew as well that these investors were watching warily as his nation descended into a postwar recession. Notwithstanding the wariness of some Western businessmen, many remained sufficiently sanguine about Japan's prospects for sustained economic growth that they continued to seek ways of penetrating its markets. Accordingly, Seki encouraged the Japanese leadership to steel its postwar resolve to increase tariffs and thereby protect infant industries.

109. Howe, *Origins of Japanese Trade Supremacy*, p. 161.

110. Yamazawa, *Economic Development and International Trade*, p. 149.

111. Seki Hajime, "Toshi kōtsū," p. 173.

112. Yamazawa, *Economic Development and International Trade*, p. 144.

113. Seki, "Toshi kōtsū," pp. 261–263.

114. Ibid., pp. 263–264.

115. Ibid., pp. 265–266.

116. Seki Hajime, "Beika tōki to sono chōsetsu saku" [Rising rice prices

and regulatory policy], *Kokumin keizai zasshi* 11, no. 8 (July 1912), pp. 11 and 12.

117. Ibid., pp. 11, 12; Seki, "Tsūshō jōyaku ron, I," pp. 8–9 and 10. See also Seki, *Shōgyō keizai seisaku*, p. 173, on the dangers of turning the clock back.

118. Seki and Fukuda, *Saikin shōsei*, p. 111.

119. Seki, "Tsūshō jōyaku ron, II," p. 86. While Seki eagerly anticipated Japan's imminent annexation of Korea, he sharply distinguished its expansionist impulse from that of the Western imperialist powers. The critical distinction that Seki and others drew between European and Japanese imperialism seems to have been lost on most historians, however. Kojita is a good case in point. In his haste to identify Seki as a closet imperialist, Kojita elides the distinction made by Seki and others between an "imperialist economy" and a "greater people's national economy." As they saw it, the critical difference between the European powers and Japan was that the Europeans were engaged in global transoceanic imperialism while Japan's annexation of Korea was a natural extension of Meiji nation building. Kojita Yasunao, *Nihon kindai toshi shi kenkyū josetsu* [An introduction to the study of modern Japanese urban history] (Tokyo: Kashiwa Shobō, 1991), p. 190.

120. Seki, *Shōgyō keizai seisaku*, p. 361.

121. Peter Duus, *The Abacus and the Sword: The Japanese Penetration of Korea, 1895–1910* (Berkeley: University of California Press, 1995), pp. 432–433.

122. Seki Hajime, "Nikoruson kyōju no teikoku ron o yomu" [On reading Professor Nicholson's theory of imperialism], *Kokumin keizai zasshi* 8, no. 6 (June 1910), pp. 107 and 95.

123. Ibid., p. 107.

124. While the annexation of Korea did not transform Japan into a colonial juggernaut, it did significantly strengthen the people's national economy. Japan remained dependent on imports for many things, including most of the raw materials and much of the machinery needed to run its industrial economy. But it finally had room to grow, literally and figuratively. To borrow Calder's vocabulary and to put a twist on his observations about the converse situation prior to 1910–1911: no longer was Japan so tightly constrained by considerations of scale and resources that it had no choice but to be "[hyper]-market sensitive." The annexation of Korea enabled Japan to "insulate" itself from the unremitting pressure to sustain "international economic competitiveness." Rather than being compelled to reactively adjust its national economic agenda to meet the challenges posed by Western competition, Japan was able to actively set an economic agenda that reflected its national(ist) aspirations. Calder, *Strategic Capitalism*, p. 24.

125. Seki Hajime, "Kokusai boeki shinkō-saku" [Measures for the promotion of international trade], *Hōgaku shinpō* 23, no. 6 (June 1913), pp. 10–13.

126. On the significance of entrepreneurs in the industrial age, Seki wrote

the following: "The special character of the machine age is not to be found simply in the utilization of machines, nor is it traceable to individual skills. Ultimately, it must be identified with those who properly implement the means of achieving its objectives. The foundation of advancement for the people's national economy is the entrepreneur who recognizes the true value of science." Seki Hajime, Kōgyō seisaku [Industrial policy] (Tokyo: Hōbunkan, 1911), p. 1:50.

127. Quoted in Hirokawa Yoshihide, "Seki Hajime no jiyūshugi shisō" [Liberalism in the ideas of Seki Hajime], Jinkun kenkyū 35, no. 5 (1983), p. 277.

128. Seki Hajime, "Kabushiki gaisha ni okeru yūgen sekininshugi no keizaijō no nedan" [The economic price of limited liability in joint-stock corporations], Hōgaku shinpō 24, no. 5 (May 1914), p. 64.

129. Ibid., p. 47.

130. Seki, Kōgyō seisaku (1913), p. 2:574.

131. Seki, "Kabushiki gaisha," passim.

132. William D. Wray, "Afterword: The Writing of Japanese Business History," in Managing Industrial Enterprise: Cases from Japan's Prewar Experience, ed. William D. Wray (Cambridge, Mass.: Harvard University Press, 1989), p. 323.

133. Seki, "Kabushiki gaisha," p. 65.

134. Ibid., p. 66.

135. Seki defined financiers as those who "supply and spend the funds necessary for the equipment and management of [industrial] enterprise." Seki Hajime, "Fuainanshā o ronzuru" [About financiers], Kokumin keizai zasshi 4, no. 2 (February 1908), p. 92.

136. Ibid., pp. 95 and 111.

137. Seki Hajime, "Keiei to kigyō to no igi ni tsuite" [Regarding the significance of management and private enterprise], Kokumin keizai zasshi 9, no. 4 (October 1910), p. 50; Seki Hajime, "Kigyōsha no honshitsu: Ueda, Fukuda ryōshi no ronbun o yomite" [The essence of the businessman: On reading the works of Messrs. Ueda and Fukuda], Kokumin keizai zasshi 16, no. 5 (May 1914), pp. 80–81.

138. Seki, "Fuainanshā o ronzuru," p. 112.

139. Ibid., pp. 112–113.

140. Seki Hajime, "Teikokushugi to shihon koku, I" [Imperialism and the capitalist nation, I], Kokumin keizai zasshi 3, no. 4 (October 1907), p. 133.

141. Seki Hajime, "Teikokushugi to shihon koku, II" [Imperialism and the capitalist nation, II], Kokumin keizai zasshi 3, no. 5 (November 1907), pp. 125–126.

142. Seki, "Fuainanshā o ronzuru," p. 113.

143. For a comprehensive history of Japanese banking, see Norio Tamaki, Japanese Banking: A History, 1859–1959 (Cambridge: Cambridge University Press, 1995). For a sweeping historical survey of modern Japanese banking,

see William M. Tsutsui, *Banking Policy in Japan: American Efforts at Reform during the Occupation* (London: Routledge, 1988), pp. 1–17.

144. Seki, *Kōgyō seisaku*, p. 1:598.

145. Ibid., p. 1:599.

146. Fuji Bank, Research Division, *Banking in Modern Japan*, p. 49.

147. Ibid., p. 50.

148. Calder, *Strategic Capitalism*, p. 26.

149. Takafusa Nakamura, *Economic Growth in Prewar Japan* (New Haven, Conn.: Yale University Press, 1983), p. 61.

150. See ibid., p. 61, and Fuji Bank, Research Division, *Banking in Modern Japan*, p. 43.

151. Tsutsui, *Banking Policy in Japan*, p. 3.

152. Seki, *Kōgyō seisaku*, p. 1:203.

153. Ibid., pp. 1:634–635.

154. Seki, "Kigyōsha no honshitsu," p. 80.

155. Seki, *Kōgyō seisaku*, p. 1:203.

156. Paraphrasing Schmoller on the subject, Seki declared that "even as humankind [seeks] generally to control nature, it must increasingly exert self-control [for] if the eternal moral ideals of society are not adapted anew to economic life, the eternal welfare of mankind will be sacrificed. . . . True human welfare is based on the preservation of a balance between impulse and ideal, between the wish to gratify desires and that which is truly possible." Quoted in ibid., p. 1:69.

157. Ibid., pp. 1:202 and 1:210.

158. Ibid, p. 1:240. See also Seki Hajime, "Kōgyō no tokka to ketsugō" [Industrial specialization and coupling], *Kokumin keizai zasshi* 6, no. 2 (February 1909), pp. 96–97; Seki Hajime, "Kōgyō no chihōteki shūchū oyobi bunsan" [The regional concentration and dispersion of industry], *Kokumin keizai zasshi* 9, no. 5 (November 1910), p. 45.

159. Seki, *Kōgyō seisaku*, pp. 1:382–383 and 1:399.

160. Seki Hajime, "Kigyō rengō oyobi gōdō no yushutsu shōrei saku" [Industrial combination and cartelization measures for the encouragement of exports], *Kokumin keizai zasshi* 4, no. 5 (May 1908), pp. 20 and 27.

161. Seki did toy briefly with several more radical solutions to the problem of trusts and cartels. At one point, he even entertained the idea of establishing state monopolies in industries of vital concern to the nation, citing as his model the German government's proposed monopoly of oil production. The prospect of state control apparently disturbed Seki's moderate regulatory sensibilities, however, for he never pursued the idea. One alternative that did keep Seki's interest was the establishment of "cooperative ventures between the private and public sectors" *(kōshi kyōdō jigyō)*. He argued compellingly that a lively combination of private and public investment would be appropriate to Japan; he bargained that a system in which the state maintained a controlling interest in such enterprises would inevitably benefit the Japanese people as a whole.

Seki Hajime, "Doitsu teikoku sekiyū senbai hōan" [The proposed state oil monopoly of imperial Germany], *Kokumin keizai zasshi* 15, nos. 4 and 5 (October and November 1913), and Seki Hajime, "Kōshi kyōdō jigyō" [Collaborative ventures by the public and private sectors], *Kokumin keizai zasshi* 16, no. 4 (April 1914), pp. 65 and 80.

162. Seki, *Kōgyō seisaku*, p. 1:7.
163. Seki, *Shōkō seisaku kōryō*, pp. 251–253.
164. Ibid., p. 240.
165. Seki, *Kōgyō seisaku*, pp. 1:16–17.
166. Ibid., pp. 2:1, 2:13.
167. Ibid.
168. Ibid., p. 2:26.
169. Ibid., p. 2:93.

CHAPTER 3. CLASS AND NATION

1. Ernest Gellner, *Encounters with Nationalism* (Oxford: Blackwell, 1994), p. 2.
2. Roman Szporluk, *Communism and Nationalism: Karl Marx versus Friedrich List* (New York: Oxford University Press, 1988).
3. Karl Marx, "Draft of an Article on Friedrich List's Book *Das System der Politischen Oekonomie*," in Karl Marx and Frederick Engels, *Collected Works*, vol. 4 (New York: International Publishers, 1975), pp. 280–281.
4. Gellner, *Encounters with Nationalism*, p. 2.
5. Ibid., p. 11.
6. Ibid., pp. 11–12.
7. Ibid., p. 13.
8. Ibid.
9. Quoted in ibid.
10. Ibid.
11. Quoted in ibid., p. 12.
12. Ibid., pp. 12–13. See also Szporluk, *Communism and Nationalism*, pp. 30–42.
13. Ibid., p. 13.
14. Nōshōmushō Shōkōkyoku, *Shokkō jijō* [The condition of the workers]. 1903 (reprint, 3 vols.; Tokyo: Shinkigensha, 1980).
15. Seki Hajime, "Zoku kōjōhō kanken" [A personal view of the Factory Law, continued], *Kokumin keizai zasshi* 8, no. 1 (January 1910), pp. 21–22.
16. Seki Hajime, *Rōdōsha hogo hō ron* (Tokyo: Ryūbunkan, 1910), p. 69.
17. Ibid.
18. David Williams, *Japan: Beyond the End of History* (London: Routledge, 1994), p. 88.
19. See Germaine A. Hoston, *Marxism and the Crisis of Development in Prewar Japan* (Princeton, N.J.: Princeton University Press, 1986).

20. Sheldon Garon, "Rethinking Modernization and Modernity in Japanese History: A Focus on State-Society Relations," *Journal of Asian Studies* 53, no. 2 (May 1994), p. 349.

21. On the early influence of Marxist thought in Japan, see the following: Tessa Morris-Suzuki, *A History of Japanese Economic Thought* (London: Routledge, 1989), pp. 73–76; Peter Duus and Irwin Scheiner, "Socialism, Liberalism, and Marxism, 1901–1931," in *The Cambridge History of Japan*, vol. 6: *The Twentieth Century*, ed. Peter Duus (New York: Cambridge University Press, 1988), pp. 657–666; and Hoston, *Marxism and the Crisis of Development*, pp. 19–23.

22. Morris-Suzuki, *A History of Japanese Economic Thought*, p. 69.

23. Seki, *Rōdōsha hogo hō ron*, pp. 78–79.

24. Kawakami Hajime, *Jisei no hen* [The changing spirit of the times] (Tokyo: Yomiuri Shinbunsha, 1911).

25. Gail Lee Bernstein, *Japanese Marxist: A Portrait of Kawakami Hajime* (Cambridge, Mass.: Harvard University Press, 1976), pp. 76–83. For a thumbnail sketch of Kawakami's Marxist economics, see also Morris-Suzuki, *A History of Japanese Economic Thought*, pp. 76–81.

26. Kawakami, *Jisei no hen*, pp. 175–176.

27. Ibid., pp. 148, 48, 45.

28. Seki Hajime, "Hōgakushi Kawakami Hajime sho: *Jisei no hen*" [By Doctor of Law Kawakami Hajime: The changing spirit of the times], *Kokumin keizai zasshi* 12, no. 2 (February 1912), p. 178.

29. Ibid., p. 177.

30. Ibid., p. 178.

31. Ibid.

32. Quoted in ibid.

33. Ibid. Seki apparently invoked the term *nigenron* here to emphasize the distinction between the different laws of action that applied to the natural and human worlds.

34. Ibid.

35. Kawakami Hajime, "Yuibutsu shikan ni tsuite Seki hakase ni kotau" [In reply to Dr. Seki concerning the materialist historical perspective], *Kokumin keizai zasshi* 12, no. 4 (April 1912), pp. 83–84.

36. Ibid., p. 84.

37. Ibid.

38. Ibid., p. 85.

39. Ibid., p. 86.

40. Seki Hajime, "Yuibutsu shikan ni tsuite Kawakami Hajime gakushi no oshie o kou" [Asking Mr. Kawakami Hajime for instruction concerning the materialist historical perspective], *Kokumin keizai zasshi* 12, no. 6 (June 1912), pp. 88 and 90.

41. Ibid., p. 90. On Eduard Bernstein's revisionism, see Stanley Pierson, *Marxist Intellectuals and the Working-Class Mentality in Germany, 1887–1912* (Cambridge, Mass.: Harvard University Press, 1993), pp. 121–124.

42. Seki, "Yuibutsu shikan ni tsuite Kawakami Hajime gakushi no oshie o kou," p. 90.

43. Ibid., p. 91.

44. Kawakami Hajime, "Yuibutsu shikan yori yuishinkan e, I" [From the materialist historical perspective to the materialist spiritual perspective, I], *Kokumin keizai zasshi* 13, no. 1 (July 1912), pp. 29 and 30.

45. Ibid., pp. 30–33.

46. Ibid., p. 38.

47. Ibid., pp. 43–44.

48. Kawakami Hajime, "Yuibutsu shikan yori yuishinkan e, II" [From the materialist historical perspective to the materialist spiritual perspective, II], *Kokumin keizai zasshi* 13, no. 2 (August 1912), p. 12.

49. Kawakami, "Yuibutsu shikan yori yuishinkan e, I," p. 52.

50. Ibid.

51. Seki Hajime, "Kawakami gakushi no 'Yuibutsu shikan yori yuishinkan e' o yomu" [Reading Mr. Kawakami's "From the materialist historical perspective to the materialist spiritual perspective"], *Kokumin keizai zasshi* 13, no. 3 (September 1912), p. 92.

52. Ibid., p. 93. On the subject of Weber's approach to social science, and particularly his indebtedness to the German historical school, see Fritz K. Ringer, *Max Weber's Methodology: The Unification of the Cultural and Social Sciences* (Cambridge, Mass.: Harvard University Press, 1997).

53. Quoted in Keith Tribe, *Strategies of Economic Order: German Economic Discourse, 1750–1950* (Cambridge: Cambridge University Press, 1995), p. 92.

54. Seki, "Kawakami gakushi no 'Yuibutsu shikan yori yuishinkan e' o yomu," p. 94.

55. Seki Hajime, *Kōgyō seisaku* (Tokyo: Hōbunkan, 1913), pp. 2:58–59 and 2:64–65.

56. Ibid., p. 2:65.

57. Ibid., pp. 2:69, 2:74, and 2:77–78.

58. Ibid., pp. 2:79 and 2:83–84.

59. Quoted in Kenneth B. Pyle, "Advantages of Followership: German Economics and Japanese Bureaucrats, 1890–1925," *Journal of Japanese Studies* 1, no. 1 (Autumn 1974), p. 134.

60. Ibid.

61. Ibid., p. 135.

62. Ernest James Notar, "Labor Unions and the *Sangyō Hōkoku* Movement 1930–1945: A Japanese Model for Industrial Relations" (Ph.D. diss., University of California, Berkeley, 1979), pp. 17–18.

63. Quoted in Pyle, "Advantages of Followership," pp. 145–146.

64. Ikeda Makoto, *Nihon shakai seisaku shisō shi ron* [On the history of Japanese social-policy thought] (Tokyo: Tokyo Keizai Shinpōsha, 1978), p. 10.

65. Ibid., pp. 6–7.

66. Notar, "Labor Unions and the *Sangyō Hōkoku* Movement," p. 18.

67. Ibid., p. 21.

68. Quoted in Pyle, "Advantages of Followership," p. 130.

69. Ikeda, *Nihon shakai seisaku*, pp. 4–5.

70. Quoted in Pyle, "Advantages of Followership," p. 130.

71. Ikeda, *Nihon shakai seisaku*, pp. 9–10.

72. Shakai Seisaku Gakkai, ed., *Kōjōhō to rōdō mondai* [The Labor Law and the labor question] (Tokyo: Dōbunkan, 1908), p. 25.

73. Ikeda, *Nihon shakai seisaku*, pp. 69–79.

74. Pyle, "Advantages of Followership," pp. 152–153. On the Kyōchōkai, see W. Dean Kinzley, *Industrial Harmony in Modern Japan: The Invention of a Tradition* (New York: Routledge, 1991).

75. Fritz K. Ringer, *The Decline of the German Mandarins: The German Academic Community, 1890–1933* (Cambridge, Mass.: Harvard University Press, 1969), pp. 145–147.

76. Morris-Suzuki, *A History of Japanese Economic Thought*, p. 63.

77. Notar, "Labor Unions and the *Sangyō Hōkoku* Movement," p. 19.

78. Pyle, "Advantages of Followership," p. 164.

79. On the prominence of Fukuda Tokuzō within the Gakkai, for example, see Morris-Suzuki, *A History of Japanese Economic Thought*, pp. 67–68.

80. Pyle, "Advantages of Followership," p. 153.

81. Ikeda, *Nihon shakai seisaku*, pp. 209–210.

82. Bernard S. Silberman, *Cages of Reason: The Rise of the Rational State in France, Japan, the United States, and Great Britain* (Chicago: University of Chicago Press, 1993), p. 222.

83. J. Mark Ramseyer and Frances M. Rosenbluth, *The Politics of Oligarchy: Institutional Choice in Imperial Japan* (Cambridge: Cambridge University Press, 1995), p. 58.

84. Daniel T. Rodgers, *Atlantic Crossings: Social Politics in a Progressive Age* (Cambridge, Mass.: Harvard University Press, 1998), p. 26.

85. Tsumura Hidematsu, *Kokumin keizaigaku genron* [Views on people's national economics] (Tokyo: Ryūbunkan, 1910), pp. 1342–1343.

86. Tribe, *Strategies of Economic Order*, p. 79.

87. Ibid., 71.

88. A good example of the confusion among historians over the scholarship of the practical-studies faction can be found in the sharply contrasting accounts of Seki's labor reformism provided respectively by Shibamura Atsuki and Kojita Yasunao. Shibamura, an unreconstructed socialist historian, has persistently teased evidence of radicalism from Seki's work, making him appear a closet socialist. Kojita, a liberal revisionist, has taken precisely the opposite tack. Claiming to have found statist nationalism in Seki's labor reformism, he has labeled him a closet rightist. So, which was he, a leftist or a rightist? The answer is neither. But before we ask just what Seki was, let us establish what he was not by subjecting Shibamura's wistfulness and Kojita's cynicism to closer scrutiny.

Little in Seki's labor reformism would lead anyone but a true believer such as Shibamura to suggest that it was thinly disguised socialism. As suggested earlier, Seki vociferously criticized socialist determinism and internationalism alike. As I shall soon illustrate, he also assiduously resisted the socialist predisposition toward unilateral state intervention in the relationship between workers and capitalists.

However, a great deal in Seki's labor reformism might lead a skeptical revisionist such as Kojita to identify an apologist for state industrial policy. In a quirky critique of Seki's economic thought, Kojita reveals his suspicions. He contends that Seki was speaking out of both sides of his mouth when he made his case for labor reform. Behind the rhetoric of "workers' rights" and "public benefit," argues Kojita, was a highly rationalistic and nationalistic scheme to "promote [labor] production" as a central element of policy for heavy industry. Yet Kojita provides little more than circumstantial evidence of this interpretation, basing his case on a tacit accusation of guilt by (state) association.

Between the lines of Kojita's argument lurks a revisionist thesis concerning the nature of political and economic power in the 1930s. But what, we might ask, does this thesis have to do with labor reformism in the 1910s and 1920s? Well, according to the revisionist historical reasoning of scholars such as Kojita, who have made it their paradoxical mission to trace the roots of Showa fascism to Taisho democracy, social reformers such as Seki were ultimately little more than sophisticated apologists for the autocratic Japanese state. Kojita, who dismisses the popular postwar thesis that monopoly capitalism was the product of a conspiracy between state leaders and powerful industrialists, links its formation instead to the steady current of "economic rationality" that surged through state policymaking in the Taisho era. In removing Seki from his reformist pedestal as just such an economic rationalist, Kojita aims to kill two birds with one stone. On the one hand, he seizes the opportunity to chasten Shibamura for his historical naivete in identifying Seki, the social reformer, as a closet socialist; on the other, he hangs this social reformer on the historical hook for the part he and others like him played in leading Japan down the road to imperialism and war.

Kojita's interpretative agenda is not dissimilar to that of Sheldon Garon, who has decried our misidentification of the 1930s as a "reactionary period" of "irrationality" and "retrogression." Against the conventional view that a historical "rupture" occurred in the 1930s—a rupture that "temporarily reversed the post-Restoration process of political modernization"—Garon traces a continuum between the recognizably rational 1920s and the seemingly insane 1930s. "In short, the illiberal New Order was more than a conservative or nativist return to premodern or Meiji-era Japan," concludes Garon. "Its modern ingredients of mass mobilization and state controls over the economy flowed, in a sense, from the democratic currents of the 1920s."

Both Kojita and Garon are intent, in Garon's words, "upon illuminating how the concept of modernization can be used to understand better the nature of Japanese authoritarianism." But in rendering "rationality" as a synonym for "modernization" and by sweepingly associating it with the decision-making efficiency of the authoritarian state, they have merely substituted one monocausal explanation of change for another. It is one thing to suggest that the state invoked a powerfully instrumentalist logic of modernization in the 1930s, as it certainly did, but it is yet another to condemn rationalist policy-making as a direct precursor of Showa authoritarianism.

If Garon is right to emphasize the collaboration between "higher civil servants" and "social policy scholars" in the formulation of the Factory Law, for example, he is much too quick to chalk up the resulting compromise to their "common backgrounds and experiences" as middle-class elites. Garon's argument here, no less than Kojita's cited earlier, rests on the premise of guilt by (state) association. Ironically, Garon himself has argued compellingly elsewhere that the Factory Law was not solely the logical consequence of rational decision making by scholars and policymakers steeped in the ideology of modernization; it was also the product of myriad pressures brought to bear on industrialists and the state alike.

Kojita Yasunari, "Nihon teikokushugi seiritsu no toshi seisaku" [Urban policy in the establishment of Japanese imperialism], *Rekishi hyōron* 393 (January 1983), pp. 187–188; Shibamura Atsuki, *Seki Hajime: Toshi shisō no paioniā* (Kyoto: Shōraisha, 1989), passim; Sheldon Garon, "Rethinking Modernization," pp. 349–351; and Garon, *The State and Labor in Modern Japan* (Berkeley: University of California Press, 1987), pp. 25–29.

89. Garon, *The State and Labor in Modern Japan*, p. 50.

90. Oka Minoru, "Kōjōhō no onjin" [Benefactor of the Factory Law], *Dai Ōsaka* 11, no. 2 (1935), p. 50.

91. Seki, *Kōgyō seisaku*, pp. 2:13–20 and 2:25.

92. Ibid., pp. 2:17, 2:18, 2:24–25; 2:13; 2:21–22.

93. Ibid., pp. 2:25 and 2:21.

94. Ibid., p. 2:25.

95. Ibid., pp. 2:21 and 2:22.

96. Ibid., p. 2:97.

CHAPTER 4. TOWARD A MODERN MORAL ECONOMY

1. At the beginning of his groundbreaking history of labor policy, Garon felt the need only to add an exclamation point to this story by quoting the "pioneer labor specialist" James Abegglen: "Whereas the Industrial Revolution occurred in Great Britain over the latter half of the eighteenth century, the process worked itself out in Japan between 1895 and 1897." Quoted in Sheldon Garon, *The State and Labor in Modern Japan* (Berkeley: University of California Press, 1987), p. 10.

2. Andrew Gordon, *The Evolution of Labor Relations in Japan: Heavy Industry, 1853–1955* (Cambridge, Mass.: Harvard University Press, 1985), p. 17.

3. Garon, *The State and Labor in Modern Japan*, pp. 12–13.

4. E. Patricia Tsurumi, *Factory Girls: Women in the Thread Mills of Meiji Japan* (Princeton, N.J.: Princeton University Press, 1990), p. 3.

5. Garon, *The State and Labor in Modern Japan*, p. 13.

6. Ibid.

7. Sumiya Mikio, "Kōjōhō taisei to rōshi kankei" [The structure of the Factory Law and the relationship between labor and capital], in *Nihon rōshi kankei shi ron* [On the history of the relationship between Japanese labor and capital] (Tokyo: Tokyo Daigaku Shuppankai, 1977), p. 7.

8. Ikeda Makoto, *Nihon shakai seisaku shisō shi ron* (Tokyo: Tokyo Keizai Shinpōsha, 1978), pp. 85 and 91–92.

9. Ibid., p. 89.

10. Rōdō Undō Shiryō Iinkai, ed., *Nihon Rōdō undō shiryō, III* [Historical documents of the Japansese labor movement, III] (Tokyo: Tokyo Daigaku Shuppankai, 1968), p. 178.

11. Byron K. Marshall, *Capitalism and Nationalism in Prewar Japan: The Ideology of the Business Elite, 1868–1941* (Stanford, Calif.: Stanford University Press, 1967), pp. 56–57.

12. Andrew Gordon, *Labor and Imperial Democracy in Prewar Japan* (Berkeley: University of California Press, 1991), p. 63.

13. See especially Stephen E. Marsland, *The Birth of the Japanese Labor Movement: Takano Fusatarō and the Rōdō Kumiai Kiseikai* (Honolulu: University of Hawaii Press, 1989), pp. 19–45, for a broad survey of early labor activism.

14. Koji Taira, "Economic Development, Labor Markets, and Industrial Relations in Japan, 1905–1955," in *The Cambridge History of Japan*, vol. 6: *The Twentieth Century*, ed. Peter Duus (New York: Cambridge University Press, 1988), p. 633.

15. Garon, *The State and Labor in Modern Japan*, p. 21.

16. Kanai Noboru, "Kōjō hōan ni taisuru rōryokusha no iken o chōsu be-shi" [Why we should solicit the opinions of workers regarding the proposal for a factory law], *Kokka gakkai zasshi* 12, no. 12 (December 1898), pp. 2172–2174.

17. Garon, *The State and Labor in Modern Japan*, pp. 25–26.

18. Quoted in ibid., p. 26.

19. Andrew Gordon, "The Invention of Japanese-Style Labor Management," in *Mirror of Modernity: Invented Traditions of Modern Japan*, ed. Stephen Vlastos (Berkeley: University of California Press, 1998), pp. 21–23.

20. Seki Hajime, *Rōdōsha hogo hō ron* (Tokyo: Ryūbunkan, 1910), pp. 92–93.

21. Gordon, "Invention of Japanese-Style Labor Management," p. 23.

22. Ibid., p. 21.

23. Quoted in ibid., pp. 22–23.

24. Quoted in Marshall, *Capitalism and Nationalism in Prewar Japan*, pp. 58–59.

25. Gordon, *The Evolution of Labor Relations in Japan*, p. 67.

26. Quoted in Seki, *Rōdōsha hogo hō ron*, pp. 92–93.

27. Ibid., pp. 93 and 90.

28. Ibid., p. 94.

29. Seki Hajime, "Zoku kōjōhō kanken," *Kokumin keizai zasshi* 8, no. 1 (January 1910), p. 21.

30. Seki, *Rōdōsha hogo hō ron*, pp. 39–40.

31. Ibid., pp. 32–33 and 19.

32. Ibid., p. 94.

33. Seki, "Zoku kōjōhō kanken," p. 23.

34. Ibid., p. 30.

35. Seki, *Rōdōsha hogo hō ron*, preface, p. 1.

36. Sumiya, "Kōjōhō taisei," pp. 6–7.

37. Seki, *Rōdōsha hogo hō ron*, p. 55.

38. Ibid., p. 5.

39. The specific works he cited were Wilhelm Roscher, *System der Volkswirtschaft* (1883–1889), and Arnold Toynbee, *Lectures on the Industrial Revolution of the 18th Century in England* (1902).

40. See Ōsaka Shōka Daigaku, ed., *Seki bunko mokuroku* [Catalogue of the Seki collection] (Osaka: Ōsaka Shōka Daigaku, 1935). A representative sampling from Seki's personal library includes: J. E. Cairnes's sweeping *Character and Logical Method of Political Economy* (1857), W. Stanley Jevons's acerbic *The State in Relation to Labour* (1882), and Charles Gide's pathbreaking *Principes d'économie politique* (1884).

41. Daniel T. Rodgers, *Atlantic Crossings: Social Politics in a Progressive Age* (Cambridge, Mass.: Harvard University Press, 1998), pp. 83–84.

42. Seki Hajime, "Kōgyō no tokka to ketsugō," *Kokumin keizai zasshi* 6, no. 2 (February 1909), p. 76–77.

43. Seki Hajime, *Kōgyō seisaku* (Tokyo: Hōbunkan, 1913), p. 2:33.

44. Seki Hajime, *Kōgyō seisaku* (Tokyo: Hōbunkan, 1911), pp. 1:16–17.

45. Kojita Yasunao, "Nihon teikokushugi seiritsu no toshi seisaku," *Rekiishi hyōron* 393 (January 1983), pp. 88–89.

46. Seki, *Kōgyō seisaku*, p. 1:93.

47. Seki, "Kōgyō no tokka to ketsugō," *Kokumin keizai zasshi* 6, no. 2 (February 1909), p. 78.

48. Seki, *Kōgyō seisaku*, p. 1:139.

49. Ibid., p. 2:1.

50. Ibid., p. 1:93.

51. Seki, *Rōdōsha hogo hō ron*, pp. 5 and 6.

52. Ibid., p. 6.

53. Ibid., pp. 11–12.

54. Ibid., pp. 14–15.

55. Ibid., p. 19.

56. Ibid., p. 25.

57. Ibid., p. 15.

58. Ibid., p. 10.

59. Ibid., p. 22.

60. Ibid., pp. 23–24.

61. Ibid., pp. 13–14.

62. Ibid., p. 60.

63. Ibid., pp. 63–64 and 68.

64. Seki, *Kōgyō seisaku*, p. 2:132.

65. Seki, *Rōdōsha hogo hō ron*, p. 25.

66. Seki, *Kōgyō seisaku*, p. 2:27.

67. Ibid., pp. 2:27–28.

68. Seki, *Rōdōsha hogo hō ron*, pp. 99–100.

69. Seki, *Kōgyō seisaku*, pp. 2:22, 2:49–50, 2:50–51, 2:26–27.

70. Ibid., p. 2:7.

71. Smith and others have gone a long way toward correcting the misimpression that Meiji workers were demanding "rights" in the Western sense of that term. Smith poignantly observes that the strident workers of late Meiji said "rights" but actually meant "status": "When they [workers] spoke of rights, as they sometimes did . . . in demanding 'improvement in workers' rights and status,'" writes Smith, "the word was often given a meaning indistinguishable from that of 'status.'" T. C. Smith, "The Right to Benevolence: Dignity and Japanese Workers, 1890–1920," *Comparative Studies in Society and History* 26, no. 4 (October 1986), pp. 588–589.

72. Seki Hajime, "Kigyōka no shakaiteki setsubi" [Social provisions made by industrialists], *Kokumin keizai zasshi* 7, no. 2 (August 1909), p. 51.

73. Seki, *Kōgyō seisaku*, pp. 2:253–254.

74. Ibid., pp. 2:49–50.

75. Smith, "The Right to Benevolence," p. 595.

76. Seki, *Kōgyō seisaku*, pp. 2:50 and 2:96.

77. Seki, *Rōdōsha hogo hō ron*, pp. 99–100 and 14–15.

78. Seki, *Kōgyō seisaku*, pp. 2:23 and 2:25.

79. Ibid., p. 2:28.

80. James T. Kloppenberg, *Uncertain Victory: Social Democracy and Progressivism in European and American Thought, 1870–1920* (New York: Oxford University Press, 1986), pp. 239–246.

81. Ibid., p. 246.

82. Seki, *Rōdōsha hogo hō ron*, pp. 105–106.

83. Seki, *Kōgyō seisaku*, pp. 2:82–83.

84. Seki Hajime, "Kōjōhō to rōdōsha hoken" [The Factory Law and workmen's compensation], *Kokumin keizai zasshi* 12, no. 2 (February 1912), p. 33.

85. Seki, *Kōgyō seisaku*, pp. 2:27 and 2:25.

86. Seki Hajime, "Eikoku ni okeru shakaiteki rippō no shin keikō" [New trends in social legislation in England], *Kokka gakkai zasshi* 23, nos. 8 and 9 (August and September 1909).

87. Ibid., p. 94.

88. Seki, *Kōgyō seisaku*, p. 2:26.

89. Ibid., p. 2:28.

90. Ibid., pp. 2:9–10.

91. Ibid., p. 2:11.

92. Ibid., pp. 2:71–72.

93. Ibid., p. 2:72.

94. Ibid., p. 2:79.

95. Ibid., pp. 2:82–83 and 2:75–76.

96. Ibid., p. 2:71.

97. Ibid., p. 2:76.

98. Sidney Webb and Beatrice Webb, *Industrial Democracy*, 2 vols. (London: Longmans, Green, 1897). On the Webbs and their interest in social-reform legislation, see Kloppenberg, *Uncertain Victory*, pp. 290–291.

99. Seki, *Rōdōsha hogo hō ron*, pp. 106–107.

100. Seki, *Kōgyō seisaku*, p. 2:75.

101. Ibid., pp. 2:106, 2:107, 2:108.

102. Ibid., p. 2:98.

103. Seki Hajime, "Kōjōhō to rōdōsha mondai" [The Factory Law and the worker problem], *Kokumin keizai zasshi* 5, no. 1 (July 1908), p. 140.

104. Seki, *Rōdōsha hogo hō ron*, p. 114.

105. Seki, *Kōgyō seisaku*, pp. 2:27 and 2:633–645.

106. Ibid., p. 2:265.

107. Ibid., pp. 2:330 and 2:270.

108. Ibid., p. 2:353.

109. Ikeda, *Nihon shakai seisaku*, pp. 209–210.

110. Ibid., pp. 238–239.

111. Thorstein Veblen, "The Opportunity of Japan," *Journal of the Race Development* 6 (July 1915); reprinted in Thorstein Veblen, *Essays in Our Changing Order* (New York: Viking Press, 1934), pp. 248–266.

112. Gordon, *The Evolution of Labor Relations in Japan*, p. 65.

113. Oka Minoru, *Kōjōhō ron* [On the Factory Law] (Tokyo: Yūhikaku, 1913), p. 165.

114. Kuwata Kumazō, *Kōjōhō to rōdō hoken* [The Factory Law and workmen's compensation] (Tokyo: Ryūbunkan, 1909), pp. 198–199 and 404–405.

115. Toda Kaiichi, *Nihon no shakai* [Japanese society] (Tokyo: Hakubunkan, 1911), pp. 44–45.

116. Seki, "Kōjōhō to rōdōsha mondai," passim.

117. Ibid., pp. 141–143.

118. Seki Hajime, "Kōjōhō kanken" [A personal view of the Factory Law], *Kokumin keizai zasshi* 7, no. 5 (November 1909), passim.

119. Seki, "Zoku kōjōhō kanken," passim.

120. Ibid., pp. 18–30.

121. Seki surveyed a vast range of national examples of labor legislation across Europe, North America, Australia, and New Zealand; Seki, *Rōdōsha hogo hō ron*, pp. 365–417.

122. Ibid., 355.

123. Ibid., pp. 199–257 and 271–298.

124. Seki, *Kōgyō seisaku*, p. 2:138.

125. Ibid., p. 2:136.

126. Ibid., p. 2:153.

127. Seki Hajime, "Saitei chingin, I" [Minimum wage, I], *Kokumin keizai zasshi* 12, no. 4 (April 1912), pp. 64–65, 58, 66–67, 83–84.

128. Ibid., pp. 57–65 and 69–70.

129. Seki Hajime, "Saitei chingin, III," *Kokumin keizai zasshi* 13, no. 2 (August 1912), pp. 63, 67.

130. Ibid., pp. 82–83.

131. Ibid., pp. 83–84.

132. Seki, *Kōgyō seisaku*, p. 2:230.

133. Ibid., p. 2:253.

134. Seki Hajime, "Rōdō jikan o ronzu" [On labor hours], *Mita Gakkai zasshi* 7, no. 1 (January 1913), pp. 7–9.

135. Seki, *Kōgyō seisaku*, p. 2:253.

136. Ibid., p. 2:254.

137. Seki, "Rōdō jikan o ronzu," pp. 19 and 30.

138. Ibid., p. 29.

139. Ikeda, *Nihon shakai seisaku*, pp. 209–210.

140. Seki, *Kōgyō seisaku*, p. 2:581 and 2:265.

141. Ibid., pp. 2:264–265.

142. Seki, "Saitei chingin, III," p. 70.

143. Seki, *Kōgyō seisaku*, pp. 2:353–356.

144. Ibid., p. 2:361.

145. Ibid., p. 2:262.

146. Seki, *Rōdōsha hogo hō ron*, p. 137.

147. Seki, *Kōgyō seisaku*, pp. 2:342, 2:346.

148. Seki, "Kōjōhō to rōdōsha hoken," p. 33.

149. Rōdō Undō Shiryō Iinkai, *Nihon rōdō undō shiryō, III*, p. 265. For a history of the Yūaikai, see Stephen S. Large, *The Rise of Labor in Japan: The Yūaikai, 1912–19* (Tokyo: Sophia University Press, 1972). In an appendix listing the Yūaikai's original board members, Large mistakenly renders Seki Hajime's name as Kan Ichi.

150. Seki Hajime, "Rōdō shōkai seido, II" [The labor-referral system, II], *Kokumin keizai zasshi* 9, no. 2 (August 1910), p. 88.

151. Seki Hajime, "Rōdō shōkai seido, I," *Kokumin keizai zasshi* 9, no. 1 (July 1910), pp. 27, 32.

152. Seki, "Rōdō shokai seido II," p. 88.

153. Seki, "Rōdō shōkai seido, I," p. 33; and Seki, "Rōdō shōkai seido, II," p. 87.

154. Seki, "Kōjōhō to rōdōsha hoken," pp. 47, 48, 52.

155. Ibid., p. 33.

156. Rodgers, *Atlantic Crossings*, p. 213.

157. Seki Hajime, "Shisshoku mondai, I" [The unemployment problem,

I], *Kokumin keizai zasshi* 8, no. 5 (May 1910), pp. 3, 5, 6, 9. Persistently troubled by the issue of unemployment, Seki read a great deal on the topic over the years, including a book by the economist Percy Alden—*The Unemployable and the Unemployed* (London, 1909)—that appears to have helped him crystallize some of the issues.

158. Seki Hajime, "Shisshoku mondai, II," *Kokumin keizai zasshi* 8, no. 6 (June 1910), pp. 14–21.

159. Ibid., pp. 20, 21–28, 35–38.

160. Ibid., p. 38.

161. Seki, *Rōdōsha hogo hō ron*, pp. 419–471.

162. Ibid., pp. 470–471.

163. Quoted in R. P. Dore, "The Modernizer as a Special Case: Japanese Factory Legislation, 1882–1911," *Comparative Studies in Society and History* 11, no. 4 (October 1969), p. 445.

164. Seki, *Rōdōsha hogo hō ron*, p. 127.

165. Seki, "Rōdō jikan o ronzu," p. 28.

166. Seki, *Kōgyō seisaku*, p. 1:125.

167. Ibid., pp. 1:124–125.

168. Ibid., p. 1:141.

169. Seki Hajime, "Kōgyō no chihōteki shūchū oyobi bunsan," *Kokumin keizai zasshi* 9, no. 5 (November 1910), p. 45.

170. Ibid.

171. Seki, *Kōgyō seisaku*, p. 2:42.

172. Ibid., pp. 42–43.

173. Ibid., pp. 43 and 44.

174. Seki, *Rōdōsha hogo hō ron*, pp. 53–54.

175. Seki, *Kōgyō seisaku*, p. 2:49.

176. Here, Seki paraphrased the German political economist Carl Menger; ibid., p. 2:8.

177. Seki Hajime, *Shōgyō keizai seisaku* (Tokyo: Ōkura Shoten, 1903), p. 49.

178. Seki Hajime, *Shōkō seisaku kōryō* (Tokyo: Dōbunkan, 1909), p. 186.

179. Seki, "Toshi kōtsū kikan no hattatsu to kyojū kankei," in *Shakai Seisaku Gakkai ronsō: Kanzei mondai to shakai seisaku*, 2, ed. Shakai Seisaku Gakkai (Tokyo: Dōbunkan, 1909), pp. 275–276; Seki, *Kōgyō seisaku*, p. 2:42.

CHAPTER 5. A NEW URBANISM

1. Seki Hajime Kenkyūkai, ed., *Seki Hajime nikki: Taishō Shōwa Shoki no Ōsaka shisei* (Tokyo: Tokyo Daigaku Shuppankai, 1986), 1 January 1914, p. 54.

2. Ibid., 19 November 1913, pp. 43–44.

3. Tsumura Hidematsu, "Yūjin toshite no Ko Seki shichō" [The late Mayor Seki as a friend], in *Ko Seki shichō o shinobu* [Recalling the late Mayor Seki], ed. Osaka-shi Kyōikukai (Osaka: Osaka-shi Kyōikukai, 1935), pp. 100–101.

4. Seki, *Nikki*, 29 November 1914–16 December 1914, pp. 46–49.

5. Tsumura, "Yūjin toshite no Ko Seki shichō," p. 101.

6. Seki, *Nikki*, 18 October 1913, p. 40.

7. Shibamura Atsuki, *Seki Hajime: Toshi shisō no paioniā* (Kyoto: Shōraisha, 1989), pp. 52–53.

8. Seki, *Nikki*, 15 January 1914, p. 55.

9. Ibid.

10. Ibid., 8 February 1914, p. 58.

11. Ibid., 8 March 1914, p. 61.

12. Ibid., 9 March 1914, p. 61.

13. Ibid., 17 March 1914, p. 62.

14. Ibid., 23 April 1914, p. 66.

15. Ibid., 29 April 1914, p. 67.

16. Ibid., 30 April 1914, p. 67.

17. Ibid., 1 May 1914, p. 67.

18. Ibid., 2 May 1914, p. 68.

19. Ibid., 31 May 1914, p. 71.

20. Shibamura, *Seki Hajime*, p. 56.

21. Seki, *Nikki*, 9 June 1914, p. 73.

22. Ibid., 12 June 1914, p. 73.

23. Ibid., 3 July 1914, p. 76.

24. Ibid., 9 July 1914, p. 77.

25. Ibid., 30 July 1914–31 July 1914, pp. 80–81.

26. Ibid., 3 September 1914, p. 85.

27. Ibid.

28. Seki Hajime, "Toshi kōtsū kikan no hattatsu to kyojū kankei," in *Shakai Seisaku Gakkai ronsō: Kanzei mondai to shakai seisaku*, 2, ed. Shakai Seisaku Gakkai (Tokyo: Dōbunkan, 1909), pp. 267–268.

29. Ibid., p. 268.

30. Ibid.

31. Seki Hajime, *Shōkō seisaku kōryō* (Tokyo: Dōbunkan, 1909), p. 186.

32. Daniel T. Rodgers, *Atlantic Crossings: Social Politics in a Progressive Age* (Cambridge, Mass.: Harvard University Press, 1998), p. 47.

33. Furthermore, it does not appear as if Seki was blithely invoking the idea of evolution. Among the books in his personal library were Charles Darwin's *Origin of Species* and Herbert Spencer's *Principles of Sociology*; Seki Hajime, *Kōgyō seisaku* (Tokyo: Hōbunkan, 1911), p. 1:271.

34. Seki, "Toshi kōtsū," p. 275.

35. Seki, *Kōgyō seisaku*, p. 1:271.

36. Anthony Sutcliffe, *Towards the Planned City: Germany, Britain, the United States and France 1780–1914* (New York: St. Martin's Press, 1981), p. 56.

37. On Japanese views of the city, see Henry D. Smith II, "Tokyo as an Idea: An Exploration of Japanese Urban Thought until 1945," *Journal of Japanese Studies* 4, no. 1 (Winter 1978).

38. Ibid., p. 51.

39. Quoted in Joyce Lebra, *Okuma Shigenobu: Statesman of Meiji Japan* (Canberra: Australia National University, 1973), p. 58.

40. On Nōhonshugi, see Thomas R. H. Havens, *Farm and Nation in Modern Japan: Agrarian Nationalism, 1870–1940* (Princeton, N.J.: Princeton University Press, 1974).

41. Smith, "Tokyo as an Idea," pp. 53–57.

42. Fujimori Terunobu, *Meiji no Tōkyō keikaku* [Meiji Tokyo planning] (Tokyo: Iwanami Shoten, 1982), pp. 1–44.

43. Edward Seidensticker, *Low City, High City: Tokyo from Edo to the Earthquake: How the Shogun's Ancient Capital Became a Great Modern City, 1867–1923* (San Francisco: Donald S. Ellis and Creative Arts Book Company, 1985), p. 59.

44. Quoted in Mikuriya Takashi, *Shuto keikaku no seiji: Keisei-ki Meiji kokka no jitsuzō* [The politics of capital planning: A realistic image of the formative Meiji state] (Tokyo: Yamakawa Shuppansha, 1984), p. 17.

45. Quoted in ibid.

46. Ibid., p. 17.

47. For Ende and Böckmann's story, see Horiuchi Masaaki, *Meiji no oyatoi kenchikuka Ende & Bekkuman: Baufirma Ende & Böckmann* [Architects in government service during Meiji, Ende & Böckmann: The design firm Ende & Böckmann] (Tokyo: Inoue Shoin, 1989).

48. Fujimori, *Meiji no Tōkyō keikaku*, illustrations 50–58. For a different interpretation of this episode in early capital planning—one that stresses its transformative impact on Tokyo as the nation's "symbolic and ritual center"— see T. Fujitani, *Splendid Monarchy: Power and Pageantry in Modern Japan* (Berkeley: University of California Press, 1996), pp. 66–82.

49. On the financial debates over Meiji capital planning, see Mikuriya, *Shuto keikaku*, passim.

50. Smith, "Tokyo as an Idea," p. 55.

51. Yoshikawa Aramasa, "Shiku kaisei ikensho" [An opinion on city improvement], in *Nihon kindai shisō taikei: Toshi/kenchiku* [A collection of modern Japanese thought: Cities/architecture], ed. Fujimori Terunobu (Tokyo: Iwanami Shoten, 1990), pp. 60–85.

52. Quoted in Mikuriya, *Shuto keikaku*, p. 51.

53. Tamaki Toyojirō, *Ōsaka kensetsu shi yawa* [A tale about the history of the building of Osaka] (Osaka: Osaka Toshi Kyōkai, 1982), pp. 142–143.

54. Fujimori, *Meiji no Tōkyō keikaku*, pp. 263–264.

55. Tamaki, *Ōsaka kensetsu shi yawa*, pp. 144–145.

56. Ishida Yorifusa, *Nihon kindai toshi keikaku on hyakunen* [A century of modern Japanese urban planning] (Tokyo: Jichitai Kenkyūsha, 1988), pp. 97–99.

57. Masayoshi Chubachi and Koji Taira, "Poverty in Modern Japan: Perceptions and Realities," in *Industrialization and Its Social Consequences*, ed. Hugh Patrick (Berkeley: University of California Press, 1976), pp. 392–393.

58. Suzuki Umeshirō, "Ōsaka Nagomachi hinminkutsu shisatsu ki" [An observer's account of the Osaka Nagomachi slum], 1888; reprinted in *Meiji zenki no toshi kasō shakai* [The urban lower classes in early Meiji], ed. Nishida Taketoshi (Tokyo: Kōseikan, 1970); Yokoyama Gennosuke, *Nihon no kasō shakai* [The lower classes of Japan], 1899 (reprint; Tokyo: Iwanami Shoten, 1955); and in English, Eiji Yutani, "*Nihon no kasō shakai* of Gennosuke Yokoyama, Translated and with an Introduction" (Ph.D. diss., University of California, Berkeley, 1985).

59. Sugihara Kaoru and Kiso Junko, eds., *Taishō Ōsaka suramu: Mo hitotsu no Nihon kindai shi* [The slums of Taisho Osaka: Another modern history of Japan] (Tokyo: Shinhyōron, 1987), pp. 21–22.

60. Suzuki, "Ōsaka Nagomachi hinminkutsu shisatsu ki," p. 125.

61. Ibid., pp. 127–130.

62. Ibid., p. 128.

63. Ōhashi Kaoru, *Toshi no kasō shakai* [Urban lower-class society] (Tokyo: Seishin Shobō, 1962), pp. 117–118.

64. On the topic of slum clearance and expositions, see especially Enami Shigeyuki and Mihashi Toshiaki, *Hinminkutsu to hakurankai: Kindaisei no keifu gaku—kūkan/chigaku hen* [Slums and exhibitions: A genealogy of modernism—space/perception edition] (Tokyo: JICC Shuppankyoku, 1989).

65. Tamaki Toyojirō, "Ōsaka no toshi keisei to toshi keikaku" [Urban formation and urban planning of Osaka], *Toshi keikaku* 84 (September 1975), p. 8.

66. Katayama Sen, *Toshi shakaishugi: Waga shakaishugi* [Municipal socialism: My socialism], 1903; reprint ed. Iwamoto Eitarō (Tokyo: Jitsugyō no Nihon-sha, 1949), p. 100, preface, and p. 99. See also Abe Isoo, *Ōyō shisei ron* [On practical municipal politics] (Tokyo: Hidaka Yūrin, 1908).

67. Carol Gluck, *Japan's Modern Myths: Ideology in the Late Meiji Period* (Princeton, N.J.: Princeton University Press, 1985), p. 159.

68. Kenneth B. Pyle, "The Technology of Japanese Nationalism: The Local Improvement Movement, 1900–1918," *Journal of Asian Studies* 33, no. 1 (November 1973), p. 57.

69. Ibid., p. 58.

70. Quoted in ibid., p. 58.

71. Ibid.

72. For a rigorous examination and scathing indictment of the model-village movement, see Kim Jang-kwon, *Kindai chihō jichi no kōzō to seikaku* [The structure and character of modern local autonomy] (Tokyo: Tōsui Shobō, 1992).

73. Kuwata Kumazō, "Toshi no shakai seisaku" [Urban social policy], *Kokka gakkai zasshi* 14, no. 163 (September 1900), pp. 20, 21, 96.

74. Inoue Tomoichi, *Kyūsai seido yōgi* [Essentials of the system of poor relief] (Tokyo: Hakubunkan, 1909), passim.

75. Inoue Tomoichi, *Toshi gyōsei oyobi hōsei: Gekan* [Urban administra-

tion and law: Vol. 2] (Tokyo: Hakubunkan, 1911), pp. 395, 410–411, 414, 415, and 432–434.

76. Ibid., pp. 548–549.

77. Inoue Tomoichi, *Jichi kunren no kaihatsu* [Development of local-autonomy preparation] (Tokyo: Hakubunkan, 1909), p. 5.

78. For a sweeping survey of Meiji "city-planning" initiatives, see Ishida, *Nihon kindai toshi keikaku no hyakunen*, pp. 51–105.

79. Miyake Iwao, *Toshi no kenkyū* [Researches of the city] (Tokyo: Jitsu-gyō no Nihonsha, 1908), pp. 117–184, 34, and 25.

80. Ibid., preface.

81. Ebenezer Howard, *Garden Cities of To-morrow* (London: Faber & Faber, 1902).

82. Naimusho Chihō-kyoku, ed., *Den'en toshi* [Garden cities] (Tokyo: Hakubunkan, 1908).

83. Howard, *Garden Cities*, pp. 10–11.

84. Ibid., p. 18.

85. Rodgers, *Atlantic Crossings*, p. 179.

86. Howard, *Garden Cities*, p. 100.

87. C. B. Purdom, *The Garden City; a Study in the Development of a Modern Town* (London: J. M. Dent & Sons, 1913), p. 201.

88. Howard, *Garden Cities*, p. 18.

89. Naimusho, *Den'en toshi*, p. 3.

90. Ibid., p. 366.

91. Ibid., pp. 1–2 and 379.

92. Seki, "Toshi kōtsū," p. 270.

93. Seki Hajime, "Yanagita Kunio cho 'jidai to nōsei'" [Yanagita Kunio's "eras and agricultures"], *Kokumin keizai zasshi* 10, no. 2 (February 1911), pp. 154–155. Had Seki been feeling a bit less diplomatic, he might have expressed his criticism more directly: that Yanagita had misconstrued the process of urbanization in Japan by tendentiously extrapolating an enduring cultural pattern from a dynamic historical moment. In short, he maintained that Yanagita had removed time and change from the urban picture by inventing a timeless social tradition that speciously presumed the fundamental unity of rural and urban Japanese life.

94. Seki, "Toshi kōtsū," p. 275.

95. Seki Hajime, "Kaen toshi to toshi keikaku" [Garden cities and urban planning], *Hōgaku shinpō* 23, no. 1 (February 1913), p. 36.

96. On Ebenezer Howard and the garden-city movement more generally, see Robert Fishman, *Urban Utopias in the Twentieth Century* (New York: Basic Books, 1977).

97. Seki, "Kaen toshi to toshi keikaku," pp. 23–40.

98. Ibid., p. 37.

99. Ibid., p. 21.

100. Ibid., pp. 37 and 40.

101. Seki, "Toshi kōtsū," pp. 268–279.

102. Seki Hajime, "Shiei jigyō" [Municipal enterprise], in *Shakai Seisaku Gakkai ronsō: Shiei jigyō* [Treatises of the Japan Association for Social Policy: Municipal enterprise], ed. Shakai Seisaku Gakkai (Tokyo: Shakai Seisaku Gakkai, 1911), pp. 64 and 81.

103. Ibid., p. 76.

104. Seki Hajime, "Toshi renraku denki tetsudō" [Interurban electric railways], *Hōgaku shinpō* 22, no. 1 (January 1912), p. 55.

105. Seki, "Kōshi kyōdō jigyō," *Kokumin keizai zasshi* 16, no. 4 (April 1914), p. 61. In only one important respect did Seki find fault with urban policy in Osaka: a missed opportunity for urban social reform offered by its massive port-improvement initiative. While the city had managed to produce new urban space by successfully completing a massive landfill project, observed Seki, it had allowed huge cost overruns to undermine its original plan to dedicate the property to low-income housing. When the city sold the landfill to private business to defray expenses, it ended up squandering an urban asset that could and should have been used to improve the lives of citizens. Seki Hajime, "Shōkō ron" [On commercial ports], *Nihon keizai shinshi* 12, no. 3 (November 1912), pp. 16–18.

106. Seki Hajime, "Tochi tōki to jūkyo mondai" [Land speculation and the residential problem], in *Kokka oyobi kokka gaku* 1, no. 3 (March 1913), pp. 71–72.

107. Ibid., p. 71.

108. Seki Hajime, "Shiei jigyō ron, III" [On municipal enterprise, III], *Kokumin keizai zasshi* 11, no. 3 (September 1911), p. 62.

109. Kameda Nagashichi, "Keibo setsusetsu" [Ardent admiration], in *Ko Seki Shichō o shinobu* [Recalling the late Mayor Seki], ed. Ōsaka-shi Kyōikukai (Osaka: Ōsaka-shi Kyōikukai, 1935), p. 32.

110. Takiyama Ryōichi, "Omoide de" [In remembrance], in *Ko Seki Shichō o shinobu* [Recalling the late Mayor Seki], ed. Ōsaka-shi Kyōikukai (Osaka: Ōsaka-shi Kyōikukai, 1935), p. 79.

111. Zen-Ōsaka Shichō Ikegami Shirō-kun Shōtoku Kai, ed., *Moto Ōsaka Shichō Ikegami Shirō-kun Shōei* [A portrait of former Osaka Mayor Ikegami Shirō] (Osaka, 1941), pp. 10–11. On the politics of Meiji Osaka, see Harada Keiichi, *Nihon kindai toshi shi kenkyū* [Researches on the history of the modern Japanese city] (Kyoto: Shibunkaku Shuppan, 1997).

112. Harada Keiichi, "Toshi shihai kōzō" [The structure of city rule], *Rekishi hyōron* 393 (January 1983), p. 85.

113. Ibid., p. 84.

114. Zen Ōsaka Shichō Ikegami Shirō-kun Shōtoku Kai, ed., *Moto Ōsaka Shichō Ikegami Shirō-kun Shōei*, pp. 22 and 105.

115. Seki, *Nikki*, 14 August 1914, pp. 82–83.

116. Ibid., 21 August 1914, p. 83.

117. Quoted in Tamaki, *Ōsaka kensetsu shi yawa*, p. 156.

118. Seki, *Nikki*, 22 September 1914, p. 87.

119. Seki Hajime, "Taun puraningu ni tsuite" [About town planning], *Kobe keizaikai kōenshū* 1 (1916), pp. 157–159.

120. Ibid., pp. 159–160.

121. Ibid., p. 162.

122. Ibid., pp. 161–162.

123. Ibid., p. 162.

124. Ibid., pp. 162–163. While Seki acknowledged that the geographical and topographical differences between cities "engendered a whole host of [planning] problems," he noted as well that the conferees in Belgium had produced a workable zoning model for the world's larger cities.

125. Ibid., p.163.

126. Ibid., pp. 163–164.

127. Ibid., pp. 164–166.

128. Ibid., p. 166.

129. Nakasa Kazushige, "Toshi keikaku kara mita Seki Hajime to Ōsaka toshi keikaku no kenkyū: 'Yobō' to 'chiryō' no toshi keikaku o chūshin ni shite" [Seki Hajime seen from the angle of urban planning and researches of Osaka urban planning: Focusing on "treatment" and "prevention" in urban planning] (master's thesis, Osaka Shiritsu Daigaku, 1979), p. 270.

130. Shibamura Atsuki, "Seki Hajime to sono jidai (II): Jōyaku shūnin mondai to kome sōdō" [Seki Hajime and his era (II): The issue of his appointment as deputy mayor and the Rice Riots], *Shisei kenkyū* 58 (1982), p. 113.

131. Murashima Motoyuki, *Dontei seikatsu* [Slum life] (Tokyo: Bungadō, 1917), p. 2.

132. Ibid., preface.

133. Michael Lewis, *Rioters & Citizens: Mass Protest in Imperial Japan* (Berkeley: University of California Press, 1990), p. 252.

134. Ibid., p. 253.

135. Inoue Kiyoshi and Watanabe Tōru, *Kome Sōdō no kenkyū: II* [Rice Riots researches: II] (Tokyo: Yūhikaku, 1959), pp. 6–9 and 4–5.

136. Ibid., p. 9.

137. Shibamura, "Seki Hajime to sono jidai (II)," p. 115.

138. Matsumoto Kanzō, ed., *Ōsaka shisei 70 nen no ayumi* [The 70-year course of Osaka municipal government] (Osaka: Ōsaka Shiyakusho, 1959), pp. 48–49.

139. Osaka Shikai, ed., *Ōsaka Shikai giroku* [Proceedings of the Osaka Municipal Assembly], 30 February 1918.

140. NHK Ōsaka Hōsō-kyoku, ed., *Kindai Ōsaka nenpyō: Meiji gannen (1868)–Shōwa 57 nen (1982)* [A chronology of modern Osaka: From the first year of Meiji (1868) to Showa 57 (1982)] (Tokyo: Nippon Hōsō Shuppan Kyōkai, 1983), p. 104.

141. Lewis, *Rioters & Citizens*, p. 247.

142. On national recognition of the critical difference between "social

work" and "relief work," see Sheldon Garon, *Molding Japanese Minds: The State in Everyday Life* (Princeton, N.J.: Princeton University Press, 1997), p. 51.

143. On official aversion to the term *society,* see Lewis, *Rioters & Citizens,* p. 247.

144. On the district-commissioner system in Osaka, see Ōsaka Shi Hōmen Iin Seido Gojūnen Kinenshi Henshū Iinkai, *Ōsaka-shi hōmen iin minsei iin seido gojūnen shi* [A fifty-year history of the district-commissioner system in the city of Osaka] (Osaka: Ōsaka-shi, 1973). On the district-commissioner system in Tokyo, see Sally A. Hastings, *Neighborhood and Nation in Tokyo, 1905–1937* (Pittsburgh: Pittsburgh University Press, 1995), pp. 85–96.

145. Garon, *Molding Japanese Minds,* pp. 52–53.

146. David R. Ambaras, "Social Knowledge, Cultural Capital, and the New Middle Class in Japan, 1895–1912," *Journal of Japanese Studies* 24, no. 1 (1998), pp. 30–33.

147. Hastings, *Neighborhood and Nation in Tokyo,* pp. 86–87.

148. Ōmori Makoto, "Toshi shakai jigyō seiritsu-ki ni okeru chūkansō to minshūshugi" [The middle class and democracy during the formative period of urban social facilities], *Hisutoria* 97 (December 1982), pp. 72–73.

149. Sanctioned by the state to act as "class-neutral" moral arbiters, according to Ōmori, the district commissioners did not help the working classes get on their feet but instead taught them to stand up on their own; ibid., p. 70. See also Shibata Yoshimori, ed., *Ōsaka-shi minsei jigyō* [Public works in the city of Osaka] (Osaka: Ōsaka-shi Minsei-kyoku, 1978), pp. 15–32.

150. In 1919, the Labor Survey Unit began publishing its studies as a series, the *Rōdō chōsa hōkoku.* These surveys continue to be applauded as models of social-scientific research.

151. Nomura Yoshiki, "Nihon tokei hattatsu shi to Ōsaka-shi Shakai-bu 'Rōdō chōsa hōkoku'" [A history of the development of statistics in Japan and the labor-survey reports of the Social Bureau of the City of Osaka], *Keiei kenkyū* 33, no. 3 (September 1982), pp. 24–31. These reports have since been reissued as a set: Ōsaka Shiyakusho, ed., *Rōdō chōsa hōkoku* [Labor-survey reports] (Osaka: Ōsaka Shiritsu Chūō Toshokan, 1975).

152. Seki Hajime, "Toshi shakai seisaku" [Urban social policy], *Kyūsai kenkyū* 6, nos. 5 and 6 (May and June 1918).

153. Ibid., pp. 27–28.

154. Rodgers, *Atlantic Crossings,* p. 216.

155. Seki, "Toshi shakai seisaku," pp. 28–30.

156. Ibid., p. 30.

157. Ōsaka Toshi Kyōkai, ed., *Machi ni sumau: Ōsaka toshi jūtaku shi* [To live in the neighborhood: A history of urban housing in Osaka] (Tokyo: Heibonsha, 1989), p. 306.

158. Miyano Yūichi, "Seki Hajime to jūtaku seisaku: Dai Ichiji Taisen go Nihon jūtaku seisaku no keisei katei" [Seki Hajime and housing policy: The

process of forming post–World War I Japanese housing policy], *Ōsaka no rekishi* 18 (1986), p. 108.

159. Ōsaka Toshi Kyōkai, *Machi ni sumau*, p. 307.

160. Quoted in Miyano, "Seki Hajime to jūtaku seisaku," pp. 110–111.

161. Kiso Junko, "Nipponbashi hōmen Kamagasaki suramu ni okeru rōdō/seikatsu katei" [The ways of work and life in the Kamagasaki slum near Nipponbashi], in *Taishō Ōsaka suramu: Mo hitotsu no Nihon kindai shi* [The slums of Taisho Osaka: Another modern history of Japan], ed. Sugihara Kaoru and Kiso Junko (Tokyo: Shinhyōron, 1987), pp. 81–82.

162. Miyano, "Seki Hajime to jūtaku seisaku," p. 108.

163. Ōsaka Toshi Kyōkai, *Machi ni sumau*, pp. 304–305.

164. Quoted in Miyano, "Seki Hajime to jūtaku seisaku," p. 108.

165. Tamaki, *Ōsaka kensetsu shi yawa*, p. 146.

166. Watanabe Shun'ichi, *"Toshi keikaku" no tanjō: Kokusai hikaku kara mita Nihon kindai toshi keikaku* [The birth of "urban planning": Japan's modern urban planning in international comparison] (Tokyo: Kashiwa Shobō, 1993), pp. 151–165.

167. Seki, "Toshi shakai seisaku," p. 30, 31–32.

168. Seki Hajime, "Toshi jūtaku seisaku" [Urban housing policy], *Kenchiku zasshi* 33, no. 391 (1919), p. 74.

169. Ibid., p. 72.

170. Seki Hajime, *Bunka to jūtaku mondai* [Culture and the housing problem] (Osaka: Ōsaka-shi, 1921), p. 8.

171. Seki Hajime, "Toshi seisaku ni tsuite" [On urban policy], *Kyūsai kenkyū* 9, no. 11 (November 1921).

172. Ibid., p. 48.

173. Seki, "Toshi shakai seisaku," pp. 32–36.

174. Works by these authors in Seki's library included: George Cadbury, *Town Planning* (1915); Patrick Geddes, *Cities in Evolution* (1915); Percy A. Harris, *London and Its Government* (1913); Werner Hegemann, *Städtebau nach den Ergebnissen der Allgemeinen Städtebau-Ausstellung* (1910–1912); Prince Peter Kropotkin, *Fields, Factories, and Workshops* (1899); Nelson P. Lewis, *Planning of the Modern City* (1916); William Bennett Munro, *Government of European Cities* (1909); John Nolen, *City Planning* (1916); B. Seebohm Rowntree and A. C. Pigou, *Lectures on Housing* (1914); Raymond Unwin, *Town Planning in Practice* (1914); Lawrence Veiller, *Housing Reform* (1911); and Adolf Weber, *Grosstadt und ihre Sozialen Probleme* (1918).

CHAPTER 6. THE LIVABLE CITY

1. Seki Hajime, "Taun puraningu ni tsuite," *Kobe keizaikai kōenshū* 1 (1916), p. 160.

2. Daniel T. Rodgers, *Atlantic Crossings: Social Politics in a Progressive Age* (Cambridge, Mass.: Harvard University Press, 1998), p. 117.

3. Henry D. Smith II, "Tokyo and London: Comparative Conceptions of the City," in *Japan: Comparative View*, ed. Albert M. Craig (Princeton, N.J.: Princeton University Press, 1979), p. 88.

4. Raymond Unwin, the master planner of England's Hampstead Garden Suburb (1906), was the design pioneer of this variation on Ebenezer Howard's garden-city idea. See especially Raymond Unwin, *Town Planning in Practice: An Introduction to the Art of Designing Cities and Suburbs* (London: T. Fisher Unwin, 1911). For an overview of the garden-city movement, see Anthony Sutcliffe, *Towards the Planned City: Germany, Britain, the United States and France 1780–1914* (New York: St. Martin's Press, 1981), pp. 76–81.

5. Kojita Yasunao, *Nihon kindai toshi shi kenkyū josetsu* (Tokyo: Kashiwa Shobō, 1991), p. 187, and Kawase Mitsuyoshi, "Senzen Nihon no toshi keisei to keikaku: Ōsaka-shi no jirei o chūshin ni" [Prewar Japanese urban formation and planning: The example of the city of Osaka] (master's thesis, Kyoto University, 1982), pp. 44–45.

6. On the invented tradition of village solidarity, see Irwin Scheiner, "The Japanese Village: Imagined, Real, Contested," in *Mirror of Modernity: Invented Traditions of Modern Japan*, ed. Stephen Vlastos (Berkeley: University of California Press, 1998), pp. 67–78.

7. Seki Hajime, *Kōgyō seisaku* (Tokyo: Hōbunkan, 1913), pp. 2:920–922.

8. Kevin Lynch, *The Image of the City* (Cambridge, Mass.: The MIT Press, 1960), pp. 9–10.

9. Quoted in James C. Scott, *Seeking Like a State: How Certain Schemes to Improve the Human Condition Have Failed* (New Haven Conn.: Yale University Press, 1998), p. 62.

10. Henry D. Smith II, "Tokyo as an Idea: An Exploration of Japanese Urban Thought until 1945," *Journal of Japanese Studies* 4, no. 1 (Winter 1978), p. 61.

11. On Fukuda's New Tokyo plan, see Ishida Yorifusa, *Mikan no Tōkyō keikaku: Jitsugen shinakatta keikaku no keikaku shi* [Unfinished Tokyo plans: A planning history of unrealized plans] (Tokyo: Chikuma Shobō, 1992), pp. 64–66.

12. Miyake Iwao, *Toshi no kenkyū* (Tokyo: Jitsugyō no Nihonsha, 1908), pp. 197–198 and 230.

13. Yamazaki Rintarō, *Ōbei toshi no kenkyū* [Researches on Western cities] (Tokyo, 1911), pp. 286–287.

14. Nakagawa Masajirō, *Toshi kairyō mondai* [The urban-reform problem] (Tokyo: Akashiro Shozō, 1914), p. 1.

15. Ikeda Hiroshi, *Gendai toshi no yokkyū* [What contemporary cities require] (Tokyo: Toshi Kenkyūkai, 1919), pp. 19–20.

16. Nihon Jūtaku Sōgō Sentā, ed., *Senzen no jūtaku seisaku no hensen ni kansuru chōsa: Toshi Kenkyūkai no opinion rīdā* [A survey of the transition in prewar housing policy: Opinion leaders of the Urban Research Association] (Tokyo: Nihon Jūtaku Sōgō Sentā, 1980), p. 18.

17. Nishiyama Uzō and Yoshino Masatsugu, "Toshi keikaku gakusetsushi gaisetsu" [A brief history of urban-planning theory], in *Toshi jichi gakusetsu shi gaisetsu, III* [A brief history of urban-autonomy theory, III], ed. Tōkyō Shisei Chōsakai (Tokyo: Tōkyō Shisei Chōsakai, 1972), p. 108.

18. Toshi Keikaku Chōsa Iinkai, ed., *Toshi Keikaku Chōsa Iinkai giji sō-kiroku, I* [Complete proceedings of the Urban Planning Survey Commission, I] (Tokyo: Naimudaijin Kanbō Toshi Keikaku-ka, 1918), pp. 10–18.

19. Ikeda, *Gendai toshi no yokkyū*, p. 49.

20. Quoted in Akagi Suruki, "Toshi keikaku no keikakusei" [The planning qualities of urban planning], in *Toshi kōzō to toshi keikaku* [Urban structure and urban planning], ed. Tōkyō Toritsu Daigaku Toshi Kenkyūkai (Tokyo: Tōkyō Daigaku Shuppankai, 1969), p. 504.

21. Ikeda, *Gendai toshi no yokkyū*, pp. 55–70.

22. Quoted in Nihon Jūtaku Sōgō Sentā, *Senzen jūtaku seisaku*, p. 23.

23. Kataoka Yasushi, *Gendai toshi no kenkyū* (Tokyo: Kenchiku Kōgei Kyōkai, 1914), pp. 434–435 and 437.

24. Ibid., pp. 438, 440, 445.

25. Ibid., pp. 446, 454–456.

26. Kataoka Yasushi, "Toshi seikatsu to jūtaku, II" [Urban life and housing, II], *Kenchiku to shakai* 4, no. 4 (April 1921), pp. 5 and 3–5.

27. Kataoka, "Toshi seikatsu to jūtaku, I," pp. 4–7.

28. Kataoka figured prominently in the urban planning of Osaka both as a local architect and as a member of the regional planning committee. Nihon Jūtaku Sōgō Sentā, *Senzen jūtaku seisaku*, p. 51.

29. Miyao Shunji, *Toshi keikaku ni kansuru kōwa* [Lectures on urban planning] (Nagoya: Toshi Keikaku Nagoya Chihō Iinkai, 1921), p. 18.

30. Ibid., pp. 18–19 and 26.

31. Kishi Kazuta, *Seibutsugakuteki toshi keiei ron* [On biology-like urban management] (Tokyo: Sanseido, 1923), p. 52.

32. Tochiuchi Yoshitane, *Kankyō yori mitaru toshi mondai no kenkyū* [Researches of the urban problem as seen from the perspective of the environment] (Tokyo: Kōrindo Shoten, 1922), p. 226.

33. Ibid., pp. 53, 55, 58, 68–69, 222, 226.

34. Seinen Toshi Kenkyūkai, *Forest City: Sanrin toshi* (Nagoya: Seinen Toshi Kenkyūkai, 1922), pp. 2–13.

35. Yūge Shichirō, *Toshi no hanashi* [Speaking of cities] (Tokyo: Sekai Shichō Kenkyūkai, 1923), pp. 135–136.

36. Kōno Makoto, *Toshi ka den'en ka* [Will it be cities or fields?] (Tokyo: Matsuyamabō, 1924), pp. 17, 73, 121, 147.

37. Ibid., pp. 152–155, 158, 157, 166–168, 15.

38. Ibid., pp. 168–170.

39. Ibid., pp. 173–174.

40. Seki Hajime, "Toshi keikaku ron" [On urban planning] (undated lectures), in *Toshi seisaku no riron to jissai: Seki Hajime ikōshū* [Theory and

practice of urban policy: A posthumous collection of works by Seki Hajime], ed. Seki Hakase Ronbunshū Henshū Iinkai (Osaka: Ōsaka Toshi Kyōkai, 1968), pp. 112–113.

41. Ibid., pp. 113–114.

42. Seki Hajime, "Kinsei toshi no hatten to toshi keikaku" [Urban planning and the development of early modern cities], *Toshi kōron* 7, no. 12 (December 1924), p. 15.

43. Rodgers, *Atlantic Crossings*, p. 164.

44. Ibid., p. 114.

45. Seki, "Toshi keikaku ron," p. 111.

46. The following are representative works by these authors that were referenced by Seki: Raymond Unwin, *Town Planning in Practice* (1911); Graham Taylor, *Satellite Cities* (1915); Patrick Geddes, *Cities in Evolution* (1915).

47. Seki, "Toshi keikaku ron," p. 114.

48. Ibid., pp. 111 and 110.

49. Ibid., p. 117.

50. Seki, "Kinsei toshi no hatten to toshi keikaku," pp. 16–17; Seki, "Toshi keikaku ron," p. 117.

51. Seki Hajime, "Toshi jūtaku seisaku," *Kenchiku zasshi* 33, no. 391 (1919), p. 23.

52. Seki, "Toshi keikaku ron," pp. 118–119.

53. Seki Hajime, *Bunka to jūtaku mondai* (Osaka: Ōsaka-shi, 1921), p. 25; Seki, "Toshi jūtaku seisaku," p. 72.

54. Seki, "Toshi jūtaku seisaku," p. 74.

55. Seki, "Kinsei toshi no hatten to toshi keikaku," pp. 6 and 4–5.

56. Ibid., p. 7. On this same subject, from a similar perspective, see also Scott, *Seeing Like a State*, p. 63.

57. Seki, "Kinsei toshi no hatten to toshi keikaku," pp. 19, 21, 18.

58. Ibid., pp. 20–21. For a sweeping survey of contemporary British urban-planning ideas, see Sutcliffe, *Towards the Planned City*, pp. 47–87.

59. Seki, "Kinsei toshi no hatten to toshi keikaku," pp. 9, 10, 21.

60. Seki, "Toshi keikaku ron," p. 117.

61. Ibid., p. 124; Seki, "Kinsei toshi no hatten to toshi keikaku," p. 22.

62. Seki Hajime Kenkyūkai, ed., *Seki Hajime nikki: Taishō Shōwa Shoki no Ōsaka shisei* (Tokyo: Tokyo Daigaku Shuppankai, 1986), 7 November 1914, pp. 92–93.

63. Seki Hajime, "Kaen toshi to toshi keikaku," *Hōgaku shinpō* 23, no. 1 (February 1913), p. 21.

64. Seki, "Taun puraningu ni tsuite," p. 159.

65. Ibid., pp. 159–160.

66. Seki Hajime, *Jūtaku mondai to toshi keikaku* [The housing problem and urban planning] (Kyoto: Kubundō Shobō, 1923), p. 119.

67. See especially Norma Evenson, *Paris: A Century of Change, 1878–1978* (New Haven, Conn.: Yale University Press, 1979), pp. 2–24.

68. Carl E. Schorske, "The Ringstrasse, Its Critics, and the Birth of Urban

Modernism," in *Fin-de-Siècle Vienna: Politics and Culture* (New York: Vintage Books, 1981), pp. 24–115.

69. See, for example, Okada Shin'ichirō's article in the *Ōsaka asahi shinbun*, 2 January 1916, and the series of articles on residential reform that appeared in the *Ōsaka asahi* later that year on 14 January 1916 and 8 March 1916.

70. Honma Yoshihito, *Doboku kokka no shisō: Toshi ron no keifu* [Theories of the construction state: A genealogy of urban thought] (Tokyo: Nihon Keizai Hyōronsha, 1996), pp. 147–148. See also Hara Takeshi, *"Minto" Ōsaka tai "teito" Tōkyō: Shisō toshite no Kansai shitetsu* ["The people's capital" Osaka versus "the imperial capital" Tokyo: The Kansai private railways as an idea] (Tokyo: Kodansha, 1998), pp. 129–134.

71. Seki, *Nikki*, 11 April 1917, p. 166.

72. Seki reported attending four meetings of the Survey Association for Urban Reform Planning over the following year. See ibid., 19 April 1917, 3 May 1917, 29 November 1917, and 18 April 1918. In addition, he met with the Osaka Chamber of Commerce on 21 July 1917 and with engineers in the Tokyo city government on 19 March 1918 to discuss "progress" on Osaka's urban plan.

73. Ibid., 19 March 1918, p. 198.

74. Watanabe Shun'ichi, *"Toshi keikaku" no tanjō: Kokusai hikaku kara mita Nihon kindai toshi keikaku* (Tokyo: Kashiwa Shobō, 1993), pp. 155–157.

75. Seki, *Nikki*, 7 June 1918, p. 205.

76. Toshi Keikaku Chōsa Iinkai, *Toshi Keikaku Chōsa Iinkai giji sōkiroku*, I, p. 29.

77. Ibid., p. 29.

78. Toshi Keikaku Chōsa Iinkai, *Toshi Keikaku Chōsa Iinkai giji sōkiroku*, II, pp. 69–70.

79. Ibid., p. 2.

80. Ibid., pp. 86–87.

81. Watanabe, *"Toshi keikaku" no tanjō*, pp. 151–161.

82. Seki Hajime, "Toshi keikaku ni tsuite" [About urban planning], *Nihon Shakai Gakuin nenpō* 5, nos. 1–3 (February 1918), p. 357.

83. Ibid., pp. 356–358.

84. Ibid., p. 359.

85. Ibid., p. 356, 361, 358.

86. Ibid., p. 366.

87. Ibid., pp. 363–364.

88. Seki, *Nikki*, 13, 15, and 17 June 1918, pp. 206–207.

89. Ibid., 22 June 1918, p. 207.

90. Ibid., 3, 13, and 31 July 1918, pp. 208–209, 211.

91. Ibid., 15 July 1919, pp. 256–257.

92. Ōsaka Shikai, ed., *Ōsaka shikai kaigiroku* [Proceedings of the Osaka Municipal Assembly], 23 December 1919.

93. Seki Hajime, "Ōsaka toshi keikaku jūnen no kaisō" [A reminiscence of ten years of Osaka urban planning], *Dai Ōsaka* 7, no. 7 (July 1931), p. 10.

94. Kawase, "Senzen Nihon no toshi keisei to keikaku," pp. 118, 123.

95. Ōsaka Shikai, ed., *Ōsaka shikai kaigiroku*, 6 July 1920.

96. For a copy of the plan approved by the central government on 19 March 1921, see Nakagawa Hitoshi, *Shin Ōsaka taikan* [A gazeteer of the new Osaka] (Osaka: Shin Ōsaka Taikan Kankōjo, 1923), pp. 654–663.

97. Kawabata Naomasa, *Ōsaka no gyōsei* [The administration of Osaka] (Osaka: Mainichi Hōsō, 1973), p. 173.

98. Seki Hajime, "Dai Ōsaka no kensetsu" [The building of greater Osaka], *Dai Ōsaka* 4, no. 6 (June 1928), p. 3.

99. Seki, "Ōsaka toshi keikaku jūnen no kaisō," p. 10.

100. Ibid., pp. 8–10.

101. Ibid., p. 10.

102. Kawase, "Senzen Nihon no toshi keisei to keikaku," pp. 64–65.

103. Seki, "Ōsaka toshi keikaku jūnen no kaisō," pp. 8 and 10.

104. Ibid., p. 8.

105. Ibid., p. 9.

106. Ibid., pp. 10–11.

107. Seki, "Toshi keikaku ron," p. 109.

108. Seki, *Nikki*, 7 April 1921, p. 341.

109. Ibid., 22 November 1921, p. 369.

110. Seki, "Toshi keikaku ron," p. 107.

111. Beard spoke of the need for proactive urban management and apparently caused something of a stir when he proceeded to survey urban administration in Tokyo. Watanabe, *"Toshi keikaku" no tanjō*, pp. 219–225.

112. Charles A. Beard, *The Administration and Politics of Tokyo: A Survey and Opinions* (New York: Macmillan, 1923), p. 11.

113. Shibata Tokue, *Nihon no toshi seisaku* [Japanese urban policy] (Tokyo: Yūhikaku, 1978), pp. 60–62.

114. Ibid., p. 63.

115. As a disbelieving nation slowly learned, the Great Kanto Earthquake was a living hell that had provoked mass hysteria and had ultimately driven some to mass murder. Amid the chaos of the conflagration, rumors flew wildly, and conspiracy theories ran rampant. One such rumor, which spread through a populace already half-crazed by aftershocks and firestorms—of a Korean conspiracy to set fires and to poison wells—turned neighborhood-watch groups into mobs of vigilantes bent on the crudest form of street justice. Untold thousands of Koreans, Chinese, and unfortunate members of other groups were brutally murdered—their battered corpses heaped indiscriminately atop the piles of crushed, incinerated, asphyxiated, and drowned bodies that littered the city. For a post-earthquake narrative laced with firsthand accounts, see Nakajima Tōichirō, *Kantō Daishinsai* [The Great Kanto Earthquake] (Tokyo: Yūzankaku, 1995). See also Jeffrey E. Hanes, "Urban Planning as an Urban

Problem: The Reconstruction of Tokyo after the Great Kanto Earthquake," *Seisaku kagaku* 7, no. 3 (March 2000), pp. 125–127.

116. Ikeda Hiroshi, "Toshi keikaku no gainen" [The category of urban planning], in *Toshi to kōen* [Cities and parks], ed. Teien Kyōkai (Tokyo: Seibidō, 1924), pp. 15–16.

117. Uchida Toshikazu, "Toshi keikaku no shitsetsu ni tsuite" [About urban-planning facilities], in *Toshi to kōen* [Cities and parks], ed. Teien Kyōkai (Tokyo: Seibidō, 1924), pp. 1–2.

118. Takahashi Usaburō, "De'en toshi ni tsuite" [About garden cities], in *Toshi to kōen* [Cities and parks], ed. Teien Kyōkai (Tokyo: Seibidō, 1924), pp. 1–2.

119. Nakagawa Nozomu, "Toshi keikaku no kōjō" [The rise of urban planning], *Dai Ōsaka* 1, no. 1 (December 1925), p. 13.

120. Hashimoto Seinosuke, *Saikin Ōbei toshi no hattatsu* [Recent advances of Western cities] (Tokyo: Shinseisha, 1925), p. 83.

121. Tagawa Daikichirō, *Tsukurarubeki Tōkyō* [The Tokyo we should build] (Tokyo, 1923).

122. Seki, *Nikki*, 1 September 1923–31 December 1923, pp. 458–476. On the subject, see Hanes, "Urban Planning as an Urban Problem," pp. 128–136, and Jeffrey E. Hanes, "Earthquake Hazard Mitigation and Urban Planning in Japan: Historical Lessons, Cultural Constraints, Future Prospects," in *Proceedings of the 5th United States/Japan Workshop on Urban Earthquake Hazard Reduction: Recovery and Reconstruction from Recent Earthquakes*, ed. Earthquake Engineering Research Institute (Oakland, Calif.: Earthquake Engineering Research Institute, 1997).

123. Seki, *Nikki*, 28 January 1924, p. 482.

124. The one truly positive housing initiative that came out of the reconstruction era was the semipublic Dōjunkai. For an excellent account of the Dōjunkai's apartment-building construction spree, see Maruku Burudeie [Marc J. F. Bourdier], *Dōjunkai apāto genkei: Nihon kenchiku shi ni okeru yakuwari* [The original scene of the Dōjunkai Apartments: Its place in Japanese architectural history] (Tokyo: Sumai no Toshokan Shuppan-kyoku, 1992).

125. Quoted in Shibamura Atsuki, *Toshi no kindai: Ōsaka no 20 seiki* [The modern age of the city: Osaka in the 20th century] (Kyoto: Shibunkaku, 1999), pp. 18–19.

126. On Seki as mayor, see Blair A. Ruble, *Second Metropolis: Pragmatic Pluralism in Gilded Age Chicago, Silver Age Moscow, and Meiji Osaka* (New York: Woodrow Wilson Center Press and Cambridge University Press, 2001), pp. 349–355.

127. Nakasa Kazushige, "Toshi keikaku kara mita Seki Hajime to Ōsaka toshi keikaku no kenkyū: 'Yobō' to 'chiryō' no toshi keikaku o chūshin ni shite" (master's thesis, Osaka Shiritsu Daigaku, 1979), p. 41.

128. Ōsaka Shikai, ed., *Setsuzoku chōson hennyū ni kansuru shimon no kudari, ku no haichi ni kansuru shimon no kudari: Iinkai sōkiroku* [Interviews

on the incorporation of adjoining towns and villages, interviews on apportioning districts: Commission proceedings] (Osaka: Ōsaka Shikai, 1924), 5 December 1924, p. 57.

129. Ibid., 8 December 1924, pp. 11 and 12.

130. Matsumoto Kanzō, ed., *Ōsaka shisei 70 nen no ayumi* (Osaka: Ōsaka Shiyakusho, 1959), pp. 60–62.

131. Kawase, "Senzen Nihon no toshi keisei to keikaku," pp. 44–45, 177.

132. Kodera Shōzō, *Ōsaka han'eishi* [A history of prosperity in Osaka] (Osaka: Shijō Shunjūsha, 1983), p. 230.

133. Seki Hajime, "Daitoshi ni tsuite no ni-san no kōsatsu" [A couple of observations about big cities], in *Dai Ōsaka* 6, no. 9 (September 1930), pp. 23–24.

134. Kanbara Ryūji, *Minami Ōsaka hennyū kinen shi* [A commemorative history of the urban incorporation of southern Osaka] (Osaka: Minami Ōsaka Hennyū Kinen Shi Hakkōkai, 1925), pp. 1–2, 5.

135. Kawase, "Senzen Nihon no toshi keisei to keikaku," pp. 151–168.

136. Seki Hajime, "Toshi keikaku ni kansuru shin rippō" [New legislation concerning urban planning], *Dai Ōsaka* 2, no. 4 (April 1926), p. 11.

137. Seki Hajime, "Ōsaka-shi no sho mondai" [The various problems of Osaka City], *Dai Ōsaka* 1, no. 1 (December 1925), pp. 3 and 2.

138. Ibid., p. 2.

139. Seki, *Nikki*, 31 December 1924, p. 527.

140. Tanaka Kiyo, *Ōsaka no toshi keikaku* [Urban planning of Osaka] (Osaka: Hinoshita Wagakujiya, 1925).

141. Ibid., plates.

142. Ibid., preface and pp. 39–40.

143. Seki, "Ōsaka-shi no sho mondai," p. 3.

144. Shibamura Atsuki, "Taishō-ki Ōsaka no sangyō to shakai" [Industry and society in Taisho Era Osaka], in *Ōsaka no sangyō to shakai* [Industry and society in Osaka], ed. Kitazaki Toyoji (Osaka: Mainichi Hōsō, 1973), pp. 233–235.

145. Tanaka, *Ōsaka no toshi keikaku*, pp. 181–182.

146. Seki, "Toshi keikaku ni kansuru shin rippō," pp. 14–15.

147. Seki Hajime, "Kōtaishi denka gyōkei isshūnen ni saishi" [In commemoration of the progress by the imperial prince], *Dai Ōsaka* 2, no. 6 (June 1926), p. 3.

148. Ibid.

149. Seki, "Dai Ōsaka no kensetsu," pp. 3, 4, 7.

150. Seki, "Toshi keikaku ron," p. 110.

151. Seki, "Kōtaishi denka gyōkei isshūnen ni saishi," p. 3.

152. Seki, "Toshi keikaku ron," pp. 119–124.

153. M. Christine Boyer, *Dreaming the Rational City: The Myth of American City Planning* (Cambridge, Mass.: MIT Press, 1983), p. 174.

154. Seki, "Toshi keikaku ni kansuru shin rippō," pp. 12–15.

155. Seki, "Kōtaishi denka gyōkei isshūnen ni saishi," p. 4.

156. Seki Hajime, "Jiyū kūchi" [Open land], in *Dai ikkai zenkoku Toshi mondai kaigiroku* [Proceedings of the First National Conference on the Urban Problem], ed. Ōsaka Toshi Kyōkai (Osaka: Ōsaka Toshi Kyōkai, 1927), pp. 181–182.

157. Seki, "Toshi jūtaku seisaku," p. 72.

158. Seki, *Jūtaku mondai to toshi keikaku*, p. 2.

159. Rodgers, *Atlantic Crossings*, p. 163.

160. On Dawson, see ibid., pp. 61–62. For a taste of the descriptive detail and analytical precision that characterized Dawson's work, see especially William Harbutt Dawson, *Municipal Life and Government in Germany* (London: Longmans, Green, 1914).

161. On Lewis, see Sutcliffe, *Towards the Planned City*, p. 125, and Boyer, *Dreaming the Rational City*, pp. 84–85.

162. On Hegemann, see Sutcliffe, *Towards the Planned City*, pp. 45 and 174.

163. On Nolen, see Boyer, *Dreaming the Rational City*, pp. 74–75 and 144. According to Sutcliffe, *Towards the Planned City*, p. 125, Nolen's edited volume *City Planning: A Series of Papers Presenting the Essential Elements of a City Plan* (1916), along with Nelson P. Lewis's *The Planning of the Modern City* (1916), witnessed the coming-of-age of urban planning as a discipline in the United States. Both books were in Seki Hajime's library.

164. On Eberstadt, see Brian Ladd, *Urban Planning and Civic Order in Germany, 1860–1914* (Cambridge, Mass.: Harvard University Press, 1990), pp. 178–179.

165. Seki, *Nikki*, 30 September 1919, p. 265.

166. Ibid., 7 October 1919, p. 266.

167. Ōsaka Toshi Kyōkai, ed., *Machi ni sumau: Ōsaka toshi jūtaku shi* (Tokyo: Heibonsha, 1989), pp. 309–312.

168. Seki, "Toshi jūtaku seisaku," blueprint.

169. Ibid., pp. 74, 72.

170. Ibid., pp. 81–86.

171. Seki, *Nikki*, 17 May 1921, p. 347.

172. For an engaging history of the Ōsaka Shakkajin Dōmeikai, see Tamagawa Shinmei and Shirai Shinpei, *Jūmin undō no genzō: Shakkajin Dōmei to Itsumi Naozō* [Development of a residents' movement: The Renters' Alliance and Itsumi Naozō] (Tokyo: JCA Shuppan, 1978).

173. Ōsaka Toshi Kyōkai, *Machi ni sumau*, p. 307.

174. Ōsaka Shiyakusho Rōdō Chōsa-ka, "Jūtaku chōsa" [A housing survey], *Rōdō chōsa hōkoku* 7 (February 1921), preface, p. 7.

175. Ibid., preface, pp. 17–18.

176. Seki, *Bunka to jūtaku mondai*, p. 2.

177. Ibid., p. 1.

178. Ibid., pp. 1–3, 5, 8.

179. Ibid., p. 24.

180. Seki, *Jūtaku mondai to toshi keikaku*, p. 65.

181. Seki, "Ōsaka toshi keikaku jūnen no kaisō," pp. 8–9.

182. Seki, "Toshi keikaku ron," p. 119.

183. Ibid., p. 124.

184. Seki, Jūtaku mondai to toshi keikaku, p. 72.

185. Seki Hajime, "Jūtaku mondai no kaiketsunan" [The difficulty in solving the housing problem], Ōsaka-shi shōkō jihō 316 (1921), p. 19.

186. Seki, Jūtaku mondai to toshi keikaku, p. 74.

187. Seki, Bunka to jūtaku mondai, p. 12.

188. On German multistory housing, see Sutcliffe, Towards the Planned City, p. 15.

189. Seki, Jūtaku mondai no toshi keikaku, p. 65.

190. Ibid., p. 6.

191. See Schorske, Fin-de-Siècle Vienna, p. 25.

192. Seki, Jūtaku mondai to toshi keikaku, p. 120.

193. Seki, "Kotaishi denka gyōkei isshūnen ni saishi," p. 3.

194. Ibid., p. 5.

195. Seki, "Jiyū kūchi," pp. 181–182.

196. In this connection, Seki related the case of a worker in New York suffering from "nervous exhaustion" who had been ordered by his doctor to seek out "free and open space." See Seki, Jūtaku mondai to toshi keikaku, p. 65, and Seki Hajime, "Shinkei suijaku no yobō" [Prevention of nervous exhaustion], Dai Ōsaka 5, no. 3 (March 1929), p. 2.

197. Seki Hajime, "Ōsaka shiiki no kakuchō to shin shiiki ni shikkō shitaru shōban no shisetsu" [The expansion of Osaka's boundaries and facilities ready to go within the new urban boundary], in Dainikai zenkoku toshi mondai kaigi: Kenkyū hōkoku [Second National Conference on the Urban Problem: Research presentations], ed. Tōkyō Shisei Chōsakai (Tokyo: Tōkyō Shisei Chōsakai, 1930), p. 89.

198. The Hannan development survives even today as an urban oasis in southern Osaka.

199. Ōsaka Toshi Kyōkai, Machi ni sumau, p. 312.

200. Tamai Kingo, "Nihon Shihonshugi to (toshi) shakai seisaku: Ōsaka-shi shakai jigyō o chūshin ni" [Japanese capitalism and (urban) social policy: Social facilities in Osaka], in Taishō Ōsaka suramu: Mo hitotsu no Nihon kindai shi [The slums of Taisho Osaka: Another modern history of Japan], ed. Sugihara Kaoru and Kiso Junko (Tokyo: Shinhyōron, 1987), pp. 275–276.

201. Kawase, "Senzen Nihon no toshi keisei to keikaku," pp. 27–34.

202. For a descriptive survey of these different garden suburbs, see Katagi Atsushi, Fujiya Yōetsu, and Kadono Yukihiro, eds., Kindai Nihon no kōgai jūtakuchi [The suburban residential land of modern Japan] (Tokyo: Kajima Shuppankai, 2000), pp. 241–438.

203. Robert Fishman, Bourgeois Utopias: The Rise and Fall of Suburbia (New York: Basic Books, 1987).

204. Ōsaka Toshi Kyōkai, Machi ni sumau, pp. 346–349.

205. Seki, "Ōsaka-shi no sho mondai," p. 2.

206. Ibid., p. 4.

207. Miyamoto Ken'ichi, "Dai ichiji taisen-go chiiki keizai no henbō to chihō gyō-zaisei no kiki" [Transformation of the regional economy and the crisis of local administration and finance following World War I], *Ōsaka Keidai ronshū* 133 (January 1980), p. 27.

208. Seki, "Ōsaka-shi no sho mondai," p. 5.

209. Seki Hajime, "Shisei no konpon mondai" [Fundamental problems of municipal administration], *Dai Ōsaka* 8, no. 7 (July 1932).

210. Rodgers, *Atlantic Crossings*, p. 113.

211. Ōsaka Shiyakusho, *Tosei-an* [Metropolitan policy proposal] (Osaka: Ōsaka Shiyakusho, 1932).

212. Seki Hajime, "Shisei manpitsu, I" [Stray notes on municipal government, I], *Dai Ōsaka* 5, no. 7 (July 1929), p. 81.

213. Seki Hajime, "Jūekisha futankin sei no genjō to sono kaizen sho saku" [Current condition of the system of public-use assessment and several measures for its improvement], in *Dai Ni Zenkoku Toshi Mondai Kaigi: Kenkyū hōkoku* [Second National Urban Problem Conference: Research reports], ed. Tōkyō Shisei Chōsakai (Tokyo: Tōkyō Shisei Chōsakai, 1930).

214. Seki Hajime, "Shiei jigyō no honshitsu" [The essence of municipal enterprise], *Toshi mondai panfureto* (Tōkyō Shisei Chōsakai), no. 5 (1928). On Seki's urban policymaking generally, see Miyamoto Ken'ichi, *Toshi Seisaku no shisō to genjitsu* [Ideas and realities of urban policy] (Tokyo: Yūhikaku, 1999), pp. 169–214.

215. Ōsaka Toshi Kyōkai, *Machi ni sumau*, p. 332.

216. Kawase, "Senzen Nihon no toshi keisei to keikaku," p. 104.

217. Miyano Yūichi, "Seki Hajime to jūtaku seisaku: Dai Ichiji Taisen go Nihon jūtaku seisaku no keisei katei," *Ōsaka no rekishi* 18 (1986), p. 110.

218. Ibid., p. 111.

219. Seki Hajime, "Daitoshi ni tsuite no ni-san no kōsatsu," p. 23.

220. Kodera, *Ōsaka han'ei shi*, pp. 186–201.

221. Ibid.

222. Seki Hajime, "Ōsaka chikatetsu no kaitsū ni saishite" [On the occasion of the opening of Osaka's subway], *Dai Ōsaka* 9, no. 5 (May 1933), p. 22.

223. Ōsaka Shikai, *Setsuzoku chōson hennyū ni kansuru shimon no kudari*, March 1932.

224. Seki's diary provides us with a detailed recorded of his personal, as well as his professional, comings and goings. See Seki, *Nikki*, passim.

225. Ogawa Ichitarō, "Seki shichō o omou" [Some thoughts about Mayor Seki], *Dai Ōsaka* 11, no. 2 (1935), pp. 30–31.

226. Miyamoto Ken'ichi, "'Gakusha shichō' Seki Hajime no 'shōshaku.'" [The sake sipping of the scholar-mayor Seki Hajime], *Sake bunka kenkyū* 4 (1994), pp. 56–57.

227. Ibid., 8 December 1924.

228. On the slums of prewar Osaka, see Sugiwara and Tamai, *Taishō Ōsaka suramu*. On the Korean exodus to Osaka, see Sugihara Tōru, *Ekkyō suru min:*

Kindai Ōsaka no Chōsenjin shi kenkyū [People transgressing borders: Researches on the history of Koreans in Osaka] (Tokyo: Shinkansha, 1998).

229. On the modern impulse toward "creative destruction" in urban planning, see especially the following: David Harvey, *The Condition of Postmodernity: An Enquiry into the Origins of Cultural Change* (Cambridge, Mass.: Blackwell, 1989), pp. 16–18; Marshall Berman, *All That Is Solid Melts into Air* (New York: Penguin Books, 1988), pp. 290–348; and Robert A. Caro, *The Power Broker: Robert Moses and the Fall of New York* (New York: Vintage Books, 1974).

230. Scott, *Seeing Like a State*, pp. 87–117.

231. They are so identified by Scott himself in ibid. Seki owned the following works by these "high modernists": Walther Rathenau, *In Days to Come* (1921); Frederick W. Taylor, *The Principles of Scientific Management* (1911); Gustave Le Bon, *The Crowd* (1896); and Le Corbusier, *City of Tomorrow and Its Planning* (1929).

232. Seki Hajime, "Fūsuigai to Ōsaka-shi no fukkō" [Storm and flood damage and the reconstruction of Osaka], *Dai Ōsaka* 10, no. 11 (November 1934), p. 41.

233. Paraphrased in Shibamura Atsuki, *Seki Hajime: Toshi shisō no paioniā* (Kyoto: Shōraisha, 1989), p. 209.

234. Seki, *Nikki*, 16 August 1933, pp. 913–914.

235. Ibid., 27 December 1933, p. 930.

236. Ibid., 5 January 1934, p. 930.

237. Ibid., 7 January 1934, p. 930.

Bibliography

Abe Isoo. *Ōyō shisei ron* [On practical municipal politics]. Tokyo: Hidaka Yū-rin, 1908.

Akagi Suruki. "Toshi keikaku no keikakusei" [The planning qualities of urban planning]. In *Toshi kōzō to toshi keikaku* [Urban structure and urban planning], edited by Tōkyō Toritsu Daigaku Toshi Kenkyūkai. Tokyo: Tōkyō Daigaku Shuppankai, 1969.

Ambaras, David R. "Social Knowledge, Cultural Capital, and the New Middle Class in Japan, 1895–1912." *Journal of Japanese Studies* 24, no. 1 (1998).

Amin, Samir. *Unequal Development: An Essay on the Social Formations of Peripheral Capitalism.* New York: Monthly Review Press, 1976.

Barkin, Kenneth D. *The Controversy over German Industrialization, 1890–1902.* Chicago: University of Chicago Press, 1970.

Barshay, Andrew E. *State and Intellectual in Imperial Japan: The Public Man in Crisis.* Berkeley: Univesity of California Press, 1988.

Beard, Charles A. *The Administration and Politics of Tokyo: A Survey and Opinions.* New York: Macmillan, 1923.

Berger, John. "Uses of Photography." In *About Looking.* New York: Vintage Books, 1991.

Berghahn, V. R. *Imperial Germany, 1871–1914: Economy, Society, Culture, and Politics.* Providence, R.I.: Berghahn Books, 1994.

Berman, Marshall. *All That Is Solid Melts into Air.* New York: Penguin Books, 1988.

Bernstein, Gail Lee. *Japanese Marxist: A Portrait of Kawakami Hajime.* Cambridge, Mass.: Harvard University Press, 1976.

Bourdieu, Pierre, with Luc Boltanski. *Photography: A Middle-Brow Art.* Translated by Shaun Whiteside. Stanford, Calif.: Stanford University Press, 1990.

Boyer, M. Christine. *Dreaming the Rational City: The Myth of American City Planning.* Cambridge, Mass.: MIT Press, 1983.

Brophy, James P. *Capitalism, Politics, and Railroads in Prussia, 1830–1870.* Columbus: Ohio State University Press, 1998.

Burgess, John W. *Reminiscences of an American Scholar.* New York: Columbia University Press, 1934.

Burrows, Edwin G., and Mike Wallace. *Gotham: A History of New York City to 1898.* New York: Oxford University Press, 1999.

Burudeie, Maruku [Marc J. F. Bourdier]. *Dōjunkai apāto genkei: Nihon kenchiku shi ni okeru yakuwari* [The original scene of the Dōjunkai Apartments: Its place in Japanese architectural history]. Tokyo: Sumai no Toshokan Shuppan-kyoku, 1992.

Calder, Kent E. *Strategic Capitalism: Private Business and Public Purpose in Japanese Industrial Finance.* Ithaca, N.Y.: Cornell University Press, 1994.

Caro, Robert A. *The Power Broker: Robert Moses and the Fall of New York.* New York: Vintage Books, 1975.

Chubachi, Masayoshi, and Koji Taira. "Poverty in Modern Japan: Perceptions and Realities." In *Industrialization and Its Social Consequences,* edited by Hugh Patrick. Berkeley: University of California Press, 1976.

Cortazzi, Hugh, and Terry Bennett. *Japan: Caught in Time.* New York and Tokyo: Weatherhill, 1995.

Cronon, William. *Nature's Metropolis: Chicago and the Great West.* New York: Norton, 1991.

Dawson, William Harbutt. *Municipal Life and Government in Germany.* London: Longmans, Green, 1914.

Doak, Kevin M. "What Is a Nation and Who Belongs? National Narratives and the Ethnic Imagination in Twentieth-Century Japan." *American Historical Review* 102, no. 2 (April 1997).

Dore, R. P. "The Modernizer as a Special Case: Japanese Factory Legislation, 1882–1911." *Comparative Studies in Society and History* 11, no. 4 (October 1969).

Dower, John. "Ways of Seeing, Ways of Remembering: The Photography of Prewar Japan." In *A Century of Japanese Photography,* edited by Japan Photographers Association. New York: Pantheon Books, 1980.

Duus, Peter. *The Abacus and the Sword: The Japanese Penetration of Korea, 1895–1910.* Berkeley: University of California Press, 1995.

Duus, Peter, and Irwin Scheiner. "Socialism, Liberalism, and Marxism, 1901–1931." In *The Cambridge History of Japan,* vol. 6: *The Twentieth Century,* edited by Peter Duus. New York: Cambridge University Press, 1988.

Enami Shigeyuki and Mihashi Toshiaki. *Hinminkutsu to hakurankai: Kindaisei no keifu gaku—kūkan/chikaku hen* [Slums and exhibitions: A genealogy of modernism—space/perception edition]. Tokyo: JICC Shuppan-kyoku, 1989.

Ericson, Stephen J. *The Sound of the Whistle: Railroads and the State in Meiji Japan.* Cambridge, Mass.: Harvard University Press, 1996.

Evenson, Norma. *Paris: A Century of Change, 1878–1978.* New Haven, Conn.: Yale University Press, 1979.

Fishman, Robert. *Bourgeois Utopias: The Rise and Fall of Suburbia*. New York: Basic Books, 1987.

———. *Urban Utopias in the Twentieth Century*. New York: Basic Books, 1977.

Fridell, Wilbur M. "Government Ethics Textbooks in Late Meiji Japan." *Journal of Asian Studies* 29, no. 3 (August 1970).

Fritzsche, Peter. *Reading Berlin 1900*. Cambridge, Mass.: Harvard University Press, 1996.

Fuji Bank, Research Division. *Banking in Modern Japan*. Tokyo: Fuji Bank, 1967.

Fujimori Terunobu. *Meiji no Tōkyō keikaku* [Meiji Tokyo planning]. Tokyo: Iwanami Shoten, 1982.

Fujitani, T. *Splendid Monarchy: Power and Pageantry in Modern Japan*. Berkeley: University of California Press, 1996.

Gao, Bai. *Economic Ideology and Japanese Industrial Policy: Developmentalism from 1931 to 1965*. New York: Cambridge University Press, 1997.

Garon, Sheldon. *Molding Japanese Minds: The State in Everyday Life*. Princeton, N.J.: Princeton University Press, 1997.

———. "Rethinking Modernization and Modernity in Japanese History: A Focus on State-Society Relations." *Journal of Asian Studies* 53, no. 2 (May 1994).

———. *The State and Labor in Modern Japan*. Berkeley: University of California Press, 1987.

Gellner, Ernest. *Encounters with Nationalism*. Oxford: Blackwell, 1994.

Gerschenkron, Alexander. *Economic Backwardness in Historical Perspective*. Cambridge, Mass.: Harvard University Press, 1962.

Gluck, Carol. *Japan's Modern Myths: Ideology in the Late Meiji Period*. Princeton, N.J.: Princeton University Press, 1985.

Gordon, Andrew. *The Evolution of Labor Relations in Japan: Heavy Industry, 1853–1955*. Cambridge, Mass.: Harvard University Press, 1985.

———. "The Invention of Japanese-Style Labor Management." In *Mirror of Modernity: Invented Traditions of Modern Japan*, edited by Stephen Vlastos. Berkeley: University of California Press, 1998.

———. *Labor and Imperial Democracy in Prewar Japan*. Berkeley: University of California Press, 1991.

Hammack, David C. *Power and Society: Greater New York at the Turn of the Century*. New York: Russell Sage Foundation, 1982.

Hanes, Jeffrey E. "Contesting Centralization? Space, Time, and Hegemony in Meiji Japan." In *New Directions in the Study of Meiji Japan*, edited by Helen Hardacre and Adam L. Kern. Leiden: Brill, 1997.

———. "Earthquake Hazard Mitigation and Urban Planning in Japan: Historical Lessons, Cultural Constraints, Future Prospects." *Proceedings of the 5th United States/Japan Workshop on Urban Earthquake Hazard Reduction: Recovery and Reconstruction from Recent Earthquakes*, edited by

Earthquake Engineering Research Institute. Oakland, Calif.: Earthquake Engineering Research Institute, 1997.

———. "Urban Planning as an Urban Problem: The Reconstruction of Tokyo after the Great Kanto Earthquake." *Seisaku kagaku* 7, no. 3 (March 2000).

Hara, Takeshi. *"Minto" Ōsaka tai "teito" Tōkyō: Shisō toshite no Kansai shitetsu* ["The people's capital" Osaka versus "the imperial capital" Tokyo: The Kansai private railways as an idea]. Tokyo: Kodansha, 1998.

Harada Keiichi. *Nihon kindai toshi shi kenkyū* [Researches on the history of the modern Japanese city]. Kyoto: Shibunkaku Shuppan, 1997.

———. "Toshi shihai kōzō" [The structure of city rule]. *Rekishi hyōron* 393 (January 1983).

Harvey, David. *The Condition of Postmodernity: An Enquiry into the Origins of Cultural Change.* Cambridge, Mass.: Blackwell, 1989.

Hashimoto Seinosuke. *Saikin Ōbei toshi no hattatsu* [Recent advances of Western cities]. Tokyo: Shinseisha, 1925.

Hastings, Sally A. "The Empress' New Clothes and Japanese Women, 1868–1912." *Historian* 55, no. 4 (Summer 1993).

———. *Neighborhood and Nation in Tokyo, 1905–1937.* Pittsburgh: Pittsburgh University Press, 1995.

Havens, Thomas R. H. *Farm and Nation in Modern Japan: Agrarian Nationalism, 1870–1940.* Princeton, N.J.: Princeton University Press, 1974.

Hidaka Kisaburō. "Kōfūkai to bōto no omoide" [A recollection of the Kōfūkai and rowing]. *Dai Ōsaka* 11, no. 2 (1935).

Hirokawa Yoshihide. "Seki Hajime no jiyūshugi shisō" [Liberalism in the ideas of Seki Hajime]. *Jinkun kenkyū* 35, no. 5 (1983).

Hirsch, Julia. *Family Photographs: Content, Meaning, and Effect.* New York: Oxford University Press, 1981.

Honma Yoshihito. *Doboku kokka no shisō: Toshi ron no keifu* [Theories of the construction state: A genealogy of urban thought]. Tokyo: Nihon Keizai Hyōronsha, 1996.

Horiuchi Masaaki. *Meiji no oyatoi kenchikuka Ende & Bekkuman: Baufirma Ende & Böckmann* [Architects in government service during Meiji, Ende & Böckmann: The design firm Ende & Böckmann]. Tokyo: Inoue Shoin, 1989.

Hoston, Germaine A. *Marxism and the Crisis of Development in Prewar Japan.* Princeton, N.J.: Princeton University Press, 1986.

Howard, Ebenezer. *Garden Cities of To-morrow.* London: Faber & Faber, 1902.

Howe, Christopher. *The Origins of Japanese Trade Supremacy: Development and Technology in Asia from 1540 to the Pacific War.* Hong Kong: University of Chicago Press, 1996.

Ikeda Hiroshi. *Gendai toshi no yokkyū* [What contemporary cities require]. Tokyo: Toshi Kenkyūkai, 1919.

———. "Toshi keikaku no gainen" [The category of urban planning]. In *Toshi to kōen* [Cities and parks], edited by Teien Kyōkai. Tokyo: Seibidō, 1924.

Ikeda Makoto. *Nihon shakai seisaku shisō shi ron* [On the history of Japanese social-policy thought]. Tokyo: Tokyo Keizai Shinpōsha, 1978.

Inoue Kiyoshi and Watanabe Tōru. *Kome Sōdō no kenkyū: II* [Rice Riots researches: II]. Tokyo: Yūhikaku, 1959.

Inoue Tomoichi. *Jichi kunren no kaihatsu* [Development of local-autonomy preparation]. Tokyo: Hakubunkan, 1909.

———. *Kyūsai seido yōgi* [Essentials of the system of poor relief]. Tokyo: Hakubunkan, 1909.

———. *Toshi gyōsei oyobi hōsei: Gekan* [Urban administration and law: Vol. 2]. Tokyo: Hakubunkan, 1911.

Iriye, Akira. "Japan's Drive to Great-Power Status." In *The Cambridge History of Japan*, vol. 5: *The Nineteenth Century,* edited by Marius B. Jansen. New York: Cambridge University Press, 1989.

Ishida Yorifusa. *Mikan no Tōkyō keikaku: Jitsugen shinakatta keikaku no keikaku shi* [Unfinished Tokyo plans: A planning history of unrealized plans]. Tokyo: Chikuma Shobō, 1992.

———. *Nihon kindai toshi keikaku no hyakunen* [A century of modern Japanese urban planning]. Tokyo: Jichitai Kenkyūsha, 1988.

Ito, Taketoshi. *The Japanese Economy.* Cambridge, Mass.: MIT Press, 1992.

Kameda Nagashichi. "Keibo setsusetsu" [Ardent admiration]. In *Ko Seki Shichō o shinobu* [Recalling the late Mayor Seki], edited by Ōsaka-shi Kyōikukai. Osaka: Ōsaka-shi Kyōikukai, 1935.

Kanai, Noboru. "Kōjō hōan ni taisuru rōryokusha no iken o chōsu beshi" [Why we should solicit the opinions of workers regarding the proposal for a factory law]. *Kokka gakkai zasshi* 12, no. 12 (December 1898).

Kanbara Ryūji. *Minami Ōsaka hennyū kinen shi* [A commemorative history of the urban incorporation of southern Osaka]. Osaka: Minami Ōsaka Hennyū Kinen Shi Hakkōkai, 1925.

Katagi Atsushi, Fujiya Yōetsu, and Kadono Yukihiro, eds. *Kindai Nihon no kōgai jūtakuchi* [The suburban residential land of modern Japan]. Tokyo: Kajima Shuppankai, 2000.

Kataoka Yasushi. *Gendai toshi no kenkyū* [Researches of the contemporary city]. Tokyo: Kenchiku Kōgei Kyōkai, 1914.

———. "Toshi seikatsu to jūtaku, I–III" [Urban life and housing, I–III]. *Kenchiku to shakai* 4, no. 4 (April 1921).

Katayama Sen. *Toshi shakaishugi: Waga shakaishugi* [Municipal socialism: My socialism]. Reprint edited by Iwamoto Eitarō; Tokyo: Jitsugyō no Nihon-sha, 1949.

Kawabata Naomasa. *Ōsaka no gyōsei* [The administration of Osaka]. Osaka: Mainichi Hōsō, 1973.

———. *Seki shichō shōden* [A brief biography of Mayor Seki]. Osaka: Ko Ōsaka Shichō Seki Hajime Hakase Itoku Kenshō Iinkai, 1956.

Kawakami Hajime. *Jisei no hen* [The changing spirit of the times]. Tokyo: Yomiuri Shinbunsha, 1911.

———. "Yuibutsu shikan ni tsuite Seki hakase ni kotau" [In reply to Dr. Seki concerning the materialist historical perspective]. *Kokumin keizai zasshi* 12, no. 4 (April 1912).

———. "Yuibutsu shikan yori yuishinkan e, I and II" [From the materialist historical perspective to the materialist spiritual perspective, I and II]. *Kokumin keizai zasshi* 13, nos. 1 and 2 (July and August 1912).

Kawase Mitsuyoshi. "Senzen Nihon no toshi keisei to keikaku: Ōsaka-shi no jirei o chūshin ni" [Prewar Japanese urban formation and planning: The example of the city of Osaka]. Master's thesis, Kyoto University, 1982.

Kawashima Yasuyoshi. *Fujin/kateiran koto hajime* [The advent of the women's/home-life page]. Tokyo: Seiabō, 1996.

Kim Jang-kwon. *Kindai chihō jichi no kōzō to seikaku* [The structure and character of modern local autonomy]. Tokyo: Tōsui Shobō, 1992.

Kinmonth, Earl H. *The Self-Made Man in Meiji Japanese Thought: From Samurai to Salary Man*. Berkeley: University of California Press, 1981.

Kinoshita Naoyuki. *Shashinga ron: Shashin to kaiga no kekkon* [On photographic pictures: The marriage of photographs and pictures]. Tokyo: Iwanami Shoten, 1996.

Kinzley, W. Dean. *Industrial Harmony in Modern Japan: The Invention of a Tradition*. New York: Routledge, 1991.

Kishi Kazuta. *Seibutsugakuteki toshi keiei ron* [On biology-like urban management]. Tokyo: Sanseidō, 1923.

Kiso Junko. "Nipponbashi hōmen Kamagasaki suramu ni okeru rōdō/seikatsu katei" [The ways of work and life in the Kamagasaki slum near Nipponbashi]. In *Taishō Ōsaka suramu: Mo hitotsu no Nihon kindai shi* [The slums of Taisho Osaka: Another modern history of Japan], edited by Sugihara Kaoru and Kiso Junko. Tokyo: Shinhyōron, 1987.

Kloppenberg, James T. *Uncertain Victory: Social Democracy and Progressivism in European and American Thought, 1870–1920*. New York: Oxford University Press, 1986.

Kodera Shōzō. *Ōsaka han'ei shi* [A history of prosperity in Osaka]. Osaka: Shijō Shunjūsha, 1983.

Kojita Yasunao. *Nihon kindai toshi shi kenkyū josetsu* [An introduction to the study of modern Japanese urban history]. Tokyo: Kashiwa Shobō, 1991.

———. "Nihon teikokushugi seiritsu no toshi seisaku" [Urban policy in the establishment of Japanese imperialism]. *Rekishi hyōron* 393 (January 1983).

Kōno Makoto. *Toshi ka den'en ka* [Will it be cities or fields?]. Tokyo: Matsuyamabō, 1924.

Koyama Kenzō. *Koyama Kenzō den* [Biography of Koyama Kenzō]. Osaka: Sanjūyon Ginkō, 1930.

Kumamoto Kenritsu Bijutsukan, ed. *Tomishige Shashinjo no 130 nen* [130 years of the Tomishige Photographic Studio]. Kumamoto: Kumamoto Kenritsu Bijutsukan, 1993.

Kuwata Kumazō. *Kōjōhō to rōdō hoken* [The Factory Law and workmen's compensation]. Tokyo: Ryūbunkan, 1909.

———. "Toshi no shakai seisaku" [Urban social policy]. *Kokka gakkai zasshi* 14, no. 163 (September 1900).

Ladd, Brian. *Urban Planning and Civic Order in Germany, 1860–1914.* Cambridge, Mass.: Harvard University Press, 1990.

Laffut, Michel. "Belgium." In *Railways and the Economic Development of Western Europe, 1830–1914,* edited by Patrick O'Brien. New York: St. Martin's Press, 1983.

Lalvani, Suren. *Photography, Vision, and the Production of Modern Bodies.* Albany: State University of New York Press, 1996.

Large, Stephen S. *The Rise of Labor in Japan: The Yūaikai, 1912–19.* Tokyo: Sophia University Press, 1972.

Lebra, Joyce. *Okuma Shigenobu: Statesman of Meiji Japan.* Canberra: Australia National University, 1973.

Lebra, Takie Sugiyama. *Above the Clouds: Status Culture of the Modern Japanese Nobility.* Berkeley: University of California Press, 1993.

Lefebvre, Henri. *The Production of Space.* Translated by Donald Nicholson-Smith. Oxford: Blackwell, 1991.

Lewis, Michael. *Rioters & Citizens: Mass Protest in Imperial Japan.* Berkeley: University of California Press, 1990.

Linkman, Audrey. *The Victorians: Photographic Portraits.* London: Tauris Parke Books, 1993.

List, Friedrich. *The National System of Political Economy.* Translated by Sampson S. Lloyd. New York: Longmans, Green, 1904.

Lynch, Kevin. *The Image of the City.* Cambridge, Mass.: MIT Press, 1960.

Mandell, Richard D. *Paris 1900: The Great World's Fair.* Toronto: University of Toronto Press, 1967.

Marshall, Byron K. *Capitalism and Nationalism in Prewar Japan: The Ideology of the Business Elite, 1868–1941.* Stanford, Calif.: Stanford University Press, 1967.

———. *Learning to Be Modern: Japanese Political Discourse on Education.* Boulder, Colo.: Westview Press, 1994.

Marsland, Stephen E. *The Birth of the Japanese Labor Movement: Takano Fusatarō and the Rōdō Kumiai Kiseikai.* Honolulu: University of Hawaii Press, 1989.

Marx, Karl. "Draft of an Article on Friedrich List's Book *Das System der Politischen Oekonomie.*" In Karl Marx and Friedrich Engels, *Collected Works,* vol. 4. New York: International Publishers, 1975.

Matsumoto Kanzō, ed. *Ōsaka shisei 70 nen no ayumi* [The 70-year course of Osaka municipal government]. Osaka: Ōsaka Shiyakusho, 1959.

Matsuura Shigeki. *Meiji no kokudo kaihatsu shi: Kindai doboku gijutsu no ishizue* [A history of national land development in Meiji: The foundation of modern construction technology]. Tokyo: Kajima Shuppankai, 1992.

Matzerath, Horst. "Berlin, 1890–1940." In *Metropolis 1890–1940*, edited by Anthony Sutcliffe. Chicago: University of Chicago Press, 1984.

Mikuriya Takashi. *Shuto keikaku no seiji: Keisei-ki Meiji kokka no jitsuzō* [The politics of capital planning: A realistic image of the formative Meiji state]. Tokyo: Yamakawa Shuppansha, 1984.

Miller, Frank O. *Minobe Tatsukichi: Interpreter of Constitutionalism in Japan.* Berkeley: University of California Press, 1965.

Miyake Iwao. *Toshi no kenkyū* [Researches of the city]. Tokyo: Jitsugyō no Nihonsha, 1908.

Miyamoto, Ken'ichi. "Dai ichiji taisen-go chiiki keizai no henbō to chihō gyōzaisei no kiki" [Transformation of the regional economy and the crisis of local administration and finance following World War I]. *Ōsaka Keidai ronshū* 133 (January 1980).

———. "'Gakusha shichō' Seki Hajime no 'shōshaku'" [The sake sipping of the scholar-mayor Seki Hajime]. *Sake bunka kenkyū* 4 (1994).

———. *Toshi seisaku no shisō to genjitsu* [Ideas and realities of urban policy]. Tokyo: Yūhikaku, 1999.

Miyano Yūichi. "Seki Hajime to jūtaku seisaku: Dai Ichiji Taisen go Nihon jūtaku seisaku no keisei katei" [Seki Hajime and housing policy: The process of forming post–World War I Japanese housing policy]. *Ōsaka no rekishi* 18 (1986).

Miyao Shunji. *Toshi keikaku ni kansuru kōwa* [Lectures on urban planning]. Nagoya: Toshi Keikaku Nagoya Chihō Iinkai, 1921.

Miyoshi, Masao. *As We Saw Them: The First Japanese Embassy to the United States (1860).* Berkeley: University of California Press, 1979.

Morris-Suzuki, Tessa. *A History of Japanese Economic Thought.* London: Routledge, 1989.

Murashima Motoyuki. *Dontei seikatsu* [Slum life]. Tokyo: Bungadō, 1917.

Muta Kazue. "Images of the Family in Meiji Periodicals: The Paradox Underlying the Emergence of the 'Home.'" *U.S.-Japan Women's Journal English Supplement* 7 (1994).

———. *Senryaku toshite no kazoku: Kindai Nihon no kokumin kokka keisei to josei* [The family as a strategy: Women and the formation of the modern Japanese family state]. Tokyo: Shinyōsha, 1996.

Naimushō Chihō-kyoku, ed. *Den'en toshi* [Garden cities]. Tokyo: Hakubunkan, 1908.

Nakagawa Hitoshi. *Shin Ōsaka taikan* [A gazeteer of the new Osaka]. Osaka: Shin Ōsaka Taikan Kankōjo, 1923.

Nakagawa Masajirō. *Toshi kairyō mondai* [The urban-reform problem]. Tokyo: Akashiro Shozō, 1914.

Nakagawa Nozomu. "Toshi keikaku no kōjō" [The rise of urban planning]. *Dai Ōsaka* 1, no. 1 (December 1925).

Nakajima Tōichirō. *Kantō Daishinsai* [The Great Kanto Earthquake]. Tokyo: Yūzankaku, 1995.

Nakamura, Takafusa. *Economic Growth in Prewar Japan*. New Haven, Conn.: Yale University Press, 1983.

Nakano Makiko. *Makiko's Diary: A Merchant Wife in 1910 Kyoto*. Translated by Kazuko Smith. Stanford, Calif.: Stanford University Press, 1995.

Nakasa Kazushige. "Toshi keikaku kara mita Seki Hajime to Ōsaka toshi keikaku no kenkyū: 'Yobō' to 'chiryō' no toshi keikaku o chūshin ni shite" [Seki Hajime seen from the angle of urban planning and researches of Osaka urban planning: Focusing on "treatment" and "prevention" in urban planning]. Master's thesis, Osaka Shiritsu Daigaku, 1979.

NHK Ōsaka Hōsō-kyoku, ed. *Kindai Ōsaka nenpyō: Meiji gannen (1868)– Shōwa 57 nen (1982)* [A chronology of modern Osaka: From the first year of Meiji (1868) to Showa 57 (1982)]. Tokyo: Nippon Hōsō Shuppan Kyōkai, 1983.

Nihon Jūtaku Sōgō Sentā, ed. *Senzen no jūtaku seisaku no hensen ni kansuru chōsa: Toshi Kenkyūkai no opinion rīdā* [A survey of the transition in prewar housing policy: Opinion leaders of the Urban Research Association]. Tokyo: Nihon Jūtaku Sōgō Sentā, 1980.

Nomura Yoshiki. "Nihon tokei hattatsu shi to Ōsaka-shi Shakai-bu 'Rōdō chōsa hōkoku'" [A history of the development of statistics in Japan and the labor-survey reports of the Social Bureau of the City of Osaka]. *Keiei kenkyū* 33, no. 3 (September 1982).

Nōshōmushō Shōkōkyoku. *Shokkō jijō* [The condition of the workers]. 1903. Reprint (3 vols.), Tokyo: Shinkigensha, 1980.

Notar, Ernest James. "Labor Unions and the *Sangyō Hōkoku* Movement 1930– 1945: A Japanese Model for Industrial Relations." Ph.D. diss., University of California, Berkeley, 1979.

Ogawa Ichitarō. "Seki shichō o omou" [Some thoughts about Mayor Seki]. *Dai Ōsaka* 11, no. 2 (1935).

Ōhashi Kaoru. *Toshi no kasō shakai* [Urban lower-class society]. Tokyo: Seishin Shobō, 1962.

Oka Minoru. "Kōjōhō no onjin" [Benefactor of the Factory Law]. *Dai Ōsaka* 11, no. 2 (1935).

———. *Kōjōhō ron* [On the Factory Law]. Tokyo: Yūhikaku, 1913.

Ōmori Makoto. "Toshi shakai jigyō seiritsu-ki ni okeru chūkansō to minshū-shugi" [The middle class and democracy during the formative period of urban social facilities]. *Hisutoria* 97 (December 1982).

Ōsaka Shi. "Ko Seki shichō tsuitō gō" [Memorial issue for the late Mayor Seki]. *Dai Ōsaka* 11, no. 2 (February 1935).

Ōsaka Shi Hōmen Iin Seido Gojūnen Kinenshi Henshū Iinkai. *Ōsaka-shi hōmen iin minsei iin seido gojūnen shi* [A fifty-year history of the district-commissioner system in the city of Osaka]. Osaka: Ōsaka-shi, 1973.

Ōsaka Shikai, ed. *Setsuzoku chōson hennyū ni kansuru shimon no kudari, ku no haichi ni kansuru shimon no kudari: Iinkai sōkiroku* [Interviews on the incorporation of adjoining towns and villages, interviews on apportioning districts: Commission proceedings]. Osaka: Ōsaka Shikai, 1924.

Ōsaka Shi Shakaibu. "Furyō jūtaku chiku zushū" [Collected illustrations of tenement housing]. *Shakaibu hōkoku,* no. 236 (1938).

Ōsaka Shiyakusho. *Tosei-an* [Metropolitan policy proposal]. Osaka: Ōsaka Shiyakusho, 1932.

Ōsaka Shiyakusho, ed. *Rōdō chōsa hōkoku* [Labor-survey reports]. Osaka: Ōsaka Shiritsu Chūō Toshokan, 1975.

Ōsaka Shiyakusho Rōdō Chōsa-ka. "Jūtaku chōsa" [A housing survey]. *Rōdō chōsa hōkoku* 7 (February 1921).

Ōsaka Shōka Daigaku, ed. *Seki bunko mokuroku* [Catalogue of the Seki collection]. Osaka: Ōsaka Shōka Daigaku, 1935.

Ōsaka Toshi Kyōkai, ed. *Machi ni sumau: Ōsaka toshi jūtaku shi* [To live in the neighborhood: A history of urban housing in Osaka]. Tokyo: Heibonsha, 1989.

Pierson, Stanley. *Marxist Intellectuals and the Working-Class Mentality in Germany, 1887–1912.* Cambridge, Mass.: Harvard University Press, 1993.

Pike, Fredrick B. *The Politics of the Miraculous in Peru: Haya de la Torre and the Spiritualist Tradition.* Lincoln: University of Nebraska Press, 1986.

Purdom, C. B. *The Garden City; a Study in the Development of a Modern Town.* London: J. M. Dent & Sons, 1913.

Pyle, Kenneth B. "Advantages of Followership: German Economics and Japanese Bureaucrats, 1890–1925." *Journal of Japanese Studies* 1, no. 1 (Autumn 1974).

———. "Meiji Conservatism." In *The Cambridge History of Modern Japan,* vol. 5: *The Nineteenth Century,* edited by Marius B. Jansen. New York: Cambridge University Press, 1989.

———. *The New Generation in Meiji Japan: Problems of Cultural Identity, 1885–1895.* Stanford, Calif.: Stanford University Press, 1969.

———. "The Technology of Japanese Nationalism: The Local Improvement Movement, 1900–1918." *Journal of Asian Studies* 33, no. 1 (November 1973).

Ramseyer, J. Mark, and Frances M Rosenbluth. *The Politics of Oligarchy: Institutional Choice in Imperial Japan.* Cambridge: Cambridge University Press, 1995.

Ringer, Fritz K. *The Decline of the German Mandarins: The German Academic Community, 1890–1933.* Cambridge, Mass.: Harvard University Press, 1969.

———. *Max Weber's Methodology: The Unification of the Cultural and Social Sciences.* Cambridge, Mass.: Harvard University Press, 1997.

Roden, Donald. *Schooldays in Imperial Japan: A Study in the Culture of a Student Elite.* Berkeley: University of California Press, 1980.

Rodgers, Daniel T. *Atlantic Crossings: Social Politics in a Progressive Age.* Cambridge, Mass.: Harvard University Press, 1998.

Rōdō Undō Shiryō Iinkai, ed. *Nihon Rōdō undō shiryō, III* [Historical documents of the Japanese labor movement, III]. Tokyo: Tokyo Daigaku Shuppankai, 1968.

Roscher, William. *Principles of Political Economy.* 2 vols. Translated by John J. Lalor. Chicago: Callaghan, 1882.

Ross, Dorothy. "American Social Science and the Idea of Progress." In *The Authority of Experts: Studies in History and Theory,* edited by Thomas L. Haskell. Bloomington: Indiana University Press, 1984.

Ruble, Blair A. *Second Metropolis: Pragmatic Pluralism in Gilded Age Chicago, Silver Age Moscow, and Meiji Osaka.* New York: Woodrow Wilson Center Press and Cambridge University Press, 2001.

Samuels, Richard J. *"Rich Nation, Strong Army": National Security and the Technological Transformation of Japan.* Ithaca, N.Y.: Cornell University Press, 1994.

Sand, Jordan. "At Home in the Meiji Period: Inventing Japanese Domesticity." In *Mirror of Modernity: Invented Traditions of Modern Japan,* edited by Stephen Vlastos. Berkeley: University of California Press, 1998.

Sano Zensaku. "Tokyo kōshō kyōju jidai no Seki hakase" [Dr. Seki during his days as a Tokyo Commercial College professor]. *Dai Ōsaka* 11, no. 2 (1935).

Scheiner, Irwin. "The Japanese Village: Imagined, Real, Contested." In *Mirror of Modernity: Invented Traditions of Modern Japan,* edited by Stephen Vlastos. Berkeley: University of California Press, 1998.

Schivelbusch, Wolfgang. *The Railway Journey: The Industrialization of Time and Space in the 19th Century.* Berkeley: University of California Press, 1986.

Schorske, Carl E. *Fin-de-Siècle Vienna: Politics and Culture.* New York: Vintage Books, 1981.

Scott, James C. *Seeing Like a State: How Certain Schemes to Improve the Human Condition Have Failed.* New Haven, Conn.: Yale University Press, 1998.

Seidensticker, Edward. *Low City, High City: Tokyo from Edo to the Earthquake: How the Shogun's Ancient Capital Became a Great Modern City, 1867–1923.* San Francisco: Donald S. Ellis and Creative Arts Book Company, 1985.

Seinen Toshi Kenkyūkai. *Forest City: Sanrin toshi* [Forest City: Forest City]. Nagoya: Seinen Toshi Kenkyūkai, 1922.

Seki Hajime. "Anmelds Buch" [Class record]. October 23, 1900. Osaka City History Archive.

———. "Beika tōki to sono chōsetsu saku" [Rising rice prices and regulatory policy]. *Kokumin keizai zasshi* 11, no. 8 (July 1912).

———. "Berugi chōson tetsudō no kinkyō" [Recent conditions of Belgium's local railways]. *Kokumin keizai zasshi* 2, no. 6 (June 1907).

———. *Bunka to jūtaku mondai* [Culture and the housing problem]. Osaka: Ōsaka-shi, 1921.

———. "Chihō tetsudō ron, I and II" [On local railways, I and II]. *Kokumin keizai zasshi* 1, no. 7 (December 1906), and 2, no. 1 (January 1907).

————. "Dai Ōsaka no kensetsu" [The building of greater Osaka]. *Dai Ōsaka* 4, no. 6 (June 1928).

————. "Daitoshi ni tsuite no ni-san no kōsatsu" [A couple of observations about big cities]. *Dai Ōsaka* 6, no. 9 (September 1930).

————. "Doitsu teikoku sekiyū senbai hōan" [The proposed state oil monopoly of imperial Germany]. *Kokumin keizai zasshi* 15, nos. 4 and 5 (October and November 1913).

————. "Eikoku ni okeru shakaiteki rippō no shin keikō" [New trends in social legislation in England]. *Kokka gakkai zasshi* 23, nos. 8 and 9 (August and September 1909).

————. "Fuainanshā o ronzuru" [About financiers]. *Kokumin keizai zasshi* 4, no. 2 (February 1908).

————. "Fūsuigai to Ōsaka-shi no fukkō" [Storm and flood damage and the reconstruction of Osaka]. *Dai Ōsaka* 10, no. 11 (November 1934).

————. "Gaikoku shōsei gairon, I" [An introduction to foreign commercial policy, I]. *Kokumin keizai zasshi* 2, no. 6 (June 1907).

————. "Hōgakushi Kawakami Hajime sho: *Jisei no hen*" [By Doctor of Law Kawakami Hajime: The changing spirit of the times]. *Kokumin keizai zasshi* 12, no. 2 (February 1912).

————. "Jiyū kūchi" [Open land]. In *Dai ikkai zenkoku Toshi mondai kaigiroku* [Proceedings of the First National Conference on the Urban Problem], edited by Ōsaka Toshi Kyōkai. Osaka: Ōsaka Toshi Kyōkai, 1927.

————. "Jūekisha futankin sei no genjō to sono kaizen sho saku" [Current condition of the system of public-use assessment and several measures for its improvement]. In *Dai Ni Zenkoku Toshi Mondai Kaigi: Kenkyū hōkoku* [Second National Urban Problem Conference: Research reports], edited by Tōkyō Shisei Chōsakai. Tokyo: Tōkyō Shisei Chōsakai, 1930.

————. "Jūtaku mondai no kaiketsunan" [The difficulty in solving the housing problem]. *Ōsaka-shi shōkō jihō* 316 (1921).

————. *Jūtaku mondai to toshi keikaku* [The housing problem and urban planning]. Kyoto: Kubundō Shobō, 1923.

————. "Kabushiki gaisha ni okeru yūgen sekinin shugi no keizaijō no nedan" [The economic price of limited liability in joint-stock corporations]. *Hōgaku shinpō* 24, no. 5 (May 1914).

————. "Kaen toshi to toshi keikaku" [Garden cities and urban planning]. *Hōgaku shinpō* 23, no. 1 (February 1913).

————. "Kangyō tetsudō no keizai shugi" [The economics of state-run railways]. *Kokumin keizai zasshi* 1, no. 1 (June 1906).

————. "Kawakami gakushi no 'Yuibutsu shikan yori yuishinkan e' o yomu" [Reading Mr. Kawakami's "From the materialist historical perspective to the materialist spiritual perspective"]. *Kokumin keizai zasshi* 13, no. 3 (September 1912).

————. "Keiei to kigyō to no igi ni tsuite" [Regarding the significance of management and private enterprise]. *Kokumin keizai zasshi* 9, no. 4 (October 1910).

———. "Kigyōka no shakaiteki setsubi" [Social provisions made by industrialists]. *Kokumin keizai zasshi* 7, no. 2 (August 1909).

———. "Kigyō rengō oyobi gōdō no yushutsu shōrei saku" [Industrial combination and cartelization measures for the encouragement of exports]. *Kokumin keizai zasshi* 4, no. 5 (May 1908).

———. "Kigyōsha no honshitsu: Ueda, Fukuda ryōshi no ronbun o yomite" [The essence of the businessman: On reading the works of Messrs. Ueda and Fukuda]. *Kokumin keizai zasshi* 16, no. 5 (May 1914).

———. "Kinsei toshi no hatten to toshi keikaku" [Urban planning and the development of early modern cities]. *Toshi kōron* 7, no. 12 (December 1924).

———. "Kōgyō no chihōteki shūchū oyobi bunsan" [The regional concentration and dispersion of industry]. *Kokumin keizai zasshi* 9, no. 5 (November 1910).

———. "Kōgyō no tokka to ketsugō" [Industrial specialization and coupling]. *Kokumin keizai zasshi* 6, no. 2 (February 1909).

———. *Kōgyō seisaku* [Industrial policy]. 2 vols. Tokyo: Hōbunkan, 1911 and 1913.

———. "Kōjōhō kanken" [A personal view of the Factory Law]. *Kokumin keizai zasshi* 7, no. 5 (November 1909).

———. "Kōjōhō to rōdōsha hoken" [The Factory Law and workmen's compensation]. *Kokumin keizai zasshi* 12, no. 2 (February 1912).

———. "Kōjōhō to rōdōsha mondai" [The Factory Law and the worker problem]. *Kokumin keizai zasshi* 5, no. 1 (July 1908).

———. "Kokusai boeki shinō-saku" [Measures for the promotion of international trade]. *Hōgaku shinpō* 23, no. 6 (June 1913).

———. *Koruson-shi kōtsū seisaku* [C. Colson on transportation policy]. Tokyo: Dōbunkan, 1903.

———. "Kōshi kyōdō jigyō" [Collaborative ventures by the public and private sectors]. *Kokumin keizai zasshi* 16, no. 4 (April 1914).

———. "Kōtaishi denka gyōkei isshūnen ni saishi" [In commemoration of the progress by the imperial prince]. *Dai Ōsaka* 2, no. 6 (June 1926).

———. "Nikoruson kyōju no teikoku ron o yomu" [On reading Professor Nicholson's theory of imperialism]. *Kokumin keizai zasshi* 8, no. 6 (June 1910).

———. "Ōsaka chikatetsu no kaitsū ni saishite" [On the occasion of the opening of Osaka's subway]. *Dai Ōsaka* 9, no. 5 (May 1933).

———. "Ōsaka shiiki no kakuchō to shin shiiki ni shikkō shitaru shōban no shisetsu" [The expansion of Osaka's boundaries and facilities ready to go within the new urban boundary]. In *Dainikai zenkoku toshi mondai kaigi: Kenkyū hōkoku* [Second National Conference on the Urban Problem: Research presentations], edited by Tōkyō Shisei Chōsakai. Tokyo: Tōkyō Shisei Chōsakai, 1930.

———. "Ōsaka-shi no sho mondai" [The various problems of Osaka City]. *Dai Ōsaka* 1, no. 1 (December 1925).

———. "Ōsaka toshi keikaku jūnen no kaisō" [A reminiscence of ten years of Osaka urban planning]. *Dai Ōsaka* 7, no. 7 (July 1931).

———. "Rōdō jikan o ronzu" [On labor hours]. *Mita Gakkai zasshi* 7, no. 1 (January 1913).

———. "Rōdō shōkai seido, I and II" [The labor-referral system, I and II]. *Kokumin keizai zasshi* 9, nos. 1 and 2 (July and August 1910).

———. *Rōdōsha hogo hō ron* [On a worker-protection law]. Tokyo: Ryūbunkan, 1910.

———. "Saitei chingin, I, II, and III" [Minimum wage, I, II, and III]. *Kokumin keizai zasshi* 12, no. 4 (April 1912), and 13, nos. 1 and 2 (July and August 1912).

———. "Shiei jigyō" [Municipal enterprise]. In *Shakai Seisaku Gakkai ronsō: Shiei jigyō* [Treatises of the Japan Association for Social Policy: Municipal enterprise], edited by Shakai Seisaku Gakkai. Tokyo: Shakai Seisaku Gakkai, 1911.

———. "Shiei jigyō no honshitsu" [The essence of municipal enterprise]. *Toshi mondai panfureto* (Tōkyō Shisei Chōsakai), no. 5 (1928).

———. "Shiei jigyō ron, III" [On municipal enterprise, III]. *Kokumin keizai zasshi* 11, no. 3 (September 1911).

———. "Shinkei suijaku no yobō" [Prevention of nervous exhaustion]. *Dai Ōsaka* 5, no. 3 (March 1929).

———. "Shisei manpitsu, I and II" [Stray notes on municipal government, I and II]. *Dai Ōsaka* 5, nos. 7 and 8 (July and August 1929).

———. "Shisei no konpon mondai" [Fundamental problems of municipal administration]. *Dai Ōsaka* 8, no. 7 (July 1932).

———. "Shisshoku mondai, I and II" [The unemployment problem, I and II]. *Kokumin keizai zasshi* 8, nos. 5 and 6 (May and June 1910).

———. *Shōgyō keizai seisaku* [Commercial economic policy]. Tokyo: Ōkura Shoten, 1903.

———. *Shōgyō keizai taii* [An outline of commercial economics]. Tokyo: Dōbunkan, 1898.

———. "Shōkō ron" [On commercial ports]. *Nihon keizai shinshi* 12, no. 3 (November 1912).

———. *Shōkō seisaku kōryō* [Essential principles of commercial and industrial policy]. Tokyo: Dōbunkan, 1909.

———. "Tabi nikki" [Travel diary]. 1900. Osaka City History Archive.

———. "Taun puraningu ni tsuite" [About town planning]. *Kobe keizaikai kōenshū* 1 (1916).

———. "Teikokushugi to shihon koku, I and II" [Imperialism and the capitalist nation, I and II]. *Kokumin keizai zasshi* 3, nos. 4 and 5 (October and November 1907).

———. "Tetsudō gakkō" [The railroad school]. 1899–1900. Osaka City History Archive.

———. "Tetsudō keizai ni kansuru shinsho" [New works concerning railway economics]. *Kokumin keizai zasshi* 1, no. 5 (October 1906).

―――. "Tochi tōki to jūkyo mondai" [Land speculation and the residential problem]. *Kokka oyobi kokka gaku* 1, no. 3 (March 1913).

―――. "Toshi jūtaku seisaku" [Urban housing policy]. *Kenchiku zasshi* 33, no. 391 (1919).

―――. "Toshi keikaku ni kansuru shin rippō" [New legislation concerning urban planning]. *Dai Ōsaka* 2, no. 4 (April 1926).

―――. "Toshi keikaku ni tsuite" [About urban planning]. *Nihon Shakai Gakuin nenpō* 5, nos. 1–3 (February 1918).

―――. "Toshi keikaku ron" [On urban planning]. (Undated lectures.) In *Toshi seisaku no riron to jissai: Seki Hajime ikōshū* [Theory and practice of urban policy: A posthumous collection of works by Seki Hajime], edited by Seki Hakase Ronbunshū Henshū Iinkai. Osaka: Ōsaka Toshi Kyōkai, 1968.

―――. "Toshi kōtsū kikan no hattatsu to kyojū kankei" [The development of urban transit facilities and their relationship to residence]. In *Shakai Seisaku Gakkai ronsō: Kanzei mondai to shakai seisaku*, 2 [Treatises of the Japan Association for Social Policy: The tariff issue and social policy, 2], edited by Shakai Seisaku Gakkai. Tokyo: Dōbunkan, 1909.

―――. "Tōshin tetsudō no shūeki ryoku" [Earning power of the railways of eastern China]. *Kokumin keizai zasshi* 1, no. 3 (August 1906).

―――. "Toshi renraku denki tetsudō" [Interurban electric railways]. *Hōgaku shinpō* 22, no. 1 (January 1912).

―――. "Toshi seisaku ni tsuite" [On urban policy]. *Kyūsai kenkyū* 9, no. 11 (November 1921).

―――. "Toshi shakai seisaku" [Urban social policy]. *Kyūsai kenkyū* 6, nos. 5 and 6 (May and June 1918).

―――. "Tsūshō jōyaku ron, I and II" [On commercial treaties, I and II]. *Kokumin keizai zasshi* 5, nos. 3 and 4 (September and October 1908).

―――. "Unchin ron" [On fares]. *Kokka gakkai zasshi* 19, no. 11 (November 1905).

―――. "Yanagita Kunio cho 'jidai to nōsei'" [Yanagita Kunio's "eras and agricultures"]. *Kokumin keizai zasshi* 10, no. 2 (February 1911).

―――. "Yuibutsu shikan ni tsuite Kawakami Hajime gakushi no oshie o kou" [Asking Mr. Kawakami Hajime for instruction concerning the materialist historical perspective]. *Kokumin keizai zasshi* 12, no. 6 (June 1912).

―――. "Zoku kōjōhō kanken" [A personal view of the Factory Law, continued]. *Kokumin keizai zasshi* 8, no. 1 (January 1910).

Seki Hajime and Fukuda Tokuzō, eds. and trans. *Saikin shōsei keizai ron* [On the economics of contemporary commercial politics]. Tokyo: Ōkura Shoten, 1902.

Seki Hajime Kenkyūkai, ed. *Seki Hajime nikki: Taishō Shōwa Shoki no Ōsaka shisei* [Seki Hajime diary: Taisho–Early Showa Osaka municipal government]. Tokyo: Tokyo Daigaku Shuppankai, 1986.

Shakai Seisaku Gakkai, ed. *Kōjōhō to rōdō mondai* [The Labor Law and the labor question]. Tokyo: Dōbunkan, 1908.

Shibamura Atsuki. *Seki Hajime: Toshi shisō no paioniā* [Seki Hajime: Pioneer of urban thought]. Kyoto: Shōraisha, 1989.

———. "Seki Hajime to sono jidai (I): Shisei tantō izen no shiseki to shisō" [Seki Hajime and his era: Historical landmarks and ideas prior to becoming a municipal manager]. *Shisei kenkyū* 56 (July 1982).

———. "Seki Hajime to sono jidai (II): Jōyaku shūnin mondai to kome sōdō" [Seki Hajime and his era (II): The issue of his appointment as deputy mayor and the Rice Riots]. *Shisei kenkyū* 58 (1982).

———. "Taishō-ki Ōsaka no sangyō to shakai" [Industry and society in Taisho Era Osaka]. In *Ōsaka no sangyō to shakai* [Industry and society in Osaka], edited by Kitazaki Toyoji. Osaka: Mainichi Hōsō, 1973.

———. *Toshi no kindai: Ōsaka no 20 seiki* [The modern age of the city: Osaka in the 20th century]. Kyoto: Shibunkaku, 1999.

Shibata Tokue. *Nihon no toshi seisaku* [Japanese urban policy]. Tokyo: Yūhikaku, 1978.

Shibata Yoshimori, ed. *Ōsaka-shi minsei jigyō* [Public works in the city of Osaka]. Osaka: Ōsaka-shi Minsei-kyoku, 1978.

Silberman, Bernard S. *Cages of Reason: The Rise of the Rational State in France, Japan, the United States, and Great Britain.* Chicago: University of Chicago Press, 1993.

Smith, Henry D., II. "Tokyo and London: Comparative Conceptions of the City." In *Japan: A Comparative View,* edited by Albert M. Craig. Princeton, N.J.: Princeton University Press, 1979.

———. "Tokyo as an Idea: An Exploration of Japanese Urban Thought until 1945." *Journal of Japanese Studies* 4, no. 1 (Winter 1978).

Smith, T. C. "The Right to Benevolence: Dignity and Japanese Workers, 1890–1920." *Comparative Studies in Society and History* 26, no. 4 (October 1986).

Sontag, Susan. *On Photography.* New York: Dell, 1977.

Sugihara Kaoru and Kiso Junko, eds. *Taishō Ōsaka suramu: Mo hitotsu no Nihon kindai shi* [The slums of Taisho Osaka: Another modern history of Japan]. Tokyo: Shinhyōron, 1987.

Sugihara Tōru. *Ekkyō suru min: Kindai Ōsaka no Chōsenjin shi kenkyū* [People transgressing borders: Researches on the history of Koreans in Osaka]. Tokyo: Shinkansha, 1998.

Sugiyama, Chūhei. *Origins of Economic Thought in Modern Japan.* London: Routledge, 1994.

Sugiyama, Chūhei, and Tamotsu Nishizawa. "'Captain of Industry': Tokyo Commercial School at Hitotsubashi." In *Enlightenment and Beyond: Political Economy Comes to Japan,* edited by Chūhei Sugiyama and Hiroshi Mizuta. Tokyo: University of Tokyo Press, 1988.

Sumiya, Mikio. "Kōjōhō taisei to rōshi kankei" [The structure of the Factory Law and the relationship between labor and capital]. In *Nihon rōshi kankei shi ron* [On the history of the relationship between Japanese labor and capital]. Tokyo: Tokyo Daigaku Shuppankai, 1977.

Sutcliffe, Anthony. *Towards the Planned City: Germany, Britain, the United States and France 1780–1914.* New York: St. Martin's Press, 1981.

Suzuki Umeshirō. "Ōsaka Nagomachi hinminkutsu shisatsu ki" [An observer's account of the Osaka Nagomachi slum]. 1888. Reprinted in *Meiji zenki no toshi kasō shakai* [The urban lower classes in early Meiji], edited by Nishida Taketoshi. Tokyo: Kōseikan, 1970.

Szporluk, Roman. *Communism and Nationalism: Karl Marx versus Friedrich List.* New York: Oxford University Press, 1988.

Tagawa Daikichirō. *Tsukurarubeki Tōkyō* [The Tokyo we should build]. Tokyo, 1923.

Taira, Koji. "Economic Development, Labor Markets, and Industrial Relations in Japan, 1905–1955." In *The Cambridge History of Japan,* vol. 6: *The Twentieth Century,* edited by Peter Duus. New York: Cambridge University Press, 1988.

Takahashi Usaburō. "Den'en toshi ni tsuite" [About garden cities]. In *Toshi to kōen* [Cities and parks], edited by Teien Kyōkai. Tokyo: Seibidō, 1924.

Takiyama Ryōichi. "Omoide de" [In remembrance]. In *Ko Seki Shichō o shinobu* [Recalling the late Mayor Seki], edited by Ōsaka-shi Kyōikukai. Osaka: Ōsaka-shi Kyōikukai, 1935.

Tamagawa Shinmei and Shirai Shinpei. *Jūmin undō no genzō: Shakkajin Dōmei to Itsumi Naozō* [Development of a residents' movement: The Renters' Alliance and Itsumi Naozō]. Tokyo: JCA Shuppan, 1978.

Tamai Kingo. "Nihon Shihonshugi to (toshi) shakai seisaku: Ōsaka-shi shakai jigyō o chūshin ni" [Japanese capitalism and (urban) social policy: Social facilities in Osaka]. In *Taishō Ōsaka suramu: Mo hitotsu no Nihon kindai shi* [The slums of Taisho Osaka: Another modern history of Japan], edited by Sugihara Kaoru and Kiso Junko. Tokyo: Shinhyōron, 1987.

Tamaki, Norio. *Japanese Banking: A History, 1859–1959.* Cambridge: Cambridge University Press, 1995.

Tamaki Toyojirō. *Ōsaka kensetsu shi yawa* [A tale about the history of the building of Osaka]. Osaka: Osaka Toshi Kyōkai, 1982.

———. "Ōsaka no toshi keisei to toshi keikaku" [Urban formation and urban planning of Osaka]. *Toshi keikaku* 84 (September 1975).

Tanaka Kiyo. *Ōsaka no toshi keikaku* [Urban planning of Osaka]. Osaka: Hinoshita Wagakujiya, 1925.

Toby, Ronald P. *State and Diplomacy in Early Modern Japan: Asia in the Development of the Tokugawa Bakufu.* Princeton, N.J.: Princeton University Press, 1984.

Tochiuchi Yoshitane. *Kankyō yori mitaru toshi mondai no kenkyū* [Researches of the urban problem as seen from the perspective of the environment]. Tokyo: Kōrindo Shoten, 1922.

Toda Kaiichi. *Nihon no shakai* [Japanese society]. Tokyo: Hakubunkan, 1911.

Tokyo Metropolitan Museum of Photography and Hakodate Museum of Art, Hokkaido, eds. *The Advent of Photography in Japan.* Tokyo: Tokyo Metropolitan Museum of Photography, 1997.

Tokyo Municipal Office. *The Reconstruction of Tokyo.* Tokyo, 1933.

Toshi Keikaku Chōsa Iinkai, ed. *Toshi Keikaku Chōsa Iinkai giji sōkiroku, I, II* [Complete proceedings of the Urban Planning Survey Commission, I, II]. Tokyo: Naimudaijin Kanbō Toshi Keikaku-ka, 1918.

Tribe, Keith. *Strategies of Economic Order: German Economic Discourse, 1750–1950.* Cambridge: Cambridge University Press, 1995.

Tsumura Hidematsu. *Kokumin keizaigaku genron* [Views on people's national economics]. Tokyo: Ryūbunkan, 1910.

———. "Waga hansei no tomo o kataru" [About my lifelong friend]. *Dai Ōsaka* 11, no. 2 (1935).

———. "Yūjin toshite no Ko Seki shichō" [The late Mayor Seki as a friend]. In *Ko Seki shichō o shinobu* [Recalling the late Mayor Seki], edited by Osaka-sh Kyōikukai. Osaka: Osaka-shi Kyōikukai, 1935.

Tsurumi, E. Patricia. *Factory Girls: Women in the Thread Mills of Meiji Japan.* Princeton, N.J.: Princeton University Press, 1990.

Tsutsui, William M. *Banking Policy in Japan: American Efforts at Reform during the Occupation.* London: Routledge, 1988.

Uchida Toshikazu. "Toshi keikaku no shisetsu ni tsuite" [About urban-planning facilities]. In *Toshi to kōen* [Cities and parks], edited by Teien Kyōkai. Tokyo: Seibidō, 1924.

Ueno Chizuko. *Kindai kazoku no seiritsu to shūen* [The formation and the demise of the modern family]. Tokyo: Iwanami Shoten, 1994.

Uno, Kathleen S. *Passages to Modernity: Motherhood, Childhood, and Social Reform in Early Twentieth Century Japan.* Honolulu: University of Hawai'i Press, 1999.

Unwin, Raymond. *Town Planning in Practice: An Introduction to the Art of Designing Cities and Suburbs.* London: T. Fisher Unwin, 1911.

Veblen, Thorstein. "The Opportunity of Japan." *Journal of the Race Development* 6 (July 1915). Reprinted in Thorstein Veblen, *Essays in Our Changing Order.* New York: Viking Press, 1934.

Wajda, Shirley Teresa. "The Artistic Portrait Photograph." In *The Arts and the American Home, 1890–1930,* edited by Jessica H. Foy and Karal Ann Marling. Knoxville: University of Tennessee Press, 1994.

Watanabe Shun'ichi. *"Toshi keikaku" no tanjō: Kokusai hikaku kara mita Nihon kindai toshi keikaku* [The birth of "urban planning": Japan's modern urban planning in international comparison]. Tokyo: Kashiwa Shobō, 1993.

Webb, Sidney, and Beatrice Webb. *Industrial Democracy.* 2 vols. London: Longmans, Green, 1897.

Williams, David. *Japan: Beyond the End of History.* London: Routledge, 1994.

Wray, William D. "Afterword: The Writing of Japanese Business History." In *Managing Industrial Enterprise: Cases from Japan's Prewar Experience,* edited by William D. Wray. Cambridge, Mass.: Harvard University Press, 1989.

Yamaori Tetsuo. *Nihonjin no kao: Zuzō kara bunka o yomu* [The face(s) of Japanese: Reading culture from icons]. Tokyo: NHK Bukkusu, 1995.

Yamazaki Rintarō. *Ōbei toshi no kenkyū* [Researches on Western cities]. Tokyo, 1911.

Yamazawa, Ippei. *Economic Development and International Trade: The Japanese Model.* Honolulu: East-West Center Resource Systems Institute, 1990.

Yokoyama Gennosuke. *Nihon no kasō shakai* [The lower classes of Japan]. 1899. Reprint, Tokyo: Iwanami Shoten, 1955.

Yoshida Mitsukuni et al., eds. *Zusetsu bankoku hakurankai shi, 1851–1942* [An illustrated history of international expositions, 1851–1942]. Kyoto: Shibunkaku Shuppan, 1985.

Yoshikawa Aramasa. "Shiku kaisei ikensho" [An opinion on city improvement]. In *Nihon kindai shisō taikei: Toshi/kenchiku* [A collection of modern Japanese thought: Cities/architecture], edited by Fujimori Terunobu. Tokyo: Iwanami Shoten, 1990.

Yoshimi Shunya. *Hakurankai no seiji gaku: Manazashi no kindai* [The politics of exhibitions: The modern gaze]. Tokyo: Chūkō Shinsho, 1992.

Yūge Shichirō. *Toshi no hanashi* [Speaking of cities]. Tokyo: Sekai Shichō Kenkyūkai, 1923.

Yutani, Eiji. "*Nihon no Kasō Shakai* of Gennosuke Yokoyama, Translated and with an Introduction." Ph.D. diss., University of California, Berkeley, 1985.

Zen Ōsaka Shichō Ikegami Shirō-kun Shōtoku Kai, ed. *Moto Ōsaka Shichō Ikegami Shirō-kun Shōei* [A portrait of former Osaka Mayor Ikegami Shirō]. Osaka, 1941.

Index

Text:	10/13 Aldus
Display:	Aldus
Cartographer:	Bill Nelson
Compositor:	Binghamton Valley Composition, LLC
Printer and Binder:	Malloy Lithographing, Inc.